The Conscience of the City

THE DAEDALUS LIBRARY

The Conscience

of the City

Edited by

MARTIN MEYERSON

GEORGE BRAZILLER
NEW YORK

CONTENTS

Acknowledgments

Thanks must be given to those who assisted in the preparatory delibera-
tions leading to the publication of this study: John E. Burchard, Louis
DeLuca, Karl W. Deutsch, Scott A. Greer, Fred Charles Iklé, Edward
Logue, Frederic A. Mosher, Daniel P. Moynihan, Lloyd Rodwin, John H.
Rubel, Sterling Tucker, Christopher Tunnard, and Paul N. Ylvisaker.
These people, with the authors who have written for the volume, and
with Stephen R. Graubard the brilliant editor of *Dædalus,* made this
publication possible. The late Stephen R. Currier inspired all of us in
the writing of this book.

This study also owes much to the generosity of the Carnegie Corporation for its grant to the American Academy of Arts and Sciences.

MARTIN MEYERSON

Introduction

As AN abstraction, "the city" has no conscience. As a collection of persons—in the late Louis Wirth's terms, as a "relatively large, dense, and permanent settlement of socially heterogeneous individuals"— the city is composed of many consciences. Admitting both logical and definitional caveats, we have titled this volume of essays "The Conscience of the City" because nothing else would have captured so well the sense of moral imperative of the authors. Moral imperative toward the city is not new; perhaps it has existed as long as cities have existed. But the nature of the moral imperative has changed; it has intensified as well as broadened. Herein the authors stress the feelings and experiences of people living in the city, particularly the poor and the black, and do not look at their problems only as products of economic and social systems subject to rational analysis; they bring to the volume themes of concern and commitment.

If we look backward only so far as the beginning of the decade of the sixties, we can see the shift in mood. Then the emphasis by both urban experts and popular and political commentators was on establishing a cabinet-level department of urban development, on increasing the production of new housing and razing blight, on protecting real-estate investment and centralized cultural facilities downtown, on highways and parking, on zoning and other land-use controls, on promoting metropolitan government. City planners, reinforced with new tools of analysis, continued in the early sixties their insistence that the goals for the far future should guide any action in the present or near future.

At the end of the decade, as the essays in the volume testify, the concerns remain for housing, for transportation, for national attention to urban problems, for governmental solutions more satisfactory than those arbitrary existing municipalities can provide. But these concerns are overshadowed by a rising set of concerns for people rather than things, and especially for poor people and others who are disenfranchised, for the here and now rather than for a far future, for direct involvement of those affected by urban policies rather than for delegation to experts in a Washington agency or a metropolitan government.

The shift in emphasis is not due merely to a sensitivity of the participants to fashions in thought or to a shared creation of and rapid dissemination of a new conventional wisdom. It is rather a response to the working conference-working paper method in which all of the participants, none of whom are novices to urban analysis and to urban policy-making, consciously and unconsciously reviewed past approaches to urban problems, took note of what was most deeply disturbing to each of them, and prepared essays that complemented one another. The call to the conferences and the initial request to authors did not anticipate that all the articles would converge, as they have, on urban neglect—the plight and needs and possibilities for the undereducated, underemployed, undercared for, and underappreciated. The original intention of the study initiated by the American Academy of Arts and Sciences and entitled "1976: Planning the American Future" was to develop for urban affairs (as for several other critical fields, such as health, education, and conservation) "recommendations for ten-year development programs that would make the United States in the two-hundredth year of its independence a nation more capable of coping with the large social and economic problems characteristic of an advanced industrial group." The study group for each field was to concern itself with fundamental changes and to disregard economic and political feasibility in the hope that compelling recommendations would generate support.

With idealism unfettered, the urban-study group began its explorations. Should urban policy give highest priority to the achievement of social and economic goals, particularly those of the poor (family income stabilization, improvement and extension of education and health services, development of occupational skills)? Should it focus on social and economic goals without special attention to the poor (for example, diversification of cultural, educational, and recreation opportunities and encouragement of greater skills in the service sector)? Or should it concentrate on the physical manifestation of social and economic programs? (For example, would the cause of education be furthered by educational parks or storefront outposts? Should city and county functions be visibly decentralized in neighborhoods? Should publicly subsidized housing be scattered throughout the urban area or concentrated in easily managed units?)

Or should urban policy aim to achieve within a decade certain specific environmental standards that are unobtainable through ordinary individual and governmental actions? For example, given the base of public opinion, legislation, funds, and technological information, it would be possible to prevent an escalation of air and water pollution. To return to sparkling air and water, however, many urban patterns would have to be changed—such as the reliance on the private internal-combustion vehicle, low-density settlement, individual heating plants, and so forth.

Or should urban policy make a dramatic plea for the fruits of technology? For example, it might call for scores of new cities, built for control of the elements, so that roofed-over, air-conditioned communities could simulate California in North Dakota. Or should new technology suffuse the city to provide for automatized production, programmed teaching, municipal heating, and instant communications?

What kinds of measures might encourage metropolitan areas to solve locally what were defined politically as problems—block grants from the federal or state government, new managerial techniques, new methods of eliciting public opinion, vast increases in informational and analytic systems?

Should urban communities all be raised to some minimally defined level of environmental and service quality? Should some communities offer experimental models of improved facilities and services, such as schools or transportation? Should development be fostered in selected portions of the nation—the South, the obsolescing eastern and middle-western cities, the fast-growing West and Southwest—with the intent of redirecting population migration and settlement?

Although questions such as these were discussed, it soon became evident that the collective temper was not to delineate statistical dimensions of urban problems nor to focus on a precise set of programs or policies. Instead, the participants (many of whom are authors represented in this volume) tended to view the city and its past ameliorative programs almost as an anachronism.

According to Melvin Webber, the geographically based, traditionally bounded city is no longer the relevant unit for a discussion of what we call urban problems. It provides neither their cause nor their cure. Nor is the place-based city, in this urbanized society, the home of the most urbane population. Although it is still cheaper to minimize travel and thus to concentrate in high-density settlements, this remaining bond will be weakened further by technological improvements in transport and communications. The most critical task of the nation is to urbanize those persons whose social mobility, education, skills, and experiences have not been comparable to those of the main stream of people in America.

Kenneth Boulding, viewing the city internationally in its functional and structural setting, suggests that the city is impotent for decision-making. It cannot even provide physical security to its inhabitants and is no longer well loved. Smaller units (such as suburbs) can offer more of a sense of community and may possibly be more productive, particularly if they are federated into some kind of metropolitanism. The most satisfactory solution would come, however, if city dwellers became self-conscious about belonging to the world city and began to act through the power of that awareness. John Seeley is not so sanguine as either Webber or Boulding. He finds so much wrong with the culture of the present urbanized society that salvation may have to come from the civilization produced by small groups living away from the baleful influences of the contemporary city.

The authors represented in Part II, "Processes and Goals for Change," do not suggest that the city is fading away or that it should do so. They assume that the city will be an ongoing functioning institution and have focused on the aims of change and the methods of implementation. Lyle Fitch has chosen very large, ambitious goals, such as working toward an open, pluralistic society drawn to human scale and full of choices. He has done so because he believes that more parochial, narrow goals will result neither in solutions to particular problems nor in a desirable environment. Edmund Bacon rejects a linear sequence of goals to facts, to alternatives, to decision, and to action. He suggests circular processes of hypothesis formation and feedback, with a great deal of interplay between the professional urban planner and the members of the community. Donald Michael contends that citizens must have a level of expertise in advanced technology, particularly computers, if both long-range planning and democracy are to coexist in the future complex society.

The impact of personal intervention in society is appraised by Messrs. George, Lindsay, and Banfield. Alexander George analyzes political leadership of strong and weak mayors and its effect on urban renewal, with emphasis on Chicago and New Haven. Franklin Lindsay urges that new managerial talent be enticed into solving urban problems. He suggests that private organizations could perform, for a fee, operating functions that are now done perhaps more expensively and less efficiently by municipal employees. Edward Banfield argues that we have defined ourselves into an insoluble problem. He contends, for example, that were we to recognize reality and lower school-leaving age, we would not have a school drop-out problem.

In Part III, the authors sketch some possibilities for "New Functions for Urban Communities." It is tempting to draw a parallel between the family and the community. The family is no longer a production unit and its role in formal education, recreation, and health maintenance has been diluted. As some family functions have been assumed at least in part by other institutions, it may be increasingly imperative for the family to concentrate on the development of its members. Similarly, now that many urban functions are borne by other levels of government, the developmental service function for cities is particularly urged by Messrs. Yarmolinsky, Coleman, Carr, Lynch, and Meier. Adam Yarmolinsky stresses the necessity of services in search of clients—of having disinterested advertisers, informants, and interpreters of services so that those who are poor, uninformed, or undemanding may learn to become knowing consumers of legal, health, recreational, and educational services. His concern is for all those who are inexperienced in city living or lack skill in getting help for their problems. Carr and Lynch feel that a city should be designed like a good museum so that it would consciously foster learning experiences. For example, factories might be encouraged to make their machines visible and transportation containers might be transparent. These and other related changes would create an environment in which the form of structures and of land would communicate the activity and function of a place. Peter Drucker urges that small or medium-sized cities with strong business leadership might be the places to start breaking the lock step of formal education and job progression. He suggests that competent people without diplomas be identified and given opportunities to obtain degrees through their job performance.

While the funneling of services to individuals is seen as a major urban function, the authors do not agree as to whether all cities are to perform all services equally well or whether all cities are to offer all services to all persons. One author sees in the differential offering of services a competitive advantage to the economic well-being of cities. Richard Meier finds that in an age of affluence much of what goes on within a city is homeostatic, tending to maintain the given population, income level, and physical environment. Any city desiring to increase its population size or income level must "engage in a popularity contest for cosmopolites" since that mobile group carries with it a disproportionate share of skills, energy, and monetary resources. Thus, to Meier, services that please this subpopulation are instrumental to the economic growth of the total community.

In the view of most of the authors in the volume, however, the subject of particular specialized service attention should be the black urban dweller. In Part IV, "Ways Out of the Ghetto," Messrs. Coles, Downs, Young, and Lerner address themselves specifically to the unique situation of Negroes and to strategies and policies that would alter their plight. Robert Coles describes what life is like in a northern ghetto for nine-year-old Peter, whose playground is the alley, and for his mother, to whom "someday" probably means never. Anthony Downs discusses various strategies for ghetto dispersion and sketches the alternative futures that we might face if one rather than another strategy were adopted. Richard Rubenstein sets forth an unconventional view of the problems of law and order. After praising the Kerner Commission Report, Michael Young points out certain aspects that are clearly surprising to an Englishman: the primitive liberalism that identifies with the poor black to such an extent that it ignores the progress that has been made; the complete failure to cost the long list of recommendations and to assign priorities to them; and, most startling, the absence of any call for civil disarmament. Max Lerner argues that the problems of the city are so entrenched and massive that only a total coalition of all relevant resources and talents will enable the city and the society in general to attack them successfully.

The authors invited to contribute to this collection of essays are saying that past ameliorative programs for cities no longer suffice. They cite other needs, giving certain ones greater priority than they attach to the traditional foci of urban planning—urban renewal, downtown parking, industrial development, playgrounds. The problem is not simply to define the questions—income maintenance or income supplements, school and residential desegregation, the training of more knowledge workers, education effectively reaching more than those from middle-class backgrounds, an environment that encourages individual development and discourages violence and other criminal acts. These issues have appeared on urban agendas for many years. The question before us is to think of how one problem relates to the other, how economically and politically certain objectives can be achieved, and why an exhortation to change is not enough.

Part I:

Traditional City
in Transition

MELVIN M. WEBBER

The Post-City Age

THE PRAGMATIC traditions in American political life have led us to attack the manifest problems of the moment with heavy commitment, but to avoid the longer-term confrontation of underlying issues. The several governmental attempts to undertake long-range problem analysis, forecasting, and planning have never succeeded. We have yet to implant a counter-tradition in America that, by exploring the future, would inform a national development policy. This failing reflects, in part, the current status of the social sciences, which have not developed adequate predictive theory in most fields of national concern. It is sobering that no sociologist predicted the magnitude of the Negro Revolt, that no prewar urbanist anticipated the postwar development patterns in American cities, and that, most troubling of all, no one has yet written systematic alternative futures seeking to chart the possible course of events in these fields.

As one consequence of our political traditions and our inadequate theory, we tend to overreact to events of the day. When a curve turns upward, we expect that it will go off the top of the chart; when it turns down, we despair that it will fall off the bottom. A decade ago we were all assured that America was floating serenely in middle-class affluence and that things could only get better. Then we suddenly changed our national self-image when we discovered a large lower-class population and large-scale poverty. The demonstrations of the past five summers have alternatively been read as signs of a new egalitarianism in America or an impending *apartheid*. We had thought our public school system was unexcelled, until Sputnik shocked us into wholesale reform. We believed that suburban development was going to provide decent homes for all, and now we believe that nothing short of immediate reconstruction of the old cities can save them from disaster.

1

There can be no doubt about the imperatives for confronting the current crises that are associated with the contemporary city. The outcries from the Negro ghetto must be answered humbly, humanely, and immediately; and that will call for huge investments of intellectual capital and federal money. The scale of the current building and rebuilding enterprise in the cities is unprecedented. We shall have to double the size of our physical plant during the next thirty-five years; and that, too, must command full-scale commitment of our intellectual and financial resources. It now appears as though these investments will be forthcoming, largely because the current crisis has captured the nation's conscience and partly because it is our style to respond to emergencies in force.

But it will be an unfortunate mistake, another repetition of our traditional propensities, if we pour our resources into the manifest problems without also dealing with the less visible underlying issues. A deep-swell is shaping those curves on our month-to-month charts—a large historical change that may reshape the character of urban society in the developed world. This, too, must command our attention, for the coming changes may so inhibit future social mobility that our present short-run, ameliorative programs could prove ineffective in retrospect. If so, we had better try to anticipate those changes and then modify our action programs to conform.

Urbanization Beyond the City

We are passing through a revolution that is unhitching the social processes of urbanization from the locationally fixed city and region. Reflecting the current explosion in science and technology, employment is shifting from the production of goods to services; increasing ease of transportation and communication is dissolving the spatial barriers to social intercourse; and Americans are forming social communities comprised of spatially dispersed members. A new kind of large-scale urban society is emerging that is increasingly independent of the city. In turn, the problems of the city place generated by early industrialization are being supplanted by a new array different in kind. With but a few remaining exceptions (the new air pollution is a notable one), the recent difficulties are not place-type problems at all. Rather, they are the transitional problems of a rapidly developing society-economy-and-polity whose turf is the nation. Paradoxically, just at

2

the time in history when policy-makers and the world press are discovering the city, "the age of the city seems to be at an end."[1] Our failure to draw the rather simple conceptual distinction between the spatially defined city or metropolitan area and the social systems that are localized there clouds current discussions about the "crisis of our cities."[2] The confusion stems largely from the deficiencies of our language and from the anachronistic thought-ways we have carried over from the passing era. We still have no adequate descriptive terms for the emerging social order, and so we use, perforce, old labels that are no longer fitting. Because we have named them so, we suppose that the problems manifested inside cities are, therefore and somehow, "city problems." Because societies in the past had been spatially and locally structured, and because urban societies used to be exclusively city-based, we seem still to assume that territoriality is a necessary attribute of social systems.

The error has been a serious one, leading us to seek local solutions to problems whose causes are not of local origin and hence are not susceptible to municipal treatment. We have been tempted to apply city-building instruments to correct social disorders, and we have then been surprised to find that they do not work. (Our experience with therapeutic public housing, which was supposed to cure "social pathologies," and urban renewal, which was supposed to improve the lives of the poor, may be our most spectacular failures.) We have lavished large investments on public facilities, but neglected the quality and the distribution of the social services. And we have defended and reinforced home-rule prerogatives of local and state governments with elaborate rhetoric and protective legislation.

Neither crime-in-the-streets, poverty, unemployment, broken families, race riots, drug addiction, mental illness, juvenile delinquency, nor any of the commonly noted "social pathologies" marking the contemporary city can find its causes or its cure there. We cannot hope to invent local treatments for conditions whose origins are not local in character, nor can we expect territorially defined governments to deal effectively with problems whose causes are unrelated to territory or geography. The concepts and methods of civil engineering and city planning suited to the design of unitary physical facilities cannot be used to serve the design of social change in a pluralistic and mobile society. In the novel society now emerging—with its sophisticated and rapidly advancing sci-

3

ence and technology, its complex social organization, and its internally integrated societal processes—the influence and significance of geographic distance and geographic place are declining rapidly.

This is, of course, a most remarkable change. Throughout virtually all of human history, social organization coincided with spatial organization. In preindustrial society, men interacted almost exclusively with geographic neighbors. Social communities, economies, and polities were structured about the place in which interaction was least constrained by the frictions of space. With the coming of large-scale industrialization during the latter half of the nineteenth century, the strictures of space were rapidly eroded, abetted by the new ease of travel and communication that the industrialization itself brought.

The initial counterparts of industrialization in the United States were, first, the concentration of the nation's population into large settlements and, then, the cultural urbanization of the population. Although these changes were causally linked, they had opposite spatial effects. After coming together at a common place, people entered larger societies tied to no specific place. Farming and village peoples from throughout the continent and the world migrated to the expanding cities, where they learned urban ways, acquired the occupational skills that industrialization demanded, and became integrated into the contemporary society.

In recent years, rising societal scale and improvements in transportation and communications systems have loosed a chain of effects robbing the city of its once unique function as an urbanizing instrument of society. Farmers and small-town residents, scattered throughout the continent, were once effectively removed from the cultural life of the nation. City folks visiting the rural areas used to be treated as strangers, whose styles of living and thinking were unfamiliar. News of the rest of the world was hard to get and then had little meaning for those who lived the local life. Country folk surely knew there was another world out there somewhere, but little understood it and were affected by it only indirectly. The powerful anti-urban traditions in early American thought and politics made the immigrant city dweller a suspicious character whose crude ways marked him as un-Christian (which he sometimes was) and certainly un-American. The more sophisticated urban upper classes—merchants, landowners, and professional men—were similarly suspect and hence rejected. In contrast, the small-town merchant and the farmer who lived closer to nature were the

4

genuine Americans of pure heart who lived the simple, natural life.[3] Because the contrasts between the rural and the urban ways-of-life were indeed sharp, antagonisms were real, and the differences became institutionalized in the conduct of politics. America was marked by a diversity of regional and class cultures whose followers interacted infrequently, if ever.

By now this is nearly gone. The vaudeville hick-town and hay-seed characters have left the scene with the vaudeville act. Today's urbane farmer watches television documentaries, reads the national news magazines, and manages his acres from an office (maybe located in a downtown office building), as his hired hands ride their tractors while listening to the current world news broadcast from a transistor. Farming has long since ceased to be a handicraft art; it is among the most highly technologized industries and is tightly integrated into the international industrial complex.

During the latter half of the nineteenth century and the first third of the twentieth, the traditional territorial conception that distinguished urbanites and ruralites was probably valid: The typical rural folk lived outside the cities, and the typical urbanites lived inside. By now this pattern is nearly *reversed*. Urbanites no longer reside exclusively in metropolitan settlements, nor do rural-ites live exclusively in the hinterlands. Increasingly, those who are least integrated into modern society—those who exhibit most of the attributes of rural folk—are concentrating within the highest-density portions of the large metropolitan centers. This profoundly important development is only now coming to our consciousness, yet it points up one of the major policy issues of the next decades.

The Participants in the High-Scale Society

Cultural diffusion is integrating immigrants, city residents, and hinterland peoples into a national urban society, but it has not touched all Americans evenly. At one extreme are the intellectual and business elites, whose habitat is the planet; at the other are the lower-class residents of city and farm who live in spatially and cognitively constrained worlds. Most of the rest of us, who comprise the large middle class, lie somewhere in-between, but in some facets of our lives we all seem to be moving from our ancestral localism toward the unbounded realms of the cosmopolites.

High educational attainments and highly specialized occupations mark the new cosmopolites. As frequent patrons of the airlines and the long-distance telephone lines, they are intimately involved in the communications networks that tie them to their spatially dispersed associates. They contribute to and consume the specialized journals of science, government, and industry, thus maintaining contact with information resources of relevance to their activities, whatever the geographic sources or their own locations. Even though some may be employed by corporations primarily engaged in manufacturing physical products, these men trade in information and ideas. They are the producers of the information and ideas that fuel the engines of societal development. For those who are tuned into the international communications circuits, cities have utility precisely because they are rich in information. The way such men use the city reveals its essential character most clearly, for to them the city is essentially a massive communications switchboard through which human interaction takes place.[4]

Indeed, cities exist *only* because spatial agglomeration permits reduced costs of interaction. Men originally elected to locate in high-density settlements precisely because space was so costly to overcome. It is still cheaper to interact with persons who are nearby, and so men continue to locate in such settlements.[5] Because there *are* concentrations of associates in city places, the new cosmopolites establish their offices there and then move about from city to city conducting their affairs. The biggest settlements attract the most long-distance telephone and airline traffic and have undergone the most dramatic growth during this era of city-building.

The recent expansion of Washington, D. C. is the most spectacular evidence of the changing character of metropolitan development. Unlike the older settlements whose growth was generated by expanding manufacturing activities during the nineteenth and early-twentieth centuries, Washington produces almost no goods whatsoever. Its primary products are information and intelligence, and its fantastic growth is a direct measure of the predominant roles that information and the national government have come to play in contemporary society.

This terribly important change has been subtly evolving for a long time, so gradually that it seems to have gone unnoticed. The preindustrial towns that served their adjacent farming hinterlands were essentially alike. Each supplied a standardized array of goods and services to its neighboring market area. The industrial cities that grew after the Civil War and during the early decades of this century were oriented to serving larger markets with the manufacturing products they were created to produce. As their market areas widened, as product specialization increased, and as the information content of goods expanded, establishments located in individual cities became integrated into the spatially extensive economies. By now, the large metropolitan centers that used to be primarily goods-producing loci have become interchange junctions within the international communications networks. Only in the limited geographical, physical sense is any modern metropolis a discrete, unitary, identifiable phenomenon. At most, it is a localized node within the integrating international networks, finding its significant identity as contributor to the workings of that larger system. As a result, the new cosmopolites belong to none of the world's metropolitan areas, although they use them. They belong, rather, to the national and international communities that merely maintain information exchanges at these metropolitan junctions.

Their capacity to interact intimately with others who are spatially removed depends, of course, upon a level of wealth adequate to cover the dollar costs of long-distance intercourse, as well as upon the cognitive capacities associated with highly skilled professional occupations. The intellectual and business elites are able to maintain continuing and close contact with their associates throughout the world because they are rich not only in information, but also in dollar income.

As the costs of long-distance interaction fall in proportion to the rise in incomes, more and more people are able and willing to pay the transportation and communication bills. As expense-account privileges are expanded, those costs are being reduced to zero for ever larger numbers of people. As levels of education and skill rise, more and more people are being tied into the spatially extensive communities that used to engage only a few.

Thus, the glue that once held the spatial settlement together is now dissolving, and the settlement is dispersing over ever widening terrains. At the same time, the pattern of settlement upon the continent is also shifting (moving toward long strips along the coasts, the Gulf, and the Great Lakes). These trends are likely to be accelerated dramatically by cost-reducing improvements in transportation and communications technologies now in the research-and-development stages. (The SST, COMSAT communications, high-speed ground transportation with speeds up to 500 m.p.h., TV and

7

computer-aided educational systems, no-toll long-distance telephone service, and real-time access to national computer-based information systems are likely to be powerful ones.) Technological improvements in transport and communications reduce the frictions of space and thereby ease long-distance intercourse. Our compact, physical city layouts directly mirror the more primitive technologies in use at the time these cities were built. In a similar way, the locational pattern of cities upon the continent reflects the technologies available at the time the settlements grew.[6] If currently anticipated technological improvements prove workable, each of the metropolitan settlements will spread out in low-density patterns over far more extensive areas than even the most frightened future-mongers have yet predicted. The new settlement-form will little resemble the nineteenth-century city so firmly fixed in our images and ideologies. We can also expect that the large junction points will no longer have the communications advantage they now enjoy, and smaller settlements will undergo a major spurt of growth in all sorts of now-isolated places where the natural amenities are attractive.

Moreover, as ever larger percentages of the nation's youth go to college and thus enter the national and international cultures, attachments to places of residence will decline dramatically. This prospect, rather than the spatial dispersion of metropolitan areas, portends the functional demise of the city. The signs are already patently clear among those groups whose worlds are widest and least bounded by parochial constraints.

Consider the extreme cosmopolite, if only for purposes of illustrative cartooning. He might be engaged in scientific research, news reporting, or international business, professions exhibiting critical common traits. The astronomer, for example, maintains instantaneous contact with his colleagues around the world; indeed, he is a day-to-day collaborator with astronomers in all countries. His work demands that he share information and that he and his colleagues monitor stellar events jointly, as the earth's rotation brings men at different locales into prime-viewing position. Because he is personally committed to their common enterprise, his social reference group is the society of astronomers. He assigns his loyalties to the community of astronomers, since their work and welfare matter most to him.

To be sure, as he plays out other roles—say, as citizen, parent, laboratory director, or grocery shopper—he is a member of many other communities, both interest-based and place-defined ones. But the striking thing about our astronomer, and the millions of people like him engaged in other professions, is how little of his attention and energy he devotes to the concerns of place-defined communities. Surely, as compared to his grandfather, whose life was largely bound up in the affairs of his locality, the astronomer, playwright, newsman, steel broker, or wheat dealer lives in a life-space that is not defined by territory and deals with problems that are not local in nature. For him, the city is but a convenient setting for the conduct of his professional work; it is not the basis for the social communities that he cares most about.

Indeed, we may not be far from the time when the vernacular meaning of "community" will be archaic and disappear from common usage. It has already lost much of its traditional meaning for a great many of those on the leading edge of the society. If it is retained, it may be restricted to the provisions of children and of those adults who have not gained access to modern society.

The demise of the city is associated with far more subtle and powerful changes than the expansion of market areas for firms and the collaboration among scientists in distant nations. Behind these developments lies the internationalization of society generated by the knowledge explosion.

By its very nature, knowledge is specific to neither cities nor nations. An overriding, largely unanticipated consequence of science is its internationalizing effect—its introduction of common understandings, common libraries of information, common bases for valuation and validation, and, indeed, a common culture for men located in all parts of the world. The same consequences emanate from developments in technology, commerce, the arts, theater, literature, and virtually all areas of creative endeavor. Save for those, like Lyzenko, who hold to certain specialized epistemologies or ideologies, new discoveries and inventions are readily accepted, irrespective of their geographic origins. By now there is a large class of persons around the world who share in the world culture, while simultaneously participating in the idiosyncratic local cultures special to their regions of residence. Their range of opportunity is far larger and far more diverse than the most powerful and wealthy man of past eras could have imagined.

Knowledge is also cumulative; its store can only get larger, and the effects it generates are one-directional. We now know that the recent expansion of knowledge has triggered a rapid explosion of life-space—both geographically and cognitively. We can expect that explosion to continue, further bursting the barriers of geography and ignorance for larger proportions of the population. The counterpart of expanding life-space has been the contracting role of the cities and the nations as the organizing frameworks of societies. This is, of course, a revolutionary development. As Kenneth Boulding has synoptically put it, it portends the end of "civilization" as the culture of the *civitas*.[7] To be sure, the end of civilization has been in sight for a long time; through a telling etymological trick we have become accustomed to speaking of national *citi*zenship, and we even describe some people as "world citizens." This usage is far more prophetic than we had realized.

Although the intellectual and business elites are undoubtedly still a minority among us, the vast middle class is rapidly adopting their styles and their capabilities, and lower-class persons are aspiring to them. About 40 per cent of American youth are now going to college, and the proportion will soon be over half. (In California it is now about 80 per cent.) Television has already supplied a window to a seamless world, a world that the present generation is actively exploring firsthand. If we ever succeed in using television creatively, it could become a more powerful educational force than the public schools have been—extending the classroom to every house and the spectrum of accessible knowledge far beyond the present bounds. Americans may already be consuming more books per capita, more magazines per capita, more music, more lectures, and more art than any population in the world— certainly far more than any peoples in the past. They are traveling widely for recreational and educational purposes; and in the course of their travels, they are absorbing information, ideas, and attitudes, even as they are seeding their own along their paths.

The nationals of other countries are, of course, engaged in the same set of activities. Western Europeans may be the next most-mobile people in the world, although the Japanese probably outpace even them in the rate at which they have been scouting the planet, absorbing and then exploiting the world's knowledge. The signs of this internationalization are clear: the rise of the international business firm, the near-instantaneous diffusion of fashion in dress and the arts, the spectacular spread of the hippie culture, the new international architecture, the Europeans' sense of personal loss at the assassinations of John F. Kennedy, Martin Luther King, and Robert F. Kennedy, the acceptance of the common market idea, and the new-found racial pride among mutually supportive colored peoples.

We have little reason to doubt that the accumulation and dispersion of knowledge will continue, bringing further dissolution of local differences. The economy is expanding in precisely those service industries that demand high educational attainment and sophistication: education, research and development, health, and the information services. Concomitantly, the traditional loci of growth that marked the industrial stage of national development are already on the decline. During the past twenty years, there has been almost no expansion in manufacturing employment in the U.S.; we may soon be seeing an actual decline, despite the fantastic expansion of output. Unskilled jobs are fast disappearing, and physically exhausting work may before long be completely consigned to machines.

The processes have been mutually reinforcing. The service occupations that require high skill have been able to expand because a highly educated labor force has been developing. In turn, these occupations, particularly those within the knowledge industries, have been reproducing their own next-generations of better trained persons and their own next-generations of new knowledge. Thus, we have been riding a rising spiral that is turning the economy upside down, converting it from one in which workers produce physical products to one in which they produce services. Many of the new services are concerned with the management of information, and the information content of most of the new physical products is rising rapidly. (Compare, for example, the information content of a transistor radio with that of a trainload of coal.) In the process, the emphasis on knowledge and information has been increasing dramatically. Already the number of Americans working full time as teachers is over two million. We may now be fast approaching the day, long heralded by the ancient Greek philosophers, when our major occupation will be learning for its own sake.

The Bypassed Preindustrial Locals

As the scale of the society has been rising, carrying the bulk of the national population into the dimly seen post-industrial era, a large segment of the population is being left further and further behind. A short time ago, many of these people were living in rural areas, a high proportion in the southern and Appalachian

11

states; the migration to the cities during the past twenty-five years has by now relocated nearly all of them. Today, they are city dwellers, residing in the most dense sections of the metropolitan areas, but still living in the folk cultures their grandparents knew. Here in the Harlems and South Sides of the nation are some of the last viable remnants of preindustrial societies, where village styles are most nearly intact. Here the turf is the city block, and teenage gangs wage war in its defense. Here in the slum blocks of the central cities may be the only pure place-based social neighborhoods we have left.

American cities have always been magnets for preindustrial migrants searching for access into contemporary society. Like those who preceded them from Europe, the recent migrants are being both pushed by the hardships of their present life and pulled by the promise of opportunities that the city has traditionally held out. And yet the recent migrations occur in a very different setting. Those who now come must bridge a cultural gap far wider than the one their predecessors faced, one that is widening at an exponential rate.

Despite the suffering that accompanied nineteenth-century migration and acculturation, the stage was well set; the paths to social mobility were short and easily traversed. The new manufacturing industries called for large numbers of workers who could easily be trained to perform the standardized tasks. In turn, jobs made for income security that provided relief from the hazards of everyday life, thus fostering a non-fatalistic world-view through which future opportunities could be seen. The physical structure of the city permitted the various ethnic and national groups to settle in colonies within the cities. The transplanted old-world life styles of the ethnic ghettos eased the transition for the adult newcomers, while their children gradually introduced them to the new urban ways. The democratic institutions and the legal rules for acquiring citizenship and voting rights permitted the newcomers to control and then to use local governments instrumentally in accelerating their own development. For some, politics and government provided an important route to social mobility.

Free public schools served as an open doorway through which immigrants' children found access to semiskilled and skilled occupations and thus to higher social status than their parents enjoyed. The public schools, the free public colleges, the free libraries, the availability of free or cheap medical services, and the public life of the street became the major acculturating media. By living the city-based life, the second- and third-generation Americans acquired the social and cognitive skills and the internal psychic competencies that modern urbanism demands. In the school, on the street, and frequently in illicit enterprises, the immigrants' children learned to use the money and credit economy, to defer gratification, to anticipate future problems and opportunities, to cope with crises, and to deal with multiple options. The city was, in effect, a school where peasant migrants learned with incredible speed to be urbanized Americans. Within single generations, groups that had followed the four-hundred-year-old peasant styles of life and thought were catapulted into a society of a vastly different kind and scale. Most of them landed on their feet; some of them shot to the forefront of the society and then led it on to its next stages of development.

The setting for the massive European and Asian migrations to the city was fortuitous. They arrived just when the national economy was embarking upon unprecedented industrial development, and they came into a social system constrained by few immovable barriers of social class. In a time when small capitalization was sufficient, some succeeded in establishing small, family-based businesses; in the milieu of a rapidly expanding economy, some of these soon became big businesses. Others entered the professions, government, and the large corporations where they established themselves as leaders among the intellectual elites.

The way out of the ghetto was fast and easy for a few groups of immigrants. For many Eastern European Jews, the departure from the immigrant ghetto areas in the slums occurred very quickly. Many of the Jews were culturally urbanized when they came here; in Europe the legal prohibition against their owning land kept them in towns where many were small merchants or traders. The relatively unstructured and open-ended character of their religious doctrines led them as a group to place high value on scholarship and individual achievement, to adopt a typically critical intellectual attitude, and to be concerned with the consequences of future events. These characteristics, coupled with a solidly cohesive family structure, served them well when they reached the United States. The Chinese and Japanese, with their cohesive, patriarchal family structure and high cultural value on intellectual achievement, were also among the most upwardly mobile groups.

In contrast, mobility has come slower to the Irish, southern Italian, and Polish immigrants, whose peasant heritage had few of

13

these urbanizing attributes. Only within the past generation or two have their children been going to college in large numbers, leaving the ethnic ghetto and the working-class world-view behind them. The rigidity of traditional practices and beliefs and the emphasis on discipline and conformity exerted by the Catholic Church had previously discouraged exploration of wider conceptual worlds than those of the ethnic neighborhoods.

Whatever innate and cultural attributes may have sped social mobility for some of the early migrants to America's cities, their success was just as surely a consequence of the nation's stage of development at the time they arrived. Uneducated migrants to cities were not very far behind those who had arrived long before them. Those of quick mind could master the tasks required by the new factories speedily and then move beyond into the managerial and professional roles.

The Central Policy Issue

A far more difficult setting faces the migrants to the cities today. The explosive progress in the arts, sciences, and technologies has triggered an unprecedented rise in the scale of the national society, one marked by ever finer division of labor, calling for ever higher levels of education and training; by the shift from extractive and manufacturing industries to service industries that require long periods of preparation; by increasingly complex organization of the economy and polity; and by the expansion of the spatial and cognitive fields within which human interaction and economic transaction take place. Specialization, interdependence, and integration are the definitive traits of today's urbanism. This new scale of complexity distinguishes modern urbanism from earlier forms and is setting the policy agenda that the nation must now address.

Although it is still easy to migrate to the cities, the demands of large-scale society are making it more and more difficult for newcomers to gain entry into the new urban society. Those city dwellers who are presently least integrated into modern society are facing a series of hurdles far higher than the ones the earlier migrants found. The Appalachians, Negroes, Puerto Ricans, and Mexican Americans now concentrated within the central ghettos of metropolitan areas are not just the most recent wave of newcomers to those districts, as some scholars have suggested. The others were able to pass through, but today's residents could fail to make it.

14

The editors of *The Economist* saw the situation more clearly from London than did the American commentators who wrote in the days right after the Watts riot. In a brilliant editorial, they observed that Los Angeles symbolizes the frontier of modern society, with the technologically most advanced industries, the large numbers of research-and-development establishments, high-quality public services, and the most widespread distribution of the affluent, modern style of life. With no surprise that the first major riot should occur in Southern California, rather than Chicago or New York, they perceptively interpreted the outcry as a measure of the perceived gap between two juxtaposed populations at widely different stages of development. The Watts rioters were not striking out at the city. After all, the quality of the physical environment in south-central Los Angeles is far superior to that in the metropolitan ghettos of the East. These people were striking out at their plight—at the widening social distance that separates them from their visible neighbors and at the widening differentials in opportunity. The immediate objects of hostility in Watts and in the subsequent riots were whitey's policemen and the physical city. The police and the city were, however, merely convenient symbols of the rioters' frustrating sense of powerlessness and of the many handicaps keeping them from bridging the social gap. They were surely not the real objects of their anger.

By now the message of Watts, Newark, Memphis, and the other violent outcries is beginning to be heard in critical circles, reinforcing the earlier underlying theme of the civil rights movement. Too often the meanings are interpreted simplistically—as racial conflicts between blacks and whites, as rebellion against discriminatory practices, or as protests against the filth and depravity of the slum. The rioters are saying all these things—and more. Their docket of indictments is long and righteous; their dramatic moral censure of American society has by now provoked a crisis of conscience forcing the nation to confront the plight it had been silently ignoring for so long. The nation's response with the new civil rights legislation, new housing programs, and new policing practices is admirable and right; yet none of these is enough. The problems of the poor Negro Americans are not unique to them in America. To be sure, race has been an important exacerbating factor in retarding their progress, but preindustrial status is not a distinctive condition of Negroes. Large Mexican American, Puerto Rican, and domestic Caucasian populations are living in quite similar status, and we should not be surprised when they, too, stage revolts like those of the past three years. If disparities in stages of development are behind the current urbanization crisis, that crisis is far more deep-seated and touches far more people than the current debates recognize. It would then require a much more encompassing effort, one aimed at accelerating the urbanization of all groups whose social mobility has been retarded.

Toward an Urbanization Policy

As the scale of the society has risen, our governmental system has been slowly adapting to it. Almost without deliberate intention, the federal system has been modified to conform to the rise of the nation-state as successor to the city-state. Without an explicit policy decision, the national government has assumed responsibility for confronting the urbanization problems and opportunities, albeit often in the language of localism and home-rule.

The shift in the locus of policy-making in education clearly mirrors this important change. Education has traditionally been one of the most jealously guarded provinces of local governments. People care about their children's educational opportunities and have willingly supported public education through local taxation that permitted local control. And yet when accounted within a larger-system framework, the investment strategies have not always proved prudent. Unlike investments in roads, investments in people are easily lost because, unlike roads, people are movable. Thus, the northern and eastern cities become the beneficiaries of the poor schooling accorded Negro children in the southern states. Similarly they may attract graduates of southern colleges with few direct returns to the southern culture and economy.

Population mobility has raised a difficult dilemma for governments that were initially structured to serve geographically stable peoples. Our adaptive response has been to redistribute revenues and expenditures among geographic regions. Because only the least territorially-bounded of our governments can perform the redistributive function, we have been creating new roles for the federal government and a new set of functional relationships among our various public governments.[8]

At the same time we have been building a vast network of nonpublic organizations having a governmental character and self-assigned responsibilities. Each is organized upon an interest

16

base, rather than a territorial one. Thus, trade associations effectively exert governmental constraints upon their corporation members, and professional associations govern the conduct of physicians, engineers, lawyers, and the rest. Trade unions, churches, and recreational groups have been similarly structured to serve the special interests of their members. All these groups are governments in the essential meanings of that term; they are regulative agencies with power to exert sanctions and enforce control. Increasingly, they have come to have nationwide realms for they have arisen as manifestations of a society rapidly moving into the post-industrial, post-city stage of its development. Combined with the thousands of "public governments," they contribute to a complex network of policy and decision centers.

With so complex a governing apparatus in this country, it is not possible to formulate a unitary set of policies for national development or a unitary mutually reinforcing set of programs. Nor is it possible to erect a unitary set of controls guided from a central command post. Goals for the nation are surely as pluralistic and competitive as the diverse groups that might formulate them. And yet there may be a national consensus that would permit us to pursue some common objectives in a directed and deliberate fashion. The complexity of contemporary society leaves no group independent of the others, and the welfare of any one group is now unavoidably bound up with the welfare of the others.

The United States has not until recently sensed the need for a national strategy that would accelerate economic and human development, for we have prospered well without one. Moreover, such a development policy has seemed to require far more centralization of authority and control than is tolerable or possible in this nation. Nevertheless, although the nation has prospered, all its members have not. If the left-behinds are to find access to modern society, we are going to have to launch as concerted a programmatic effort as the Latin American attempts to accelerate the social mobility of their *marginalidad*. We now have a considerable intellectual capability for developmental planning that we have so far been exporting. By exploiting those capabilities, while operating within the framework of our contemporary pluralistic governmental system, we should be able to increase the odds that the transition to the post-industrial age can be eased. If we can but use our available intelligence, we should be able to accelerate the social mobility of those who might otherwise never catch up.

"The city" can no longer serve as the central organizing idea behind such a planning effort. The next stage of urbanization planning will be guided by the concept of selective development—by the formulation of tactical programs that conform to strategic plans aimed at bringing the left-behind groups into contemporary urban society.

Some of the programmatic imperatives can be read in the very character of post-industrialism and suggest investment strategies for that human-development effort. The nation is surely rich enough to raise all incomes above the poverty line, and the means for doing so are now being invented at a rising rate. Family allowances and guaranteed minimum incomes appear to be economically feasible.

New jobs are needed in large volumes, particularly for those who are presently the least skilled. The need is most likely to be satisfied in the service occupations, and a wave of social invention under way suggests possibilities for creating new subprofessional careers that carry dignity and status—careers that might serve the recent migrants to cities as the earlier industrial jobs served the earlier arrivals. The poor quality of housing need no longer be the norm for the metropolitan centers. Again some imaginative new schemes are being devised that would merge public and private enterprises in mutually profitable and potentially productive house-building ventures—inside the cities and elsewhere. There is no imperative of the emerging new society so demanding as high-quality educational services, from prekindergarten to postdoctoral levels. Although the nation is now spending heavily in this sector of the economy, large expansion is needed. In parallel, the spectrum of public recreational services—ranging from parks and other outdoor facilities to high-brow museums and low-brow pool halls—are becoming near-necessary attributes of the new style of life. Medical and health services have never been adequate to the standards of health to which we have aspired, so a massive new effort is being aimed at planned improvement of people's physical and mental well-being, whether they live in cities or not.

The designs for such a strategy for national development can never be fitted into coherent and mutually reinforcing wholes. The pluralistic structure of American society would never permit that. Moreover, the dangers are likely to exceed the advantages, and it is wholly unlikely that we would ever know enough even to make such an attempt anyway. Some general policy guides, however, are both economically possible and politically feasible.

The Post-City Age

In this volume of essays, a group of colleagues sets forth a series of targets for the nation's development. It is our hope to encourage a debate that, in turn, might lead to a national consensus on the accomplishments we desire. Two hundred years after we declared our capacity to achieve freedom for all Americans, we have the capability of making that freedom real and operational. The nation has developed through several historic stages during that brief period. We passed through the vestiges of the agrarian-preindustrial era, led the world through the industrial age of cities, and are now emerging into a still uncharted era when few men will pursue the manual occupations and most will devote their energies to serving others and to learning. The next generation of middle-class Americans is destined to enjoy the unprecedently rich life that the post-industrial, national urban society will offer. Our central domestic task now is deliberately to invent ways of extending those opportunities to those groups that future history threatens to exclude.

REFERENCES

1. The phrase is Don Martindale's; it closes his "Introduction" to Max Weber's *The City* (New York, 1962), p. 67. The theme is being sounded in many quarters nowadays. See especially, Scott Greer, *The Emerging City* (New York, 1962); Kenneth Boulding, *The Meaning of the Twentieth Century* (New York, 1965); York Willburn, *The Withering Away of the City* (Tuscaloosa, 1964); and Janet Abu-Lhughod, "The City Is Dead—Long Live the City" (Center for Planning and Development Research, University of California, Berkeley, 1966, mimeo.).

2. John Friedman presents a crisp clarification of the distinction in "Two Concepts of Urbanization," *Urban Affairs Quarterly*, Vol. 1, No. 4 (June, 1966), pp. 78-84.

3. Richard Hofstadter, *The Age of Reform* (New York, 1955) and *Anti-Intellectualism in America* (New York, 1963). Morton and Lucia White, *The Intellectuals Against the City* (Cambridge, 1964).

4. Richard L. Meier, *A Communications Theory of Urban Growth* (Cambridge, 1962).

5. I have elaborated this thesis in "Order in Diversity: Community Without Propinquity," in Lowdon Wingo, Jr. (ed.), *Cities and Space* (Baltimore, 1963), pp. 23-54.

6. For example, the first-generation jet airplanes, like the first railroads, accelerated the growth of the largest settlements. The big jets could land at only those airports with long runways and specialized facilities. The second-

and third-generation jets are fast equalizing accessibility among settlements, recapitulating the accessibility effects of the railroads and then the highways.

7. Boulding, *The Meaning of the Twentieth Century.*

8. See Morton Grodzin's classic essay "The Federal System," in *Goals for Americans: The Report of the President's Commission on National Goals* (Englewood Cliffs, 1960), pp. 265-84.

KENNETH E. BOULDING

The City as an Element in the International System

AN INTERNATIONAL system may be defined as a set of social organizations or organized groups of people whose relations are governed mainly by threat and the perception of threat. Defined this broadly, the international system goes back a long way in human experience, and the primitive international systems of the paleolithic era may seem to have little resemblance to the complex international system of today. Nevertheless, in social evolution something like an international system has nearly always been present and can be thought of as a segment of the total ecological system of mankind that is at least moderately recognizable and has something of an evolutionary pattern of its own.

In spite of the observation that even very primitive peoples have organized groups, the relations among which are governed by some kind of threat system, a case can be made for the proposition that the international system as we would recognize it today emerges only with the development of cities and civilization—civilization, of course, being what goes on in cities. The threat relations among paleolithic people seem to be sporadic and very casual. In any case, before the invention of agriculture man was too near the margin of subsistence in most places to have any surplus left over, either for more elaborate organization or for organized fighting.

The domestication of plants and animals seems to have led at first to a degree of relative affluence in which productive activity paid off better than predatory, and hence the threat system seems to have been fairly well muted. A great many neolithic villages seem to have been undefended.

As long as population was sparse in relation to agricultural land, this idyllic Garden of Eden could persist. The rise of cities may well have been associated with population pressure that made simple

21

expansion of the old way of life impossible. The first cities seem to have been created by internal threat systems. In the early days, this appears to have been mainly a spiritual threat. A charismatic priesthood somehow persuades the farmer to hand over some of his surplus food, and with this food the priests, the artisans, and the builders of temples, houses, and walls are fed, but not much comes back to the farmer.

The simplest model both of the city-state and of the international system would suppose each city to have a small agricultural hinterland around it, from which the surplus of food flows into the city and which receives from the city primarily spiritual goods or threats. At this stage at any rate, the city would have little in the way of products to export. The spiritual threat of the priest is usually succeeded by the more material threat of the king who uses the food that he extracts from the farmers to feed soldiers who can extract the surplus that feeds them by material threat. An international system develops out of this because of the fundamental principle that threat capability and credibility diminish with distance from the origin of the threat, since threat capability has a cost of transport. Consequently at a certain distance from the king or the city, its threat capability and credibility decline to the point where they can no longer control behavior. At this point, there is an opportunity for another king or city. Once the second city is established there comes to be a boundary of equal strength between the two cities, and we have an international system.

A model as simple as this, of course, could never have described a real situation, even in the earliest times. The system is always more complex than we have indicated. Even in the neolithic era, for instance, there seems to have been extensive trade covering thousands of miles. The development of metallurgy meant a quite early development, at least of specialized villages that exported metals in return for food. The development of pottery, jewelry, weaving, and crafts producing transportable articles led to the development of organized trade; and trading cities, such as Tyre, had economic structures very different from the simple exploitative city and also played a very different role in the international system. The threat capability of a trading city, for instance, may be used not so much simply for the extraction of commodities from unwilling producers, as for the monopolization of trade opportunities, as in the case of Venice.

The next stage of development of the city and the international system is empire, which begins when one city conquers another without destroying it. A system of city-states is only stable if what I have called the "loss of strength gradient"—that is, the decline in threat capability and (or credibility)[1] per mile of distance traveled away from its origin—is very high. Thus, for the system of city-states to be stable, the threat capability of the city must be exhausted once it has covered an area that is capable of feeding the city from its food surplus. One city, then, cannot conquer another, for as it expands its threats beyond its own territory, it becomes too weak, and the other city becomes too strong.

The cost of transport of threat capability however, for instance in the shape of organized armies, soon fell below the critical limit that would permit the city-state to be stable. This happened first along the great river valleys simply because water transportation of anything, including threats, is very cheap. It is not surprising, therefore, that we get empires along the Nile, along the Tigris and the Euphrates, along the Indus, and along the Hoang-Ho. One of the puzzling questions of human history, incidentally, is why the pattern in America was so different, where the great river valleys like the Mississippi did not produce any early civilizations, but the wild mountains of Mexico and Peru did. The answer may be that a river had to flow through at least a semi-arid region in order to support an empire due to the extraordinary difficulties of transportation through forests. Certainly the desert plays something of the role of the sea in transportation. Just as the Roman Empire was the product of the Mediterranean and of sea transport, so the empires of the nomads of Central Asia were a product of relatively unobstructed land transportation in semi-arid regions. Forests grow faster than man, with primitive tools, can cut them down. He can only conquer the forested regions once the techniques of clearing have gone beyond a certain point. Even the arid lands cannot support an empire without something like a horse, which is probably why the incipient city-states of the Southwest Pueblos in the United States never developed into empires, having neither navigable rivers nor horses.

In the empire, there is a sharp distinction between the capital city and the provincial cities. The capital city is more purely exploitative, though the empire as a system usually involves the collection of surplus food by the provincial cities, some of which is retained and some of which is passed on to the capital city. There is probably more incentive, however, for the provincial cities to become producers of specialized manufactures and to begin to exchange these with food producers for food. Here the exchange system slowly develops and spreads as an alternative to the threat system. Finally, with the advent of the so-called Industrial Revolution and the rise of science-based technology, we begin to get virtually a-political cities like Birmingham (England) or Detroit, which grow up on a basis of pure production and exchange, usually outside the old political structures. These commercial and industrial cities play virtually no direct role in the international system though their indirect influence may be great in strengthening the power of the nation-state and the capital city to which they happen to be attached. Thus the rise of cities like Birmingham, Manchester, and Sheffield undoubtedly increased the power of Great Britain in the international system from the eighteenth century on. This increase in power, however, was largely accidental in the sense that it was not particularly planned by the central authorities and owed little to success or failure in war. What we had here was a quite independent dynamic of the exchange system that had a spillover effect on the international system.

The United States is an even more striking example of a country that has risen to power in the international system largely because of economic development through production and exchange. In the United States, the fact that the capital city of Washington was relatively insignificant over most of its history and even today is far from being the largest city symbolizes and illustrates the peculiar nature of this political organism. In the ideal type of national state, the capital city is the largest city in the country and dominates the life of the country, acting as a centralized focus for inputs of information and outputs of authority and, as the derivation of the word implies, as a "head" to the body of the rest of the country. One thinks of Paris, Rome, Madrid, Vienna, Warsaw, Copenhagen, Tokyo. The list could be extended. By contrast, Washington, Canberra, Ottawa, and, one should no doubt add, Brasilia play a different role in their respective countries. These might almost be called "economic" as opposed to "political" countries in which the major centers, such as New York, Montreal, Sydney, São Paulo are commercial and industrial cities rather than administrative and military centers. In this connection, it is interesting to note that even the state capitals of many American states are relatively minor cities like Lansing, Springfield, and Sacramento, and it is highly significant that the capital of West Germany is

Bonn. One feels that it is almost a pity that the capital of France did not remain permanently at Vichy!

Another important aspect of the city in the international system is its role in creating security against threats and violence. In classical civilization, human life was frequently more secure against violence in the city than it was in the country. Adam Smith observes, for instance, that "order and good government, and along with them the liberty and security of individuals, were, in this manner, established in cities at a time when the occupiers of land in the country were exposed to every sort of violence."[2] Even today, one sees the contrast between the landscape of France and England where the greater authority of the central power permitted men to live in open farmsteads in the country without undue fear of violence and the landscape of Germany where farmers still huddle together in villages and the countryside between villages is empty of habitation. In earlier times the city wall was a symbol of the security of the city's inhabitants. Like all forms of security, this tended to break down in the long run, and virtually all walled cities have been destroyed at some time or another. Nevertheless, in what children call the "olden days," the inhabitant of the city did enjoy at least a temporary security frequently superior to that of his rural brother. Without this, indeed as Adam Smith again points out, the accumulation that went on in the cities, the increasing division of labor, and the improvement of technology would probably have been impossible, for unless the fruits of accumulation are reasonably secure, people will not accumulate.

With the advent of aerial warfare and especially the nuclear weapon, the position of the city is radically changed. The city and the civilian who lives in it have now become hostages, and the civilian's chances of survival in a major war are much less than that of his rural brother or even that of a member of the Armed Forces. In the modern world, both the city and the civilian are expendable to the lust of the national state. This has created a complete reversal of the traditional pattern. Whereas in the earlier period the national state fostered the growth of nonpolitical cities by creating relatively large areas free from the threat of serious violence, today the national state is one of the greatest threats to its cities. Hiroshima and Nagasaki, after all, were commercial not political cities and were sacrificed to the senseless ambition of the national state. It would be very surprising if in the next "X" years Boston, Cleveland, Seattle, and so on are not similarly sacrificed on the altar of the present national system. The cities have become helpless pawns in an international system that is developing rapidly toward a major breakdown.

I have argued on another occasion that there are many reasons why the classical city, clearly bounded in space and organized from within by a strong sense of community, is incompatible with modern technology and is likely to survive only in special cases as a kind of anomaly.[3] The ecological structure of the classical city depended on a high resources cost, both of transportation and communication. The city was clustered and bounded; spatially it tended to have a ring structure centered around a market square, a cathedral, or some other civic center. Its population density was high, and there was usually a fairly sharp boundary that separated it from the countryside.

Both the economic and the political structures of the modern world are dominated by the reduction in cost of transport of people, commodities, information, and violence. Clustering of any kind is a result of cost of transport of something. If cost of transport was zero, we would expect activity of all kinds to be uniformly spread over space. The lowering of cost of transport, therefore, inevitably reduces clustering and increases dispersion. We see this very clearly in what is happening to the cities. The central cities are decaying and disintegrating. The level of amenity in them has fallen, the level of violence has risen. The central cities may decay completely, and an urban structure may emerge that looks something like chicken wire; a network of ribbon development enclosing areas of country and rural settlement. The automobile, the telephone, the television, and the missile with a nuclear warhead—all move the ecological system in the same direction.

The critical question under these circumstances is what happens to the structure of community. Before the twentieth century, community was structured geographically in fairly well-defined ways. In his political role especially, a citizen belonged to a well-defined local community, whether village, town, or city, toward which he felt some attachment and some obligations. Beyond this were regional political organizations, such as counties and states, and beyond these again the national state. A great deal can be learned about the prevailing image of community by simply asking large numbers of people "Where do you live?" or "Where do you come from?" The answer, of course, depends somewhat on the context. If one is abroad, for instance, one would tend to respond by giving the name of one's national state. In the United States, one would be unlikely to respond by giving the name of one's county. A great many people probably do not even know it, for this is not a salient community. One suspects there might be almost an even chance of giving the name of a state or the name of a city. Some people would say "I come from Dedham," some might say "I come from Massachusetts." A person from Syracuse might even say "I come from upstate New York," thereby dissociating himself from the appendage at the lower end of the Hudson. On the other hand, a man may say "I come from Boston" when he actually lives in Concord, or "I come from New York" when he really lives in Scarsdale.

There can be little doubt that the impact of the modern world is to diminish allegiance to the local community and especially to the central city. The increase in mobility assures this. In the days when a man lived all his life in the place where he was born and where his forefathers had lived for generations, there was a strong tie to the local community. In the modern world, hardly anybody lives where he was born and a man changes his location many times during his life. Under these circumstances the sense of allegiance to the local community as something special declines, and if the local political community is to be run successfully, it must rely less and less on allegiances and sentiment. It will have to rely on professionalization and the use of exchange in order to attract the kind of support necessary. Everybody recognizes that the great problem of the central city today is that the people who make the decisions about it do not live there and do not feel themselves to be part of its community. They may live in the suburbs or in another part of the world altogether. Hence the city as a decision-making unit is really disintegrating. From being a social organism, it has declined to being a chance aggregation without even the organizational structure that permits the decisions to be made that will affect the local community. One sees this, for instance, in the field of banking, finance, and corporate management where decisions may be made that profoundly affect the future of a particular community by people who have never even seen it. We see this even more dramatically in the international system where the decision of a man in the White House consigns the people of cities on the other side of the world to the flames. We have passed from the stage where the cities nurtured civilization to a world in which the city is simply a victim of forces far beyond its own control, a sacrificial lamb on the altar

27

of corporate or national ambition. The great danger here is that the sense of local community will be wholly eroded by the sense of impotence on the part of local people and local decision-makers. This can create a situation in which the cities almost literally fall apart. The city is something that nobody loves, and what nobody loves will die.

It is not surprising, therefore, that in the modern world the city is in deep crisis. It is an aggregation of humanity that has lost its sense of community and cannot, therefore, provide a human identity. St. Paul was able to say with pride that he was a citizen of no mean city. Would the same be said by a resident of Harlem or of any of our central cities? The cities of today that are not mean, like Venice, Florence, Kyoto, and one might almost add Williamsburg, are the fossil relics of a departed age. There are a great many things in our own age and in our society in which we can take great pride—the pictures of Mars, the conquest of disease, the great universities, even let me say with some trepidation, the middle-class suburbs with pleasant lawns, solid comforts, and relaxed neighborliness. The city, however, is not on this list, perhaps because it is really a survival from a past age, and we have not yet made the adjustments that can transform it into something worthy of the rest of our accomplishments.

The crux of the problem is that we cannot have community unless we have an aggregate of people with some decision-making power. The impotence of the city, perhaps its very inappropriateness as a unit, is leading to its decay. Its impotence arises, as I have suggested earlier, because it is becoming a mere pawn in economic, political, and military decision-making. The outlying suburb is actually in better shape. It is easier for a relatively small unit to have some sense of community, and the suburb at least has a little more control over its own destiny. It is somewhat less likely to be destroyed in war. Its economic base tends to be diversified as its residents commute over a wide area; hence its fate is not in the hands of a single decision-maker. Its local government, its school board, and other community agencies often are able to gather a considerable amount of support and interest from the people they serve.

It is not wholly absurd to ask whether we should not abolish the city altogether as a political organization. Let us divide Chicago and Detroit into thirty suburbs, small enough so that they have some chance of achieving a sense of local community and local responsibility for things that can be done locally. Then, of course, we would need "functional federalism"—metropolitan water boards covering a wide area, air-pollution agencies, educational finance institutions that would equalize local opportunities without destroying local initiative, police forces of different levels of size and function, and so on. Political scientists have often lamented about the multitude of political agencies in the United States, but the case against this may easily have arisen out of a prissy desire for tidiness. In terms of productivity, a multiplicity of agencies may be precisely what the times require. We seem quite incapable of expanding the central cities out into their suburban environment. Perhaps we should try reversing the recipe and move the suburbs into the city, building up around them a network of functional agencies.

The problem of integrating the city into the world community is much more difficult than the problem of reorganizing it locally. Nevertheless, the future of the city as an institution probably depends more on the future of the international system than it does on any other aspect of social life. More than any other aspect of the sociosphere, the international system is destroying the city, either physically by bombing or more critically by eroding its problem-solving capacity through the withdrawal of both intellectual and physical resources into the international system itself. The brain drain into the international system and the war industry is one of the principal reasons why the city receives so little attention and why what attention it has received in such efforts as urban renewal and public housing has been largely disastrous. The impact of urban renewal and of throughways on a city is physically not unlike that of a small nuclear weapon, but with less damage to bodies and perhaps more damage to minds. Both urban renewal and nuclear destruction come from the national state. They are both thunderbolts hurled at the city from afar without regard to the tender ecological structure of its life and community. The cities by themselves, of course, cannot solve the problem of the world community, though one would think they might exercise a little bargaining power on it. The difficulty here is twofold. In the first place, the cities seem to have astonishingly little bargaining power in general. This is a puzzling phenomenon. One looks, for instance, in the United States at the extraordinary bargaining power of the agricultural interest, even at a time when it has shrunk to an almost insignificant proportion of the total electorate. By comparison with the apparent impotence of the cities, one sees the even more astonishing bargaining power of the military, who both starve and threaten the cities and eat high off the hog at a time when the cities have to be content with scraps. The second difficulty is that the international system is not really salient to the people who live in cities, even though it affects them so profoundly. The decision-makers in the international system are few, they are remote, and it all seems a long way from the experience of the ordinary citizen. Hence he is inclined to "leave this to father" even when the great White House father is dangerously incompetent in these matters. It is not the importance of a problem that determines how much attention will be paid to it, but its salience. Unfortunately, importance and salience are very loosely related, sometimes even negatively related.

All these difficulties resolve themselves into a single structural deficiency. There are virtually no channels in society or in the world at large by which the city as such can exercise bargaining power. One wonders what would happen if the cities were represented directly, as states, not only in the United States Senate, but in the United Nations. Could we envisage a new Hanseatic League of cities against the national state and the military establishments that are threatening to destroy them? All these suggestions, alas, sound like brainstorming and pipe dreams.

Nevertheless, what we face here is perhaps the most important single example of a much larger problem of political and social organization. The conflict in the world today—underlying the cold war at the international level, civil rights and the Black Power movement in the United States, and the inability of so many tropical countries to resolve their internal conflicts to the point where economic development becomes possible—is a conflict of two political concepts. The names "individualism" and "collectivism" are quite inadequate to describe these concepts, but these are probably the best words we have. On the one hand, there is the political ideal of the individual acting as an individual and independent person in a larger community, exchanging his capacities with other individuals in a social contract and in a market economy, expressing his political activity primarily by voting in elections on the one-man, one-vote basis. In political organization, this leads to what we might call "atomistic parliamentarism." In economic organization, it leads to capitalism and the free market. In religious organization, it leads to Protestantism and sectarianism; in family life, to the free choice of partners. It goes along with the life style of mobility and rootlessness, entrepreneurship, achieved rather than ascribed status, and so on. On the other side, we have the collective ideal stressing the notion that the identity of the individual is so bound up with the community with which he identifies that he can only become an individual as part of a community. His political activity here is exercised by activity influencing the decisions and the bargaining power of a series of concentric communities, rather than as an individual among other individuals. This leads toward a consensus-oriented society, totalitarianism, socialism, catholicism, monasticism, associationism, such things as trade unions and professional associations, collective rather than individual bargaining, and the corporate rather than the parliamentary state. Each of these philosophies has its own virtues and vices, and almost any political system is some sort of uneasy compromise between the two. Some lean toward one side, and some toward the other. At the present moment in history, the crisis of the cities has arisen because in *no* political structure is the city adequately represented. At the level of individualistic democracy, the city has lost its sovereignty and independence. It has become a pawn in the sense that its local autonomy has been destroyed. At the level of collective organization, the city is not organized as a bargaining unit. It does not bargain with the other agencies of society, such as the national state or the corporation, as effectively, shall we say, as the labor unions bargain with the employers. The city, therefore, gets the worst of both worlds. Its citizens as such are effective neither as political individuals nor as members of a bargaining collectivity.

Much of the same problem is seen in the Negro or other minority groups. The rise of the Black Power movement is in a sense a breakdown of individualistic democracy at this level. On the other hand, the Black Power solution is also likely to fail, because black power is not very great and the movement is likely to raise expectations that will probably be disastrously disappointed. One sees the same problem in the demands for "student power," which are simply not constructive, though occasionally they can be destructive, as in Latin America and Japan. Nevertheless, the student is not satisfied to be a mere individual and feels the need of identifying himself with a collectivity.

The synthesis and reconciliation in both structure and philosophy of the two political "modes," as they might be called, of individualism and collectivism perhaps represent the greatest single

31

long-run problem of the human race at its present state of development. The city, or at least the urban collectivity, is one of the principal arenas in which this problem is or is not being worked out, as the case may be. Almost the only consideration that leads to any hopefulness about the future is that communication and aggregation foster the process of human learning. In the age of civilization, the concentration of people in cities unquestionably contributed to the slow growth of knowledge, simply because of the facilitation of communication that this concentration implied. Rural isolation leads to rural backwardness and cloddishness. The implications of the words "civilized," "civil," "urbane," and even "civilian," as over against "rustic" and "bucolic," suggest the values that have arisen from easy urban communication. The country may be the depository of traditional virtue, but new ideas come out of the wicked city. The city, therefore, historically has been the main source of change, both in the international system and in all aspects of the social system, as it has produced new ideas, new ideologies, new philosophies, and new technologies. The towns, as Adam Smith observes, improve the country. The decay of the city today does not represent a return to rural virtue or to rural ignorance. It is a symptom, if anything, of the urbanization of the whole world. The communications revolution has created, in effect, a world city, and this is why the local cities are in decay. It is to be hoped, therefore, that we can look forward to new knowledge, new ideas, and even a transformation of the international system that will give us security, arising out of the knowledge process of the world.

The essential key to this process may be the development of self-consciousness in the city dweller that he is a member of a city and indeed of the world city. One suspects that the unexploited bargaining power of the city is great simply because the city, disorganized as it is, is inevitably a focus or nodal point of the world network of communication. Airports are the synapses of the world communications network; so in a sense are the television stations and the newspapers of the city. So are its universities. It is a pretty fair generalization in the theory of location to say that the synapses, the gaps, or the switches in the communications and transportation network produce the city in the first place. This is why, for instance, so many cities have arisen at ports, at heads of navigation, and at points of trans-shipment. In a world in which the transportation of communication is beginning to overshadow the transportation of commodities, the city—because of its position in the communications network—has real power that is as yet unexploited, mainly because it is not self-conscious. If I can take a leaf out of the book of Karl Marx, and this is one occasion where the leaf may be better than the book, we may urge the rise of self-consciousness in the cities, a rise of their joint self-consciousness of the community as a world city representing the constructive and developmental forces of humanity as against the essentially backward-looking or destructive tendencies of the country and the military. Our motto, therefore, perhaps should be "Cities of the world unite, you have nothing to lose but your slums, your poverty, and your military expendability." On this note of modest long-run optimism, I had better conclude for fear that the pessimism of the short run catches up with us first.

REFERENCES

1. It is the credibility of the threat which really matters from the point of view of its ability to organize social systems. Credibility in very complex ways is related to capability. The relationship is closer in the case of material threat than in the case of spiritual threat where capability is hard to demonstrate, but where the threat often justifies itself: for example, the fear of Hell. Even in the case of material threat, credibility can remain long after capability has disappeared. Nevertheless, in the long run there must be a tendency for capability and credibility at least to run parallel.

2. Adam Smith, *The Wealth of Nations*, Book 3, Ch. 3.

3. Kenneth E. Boulding, "The Death of the City: A Frightened Look at Post-civilization," in *The Historian and the City*, eds. Oscar Handlin and John Burchard (Cambridge, 1963), pp. 133-45.

JOHN R. SEELEY

Remaking the Urban Scene: New Youth in an Old Environment

I

THERE IS something fatal to the understanding of urban problems in the means by which we seek it. The means are, conventionally, the orderly presentation of facts as complete, accurate, and sure as possible, in the context of argument as lucid and precise as possible, with a view to the persuasion or conviction of "rational" minds that think that way. We all know, I think, the roles, rules, and skills involved. But if this procedure has brought us to the present sorry pass, it is ironic that it should be held that necessities of communication require that the fatal process be continued in order to persuade any of its fatality.

Let no one fail to appreciate the difficulty. Imagine a patient in psychoanalysis whose central defense is "intellectualization." His analyst would like him for his own benefit to appreciate the harm he thus does himself. The patient might sense, intuit, appreciate what is lost to him *if* he will not abandon the defense enough to enter as a whole man (as nearly as he can) into the drama that he and his doctor (as representative of "the world") are playing out. But before he will engage, he says: "Prove it to me. Marshal your arguments. Show me a fourfold table of harms and goods cross-classified by intellectualization and whatever is the alternative." If the analyst yields, he and the patient are probably lost in one of two ways: Either it cannot be shown intellectually that intellectualization is as bad for this patient as it actually is, or, if it can, that this would be the worst possible way for him to reach that conclusion, since at the very least it would deepen his reliance on what he already over-relies on.

We cannot reach to the question of "the conscience of the city"

34

by means of a conscience that I hold to be in a radical sense false. It is ironic (and probably self-defeating) to seek to secure conviction on that point by the very methods that the argument impugns.

It might be noted as an intellectual *curiosum* that each of the two courses open *is* subject to and the object of attack. If a psychoanalyst maintains that there is no way to the understanding of analysis except by the experience of it—that, in effect, the abstraction and "precision" characterizing scientific speech about it inevitably falsify and misrepresent its nature—he is accused of practicing mysticism, magic, or mumbo-jumbo. If, on the other hand, a McLuhan—no matter what the merit of his contentions—argues by means of a linear logic sequentially presented against "linear logic," books, and sequential as against simultaneous presentation, his critics hold that he cannot believe what he asserts since his practice is incompatible with his theory. The two arguments, taken together, seem to substantiate the conclusion of the dean of an eminent medical school: "There is no learning," he said, "among doctors; only biological replacement by those with new ideas." They might also make intelligible the distress of the young at the difficulties or impossibilities of communication with "anyone over thirty."

In any case, what is here undertaken is a self-contradictory attempt to marshal an over-ordered argument against over-order, an attack on the undue reliance on logic relying unduly on logic, a managerial-type assault on management, a prosaic *demarche* against prosaism, an attempt to convince some colleagues by these methods that they cannot be convinced by such methods, and that failing such conviction they will mistake the future because, so restricted, they misapprehend the present in its most vital particulars.

II

The West (in which must now be included the Westernized or Westernizing nations) has reached a climax. The climax refers both to personal and institutional practices and to those reflective methods by which "adaptation" is secured and operability maintained. By a "climax" I mean that point of highest development precedent to fission, explosion, or exhaustion and replacement by another form. By "another form," I no more mean a minor modification of the old form than the so-called Dark Ages represented in relation to the preceding Roman Empire.

We may discern some intimations as to the probable shape of that successor form by attending to two classes of facts: those connected with alienation and those connected with such alternative and separate integrations as we see beginning. Alienation here means the dissolution of a civilization—not some untoward cause or consequence of it—since civilization exists in attachment, devotion, as community exists (to quote John Dewey) in communication.

If this is what is afoot, and if it can by no means—or at least not much or for very long—be contained, any treatment of "the conscience of the city" must take this development at least for its context or, if approved, for its aim. If the view is correct, there is something tragicomic about sitting around "planning" to secure, extend, and improve what is to be shortly swept away—like Roman generals plotting reparative wars abroad and placatory redistribution of bread and amusement at home, just as a double, irresistible assault striking at the roots of the very idea of Rome was being mounted by "barbarians" abroad and "riff-raff" in catacombs in the heart of the heartland at home.

Just as the city is in normal times that place where the civilization reaches the high point of its gradient, where the civilization is refined, developed, elaborated, and fed back to the hinterland, so in abnormal times the city is that place where its successor is being incubated, nurtured, fostered, or developed. And the conscience of the city lies at that *nucleus nucleorum*, wherever it may be, where most actively, most passionately, most devotedly, most integrally the foundations of the new civilizations are being in action and interaction conceived, incarnated, tested, and worked out.

Most of the thoughts and plans for the future of the city are exacerbation or mere mitigation or fond folly: mitigation if we agree to give cups of water to thirsty children while the world shifts seismically in its shape and center of gravity; folly, if we imagine that we are doing more, or that we are dealing at all with the main and significant flow of events; exacerbation if the plans perfect exactly that which leads the list of *repudianda*.

III

The crisis of the West, the great movement (or drift) toward universal alienation, is attested to by the absence of response appropriate to the very idea of crisis despite or because of endless discussion and attendant handwringing. If your patient, child, or colleague talked endlessly of a crisis or series of crises in his life, of a growing feeling of depersonalization, while over some very long period the crises grew worse and the depersonalization greater, surely you would begin to suspect that the crisis lay at another, a different, a deeper level: that perhaps the talk about crises or that way of talking about crisis was intrinsic and contributory to the crisis and its exacerbation. You would be forced to conclude that the talk (and the action "based" upon it) was insufficient as remedy; you might suspect it was unnecessary (and hence diversionary); you might well entertain the idea that that way of analyzing and dealing with crisis was at or near the core of what generates it. It is not enough to "recognize" and plan against the Kafkaesque —indeed, by now, ultra-Kafkaesque—quality of modern life, if it is precisely the kind of recognition and response that we give to the quality of life that is the source supreme of its increasingly Kafkaesque character. Some people, even if they allow that we have thought our way into the crisis, evidently believe we can think ourselves out of it. Even where they will allow that our way of conceiving and perceiving the world has brought us to this pass, they seem to hold that some continuation of the same or some relatively minor modification will see us through or out. That the whole set of ways of thinking and their attendant ways of acting themselves constitute the crisis is evidently, for them, hard to believe.

It seems evident to me and many that the world may be loosely divided, like Caesar's Gaul, into three parts: a relatively "affluent" part more or less conscious of, more or less disgusted with, and alienated from the "good life" they have finally achieved; a moderately well-off part, some still coasting on the momentum of getting there, but most more or less numbed and indifferent; a needy part desperately struggling by every means to get into the desperate straits of the other two. Such a distribution characterizes not only any single nation (this one especially), but the relations among nations as well. By a developing or an underdeveloped nation, we mean one aspiring or being pressed or maneuvered to get into the state we are in. Those who have qualms about getting them into that state console themselves by supposing that the "beneficiary" nations can at one and the same time commit themselves to our major ways of doing, being, thinking, feeling in the world, and save and preserve "the best of their culture." For people who believe that cultures are or ought to be in a profound and pervasive sense wholes, such a prescription is very strange—so strange, in fact, that one is driven to wonder what vital irrationality the proposal is meant to protect and conceal. Surely if someone had suggested we might graft the business practices of Manchester in the 1890's onto, say, Periclean Greek culture and thus have the double virtue of "cheap goods" (whatever that would have meant to our neo-Pericleans) and high-minded balance (whatever that could have meant to our neo-entrepreneurs), one would have judged the proposing someone crazy. That one or another cultural logic would have had to pervade and prevail, giving everything its ulterior significance and destroying or eliminating whatever was radically incompatible, is as certain as anything human can be, and, if not implicit in the notion of culture, most definitely confirmed by everything we know about it.

Thus the dream of a pluralism in essentials is idle. We are destined, I think, to a cultural unity. And that unity to be achieved in some historically brief interval, a virtual next instant, is unity under the sign of affluence and emptiness, plenitude of "means" and vacuum of satisfactions, satiation, disgust, "power," and nausea that now marks and distinguishes some considerable portion of our own society and a lesser portion of all Western ones.

I can hardly avoid "talking past" those who believe that the source of the deep and pervasive disgust, the *nausée générale*, has to do with "our failures." To be sustained, this view requires either a special meaning for the word "failure" or the recognition that what disgusts us is our success. The alienation, the misery, the nausea are intrinsic to our culture and its essence, implicit in its organizing principles, and most present, most visible, most palpable when and where it is most perfected.

Does anyone have serious difficulty identifying the arch-achievements and most characteristic products of our civilization? Surely some unique supremacy would have to be accorded our "production," our characteristic social organization, our "educational system," our "middle-class way of life"—as much a climax and a hallmark for us this hour as the "gentleman" was for England in the age just past. But a deeper supremacy would have to be our science and technology—now a technology of men as well as of things. And behind and below these are the ways of thinking, being, and acting of which they are the product. Those surely are our grand achievements—indeed, they are us in our distinct us-ness, in motion. These are not our aberrations, but our essential and crowning glories. Indeed they are that to which we do look when we wish or think we wish to correct what we truly consider aberrations: minor departures from expectation, such as air pollution or ghetto "housing." When Rap Brown said, "Violence is as American as cherry pie," he too was trying to get us to cease pretending that an endemic condition connected with our dearest aims and efforts may (for the sake of self-deceit and in order *not* to deal with real problems) be ignored or relegated to special, extraordinary, and disclaimed status. Our violence, both in its "spontaneous" and organized forms, I would have to list also among our arch-achievements: Mace, napalm, and person-shredding devices are as much our lovingly labored products, responsive in use to our deepest needs, as the Lincoln Memorial, the Medical Corps, or the Library of Congress. Indeed, not these severally, but their bonding or welding or wedding is what interests us here.

It would be idle to deny that a variety of responsive opinion obtains even among those who see "the phenomena" with distress or disgust. There are those who regard the phenomena as expressions of human nature, rather than our particular civilizational nature, and who look hence to resignation, "realism," or minor mitigatory measures as appropriate. These are those "reformers"—for want of a better word—who regard what presents itself as evidence of the *immaturity* of a system that is essentially good or potentially viable, and their remedy, of course, is to press on to more of the same planning, control, "education," "resource-utilization," correction of blatant injustice, and the like. There are those who profess and call themselves "radicals," who look to such remedies as new laws—or constitutions even—redefinitions of property or redistributions of titles thereto, the substitution of one elite for another (the inauguration of "meritocracy," for instance). These three seem so much alike as to appear bedfellows squabbling familiarly within the standard Western family. A fourth opinion holds that none of these views touches that which gnaws at the very marrow of the civilization, renders it intrinsically dehumanizing, inevitably corrupting of man and nature. The view ought not to be thought entirely novel even in modern times. Freud seriously raised and left open (in *Civilization and Its Discontents*) the question whether any civilization—viewed as a system protecting people from the threats of nature, the body, and one another—did not of its nature so empty life of pleasure and the possibility of pleasure that the motive for and

39

capacity to sustain the civilization must be in time undercut and destroyed. Not necessarily civilization generally, but certainly *this* civilization is, in a rapidly mounting crescendo, showing itself to be a Moloch at its heart and core.

The evidence lies not in our peccadilloes, sins, and deviations, but in our central and crowning achievements: the most basic kinds of relations among the kinds of persons we have most basically made ourselves. The allegation that we are all "plastic people" loses too much in translation to carry the force, richness, or meaning that belongs to it.

IV

If I try to bring back out of the rich and allusive "language"— words, acts, musics, postures, gestures, shaded and subtle ways of being, breathing, reaching, touching—whatever I can put into "straight" language, what shall I say? How shall I locate in "our" language the source of a *dégoût total*, a *nausée générale*, a large part of which stems from the very nature of that language and the uses to which it is put, the only uses to which it *can* be put since it was developed for just such use.

The central thrusts of the civilization are clearly conquest, control, mastery, subordination, domestication, domination, the bending of all to what is taken to be the human will. It is the apotheosis of willfulness. We appear in the Universe as Conquistadors—no matter what minor modifications we may in our odd moments permit ourselves. Agency is all; patience nothing, except as another way of mastery in rare circumstances, such as terminal cancer. We prefer in practice (whatever we may say abstractly) the effective to the harmless. Nazi soldiers were to Americans part of the family, perhaps in misconduct or error; Balinese non-soldiers are quaint or a mystery, but not serious human beings. All is reduced to the test of use—use in the peculiar "military" sense of the conqueror looking for further conquest. We sometimes smile when the claim is made explicitly that music is to be used to "tame the savage breast" or religion to maintain mental health or serve social solidarity, but in fact we can hardly accredit either comfortably until the claims (or analogical ones) have been made. To be in the world in the mode of lovers or children is so nearly unthinkable a thought that we should reject it, if we could imagine what it implied, as certainly un-American and non-Western and, perhaps, not fully hu-

man. We are the society of the girded loin, and what is in our hand
is the crook at best and the sword at worst, the two being in our
scheme so closely connected anyway as to represent phases in one
act, the appropriate act, our paradigm-universal. The questions that
divide men politically—the few capable of causing cold wars, of
threatening hot ones, and generally of promoting passion—are not
about the *whether* of appropriation, but the *whom*. Who is to take
title to and exercise dominion over the farthest reaches of space and
the uttermost depths of the sea has become an urgent question for
us. Our highest imaginative flights suggest "all of us" as the answer,
but a non-proprietary, non-possessory relation is outside the ambit
of our imagination or beyond the pale of our political practice. The
Universe is "ours"—either distributively or collectively. Indeed
property, propriety, and the proper (*propre à moi*, the essence of
the egoid) are so closely connected conceptually and practically,
psychologically and etymologically that it is impossible to think at
all in our thought-system without implying (assuming) the relations as given. Freedom is even defined as the condition under
which "I am my own man," a statement that on its face seems to
imply that slave and slaveholder, owner and owned, are one. We
cannot, dare not, would not leave ourselves unconquered, uncontrolled, unowned. We speak severally of "myself" and "my self,"
and the practice seems so close to common sense, to something
given in the nature of things, that any alternative formulation, even
a silence before the ineffable, appears needless or misleading or
both. The notion that your self is not yours, nor anyone else's, and
not in the order of things to which possessory ideas or feelings are
appropriate is so patently violative of our ideas, attitudes, practices,
and assumptions that it can barely be appreciated as a serious and
radically transforming perception. Indeed, it is in a sense an untrue,
a false statement. Starting with the assumption with which we all
start, we have evolved—or, rather, involuted—selves so truncated,
trivialized, narrowed, and ill-nourished that they probably *are*
nearly capable of being "owned," used, and held in fee.

The controlling, mastering, conquering, subordinating set is so
built into our practices, our psychology, our psyches, our episte-
mology, our ways of "knowing," and our language that extrication
or escape by means of these is actually or virtually barred. Had I
prefaced the preceding sentence by saying, "I think that. . . . ," the
very "I" used would have evoked inevitably in the mind of the
reader exactly that controlling, mastering "I," engaged in one more

act of control and mastery. That "I"—overly, formally, totally disjunctive from every we, actual and virtual, from every they, from all its and the It—is the condition, cause, consequence, and beginning of the Conquistadorial set and the conquest. It is a particular way of being in the world. Since of its nature it drives toward its own logical conclusion, it progressively bars all other ways totally.

This set, now reaching its climactic elaboration in thought and practice, has given us victory, but victory of the most Pyrrhic kind. Not the unexamined life, but the life of conquest turns out to be not worth living. The stars and the atom's powers and secrets are now ours; the biosphere is our family farm. With every promise of "success," we turn upon ourselves and one another, through "social science," the scopes (whether tele- or micro-) that bid fair to bring our own refractory selves, severally and collectively, also into our service in our severalty or collectivity. The heady hope of a "social science" that will let us truly know ourselves and one another, conjoined to a "planning" that will allow this us in effect to manage that us, is the epitomic expression of the Western dream.

The disease or dream is variously seen: by a Mannheim as a virtually limitless increase in "functional rationality" accompanied by and based upon a virtually limitless decrease in "substantive rationality"; by a Freud as the sacrifice of all pleasures to the point where the will to live is itself overcome by the elaboration of those "defenses" which this civilization represents; by others as the ever more dangerous, ever more irrepressible return of the repressed moves to aggression, the genocidal-suicidal super-achievements of our age; by a Marcuse as the topological transformation of many-sided, multiform man into "one-dimensionality." These men agree that we do ever better what makes no sense, that joy and bliss are dead on the altar of armor, that we are other and strange to all including "our own selves," hell-bound to wed death, already all but dead, reduced to a single, last dimension. Those professionals who hear these voices, however, seem dominantly to respond to the vision they evoke with a heightening of the activity which is the cause and expression of the state that the vision recognizes. They seem to hold that either more of the medicine that caused the sickness or a minor variant of the same must be the source of its cure. That senselessness, joylessness, alienation, limitless aggression, the basic alliance with death, and the final reduction of all to nothing are built into the primordial roots and presuppositions of our culture is rarely concluded and still less acted upon. We rely most desperately on what has failed us first. We cannot believe that a world conceived, organized, and related to as we have done may be finally uninhabitable, and the selves correspondingly cast over and over against such a world empty and inoperable. Even when the problem is "located" within the self, we make of that self a "that" in order to "deal with" the problem in our customary fabricant fashion. Our answer to the problems that arise is further and finer fragmentation (so that conquest can continue even as its fruits taste ever more ashen in our mouths). Dissevered each from himself, everyone from everyone else, all from nature, and each more and more from the All, we seek our salvation in one more analytic effort to be followed by one more organizational thrust, a new battle plan for triumph when what is killing us is war.

What we have perfected is technology, and it is technology on which most men, most places, most times rest such vague hopes as still stir. It is now in or almost in our hand to feed lavishly, clothe, and render "literate" the world, to live in virtually instantaneous, universal, continuous, ubiquitous "communication," to annihilate nearly all physical distance, to command more energy than we can use, to engineer mood and perhaps perception at will, to write such genetic prescriptions as we wish, to make such men as whim may dictate. The Universe capitulates. We are everywhere triumphant. But a premonitory smell of cosmic Neroism is in the air, and the cry of "Stop The World; I Want To Get Off" has become, whether absurd or not, pervasive and insistent.

V

There cannot, in the nature of the case, be a well-articulated theory of such things. A way would have to be found to "get out of the culture" in order to find as a new person a new and different direction. Indeed, since some sort of "opening" is of the essence, and since what will follow such opening is unforeknowable, a programmatic specification would be a double contradiction in terms. The first problem is to find the meaning of getting out and the means to do so; the second is to begin to "find one's head" in what then is opened to one; the third is to prevent one's reintegration and reassimilation; and the fourth is to live in relation to oneself, others, nature, in such fashion as to preserve and enhance the new person in the new relatedness. To look for a formula for a quest is to fail to understand what is implied in either term.

Some faint forecast of what may be before us may be provided by an ideal-typical appreciation of what was till recently known as the "hippie" phenomenon. Being "*a* hippie," largely a news-media invention, is itself very nearly a contradiction in terms; being "hippie" is a way of being in the world, of being in a different way, a mood, a social movement, a movement of religions, a quest at once personal, social, and transcendent.

The ontogeny of hippieness is as easy to abstract as it is fatal to adequate appreciation. The onset is marked by disaffection, disaffiliation, and disgust in the full and literal sense of those terms. What was libidinally invested is disendowed; one is orphaned. What had been nurturant is sensed to be poisonous to one's previously barely apprehended deeper being. These sentiments move toward repudiation, more or less clearly articulated, more and more massive. Escape and extrication from the whole fast-woven web of activities, connections, and expectations become paramount necessities, touched with the desperate character of a struggle for survival. Co-emergent is the urgency of finding an adequate experience sufficient at least to suggest or to intimate what in the self and the world has been so radically denied, distorted, and filtered out from the rich life of the rich child of the rich West. What is begun is a long, slow, agonizing quest that moves over a territory having few general and still fewer particular landmarks. Its criteria, recognized in treasured "highs," are the unitive experiences with self, others, nature, the All that depend upon and give rise to some diffusion of the already overbounded ego. The "incidentals" of location, drug-adjuvants, music, fatigue, fasting, costume, style, special language of word, touch, gesture are each less than essential, but more than adventitious. They promote and support, as do the endless but not tightly connected talks in pad and commune, the wandering, tentative searchings for one's roots and flower. Finding one's thing and doing one's thing mark stages and are intrinsic; they attest and contribute to a far-reaching transformation of the personality, whose inward signs are growth into gentleness, trust, and grace. No longer —or radically less—atomized, deracinated, homogenized, constricted, and truncated, no longer modeled on mastery, but wedded to wisdom, a recognizably new population emerges not merely bearing a new culture, but being in a new way and manifesting even in mien and posture what it is to be in that Way. For the first time since the history of the West became distinctly Western, a powerful movement emerges whose way is wisdom and whose hero is the sage. No more powerful transformation or revolution can be imagined for a society or a culture than a shift in the type of hero and the mode of self-modeling. From tycoon and bureaucrat-in-chief to sage, from conquest of whatever is to participation in it—these are great distances and direly different directions, dire at least for a civilization so singularly set as ours on so narrow and mean a course.

The first question commonly put to anyone asserting the power of the movement—"How many hippies, exactly, are there?"—attests to a culture lost in mindless counting, computation, calculation, and coping-with or conquering designs and devices. Not only do we instinctively turn to this counting device—to measure magnitude which then becomes undistinguishable from the greatness of something—but the externality, the management set, is implicit in the question. The question means "How many of *them* are there," so that "I" may know whether or how to modify my plans for containing them.

The kindest question asked will often be "How can we plan *for* them?" Dylan's answer—"Get out of the way, if you don't understand, For the times, they are a-changin'"—is evidently incomprehensible, for even the word "understand" is only "understood" by us in characteristic, fatal fashion. We think we understand something when we "grasp" it, have hold of those particulars that permit us to put it in its place. That the vital is only "understood" as it grasps you—or, more exactly, as embrace occurs—is not, it appears, except fleetingly in our understanding.

The question "How can we plan for them?" is so wrong in its every word that no answer is possible. There is an error in the word "them": It is a movement of the spirit, a genuine "change of mind" variously incarnated now in various degrees in various people, that requires a response; it is not some new "subpopulation" or sect. There is an error in the word "we": The likelihood that any intellectual-managerial "we" will be able (failing the advent of fascism) to plan or control underlying populations much longer is negligible, as dramatically attested by the progress of "pot," the development of new sex relations and gender definitions, the "troubles" in school and university and other prisons and ghettos in the last decade. There is error in the word "plan," unless its meaning is so stretched as to include voluntary abdication of the whole scheme of arranging conditions by forethought as to have pre-decided outcomes specified with some particularity. "Planning for Freedom"—the conciliatory slogan—somehow turns out in practice mostly to mean the mere imposition of order *in the name of freedom.*

VI

Even if the foregoing is correct, even if our civilization is about to founder in nuclear fire (or fascism) or to become something that "hippieness" foreshadows and forecasts, what has all this to do with "the conscience of the city"?

What is significant about the city is not that it is a "population center" or a place of intersection of roads, rail lines, waterways, or whatnot. A city is that place where whatever is highest in the civilization is being most actively, most vividly, most truly carried on. The city is the locus of the civilization's conscience. Failing that, the city is a population trap, a behavioral sink.

We must remind ourselves of the "hippie" insistence that "finding your head" and finding the appropriate supportive and promotive relation for doing so are co-emergents. No one has as yet gone beyond pad or commune scale in such a search and not abandoned the one half-aim or the other—though a loose commune of communes, not spatially concentrated, seems emerging. Most of these communes are now physically located by choice, not necessity, in the clefts of mountains, on the not-economically-arable plains, in the deserts and waste places generally, in the niches and interstices left free or sparse by the present ecological organization. At least for a while, the conscience of the city and therewith the city may well have its dwelling place anywhere but there.

Indeed, there are other reasons to think that for the near future the city will be literally the province and backwoods, filled with and ruled by provincials and backwoodsmen attempting to learn and do what the advance guard of the civilization is striving to unlearn and undo. It seems perfectly clear that the internal proletariat at home, like the external one abroad, is bound and determined to go through all the stages we have gone through in our miserable quest of this now potentially happy place. Those most external to our society want most the goods and powers, the games and their yield in differential deference, the penalties and rewards, the conquests and controls that are so bitter in our mouths. Just as the poor took on, step by step, the city's abandoned neighborhoods and mansions, so now they seem about to seize the city and with it the city ways that epitomize our maladies and miseries. It will be a "learning environment" of a sort, a learning environment to ease the learning of what we must in agony unlearn, a place to acquire the major diseases one did not have in the vain hope of curing the minor ones one had.

VII

The views and visions earlier adverted to carry with them altogether different implications for the "life of learning" (all life), the manner of learning (all modes), and the environment of learning.

Whatever else is true, the learning must come bearing the personal signature of some fully credible teacher—which is to say someone much more like a guru than our present technicians of skill or information conveyance. No mass process comparable to our present "knowledge" factories in the universities or person and "skill" factories in the schools could fill any part in any congruous "process of education." Something more reminiscent of, though not identical with, discipleship and apprenticeship must supervene. Unitive experiences—or even precessory experiences to these—may be sought, even cultivated, but not engineered. The very notion of putting soul-sustenance and soul-deepening into the grip of a vast machine, organized like an army, standardized, bureaucratized, governed, purporting to derive its authority from the state will seem among the more tragicomic departures in the tragicomic history of man.

We must take it that all large systems—except for the supply of minimum needs at the cost of minimum effort—will largely disappear. What we have to imagine, apart from this minimum, is virtually a nonsystem, and that is, of course, for us, almost beyond imagining. To picture the undesigned is almost as difficult as to design it.

Let us try, however, to imagine a situation—"a scene"—in which the immediate objectives are not so much to learn about something, as to "dig it" or to alter it so that it can be dug. The scene thus defined (to confound Burke's distinctions) includes the action and the actors and the agency. To add to confusion, the purpose—at least the immediate purpose—is to "make the scene" (in a double sense), if it is worth making. The indissoluble double sense of

47

"making the scene" is on the one hand being there and (thereby or otherwise) making it other than it would have been. Digging what there is also implies a double process, but with a tremendous preponderance of emphasis on its first element: It is both unitive and disjunctive or discriminative; it is both to be lost in and to absorb, to be comprehended and to comprehend, to be integrated into and to integrate, to yield to and not master, but embody. It is, in fact (to use Kurt Wolff's terms), to surrender in order to return transformed in order to surrender otherwise.

What is to be dug is more nearly a totality than a convenient working abstraction, though occasionally a peculiarly groovy element may be abstracted. Thus if, for instance, a mathematics lesson should survive as a scene worth making, it is barely possible (and only under peculiar leanings and circumstances) that the beauty of the mathematics will be the principal element dug. The scene (in Burke's sense), the act (as likely as not seen as the funny, pathetic, possibly interesting, peculiarly subtle interplay of personalities), the actors (including oneself, with special attention to the deeper levels of value and significance), and the agency (also dug in its fullness, rather than narrowly as means to an act of narrowly defined purpose) are to be simultaneously dug and in a special sense played into—thus altering all. The special sense of "played into" is that what is meant must have no element of "playing games." To play games is to be governed by a trinity of *repudianda:* to be acting only or dominantly out of consciousness or forethought (instead of *aus ganz Natur*), for one's advantage, and in the light of other's conscious (especially predetermined and narrowed) expectations. A particular game that has to be avoided is the game of not playing games. The knife edges are very, very fine.

Let there be no question that if "skills" are not "acquired," there will be insufferably little to dig. I have had to put both words in quotation marks because they will be—can be—no longer the same things. "Acquisition," in virtue of its active, aggressive, prehensile, and possessory overtones is the wrong word; and "skills" is unduly connotative of the narrow and the "useful," the narrowly useful. But rhetoric, music, poetry, pictorial and plastic art, not to mention domestic arts, the bread and wine of life, philosophizing and testing of philosophy in dialogue and action—all these are already in process of exceedingly rapid elaboration and development. But whatever corresponds to "skills" will appear as natural emergents from activities and experiences, creditable and valuable in their own general (total) terms, rather than as the results of a self- or other-governed rationalized process of skill production (a series of lessons or a curriculum). Put another way, the way of life will engender the skills that enhance it.

Implicit in all this is a necessity that all men, or most, be teachers (and gurus) in a way for which history affords no example. That transformation can by no means be achieved overnight, for implicit in that implication is another: that "teaching" must, in effect, become a "voluntary," "natural," amateur, continuing function of the life of many, most, or all, rather than, as at present, an involuntary, artificial, intermittent job or trade of an essentially reluctant and, of course, incompetent few. The need, place, and, indeed, possibility for "teaching" as it is presently surviving will be minuscule. The nature of the society contemplated and the likely increase in the tempo of discovery ensure that learning can no longer occur, except marginally, in any situation of unilateral expertise. Increasingly it will be the case that the relative newcomer being taught will have information required for this learning that the relative oldcomer simply cannot have. Because that information will become more and more indispensable, all teaching-learning will have to have the structure of mutuality and the character essentially of a conference. Such doctors—teachers—as remain must be doctors of dialogue. In any case, the bulk of the activity entailed will fall increasingly to the siblingship. And the siblingship will no longer be, solely or primarily, the intense tiny group of "natural" (biological) brothers and sisters nor the non-intense "peers" (friends and acquaintances), but something in between the sibs of the extended families, small "tribes," and such that now begin to dot and will presently fill the landscape.

Very little will need planning—just enough control over the spread of cities and their ways to permit the conscience of the city to find itself chiefly outside these centers, to spread through the society which, by then, may be ready, having reached its fevered climax, to abandon its delirium and search out its new way. That new way, I am confident, will not be, cannot be, in content, organization, aim, or spirit, anything like a continuation or culmination of what we have hitherto nurtured and known.

Part II:

Processes and
Goals for Change

LYLE C. FITCH

Eight Goals for an Urbanizing America

WHATEVER HAPPENS here or in the rest of the world in the final third of the twentieth century, American life will profoundly change. U. S. population will grow by 75 to 125 million, with the increase locating in urban areas. Between 150 and 250 new cities of half a million each will be the measure of minimum expansion, both physical and social, that must be accomplished in little more than thirty years. Growth of knowledge and technological potential deriving from knowledge will continue, probably at an increasing rate. The flaring discontent of Negro and other minority groups will also continue until they approach full economic and political equality.

Nothing short of catastrophic war will avert these forces or the changes which they imply. The great challenge before Americans concerns whether the forces can and will be directed toward improving the urban order.

Present trends of urban development hold out both promise and threat for the future. On the one hand, despite the glaring deficiencies in such areas as housing, transportation, crime prevention, health, education, and the quality of public services, urban life has improved enormously in this century. We have come a good way from the times when urban conditions were synonymous with periodic ravage by fire and epidemics, with muddy streets, corrupt and compliant courts and police, and large sections having no pretense to law and order. Measured by material well-being, life for the majority of American families has improved more or less steadily since the depths of the Depression. Per-family real income after taxes has risen by 50 per cent in the past two decades. Educational levels have zoomed. In 1967, the proportion of young people completing college was as great as that which completed high school in the early 1920's.

On the other hand, experience thus far gives us no basis for hop-

51

ing that the present largely unplanned processes will produce efficient, secure, and beautiful cities. Smog, pollution, and congestion, frustration, delinquency, violence, and other manifestations of social pathology are all on the rise, along with affluence. The highest rate of population increase is occurring among groups most hopelessly caught in the poverty trap.

Obsolescent commercial and industrial buildings, bad taste in design, careless destruction of open space, and residential slums manifest a failure to recognize the needs of the human spirit for variety, vistas, openness, and grandeur. Nor can we flatter ourselves that in the twentieth century we have gained the functional city or the efficient city, even by sacrificing the city beautiful.[1]

It is quite possible in the last third of the century to achieve greater variety and less dullness, more beauty and less ugliness, clean streets, pure air and water, and fast, comfortable transportation. These potentialities will not be realized, however, by way of the aspirations commonly ascribed to the middle class: a secure job, a house in the suburbs, an agreeable wife, and three lovely children. There is nothing wrong with such aspirations, but they will hardly suffice to bring forth the good urban life. Progress requires visions of what we would like to become, visions of efficiency, beauty, and social justice.

Over the objections of proponents of "disjointed incrementalism,"[2] I argue that the social-action analogue for developing and marketing products in the private sector is by formulating, debating, and getting consensus on goals that express the community's aspirations for itself. Goals provide the sense of direction essential in a purposeful, dynamic society.

We have not suffered for want of goals statements in recent years, to be sure, but these efforts have concentrated on special problems or subjects such as housing and renewal, poverty and conservation.[3] I share with many others a concern that, in overreacting to these most compelling, immediate problems, we will neglect other things equally important over a longer time-span. Thus, it is said that today's urban problem is that of the Negro; I submit that if we concentrate on the Negro "problem" alone, we will neither be solving that particular "problem" nor creating the urban society and environment we should like to see in the long run.

The eight goals listed here represent my own sense of what is most important and reasonably comprehensive. They are not presented as objectives to be realized overnight, but as suggestions of the directions in which we should be going. Moreover, in a society dominated by rapidly evolving knowledge, technology, and culture, these goals, or any other set of goals, will need to be revised and replaced as new needs and possibilities present themselves.

Goal I

An urban society with values, environment, and service systems that respond fully to the needs and wants of families and individuals; a society drawn to the "human scale." This society should be open, with freedom of choice, freedom to move up occupational and social ladders, and opportunity to participate fully in economic and political life. It should be a pluralistic society in that it honors cultural differences which particular groups may wish to maintain. It should offer a variety of ways of life and opportunity to choose among them.

I mean by "human scale" the qualities of a city that provide people with comfort, satisfaction, spiritual uplift, a sense of identification with the city and their fellow men, a care for those whose needs tend to be neglected in the hustle of the market place, a regard for graciousness in relationships, a care for beauty and grace in urban design. The city falls far short of such ideals. It is hostile to women and young children; it fails to provide a social environment for courtship, neglects recreation for adolescents, lacks trees and parks, unthinkingly destroys neighborhoods and with them neighborhood values and traditions. Relations between public servants and the public are commonly uncivil and not uncommonly brutal.

"Human scale" is implicit in the traditional American commitment to freedom; freedom has been associated, in part, with that enlargement of choice made possible by the advance of technology, output, and income on education, careers, dwellings, recreation, styles of life. But today freedom of choice is suppressed in numerous ways. The city's many people who are impoverished as to education and income are correspondingly impoverished as to choice, forever strangers to many sorts of opportunity. Those who would prefer to live and rear their children in a heterogeneous cosmopolitan environment are frustrated by the predominance of homogeneous communities ranging from the racial ghetto to the high-income suburb. We need neighborhoods for the villager and the cosmopolite, for young people, for the aged, and for mixed age groups; we need communities of low density and high density, of single, multiple, and mixed dwellings, neighborhoods which are homogeneous and neighborhoods which are mixed as to income, racial, and ethnic characteristics; we need stable and changing, historic and contemporary communities.

Along with the traditional American ideal of freedom goes its necessary complement, a pluralistic society. But it is essential that cultural differences, where they are maintained, reflect pride in race, origin, and group accomplishment—not a sense of inferiority, exploitation, and alienation.

Such adaptation to the human scale—making the city more responsive to individual need and fostering individual freedom of choice of life style—will not result from uncoordinated market decisions nor from the actions of a myriad of governments separately providing routine services. It requires of business, labor, and other private sectors as well as public leadership a commitment to the values served by a city of "human scale."

GOAL II

A national commitment to the work of developing the urban frontier, as pervasive and compelling as the national commitment to developing the western frontier in the nineteenth century. Such a commitment must draw on federal, state, and local governments, business and labor, and educational, religious, and other organizations. It must be based on a heightened sense of common interest among all urban dwellers, with increased communication and mutual understanding across class lines, and a general concern for the well-being of each community.

Although the "cultural gap" between rapid accumulation of scientific knowledge and its technological application, on one hand, and the evolution of social and political institutions capable of coping with the new technological age, on the other, cannot be measured quantitatively, it seems to widen mainly because of the unprecedented scale and speed of technological change. From electricity to nuclear power, from the first adding machine to the computer, has been only a few decades, but the difference in corresponding beliefs, customs, and institutional requirements is epochal.

Technology has made possible the great population increases, and the high-density concentrations, of today's megalopolitan and metropolitan areas. These emerging concentrations of people, wealth, talent, influence, and prestige represent a new phenomenon of power and its distribution. But we are still trying to manage them with political forms devised for cities in the nineteenth century.

To attain goals as ambitious as those listed here requires effective local government, responsive to citizens' needs and wishes. But most local governments are anachronisms, characterized by excessive numbers of units, lack of public interest, and inadequate machinery for planning, policy-making, and administration.[4]

Clearly, if states are to maintain their historic role in the federal system, state governments *must* respond more adequately to urban needs. But with a few important exceptions, most state governments have lagged in meeting responsibilities imposed by the urban revolution, refusing to come to grips with the problems created by immigration and poverty. They have deemed cities unworthy to exercise powers of home rule and have dragged their feet on needed political and governmental reorganization. State governments can assist in modernizing tax and fiscal systems and providing financial support to meet urban development needs. They must promote the organizational changes in local government necessary to meet the needs of expanding metropolitan areas. They must move into areas which, as a group, they have thus far scarcely touched: economic growth, civil rights, education of the culturally deprived, eradication of poverty, ugliness, pollution of air and water, traffic congestion, metropolitan planning, modernization of zoning and building codes, eradication of restrictions on technological progress, and assistance in raising the quality of local government personnel.

The federal government will continue to be called upon for direct and indirect assistance in obtaining funds for urban development and renewal simply because, as things now stand, the federal government alone has access to the resources necessary for underwriting the vast task of redoing the present physical environment, and bringing up to par the nation's underdeveloped human capital. And only the federal government can take into account interstate spillovers of the benefits from and costs of public services: for example, costs imposed on northern cities by the grossly inadequate education of migrants from the South.

The Congress, historically dominated by rural and conservative

55

interests, has also lagged in responding to the transition from western to urban frontier, despite the proliferation of federal assistance programs initiated since World War II, which have created the new profession of grantsmanship. In the first seven years of the 1960's, the federal government spent on net balance about $1.6 billion for housing and community development to improve the urban environment in which 70 per cent of Americans now live. Agriculture and space each got $27-$28 billion; defense and war, $384 billion.

Federal and state governments can facilitate and assist in defining what an urban community wants to do and in mobilizing resources to get it done, but they cannot provide the leadership. Such leadership must come from the community itself—out of livelier participation in public affairs. In particular, the business sector has now been challenged by social imperatives and invited by the Administration to play a leading role.

Even the most active business and political leadership will come to nought without the interest and active involvement of the citizens. The metropolitan community as a whole will fall short of its potential and may deteriorate beyond repair if its citizens accept only its amenities and evade its problems.

To the majority of Americans the personal experience of urban living is one of more or less continuous improvement. Middle- and higher-income people are highly mobile; their roots tend to be in professional, cultural, and other interests rather than in the geographic neighborhoods where they happen to be living at the moment. Manifestations of trouble tend to be concentrated in central cities; the middle class can, and frequently does, escape by moving to the suburbs where its members spend much of their civic energies building fortifications against incursions by the poor.

Interest in urban goals at the lower end of the income-culture scale has been lacking until recently; the poor have tended to look to the great welfare bureaucracies, rather than to political organization, for assistance in meeting pressing needs. In both the central cities and the suburbs, political control has tended to be dominated more by the middle class, which demands less from government, than by the lower class, which demands more. Various circumstances—one being perennial financial stringency and another unimaginative leadership—tend to magnify the negative or veto powers of groups at the urban government level. In the urban political game, the defense has dominated the offense.

But new political winds are blowing in the forms of both violent protest and more extensive political involvement. The needs of those on the lowest economic plane are being forcefully articulated by people who want employment opportunities, better housing, more adequate education facilities, and a better social environment beginning with neighborhoods free from violence, dope pushers, and vagrants. None of these things is revolutionary; all reflect existing middle-class values and middle-class opportunities. People caught in the poverty trap want mainly what the majority of Americans already have.

GOAL III

Eradication of poverty and increase of productivity by:

a. *providing job opportunities for all who wish to work and opportunities for able older people to continue contributing to society;*

b. *raising the levels and extending the coverage of social insurance and public assistance programs to promote incentives and stable family life, and to be more responsive to need.*

In 1966, about 6 million families comprising 25 million persons, and another 5 million unrelated individuals were in poverty.[5] The proportion of nonwhite households (families and single individuals) in poverty was 30 per cent, 2.5 times that of the white (12 per cent). The poverty roster in 1966 included 3.8 million one- and two-person households with head age sixty-five or over (more than 5 million persons), and 1.5 million women heading fatherless families with 4 million children under age eighteen. About 3 million families in poverty were headed by men under sixty-five, most of whom were employed full or part time during the year. Their poverty was due to low wages, intermittent employment, and large families (a principal cause of poverty).

Like the rest of America's population, the poor have been drawn into urban areas. Once there, they are confined by poverty and discrimination to large cities and to older core areas. Another large segment of the poor lives in urban communities outside metropolitan areas.

The proportion of poor people living in large cities is still increasing as middle-income residents flee to the suburbs and poor immigrants take their places. Thus between 1960 and 1966, 1.2 million whites left the nation's twenty largest central cities, and 3.2 million nonwhites moved in. Skyrocketing welfare costs are one result: 7-10,000 people were added monthly to the AFDC program in New York City alone during 1967.

Poverty is a relative not an absolute condition—people measure their well-being by comparison with the population at large, not by how far they are from starvation. If we use a relative poverty line, such as 50 per cent of median family income, we find that poverty has not decreased in the last two decades; if anything, it has increased.

The extent of persistent and rising unemployment in large-city slums is indicated by a Bureau of Labor Statistics survey of ten slum areas in eight cities in November 1966, which found an underemployment rate of 34 per cent.[6] Lack of employment opportunities, or the conviction that they will be lacking, appears to be the greatest deterrent to both aspiration and persistence.

One of the principal demands from the slum-ghetto is for jobs, and one of the principal causes of rioting is lack of economic opportunity. The notion is still widespread that those who remain unemployed in times of high prosperity lack initiative or are simply unwilling to accept work-discipline or are content to subsist on welfare. In fact, the problem is far more complicated; it reflects in part the failure of the educational process, in part lack of organization of the job market, in part timidity of individuals, in part separation of jobs from housing and deficient transportation facilities, and only in some residual part ingrained laziness or irresponsibility. Although blue-collar and less skilled jobs have moved to suburban locations, suburban communities fiercely resist efforts by Negroes to follow.

To conclude that joblessness is due in part to automation, and that income must be distributed on some basis other than productive effort is premature in my judgment. The job of maintaining the growth rate, building new cities and rebuilding old ones, and doing other necessary things will for some time require more human energy than we shall probably be able to supply.

There is no simplistic solution to the job problem. One main approach is making more employment more accessible to ghetto residents. A second is providing improved information on the labor market. A third is specific job training and other measures to equip and rehabilitate workers for available jobs. We also have to face the fact that low-pay menial jobs with no career opportunities are not going to attract, much less inspire, young people from any income or social class, even the lowest. The need is for more career opportunities which hold forth the prospect of climbing as high as one's talents permit.

Finally, the negative philosophy that attempts to shove older people out of the labor force as soon as possible to make room for younger workers should be discarded. To cite Margaret Mead:

> We have been living through a period in which the old have been recklessly discarded and disallowed. . . . Given an opportunity to participate meaningfully in new knowledge, new skills, and new styles of life, the elderly can embody the changing world in such a way that their grandchildren—and all children of the youngest generation—are given a mandate to be part of the new and yet maintain human ties with the past which, however phrased, is part of our humanity.[7]

Over time we have built up a bewildering profusion of devices for keeping individuals and families from complete destitution. The welfare system, however, militates against incentives to work, against stable family life, against effective education. It also fails to rescue from the direst poverty people unable to work—the very young, the very old, mothers of small children, the disabled. Average monthly payments for old-age assistance range, among the states, from $124 in the high state to $41 in the low state. For the Aid to Families with Dependent Children program, the range is from $51 to $8 per person. In 1966 about a third of the poor received social security benefits, but even with these they remained below the poverty line.

Clearly the whole income-maintenance system must be strengthened.[8] In June 1966, the Advisory Council on Public Welfare in a report to the Secretary of the Department of Health, Education, and Welfare recommended that public assistance be extended to "all people whose income is below the national minimum standard of health and decency, with 'need' the only criterion of eligibility." It should be possible to design a system that would create incentives rather than destroy them—a system more effective and coherent than the present hodgepodge of welfare, unemployment compensation, housing subsidies, and other income-maintenance devices. A foundation income for all households would not solve all problems, but it would be a start.[9] It does contravene long-standing notions about work incentives which are difficult to refute or to support with available statistical data. A great fear is that a foundation income would reduce the supply of labor. This concern springs from simplistic and questionable assumptions about the nature of work and why men work. First is the assumption that work is something to be avoided. Yet in the American culture, holding a job is part of the male role (from which follows the observation that denial of the opportunity to work is a form of social emasculation), and more and more women feel the same social pressures. Second, as machines take over both the ditch-digging and the dull routine, more and more of the nation's work is of the sort that gratifies the human urge to be of service and to be creative. Some imagination and conscious effort would accelerate this transformation.

The existing welfare system is one of the most effective devices yet invented for stifling incentive. For those families living in poverty who supplement earnings with public assistance and unemployment insurance, a dollar's increase in earnings has meant a dollar's cut in their welfare allotment. The 1967 amendments to the Social Security Act somewhat mitigated this harshness in the case of AFDC recipients by allowing them to keep the first $30 of earnings and 30 per cent of the excess. Even so, the marginal tax rate—70 per cent—equals the rate in the top tax bracket on income gained by other means. If a recipient is allowed to keep as much as 50 per cent of his earnings, the effective tax rate is 50 per cent.[10] (Similar problems arise under the negative income tax plan.) A foundation income to which earnings could be added would provide incentive for effort.

In addition to their other bad features, present income-maintenance systems based on detailed supervision and demeaning investigation are directly at odds with the American belief that government paternalism and coercion should be minimized. Of course, some control over such matters as insuring education and adequate health services for children is indispensable, and in some areas the need may be for more rather than less paternalism. Subject to these exceptions, a society stressing freedom and responsibility should not deny these values to the unfortunate; rather it should take the risk that those who are treated as responsible citizens will turn out to be so.

We have come a long way from the degradation of the poorhouse. We accept the principle that society owes all its members the chance of a reasonable start in life. We have not yet, however, related either the problems of an automated society or the possibilities of an enormously affluent one to the basic needs of all our citizens.

Some states, like New York, have already achieved a minimal income system in the sense that no needy person is left out. Pending a radical overhauling of the present system of social security, public assistance and other benefits in the nation at large could be strengthened greatly by raising social security payments to above-poverty levels, by reducing the discrepancies among states in levels of public assistance benefits, and by moving to eliminate the present disincentives embedded in public assistance programs.

GOAL IV

Extending new meaning to the traditional American ideal of equality of opportunity by making available to all citizens:

a. lifelong educational opportunities, through a system designed to give each person incentives and facilities to develop fully his own capacities and to contribute to society;

b. decent and adequate housing;

c. health and medical services adequate to allow each person to achieve his full potential productivity and sense of physical well-being;

d. a variety of recreational and cultural outlets.

America's high and rising productivity unquestionably rests on its broad-based educational system and rising educational levels. Education is no longer solely for the young—what with the pace of knowledge accumulation and the obsolescence of knowledge already acquired, people will spend more of their lives being educated and will go back to school at intervals for retraining and updating. And there is a growing demand for study for self-fulfillment, for developing creativity and talents.

The most difficult and complicated task of American education is raising the levels at the bottom of the scale. It is a matter not only of providing better educational opportunities, but also of persuading the children of ignorance and poverty to want to be educated.

Aspirations and incentives are even more important than the educational apparatus.

The environment in which disadvantaged children are educated, however, must be far different from that of most of today's slum schools.[11]

Supplementary and remedial programs must be made available to every person, young or old, who needs help. Present innovational programs, such as Head Start, are a step in the right direction, but so far they have reached only a small fraction of the educationally deprived.

Educational efforts cannot stop with the schools; they must reach into the home and the community. Indoctrination of parents and the cultivation of community attitudes are part of the educational process, as is employment which supplies motivation.

In the context of educational and cultural development, housing is not a consumer good, but an essential ingredient of stable family life and effective rearing of children. At least a sixth of the present housing stock is substandard. These buildings are vermin-ridden and inadequately heated, lighted, or ventilated, or lack other minimum essentials for decent family life. The number of dwelling units started in 1966, however, was the lowest of any year in the 1960's. If the goal of twenty-six million new units over the next ten years announced in the President's 1968 urban message to Congress is to be reached, the annual rate of production must more than double. Nonetheless, replacing present slums with housing and other neighborhood amenities of below-average quality is an almost certain road to new cycles of slum and blight. Low quality may be a necessary concession to political expediency in the short run, but it is likely to be very costly in the long run.

It is paradoxical that in the world's wealthiest country health standards for a considerable part of the population are in some respects below those of other advanced countries. One manifestation is in the proportion of selective service draftees rejected for medical reasons—in most years, more than 20 per cent. The importance of this datum lies less in what it implies for military recruitment than in its implications for the national economy and living standards. Poverty, with its correlatives of ignorance, bad habits, and lack of medical care, is an underlying cause of poor health, and poor health is a cause of poverty in that it reduces productivity and working time.

Health services are notoriously deficient in urban ghettos and slums, and even more deficient in rural areas. Such services as exist tend to be provided by many different programs which are frequently located in different places; people are often denied service because they go to the wrong institution, to the wrong government jurisdiction, or because they cannot pay even minimum fees. Some deficiencies are attributable to the growing shortage of hospitals and professional personnel, but they also reflect bad organization, lack of attention to education, failure to train and use paraprofessional personnel, and other factors technically manageable.

As for recreation, there are already great deficiencies resulting from lack of access to outdoor recreation and open space, inhibition of water recreation by pollution and private enclosure of beaches. Slum and ghetto residents are deprived of facilities of all kinds. Possibly because of Puritan inhibitions about the use of public funds for fun and games, public recreation tends to be poorly represented in the competition for resources, even though American life and the American economy are more and more dominated by recreational pursuits and by the recreational industries. Ubiquitous television (a type of recreation), featuring the more exotic recreation habits of the affluent, constantly fans the flames of discontent by reminding people at the bottom of the extent of their deprivation.

Goal V

Extending the meaning of individual freedom to include:

a. freedom from personal aggression, security of person and property in public and private places;

b. freedom from the physical and psychological damage caused by environmental aggression, including obtrusive noise, polluted air, overcrowding;

c. freedom from the threat of uncompensated losses by public action for the benefit of others, whether in the name of public welfare or "progress";

d. freedom from discrimination under the law: assurance of opportunity for defense against prosecution, protection against loss of rights owing to poverty or other personal circumstances, and protection against exploitation of poverty and ignorance.

Freedom from personal aggression, obviously a first essential of the good society, is increasingly endangered in city and suburb as crime and delinquency rates rise. Although all classes suffer, the incidence of crime is highest in the ghetto and slum. Moreover, the poor suffer most. Even though ghetto and slum residents complain of police brutality, they also deplore their lack of security.[12]

Eradication of slums and poverty, along with other achievements of the good society, should substantially reduce the incidence of crime. The immediate need in most cities, however, is for wholesale change in the role of the policeman, in police technology, and in parole and penal systems. The kinds of change now being proposed are implicit in the suggestions that the designation "policeman" be changed to "human relations officer," and that the rubric "law enforcement" be changed to something like "public protection."

The concept of law enforcement and which laws are to be enforced should take into account, as it now ordinarily does not, the mores of the community. It is well known that the police are highly selective in the laws they enforce. Conventional police practices arouse the animosity of the community either by imposing locally unacceptable standards of law enforcement or by conniving in violations while mulcting the violators (as by levying on numbers and bookmaking operations).

It is no more than ordinary common sense to recruit the police serving minority group neighborhoods from minority groups. But added to the difficulty of finding and preparing minority group recruits who meet acceptable standards is their reluctance to go into police work.

The consciousness of environmental aggression also rises as changing technology imposes new nuisances and as knowledge grows of the physical and psychological damage to the human machine from noise, pollution, overcrowding, and other impositions. Environmental noise frequently reaches levels which not only frazzle nerves, but damage hearing. The statement that a day of breathing New York City air is equivalent to smoking two packs of cigarettes is more than fantasy. And the economic cost, beginning with mundane cleaning bills, of stench, airborne dirt, and chemical pollution in the nation's largest cities is already reckoned in billions of dollars annually.

Congestion and overcrowding—vehicle congestion in roadways, people congestion in transit cars and buses, schools, recreation centers, and other public places—impose other economic costs and personal discomforts. It is well established by now that with most animal species overcrowding leads to neurosis and regressive behavior. Implications for *homo urbanus* have not yet been fully explored, but it is clear that environmental crowding may cause both psychological and physiological damage.[13]

The traditional principle that people should not be unduly damaged for the benefit of others and that unavoidable damage should be reasonably compensated takes on new dimensions as more and more people find themselves standing in the way of "progress." A case in point is the sonic boom: Imposing the boom on populated areas for the benefit of the relative few who would be using supersonic aircraft can hardly be labeled "progress"; for the majority it would be quite the opposite.

In theory, government can regulate much of the damage caused by private interests, or it can require private interests to pay for the social costs they impose. In practice, however, government agencies themselves are often the offenders in pre-empting private property, dispossessing people without adequate compensation, and imposing other social damages on the grounds that the "public interest" justifies such damage. Thus it is estimated that between 1964 and 1972 the Federal Urban Renewal and Interstate Highway Programs alone will uproot 625,000 families and individuals and 136,000 businesses and nonprofit organizations. There are serious questions about the equity and adequacy of many compensation provisions; in many instances, there is no relocation assistance at all. Most seriously affected are old or poor individuals and small businesses.[14]

If it is not possible to compensate within reason those who are damaged by "progress," there is good justification for not undertaking the project unless the public benefits clearly and preponderantly outweigh the aggregate damages. If some people are to be unduly penalized for the benefit of others in the name of "public interest" or "progress," the resultant controversies are likely to damage both the public interest and the cause of progress.

Not much disputed but often frustrated are the high principles of Western political philosophy and Anglo-Saxon common law that the law and its officers should not discriminate among individuals except in the interest of reasonable and constitutional objectives and that all charged with violating the law should receive equal treatment and protection. The sophisticated and affluent can protect themselves. The poor and ignorant, by and large, are without legal recourse against unscrupulous landlords, merchants, loan sharks, and other would-be exploiters; the law is usually on the side of the exploiters. Ordinarily the poor are unable to protect themselves against arbitrary treatment by the government bureaucracies on which they must so heavily depend. When they get into trouble with the law, their chances of obtaining adequate counsel, reasonable bail, expeditious hearing and trial, and other protection are far less than those of the more sophisticated and affluent. Recent court decisions respecting right to counsel improve this situation, but it is still far from satisfactory. Minimizing the extent to which exploiters can bend the law and take advantage of the poor, and providing recourse against arbitrary action by government agencies which deal with the poor are more than just additional welfare measures. It is rather a matter of maintaining traditional American principles of liberty and justice.

GOAL VI

Application of modern technology to the improvement of amenity, efficiency, and beauty of the urban environment, and development of new concepts and techniques for guiding metropolitan growth.

With the exception of television and air conditioning, there has been little hardware innovation for two generations which has bettered in any basic way the day-to-day life in cities. (The betterment that has occurred is attributable mainly to rising real incomes and marginal improvements in already existing household gadgetry. And there have been many worsements which are also attributable to technology.)

If one compares the vision, the daring, the mobilization of technical performance, the fruitful cooperation between government and private enterprise that characterize the program for outer space, it is hard to believe that the same community should deal so timidly and tardily with its inner space. The space program, uncluttered with existing institutions and vested interests, could set new aims and move forward expeditiously. But the methodology of setting objectives and organizing technology and science to meet them, assisted by new public and private instruments of collaboration, should be applicable to the urban sector.

One of the most fruitful applications might lie in joining public and private financial and technological resources to create new towns and entire new cities. The initial purpose should be primarily that of testing and demonstrating new technologies of urban life uninhibited by already existing institutions, traditions, development patterns, transportation and utility systems, and land-holding patterns, all of which have effectively frustrated innovation in and around established central cities in metropolitan areas.

GOAL VII

Maintenance of central cities as vital, healthy centers of knowledge and culture, of management and commerce, and of residence for city-lovers.[15]

The role of central cities is rapidly changing in today's world of giant metropolitan areas and emerging megalopolises. One of the things that Melvin Webber and others seem to imply is that the concept of the central city is obsolete, and that modern transportation and communication will continue their decentralizing forces to produce more and more dispersal of activities and services. This view is confirmed in part by growth patterns in Los Angeles and other new southwestern urban centers, but does not yet apply, I think, to urban areas of central cities with established patterns and traditions, institutions, monuments, and cultural centers. Moreover, the growth patterns of New York, Chicago, Atlanta, the Twin Cities, and other national and regional management and financial centers indicate a preponderant tendency for office and related industries to cluster. And there are many people who continue to value the central city for aesthetic as well as economic reasons. It offers excitement and drama in life, a sense of great activity, monuments, vistas, and cultural opportunities that can be found nowhere else.

Central cities do face many dilemmas. For the most part, they have developed to meet the needs of industry and commerce, rather than for living; they are not built to the human scale. There is also the outmovement of middle-income groups, mainly white, and their replacement by the poor, mainly nonwhite. For the latter, the city appears to be losing its effectiveness in its traditional roles of acculturating agency and melting pot. The latest waves of migrants to the central city, instead of climbing up the ladder to join other metropolitan residents, see widening gaps in social and cultural status, economic productivity, and stage of development. The job of revitalizing central cities is one of reclaiming people even more than of physical rebuilding.

There is also the cumulative obsolescence of buildings which cannot be economically replaced under present institutions because of the high costs of assembling land parcels suitable for new buildings and of demolishing old ones. Congestion of people and vehicles jumbled together frustrates the central city's prime economic function of reducing transportation friction.

The first and most important element of rejuvenation has to do with offering a greater variety of choices of residence and ways of life to people of all racial and income groups, in and out of the central city. This is the most effective answer for the person trapped in the ghetto and for the middle-class city-lover who flees to the suburbs to find amenities which the city should offer, but does not.

Separation of vehicular and pedestrian traffic, arcaded sidewalks, outdoor play and recreation facilities on rooftops or open floors, and pedestrian shopping and recreational areas are all devices for bringing beauty, style, convenience, interest, and other values of environmental design to the city. New York's Rockefeller Center, Chicago's lakefront, Philadelphia's Penn Center, and Montreal's Place Ville Marie indicate some of the potentialities.

Social and physical rebuilding will not be achieved with dabs of urban renewal here, a housing project there, and an adult education or Head Start program somewhere else. Physical and social renewal and development programs must be concentrated in specific limited areas. Billions of dollars must be invested to build new towns in town.[16] The principle of the coordinated approach is recognized in the Model Cities Program, but the program thus far provides little either in the way of integrating machinery or financing. Compared to need and to the country's resources, the funds provided thus far are no more than a token.

The immediate danger is that the cost of providing special services for, or alternatively repressing, the poor who are concentrating in central cities, to the extent that it must be financed by the cities themselves, will become one more force driving business firms and middle- and upper-income residents out of town. Fiscal reform to relieve cities of public assistance and other special social service costs must have high priority. But this is after all a matter of recognizing that it is a bizarre order of priorities which provides so little for restoring cities and so lavishly for destroying them.

GOAL VIII

Metropolitan development planning for efficiency and aesthetic appeal, and for conservation of urban natural resources and regional ecology.

The specter of endlessly sprawling urban development, heedless of any human values save the immediate need for a room and four walls, unconcerned with monotony and lack of coherence: This is the prospect for most metropolitan areas in America, even today. Existing institutions and market forces do not provide for coherent relationships or strategies for mutual benefit between central city and surrounding region, or for efficient spatial relationships between residential, employment, and other activity centers. There are no mechanisms for assembling the vast amounts of capital and talent required for large-scale innovations in design, technology, or organization.

Any alternative to unplanned urban sprawl requires an orderly expansion of existing centers and new-town building. Catherine Bauer Wurster states one philosophy of metropolitan design:

Instead of scattering houses, factories, shops, offices and services all over the landscape, we should pull them together into compact cities with adjacent open space saved for recreation, agriculture, and general amenity. . . . Suitable housing for a cross-section population should be provided, with more emphasis on row houses and garden apartments. A variety of employment opportunities should be encouraged, as well as bona fide urban centers. The cities would be readily accessible to each other and to the central city.[17]

The United States alone among advanced nations has no public policy for new-town building. For the most part, the few new towns in this country have been privately planned and financed and are necessarily small and partial. By the end of the century, however, the United States will have to build the equivalent of between 150 and 250 cities, each of 500,000 population. They will require a total investment in the magnitude of $3.5 to $5 trillion. It would be only simple prudence to undertake with public and private resources a half-dozen or so "demonstration cities" in the next decade, using all the resources of modern physical and social science, for guidance in building the remainder.

We also need new concepts of urban resources—open space, air, and water. Fields, hills and valleys, streams and wetlands purify the air, provide climatic and hydrological control, conserve wildlife, serve as spawning grounds for marine life, and affect urban man and urban environment in dozens of drastic and subtle ways. Such ecological considerations, along with the multiplying needs for public park and recreation areas, impose a new dimension on urban planning.

Economic Potential for Goal Realization

The economic potential is encouraging. The value of the Gross National Product in 1967 was $785 billion. The average annual GNP growth rate during the 1960's has been about 4.7 per cent in constant value dollars though the rate dipped to 2.4 per cent in 1967. If an average growth rate of 3 per cent is maintained for the last third of the century, the cumulative GNP would amount to some $44 trillion in 1967 prices. A 4 per cent growth rate, which many analysts consider not out of the question, would yield $54 trillion.[18]

With a 4 per cent growth rate, assuming a population increase of eighty million, we could accomplish the following by the last third of the century:

1. Double average consumption per household. The increase might be more evenly distributed by developing a higher quality in education and training for the labor force and by moving toward more generous income-maintenance programs for those not in the labor force.

2. Provide new dwellings for all new households, replace approximately three fourths of present dwelling units, and provide second units for approximately 25 per cent of all households.

3. Double, by 1975, education expenditures per pupil; eliminate elementary and secondary school dropout; increase college enrollments by 50 per cent.

4. Triple average annual expenditure over the period on public facilities, including transportation, water, and sewer lines, recreational facilities, health centers and hospitals, and so forth.

5. Increase federal, state, and local government nondefense expenditures on services by an average of 4 per cent per year.[19]

6. Allocate 1 per cent of GNP (about two and a half times the present level of effort) for expediting development of less-developed nations.

I have made some rough estimates of the amounts of Gross National Product required to meet such objectives in the last third of the century:

	Trillions of dollars
Consumption	27.2
Housing	1.6
Education	4.4
Urban public facilities (infrastructure)	2.0
Business investment (plant and equipment)	7.7
Federal government	
Defense	2.2
Other	1.2
State and local government (excluding education and public facilities)	3.1
Foreign balance and unallocated	2.1
	$51.5

A 4 per cent growth rate would supply the demands as projected; a 3 per cent rate would fall some $7.5 trillion short; with a rate substantially under 4 per cent, demands on GNP would have to be reduced accordingly.

Many things might deplete the potential resource pool. The most serious danger now apparent is the continued escalation of expenditure on defense and military adventures. A second would be a growing indifference of organized labor toward productivity or long-continued periods of wage-price inflation. A third is the possibility that as more employment shifts to service industries, the margin for productivity increases will diminish (although production of many services can be mechanized).

In my perhaps overly optimistic judgment, these factors will not preclude rising productivity and affluence. Whether or not rising productivity is used to achieve the kinds of goals suggested here[20] depends on whether such goals can win public consensus, and whether present prejudices, habits, and institutions can be bent sufficiently to implement them if they are widely accepted.

Already there is at least a half-formed consensus on all of the goals; on most of them, the nation is already committed to some measure of implementation. Policy-makers and legislatures have addressed themselves to employment, housing, urban renewal, welfare, education, recreation, and law enforcement. The difficulty rests with lack not so much of programs or program objectives, but of knowhow. Moreover, the scale of effort thus far would not in another hundred years solve the problems which we now consider urgent.

Whether we will be mentally and socially nimble enough to adapt prejudices, habits, and institutions to the needs of the fast-moving age is another question. Here, too, I am optimistic. I recall what John Maynard Keynes said in the early 1930's with reference to the Great Depression:

If we lacked material things and the resources to produce them, we could not expect to find the means to prosperity except in hard work, abstinence and invention. In fact, our predicament is notoriously of another kind. It comes from some failure in the immaterial devices of the mind. . . . Nothing is required and nothing will avail except a little, a very little, clear thinking.

With Keynes's assistance we did produce enough clear thinking to establish the means for eliminating the scourge of great depressions. The challenge now before us is to come forth with a comparable response to the multifaceted needs of the urban frontier.

REFERENCES

1. It is said that splendid and beautiful cities are not a realistic goal in a democratic society based on a mass culture, and that the grand cities of the past (notably medieval and renaissance cities) were products of autocracy. But we should not forget that the splendor of ancient Athens was a product of the world's first great democratic society.

2. See David Braybrooke and Charles E. Lindblom, *A Strategy of Decision: Policy Evaluation as a Social Process* (New York, 1963).

3. For example, the Rockefeller panel reports in *Prospect for America* (1960); the report of the President's Commission on National Goals in *Goals for America* (1960); "Urban Revival: Goals and Standards," *The Annals* (March, 1964); and numerous publications and symposia such as Werner Z. Hirsch, *Urban Life and Form* (New York, 1963); Lloyd Rodwin (ed.), *The Future Metropolis* (New York, 1961); the report of

the NASA Conference on Space, Science, and Urban Life; and Leonard Lecht's study *Goals, Priorities and Dollars* (New York, 1966), for the National Planning Association.

4. For suggested improvements, see Committee for Economic Development, *Modernizing Local Government* (1966).

5. The definition of poverty is that of the Social Security Administration: The poverty line there varies according to size of family, number of children, and farm-nonfarm status. It is equivalent to an annual income of about $3,300 for a nonfarm family of four. This amounts to about $2.25 per day per person, of which one third is allocated for food. Poverty statistics are occasionally attacked by apologists for poverty who point out (a) that some households with incomes below the poverty line can draw on previously accumulated assets, and (b) that some families on the poverty rolls at any given time are there only temporarily. But the conclusion does not follow that the statistics necessarily overstate poverty. In other special cases even an income above the arbitrarily defined poverty line may not be adequate for an above-poverty level of living.

6. The underemployed include:
   a. the unemployed (those currently seeking work);
   b. part-time workers seeking full-time jobs;
   c. heads of households under sixty-five earning less than $60 a week in full-time employment;
   d. non-heads of households under sixty-five earning less than $56 a week in full-time employment;
   e. 50 per cent of the nonparticipants in the male age group twenty to sixty-four.

7. Margaret Mead, "Establishing the Shared Culture," *Dædalus* (Winter, 1965).

8. The Ninetieth Congress moved in this direction in 1967 by amendments to increase gradually the scale of payments. At the same time, however, Congress took a backward step by limiting the number eligible for AFDC payments.

9. Under the simplest form of foundation income, every family receives a basic allowance (which may depend on size of family) to which all earned and other income can be added, income tax being based on total income including the foundation payment. Admittedly we are a long way from that goal now, either psychologically or economically. To bring families now below the "poverty line" only up to the line would cost in the neighborhood of $11 billion a year. A foundation income averaging $4,000 per family would cost approximately $200 billion a year gross, though the net cost would be very much less since from the gross there would be deducted income taxes on marginal income, public assistance, at least part of the social security payments which otherwise would be necessary, housing, food, and other subsidies. The remainder would presumably be financed by adjusting income tax rates so as to bring about some redistribution of income.

10. Under the federal income tax on ordinary income, the 50 per cent rate does not apply until taxable income (after deductions and exemptions) has reached $44,000 (for joint returns). For the affluent this high rate is ordinarily held to damage incentive.

11. See Jonathan Kozol, *Death at an Early Age: The Destruction of the Hearts and Minds of Negro Children in the Boston Public Schools* (Boston, 1967).

12. A public opinion survey conducted by John F. Kraft, Inc., in Harlem in 1966 found that in a list of complaints about neighborhood conditions the three highest were prevalence of narcotics addiction, bad housing, and crime rates (closely related to narcotics addiction).

13. See Rene J. Dubos, "Man Adapting: His Limitations and Potentialities," *Environment for Man*, ed. William R. Ewald (Urbana, 1967).

14. U.S. Congress, House Committee on Public Works, *Study of Compensation and Assistance for Persons Affected by Real Property Acquisition in Federal and Federally Assisted Programs*, 88th Cong., 2nd Sess., 1963 (U.S. Government Printing Office, 1964), p. 258; and *Metropolitan America: Challenge to Federalism*, A Study Submitted to the Advisory Commission on Intergovernmental Relations, 89th Cong. (U.S. Government Printing Office, 1966), Chapter 4.

15. This and the following goal (concerned with urbanism outside central cities) should be considered together. The metropolis is an organism of closely interacting parts and of policies pursued either in center or in periphery which interact at every point and vitally affect each other's success or failure.

16. See Harvey S. Perloff, "New Towns Intown," *Journal of the American Institute of Planners* (May, 1966).

17. Catherine Bauer Wurster, "Form and Structure of the Future Urban Complex," *Cities and Space*, ed. Lowden Wingo (Baltimore, 1963).

18. The average growth rate in real GNP between 1929 and 1966 was 3.2 per cent. This period included the Great Depression and World War II, when private capital formation for peacetime production was held back.

19. With a 3 per cent growth rate, there would be about $10 trillion less available, equivalent to about thirteen years' annual production at 1967 rates. Even this amount (a total of $44 trillion) would be a vast pool of resources compared with anything we have known in the past. The total gross production of the American nation thus far is in the magnitude of $18-20 trillion, but the amount of the potential difference does indicate the crucial importance of maintaining a high growth rate.

20. To a considerable extent, rising productivity will depend in turn on goal achievement. Thus skimping on such items as education and training, or planning for greater efficiency of urban areas will dampen productivity. The 1966 annual report of the Council of Economic Advisers stated that if nonwhite employment and productivity were equal to the white, Gross National Product would be an estimated $27 billion higher.

EDMUND N. BACON

Urban Process

THE FAILURE of cities is an intellectual one. It is brought about by the failure of the intellectuals to generate a viable concept of a modern city and a modern region. Attempts are made to deflect attention from this bald fact by laying the blame on politics, on lack of money, on any cause but the root one. Of course, all these things play their role in the total process, but until there is generated a vivid and impelling concept of what we are fundamentally driving at, the other factors cannot play their role in the total process.

In the present atmosphere, not only is the root issue—basic concepts and ways of thinking—not discussed, but it is considered slightly disreputable even to bring up the subject. The happy assumption is made that we already know how to think, and that all would be solved if only someone would listen to us. I maintain that the great majority of our discussions of the urban problem deal with secondary manifestations rather than root causes. Current teaching in the universities has much to do with this. Until we get over our insistence that everything be reduced to the comforting specificity of manageable numbers before we even consider it, until we stop using the term "intuitive" as a means to kill in the bud any creative thinking, we will not get very far along the road to dealing with the basic issues implicit in the urban crisis.

Present Background for Thought

The basic structure of assumption used by the liberal intellectual today as the springboard for his actions is largely dominated by concepts inherited from the revolutionary days of the New Deal (the middle 1930's). Circumstances have changed so much since then that these concepts are not only no longer relevant, but inhibitory to clear thinking.

75

It was natural and inevitable at the very spear point of the effort to overthrow the accumulation of deeply embedded and widely held reactionary concepts that the basic issues would be reduced to crude slogans capable of seizing the rather torpid public mind, and so generate action. Unfortunately, many of these slogans have hardened into concepts that have become working tools of minds trying to deal with the highly involved processes of contemporary life.

Key among these slogans was the categorization of vast numbers of human beings into one clearly identified class, marked with a pungent label, for easy handling.

"One third of a nation, ill housed, ill clothed, ill fed," was the kind of shocking revelation that was needed by the American people in the thirties, but the by-product has been the establishment of an intellectual model in which people disappear as individuals and become members of a vast, statistically quantifiable, but faceless uniform group. This model is all too prevalent in the background of the discussion of social problems today, even on the part of intellectuals. The restructuring of thought and the restructuring of social programs so that each person and family group are seen and treated as individual identities with their own special characteristics and needs are painful and revolutionary, but must be accomplished if we are to get on with solutions to the problems of cities.

One concrete expression of the categorization of the "ill-housed, low-income group," both as an intellectual model and a legal entity, has been the construction of vast, institutionalized public housing projects to replace the "slums." Individual families are uprooted from the individual and unique positions that they occupy in the complex of their social community, however undesirable some of these positions may be. They become one of a series of families on an essentially uniform basis. It is very much easier intellectually to categorize areas as "unsafe and unsanitary," to recommend their destruction and replacement by "safe and sanitary dwelling units," than it is to deal with the reality of the problem on an individual basis for each individual family where it exists. It requires a far more rigorous intellectual discipline to think of solutions on the latter basis and a much more vast and skilled administrative arrangement to bring them about. Yet, curiously, that approach, if it could be clarified, would probably elicit a more sympathetic political reception than does the present one. The elected representative, the politician, the community leader, indeed the Black Power advocate, is denied the opportunity to champion such an approach to the problem of cities because the intellectual has failed both to structure it into a viable and communicable conceptual model and to suggest possible action programs geared to its basic tenets.

Another manifestation of the New Deal is the "demonstration project"—witness the Greenbelt towns, the slum clearance projects, the rural resettlements. This was not only a pardonable, but a relevant and desirable concept in the 1930's. To accept this as the basis for vast public programs in the 1960's is officially to acknowledge that we still are incapable intellectually of coming to grips with the totality of the problem, an admission that is not appropriate for the present day.

Virtually the entire legal, intellectual, and administrative base of the redevelopment and urban renewal programs throughout the United States is based on the intensive treatment of a fragment of the problem. Any attempt to recast thinking about the program so that it deals with the universe of the problem runs counter to the interests of both the administrative and intellectual adherents of the program and meets massive resistance. Again, the intellectual strain required to conceive, define, and plan the "completely renewed" community is far less than that incurred in the line of thinking contending that fragmented demonstration projects simply prove we are spending more and more money in less and less area, and that from such an approach we will never get on to dealing with the total environmental problems of those who live in deteriorated areas. Thus, we should undergo the intellectual wrench of abandoning old, comforting, but outworn models of the familiar "good neighborhood" and create entirely new ones of environment and process in which every individual benefits from our efforts to do something about blight. Here, again, such basic intellectual restructuring and restatement of the nature of the problem and its possible solutions are the necessary precursors to effective political action.

A third, unfortunate, surviving result of the 1930's "liberalism" is the stereotype of private enterprise as the enemy. This has so soaked into the thinking of many who are working on the urban problem that it acts as an insulator, inhibiting a valid interlock between the intellectual and technological insights that private industry and its research arms could bring to understanding the problem of slums and the energy and action that the great corporations are capable of in the solution of these problems. Again, we face an inadequate, but prevalent stereotype that the technicians and the public administrators should write the specifications for what should be done in an atmosphere untainted by any vestige of vested interests and that these should then be put out for competitive bids by private enterprise. This approach has already been proved to be unworkable in the development of space programs. In the case of cities, it must be replaced by a process in which government officials and private enterprise explore the nature of the problems together. Out of the combined structuring of the problems can come tremendous new energies, financing, research, construction, and deepened insights into new ways in which elements of the private enterprise sector can interrelate with one another and connect with the real problems in the field in their total extent as revealed by working association with the people who have them.

The problem of the American ghetto can be solved only when the resources of the private enterprise system are redirected back into these areas. The time is ripe for a massive overture from government to the private enterprise system for help in the problem of cities. The corporations are now receptive to such an overture and are prepared to respond. But the value will lie in a new kind of association, and this also, at its root, must grow out of a new intellectual concept.

It is usual to stop at this point, and it is much more pleasant to do so because so far there is little that can be attacked. I shall go on, however, to state three basic principles that I think to be important, thereby providing ample material for others to tear apart. By this very act, the process of assertion, controversy, and feedback may be helped to move a little closer to the core issues.

From Absolutes to Process

Despite protestation to the contrary, most planning and urban development thinking is based on the linear notion of a sequential progression from goal formation to getting the facts, to analyzing the facts, to the formation of alternative plans, to the selection of a plan, to implementation. This has as much connection with the total process of city building as did the geographical comprehension of the persons in the fifteenth century, whose limited experience led them to the conclusion that the world was flat, has to the real circular world.

Until there is general understanding of the process of hypothesis formation, its injection into the tumult of democratic dispute, the generation of feedback, and the restructuring of the hypothesis in the light of that feedback, in an ever recurring cyclical interaction, little progress will be made in achieving a viable relationship between the intellectual and actual decision-making, and indeed, in the very formation of viable concepts.

Under this system the planner views himself as the source of idea formation. The ideas are then injected into the field of action where they are acted upon by the people affected through democratic institutions. Parts of the original concept are rejected by the people, parts are accepted. The product of this process is a series of fragmented elements to which new elements must be added and the whole restructured into a new hypothesis for a next go-round of democratic feedback. After the fourth or fifth trip around the cycle the elements which pass through the screen of democratic approval accord more and more closely with the value system of the people in the community. In the process, the idea formulator himself has been tempered by the heat of his confrontation with his peers, and he himself, perhaps unwittingly, has become a more sensitive instrument more closely attuned to community values.

This process, indicated in the following chart, can be further refined by distinguishing, both in idea formation and in the field of action, the general and the specific. In idea formation there are the basic principle or root idea and its expression in specific proposals or projects. The development of the expression and its testing in the field of action expose the strengths and weaknesses of the broad principle, which must then be reconsidered in the light of the experience gained with the specific application. So in the field of action there is the identifiable leadership group, an ever changing but nevertheless finite collection of people who make key decisions. In addition, there is the great mass of the people of the city, each an individual, yet each contributing to a collective state of mind, a general attitude, a prevailing community sentiment. Here again, each of these influences the other. Neither is captive of the other, and the viewing of these two in constant cyclical interaction is helpful in overcoming many of the rigid sequential concepts we have inherited in this area.

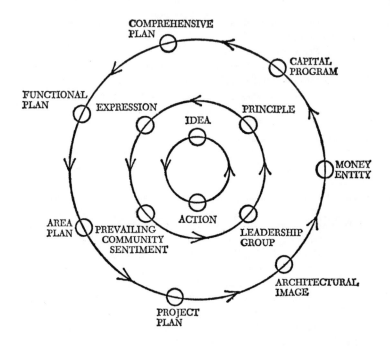

When viewed in this light, the process is not that of preparing a series of different alternatives, which relieve the planner of the necessity of thinking through the hard issues and making firm decisions, thereby escaping the most essential and disciplinary stress of the planning act. Rather, the process is seen in the binary system of the computer. The exposure of the ordered hypothesis to public attack paves the way for the division of it by the public into a series of aspects, according to the *public* value system. The public systematically accepts or rejects each of these separate aspects as it sees fit. It is then the task of the planner to pick up those aspects that survive the community value review, to restructure a hypothesis using these aspects and adding such additional elements as are necessary to create a new and enlarged system of order. So the process is repeated on and on. If done with technical competence each time, a larger proportion of the facets of the hypothesis go through the feedback filter, until finally a system of order is developed not by the planner nor by the community, but as a product of the interaction between each that is sufficiently

80

attuned to prevailing community values (as affected by the confrontation with the planner) that it becomes the basic directive for action on a large scale.

Under this approach sequence is irrelevant, just as irrelevant as the sequence in which the light beams pass through the various points on a television screen. Everything is seen as virtually simultaneous cyclical interaction, the process of idea formation with community feedback. So, also, the idea formulator sees himself and his role very differently than he does under the linear approach.

First, he recognizes that a tremendous deepening and enlarging of the original hypothesis will occur as a result of the feedback. Therefore, he recognizes at the outset that his hypothesis will be incomplete. Rather than spending huge sums of money and time on feeding every possible factor into the hypothesis before it is tested, he tries to make a powerful structure of the most essential ideas with the full confidence that enrichment and extension will occur in the restructuring process as a product of feedback.

Also, instead of attempting to determine before hypothesis formation the full range of community values by such artificial techniques as opinion polls, he respects the capacity of the community to accept and *to reject* those parts of his hypothesis which do or do not correspond with their value system. Thus, he sees his role as that of presenting the community with the finest and most complete hypothesis he can create for a better environment. Under this approach, many of the questions that plague academic discussions of planning issues disappear, and the issue of viable hypothesis formation emerges as the dominant one for the intellectual.

Unfortunately, the university, where most planners are trained, is the institution that has most systematically rejected the feedback principle and is most likely to continue to do so. The teaching profession in general has become removed from the field of action and, indeed, has tended to distrust it. This is not a question of "being practical"; it invokes the most essential part of idea formation. One consequence is a tremendous stress in education on the act of quantifying everything in a sterile pursuit of absolutes.

An illustration of this was the work on a new city in a foreign country supervised by one of our most distinguished educational institutions. In this case the economists projected the population of the city at half a million, and the computers determined the amount of land needed for shopping, housing, industry, schools, and so forth. The plan was drawn in precise accord with the quantities derived. When the economists changed their estimate of the future population, the *plan had to be done over.* Any kindergarten child could have told the planners that any city with a population of five hundred thousand started out much smaller and, having arrived at that point, would continue to grow to be somewhat larger.

The key issue is to see cities and regions in terms of growth process, including expansion and decay down to the individual units, and to see the planner as one participant in a total cyclical process of democratic interaction rather than as the manipulator of absolutes. If this can be accomplished, it will represent a great revolution in educational thinking.

The time has come for universities to re-examine their relationships with the students in the light of these new forces. Key to the whole is the development within the faculty of a respect for and confidence in the political process. The malaise that most faculties feel about politics reflects itself in such extremes as presenting advocacy planning as only a way of contributing to society's contempt for anyone who succeeds within the realities of the political process. This is partly engendered by the habit of enlisting graduate students for teaching jobs, thereby denying them successful experience in actual planning, an experience that would have supplied an essential ingredient for the formulation of their intellectual theories.

Somehow each university faculty should contain at least one person who has had a significantly successful experience in the administration of a planning program, preferably as a responsible governmental official rather than as a consultant (who by the nature of his relationship with the process is spared the ultimate accountability for his recommendations). If this cannot be done full time, the gap might be filled by getting such persons to participate in faculty discussion and to engage in part-time teaching.

Providing a real environment for student problems is most essential, but this should be connected with a public planning program so that the student sees a relationship between the field problems that he experiences and the government processes designed to correct them. This works best when there is an intimate relationship between the university and the local planning commission.

In Philadelphia, the Planning Commission, aided by a grant from the Smith, Kline & French Foundation, has established a program for hiring Master's candidates in city planning, urban design, and architecture over the summer between their first and second year, and then keeping them on part time over the last year with the idea of their taking a full-time job upon receiving their Master's degree if the association has proved to be rewarding to both the agency and the student. A valuable by-product of this program is the experience the student brings to the discussion with his fellow students over the second year. It tends to dispel the sense of unreality and even fear of reality that engulf so many educational institutions.

Particularly successful was a studio project in the second year of the Master's course where the subject was the renewal of a section of North Philadelphia which became a Model City area. Five of the students who worked on this academic project moved over into the City Planning Commission staff and continued their work on this area. The kind of involvement with the residents of the area which they had had as students was continued and intensified as they assumed the position of speaking for the government. If they are able or are asked to share their experiences with the graduate students at the university now, they cannot help but give a sense of direction and purpose and an image of purposeful action with which the students can identify.

The students recently graduated and those now in the universities have, in my opinion, a much higher motivation for social involvement and a much clearer picture of their purpose in the pursuit of their professional career than did their predecessors. It is critically important that the university and the operating planning agencies rethink and restructure their programs and especially their interrelationships so that this new thrust on the part of the students is not frustrated, but provided with channels for its exercise. Insofar as possible, it should be directed toward the central points of decision-making and not dissipated in peripheral byways.

From Building to Environment

Another inhibition to clear thinking about the plight of cities is the habit of thinking of "housing" in discrete quantitative terms as though "dwelling units" have their existence as manipulatable numbers rather than simply as fragments of an environment. This has led to many studies of numbers, based on "housing starts," "units to be demolished," and so forth, as though the individual structure could be shifted about as easily as the numbers used to represent it.

This type of thinking has led to the absurd situation where we think of family problems in terms of buildings, and we demolish the building and move the families to suit the convenience of the social and financial programs, rather than moving the abstract financial and social programs to accord with logical treatment of buildings and a rational and humane treatment of the individual families. Thus, instead of bringing the rent subsidy available under existing housing legislation to the people who need it where they already are (as integral parts of a complex community), we rip them out of their present environment and herd them all together in one great institution, the "public housing project." Then we throw them out bodily, children and all, if they succeed in bettering themselves and becoming a part of the American enterprise system. This is in contrast to the simple idea of adjusting aid programs to the needs of the people where they are, rather than moving people to the convenience of bureaucratic programs. Indeed, much of the basis of the entire national urban renewal and housing program is based on the convenience of the Washington file clerk.

By the same token, our thinking of structures purely in terms of numbers, as abstract, placeless entities, has led to an absurd situation in many cities. Thousands of vacant lots and derelict vacant and abandoned houses spread through hundreds of blocks of residential areas, crying out for new structures that would eliminate ghastly neighborhood hazards, that would infuse new life into neighborhood after neighborhood. Yet the public housing authority, following traditional molds of thinking, ignores these immediately available open sites whose use would avoid relocation and looks for project sites that mean political upheavals, physical demolition, and social and economic disruption because of the forcible uprooting of families involved.

The claim that negative "environmental factors" prevent our building new houses in these areas is totally untenable. In democratic America we cannot afford to delimit areas occupied by thousands of families as areas to stay out of. We must see the public housing program not narrowly from the viewpoint of the minority of the ill housed, who are its tenants, but rather as an instrument for getting at the root of the housing problem of everyone. This purpose can be furthered and strengthened by a shift from thinking based on housing units as abstract, placeless, mathematic entities to that concerned about the real and total environment of every underprivileged citizen in the entire city. This change of thinking perforce acts as a great catalyst, involving vast areas of social and economic programs in a systematic interrelation with the purely housing aspect of the problem. Given an underbase of a deep concern and understanding of the human need of the family not as a unit of an abstract category, but as a very real and individual entity, great energy will be released, and we will get on with the job in terms not of demonstration projects, but of an attack on the total situation.

It has been amazing to observe the response of the various institutions and of the government to these basic concepts in Philadelphia. Mayor James H. J. Tate set forth in 1967 the fundamental principle of eliminating essentially by rehabilitation or rebuilding for low-income occupancy (except where the land is needed for community facilities) all of the fifteen thousand or so vacant and open structures and the five thousand scattered vacant lots spread through some two thousand blocks in Philadelphia. Mayor Tate vigorously followed through with conferences with the Council in Philadelphia, with Congressmen in Washington, and with federal administrators. Within the city government machinery, a process was set in motion to bid in tax delinquent properties on a large scale, and even to have the city accept as a gift tax delinquent properties on which it would write off the back taxes. The city obtained approval from the Department of Housing and Urban Development for a five thousand-unit $70,000,000 public housing program consisting of the rehabilitation of vacant and derelict scattered structures in North Philadelphia.

The city set up the nonprofit Philadelphia Housing Development Corporation and provided it with a $2,000,000 revolving fund to enable it to build and rehabilitate housing for low- and moderate-income families. This agency also facilitates property transfer to developers of rehabilitated housing for the Housing Authority. A number of local groups were formed by people in the areas, often centering in churches, to act as developers of rehabilitated housing under a variety of programs. The Smith, Kline & French Foundation provided the seed money and drive for the rehabilitation of some seventy derelict dwellings in the vicinity of their building, thereby supplying homes for two hundred low-income families.

Already several hundred vacant structures have been rehabilitated throughout a large area, giving positive demonstration to the possibility of achieving Mayor Tate's vision of the complete elimination of the cancerous sores that derelict structures represent. Within the framework of this new thrust can be developed a wide range of different programs skillfully intermixed to get away from the institutionalism previously associated with public housing, to provide a variety of income groups and family structure in the same neighborhood, and to give a vehicle for rich participation to the people who live in the neighborhoods.

Relating to Ever Enlarging Systems of Order

A mother with, say, three children under four, living in a blighted area and receiving welfare assistance in the form of aid to dependent children, may function in her own world with almost no ordering of time or space in the customary sense. Much of the family life will take place in a single room. There is no requirement to get up or go to bed at any particular time. It is likely that meals, in the sense of systematic punctuation of a time sequence, do not exist.

Along comes the Head Start Program. The mother must rise at a definite time, get the child dressed, feed him, and take him on a definite route through space to the focal point of the activity, the school or another institution. The mother identifies with this point in space outside her own home—as a meeting ground with others in the community.

The mothers learn that Head Start funds are exhausted and the program is about to be terminated. Together with mothers from other areas, they go to city hall to protest, thus identifying with another point in space, relating to another hierarchical level of community involvement. They learn in city hall that the trouble is in Washington; so the system of order with which they now identify is raised one notch in the systems level. When they learn that the cause of the curtailment of funds is the Vietnam war, they become, indeed, members of the world community.

This elementary review of the process of relating to an ever enlarging system of order provides a microcosmic model for one of the most fundamental principles that should guide the planning of the physical environment. It is a primary responsibility of the planner of the environment to provide focal points of identification, placed in significant relationship to valid principles of social groupings and articulated architecturally so that they draw people to them, speak to the people in terms of their preconditioned sensory emotional and cultural responses, and engender a sense of pride in the community, a loyalty to the social entity which is the community, a feeling of identification with its purposes, a basic involvement.

The process of articulation of the environment proceeds with the interconnection of these firmly established focal points in space by structured lines of movement—garden footpaths, greenways, parkways, malls, boulevards, or expressways. It includes the establishment of new points in space based on networks of enlarged systems of order: perhaps the district center that binds together a series of neighborhood centers, the city center, the metropolitan center, regional centers, national centers, and so forth. The function of design is to touch these articulated points in space with the quality of life, thereby engaging the emotions and loyalties of the people and setting into motion the process of identification with an ever enlarging system of order. In order for a planner or designer of the environment to do this, he must be engaged in his work and in his own life in a process of enlarging his own vision and the range of his capacities.

The Role of Beauty

It is only at this point, after all these processes have been set into motion, that it is possible to talk about elegance and beauty in the environment. Only as the designer himself—the architect, the landscape architect, the sculptor, the industrial designer, the graphic artist—is involved in these processes with his whole being will he be able to reflect and express the feelings and aspirations of the people whose environment he is building; with equal force let it be said that it is only as the designer, the artist, is involved in environment-building in a valid way will the environment he builds be a proper expression of the hopes of the people, be they of the very poorest.

And the final and most important element of all is the simple requirement that the people who live there must, themselves, have a hand in shaping their own environment. So foreign is this to our

87

traditional ways of thinking that its carrying out will, indeed, require drastic changes in our customary way of doing things.

So, in my view, it is possible to create a noble and beautiful environment in cities that extends to *all* its parts, that engages the loyalty and pride of its citizens, that leads toward a greater sense of involvement than we have ever known. But in order to accomplish this, we must abandon many traditional ways of thinking. We must establish and nurture new kinds of concepts, and we must set in motion processes and systems of interaction out of which such an environment may, quite naturally, grow.

DONALD N. MICHAEL

On Coping with Complexity:
Planning and Politics

ONE FORECAST regarding the cities in 1976 can be made with considerable assurance: The requirements for urban improvement, perhaps even for urban survival, will embroil city governments in extensive efforts at long-range planning.[1]

It is becoming increasingly clear that no major social task can be realized with less than a decade or more of sustained organized effort directed at the realization of specific goals, whether they be pollution control, elimination of ghettos, mass transit, adequate education, or building new cities. Because human lives are what will be changed, the risks that can be taken in leapfrogging to the attainment of hardware goals are not ethically acceptable.

Long-range planning will be an unprecedentedly complex activity because the urban condition is complex and planning technology is increasingly using sophisticated economic and social theory, applied through systems analysis, program planning and budgeting, and the like. Since knowledge of this sort will be the basis for city management, it will also be central to attaining and maintaining political and bureaucratic power.

These circumstances presage new problems. In brief, long-range planning requires continuity and some unknown degree of stability to reap its fruits, but at the same time small percentages of the population will increasingly have the ability or inclination to upset or to perturb the "system." Planners and those responsible for managing the city will tend to do what they can to prevent their long-range plans from being upset. More often than not, this will involve partisan interpretations to the public of the purposes and prospects of the planning goals and their implementation. Given the complexity of both the planning process and the urban situation, the citizen will probably be unable to find out the implications of pursuing one plan rather than another. His option then will be disrupting protest, political withdrawal, or ritual participation. None of these will be satisfactory if we want both democracy and long-range planning. A partial solution would be for the citizen to be able to react to the plans in their full content and·intent; he would thereby appreciate what is going on and the possible consequences of the changes. Such a process would not save plans from being changed, but plans should be designed to be altered as the pertinent context evolves. Nor would such knowledge eliminate politics or passion. It would, however, increase the chances of choosing and revising plans on the basis of truly shared knowledge and interpretations about urban realities. In addition to those conventionally anticipated uses of the computer for coping with urban complexity, it could provide prerequisites for such new forms of citizen participation in democratic governance.[2]

By 1976, the population of urban environments will be so large that even small percentages will represent politically and socially significant numbers of people. Moreover, the level of communications and physical mobility will be so great that even low-probability events will occur often enough to be politically and socially significant. Indeed, low-probability events will increase simply because the larger variety of collectivities will provide a greater variety of actions and interactions.

The sit-in desegregation of the South, the Columbia demonstrations, the nationwide rioting in the ghettos, and the disruptiveness of protesting *ad hoc* groups in general all testify to the perturbing effects of very small percentages of the population. Small percentages have, of course, made big changes in the past, even when their numbers were also small. But high rates of communication and mobility and the greater numbers involved will mean that the consequences of particular actions will multiply and that these consequences will be felt in more diverse ways more quickly than in the past. Moreover, such actions will encourage further activity, thereby compounding the complications in responding to and coping with the urban scene in some coherent manner.

Meeting such demands, or simply cooling them, will become all the more complex (though perhaps more tractable, in some cases) because increased mobility and communications will facilitate their interaction and emphasize priority and resource conflicts and resolutions among them. Moreover, because the density of the human and physical environment will be so great, the number of low-probability events that do happen will increase. There will simply be more opportunities for such low-probability events to occur: power blackouts, tankers decimating shorelines with accidentally spilled cargo, assassinations, thalidomide-type tragedies, lethal atmospheric inversion layers, and so forth. In 1966, for example, only 1 per cent of the baggage checked with the airlines in the United States was mishandled, but that represented 1.7 million pieces of luggage!

In almost every area of social planning, small percentages will also represent *persisting* large numbers of people needing—often demanding—specialized attention: job opportunities or training for the unemployed, even if they are only 4 per cent (particularly if we ever give up Vietnam-type wars that skim off the marginally employable); education efforts like Head Start (for the affluent as well as the poor); more integrated and responsive local welfare services; airport noise and sonic boom protection; and so on.

When a city was run according to *ad hoc* or short-perspective considerations, the city government could respond to the actions of small percentages of the population in the same spirit. But when long-range planning becomes both the style and the necessity, these perturbations may inadvertently jeopardize long-range plans that are being implemented, or they may indicate where changes are needed in the plan's implementation. Either way, the effects of these small percentages must be incorporated into long-range programs; thus, the planning and policy models must incorporate both information about these events and conceptual schemes that attempt to discover the relation of these perturbations to the destiny of the long-range programs. The computer is, therefore, all the more necessary for the management of the city—for processing data about the present in the present, as a primary basis for planning and revising plans.

It is commonplace today to recognize the necessity for moving in this direction in order to deal more adequately with the operating requirements of day-to-day government. Crime control, tax records, urban data banks, program planning and budgeting systems, and so forth all depend or are expected to depend on the computer's data-storing and data-processing capabilities. But using the computer for long-range planning in a context of social perturbations will demand a collaboration among planners, policy-makers, and politicians that will threaten the practice of democracy. This threat can, perhaps, be mitigated by using the computer in ways

91

we shall examine later. First, however, we should be clearer about the nature of the threat.

Its source is twofold: the increasing dependence of those with political power on esoteric knowledge and the decreasing ability of the concerned citizen[3] to get the knowledge he needs to participate in matters of importance to him.

All decision-making related to a city government[4] or made by agencies of a government has a substantial political component, even those decisions based heavily on the kinds of information the computer and its human adjuncts provide. Any political decision is made with the intent of preserving or expanding the base of power, command, control, and influence of the organization or persons involved. Mayors, authorities, chiefs or commissioners of this and that do not choose to weaken their personal power, nor do their organizations deliberately act so as to lose control over their traditional mandates.

In the urban world of 1976 that control, that power, will increasingly be based on access to and control of information and the means for generating new knowledge out of it. Information will provide an increasingly potent basis for "adjusting" the outside world so that it is compatible with the survival and growth aims of the agency and for internally adjusting the agency so that it can respond to what it perceives as pertinent to it in the evolving complex environment. This is not a new situation; organizations have always acted to monopolize the knowledge they need for influence and for control of decisions and their implementation even when the knowledge served essentially a ritualistic or rationalizing purpose rather than as a realistic efficient basis for choosing options.[5]

But the situation takes on significant new aspects when the computer provides an improved basis for choosing among options. Then the politician (and I include the agency chief and the advocate planner), working in tandem with his technological advisers and program designers, is in a position to put forth interpretations of "urban reality," programs to deal with it, and evaluations of those programs as implemented based on knowledge either unavailable to those who might challenge him or unavailable at the time that a challenge might be most effective.

This situation characterizes the way military affairs and military policies are planned and operated (for example, the Vietnam war), but it is also true, and will be increasingly so, in more and more domestic areas. The partisan use of incomplete or selectively emphasized technological knowledge is already the case with regard to the justification offered for the supersonic transport or more trips to the moon. It is beginning to be so with regard to methods advocated for pollution control, mass transport, educational technology, and social welfare. As these areas of planning and operations become more rationalized, the agencies and persons responsible for such plans and programs will try to protect their decisions and actions from effective criticism or impedance. We can expect this conventional organizational reflex to continue to operate, certainly over the next decade or more when bureaucracies will still be dominated by those who were trained in and rewarded by the traditionally successful operating styles. And given the nature and the basis for decision-making and operations—increased social complexity dealt with through increased conceptual complexity—it will be easier to obscure the organizations' situation than it was in a simpler day unless we specifically design means for keeping these reflexes from operating too well.

No computer-based, technology-based set of options will be exhaustive. Our knowledge about the nature of the urban present, although greatly improved, will be incomplete and our theories for interpreting that knowledge will be flawed. And since more and more of the urban tasks will be long-range ones, policy-planners and decision-makers will have to commit themselves on the basis of estimates of an essentially unpredictable future. (And citizens, choosing among the options offered, will be even more ignorant because a realistic estimate of the long-range consequences associated with an option requires an evaluation of the knowledge on which the option is based.) The politician, when choosing among any set of options, will face two facts of life he has customarily shared with the voter as little as possible. The first is the fallibility of the programs and plans to which he commits himself and his organization, the inherent uncertainty about the nature and distribution of costs and benefits. The second is that, given this state of uncertainty about the future, present political considerations pertaining to the preservation and extension of his power through time deeply influence his decisions. In the conventional situation, the politician and professional could cover up these two facts of life quite well most of the time. In the future, it will be even easier to cover them up because computer-based options will, by virtue of their source, carry great weight with many policy people and voters. The overwhelming complexity incorporated into the derivation of the options will make it excessively difficult to know in what ways the politician is covering up conceptual and data limitations in the computer program providing those options.

By 1976 not all agencies will be using computer aids to the extent they might. In many situations the changeover to such rationalized methods will be too threatening to those in power, too upsetting to their definitions of self, purpose, and status for them to move easily and quickly into the new arrangements, styles, and rewards appropriate when computer aids are used for planning. Given the mixed bag of autonomous, interlinking, semiduplicative, and competitive agencies and activities that characterize the urban condition of governance and control, foot-dragging will be difficult to overcome. These "foot draggers" will, however, feel that they must give their clients the impression that they indeed know where they are going and that, in the mode of the times, their knowledge somehow derives from the approved, sophisticated "systems" thinking. Thereby, they will have an additional reason for hiding their interpretative and programmatic fallibility, a fallibility appearing and in fact sometimes being greater for their dependence on "old-fashioned" non-computerized approaches.

These anticipated characteristics of urban governance suggest that we should be preoccupied with developing not only the means for making the political system manipulable by the poor, but also the new means that will enable affluent, concerned citizens to get at the political system in years to come. Unless we do so, the citizen of 1976 may find himself unable to judge whether he knows enough about a particular proposed policy or a proposed or ongoing program to discern where his and the community's interests lie. He probably will not be able to identify the set of options or the conceptual model used to transform the data. He will not even know what data were fed into the program or how adequate they were.[6] Nor will he be able to judge which costs and benefits of the secondary and tertiary impacts reverberating out through the urban environment have been taken into consideration and by whom. (Given the autonomy of various agencies in the urban government, he will probably be safe in assuming that some of the "interface" issues have not been dealt with or even recognized by agencies indifferent to or ignorant of them—or by those avoiding them for political reasons.) Thus, even when he is offered a choice of programs, his ignorance about the assumptions made by the planners regarding the supposed future context in which the programs will operate and eventually "pay-off" will prevent him from choosing wisely, from committing himself to a long-range risk with an understanding of what the costs and benefits are thought to be.

If the concerned citizen felt ignorant or impotent in the past, he could take solace in the knowledge that the capacity of organizations to change things was usually small and potentially subject to some revision at the next election. That solace will disappear, however, when the requirement for long-range programs means that many programs will have to carry on through many elections if they are to have any chance of success.

This source of comfort will be gone, too, when the citizen comes to realize that computer-aided planning and operations allow programs to have a much greater impact on the urban environment, and that the intense and wide-ranging interaction within this environment encourages secondary and tertiary consequences of perhaps even greater impact than the primary ones. Obversely, the citizen will find no comfort in those cases where he wants some great impact on the environment, but where considerations—mostly unknown to him—result in choices that have little impact. The concerned citizen's discomfort will be increased in a new way: He will know he is unskilled in manipulating and evaluating the information from which the computer-based options are derived. Not only will he realize that he lacks some of the facts; he will know that he is unable to work with them, even when he has them.

These sources of discomfort suggest the direction in which we shall have to look for new arrangements allowing the citizen a meaningful role in influencing his urban destiny. The citizen must have as much access to the procedures of social planning and evaluating data as do those in the system who propose programs and evaluate their implementation. The citizen will need this access both during the period when the agencies and the politicians are developing the program and continuously once the program is in operation. The citizen would then be able to criticize more effectively a program's quality and relevancy, and he could be aided enormously in this process by the computer.

To do so, the citizen ought to be able to ask questions such as: What were the sampling procedures used to obtain the "raw data"? How accurate and how valid are they? How are they aggregated? What sensitivity to change or stasis is lost or gained by clustering the data demographically, temporally, economically, and so forth? Then he should know which conceptual models were used to relate various data so that interpretations could be made. These models may be mathematical or logical, based on economic theory or on social-psychological theories, perhaps supplemented in part by the decision-makers' hunches and wisdom. To the extent that the models provide a basis for sharing ideas and clarifying choices, they can be made explicit in words or mathematical statements. The citizen should also know how logic and data are related in the computing program. What are to be the measures of costs and benefits? What range of economic or social variation is to be considered and how are these variations related to one another? How does the computing program emphasize or alter the meanings of the data and the conceptual model for the sake of computing convenience? (For example, one way of averaging out variations in demand for a service may indicate no special need for an increase in that service; another way of averaging those variations may indicate very real needs in certain groups under certain variations in circumstances, but whose need-indicating behavior was "washed out" in the former averaging method.) What value assumptions are operating? What goals for the plan are revealed by the methods for ranking the options generated by the computer-manipulated data? Some of the options may be generated directly by computer analysis; others may use computer outputs supplemented by considerations outside the computer's option-generating program and introduced by politicians. One way or another, the variables attended to in creating the options will reveal underlying value preferences. Are economic savings to override other social gains? To what extent is the computerized option-generating model to operate within the constraints of the private enterprise value system? Is an assumption made that inequities for 4 per cent of the target population are acceptable, but unacceptable for 5 per cent? Will monitoring the plan in action require data about people presently considered private? Why is this "invasion of privacy" presumed to be worthwhile?

In principle, the citizen ought to be able to look over the shoulder of the planner and decision-maker as they prepare their plans and decisions. He ought to be able to ask all the questions of the computer that could be asked by the professionals working for the urban agencies—such questions as: "What happens to the ratio of costs to benefits when I use the same data the planners have used, but another definition of costs or benefits?" "If in *my* conceptual model the rate at which average personal income grows has consequences for the larger community that differ depending on the ethnic background of those whose income is changing, at what rate will the average personal income in district Y grow compared to district Z if the proposed industry is in location A rather than B?" Citizens with different perspectives and interests than the planners and politicians almost certainly will ask questions that the professionals forgot, thereby discovering significant implications the professionals overlooked. In this way, the professionals will have thrust on them a larger set of considerations to reconcile. Few professionals will embrace this additional decision-making burden or the challenge to their professional omniscience, but the advantages of this burden and challenge are too obvious to bear elucidation here. On the other hand, it is also obvious that the professionals could be immobilized by the effort involved in responding to the citizens; clearly, means for establishing a mutually useful balance have to be invented.

Again, in principle, the means for such citizen involvement exist today, operating in the form of multiple-access computer systems in which many people use the same computer and share one another's programs, data, thinking, and solutions. Each user has his own terminal equipment for instructing the computer and for receiving information from the computer. The terminal may be an especially adapted typewriter or a glass surface, like a television, that displays information and can receive instructions from the user via a pen that writes signals on it with a narrow beam of light to which the computer responds by a visual display on the screen or by printed symbols on paper. Thus whatever numerical data, charts, graphs, or designs are used, and whatever computer programs are used, the information can be stored in the computer and displayed through these terminals and the computer can be queried from them.

Imagine, then, similar terminals spotted around the urban area in the center cities, the suburbs, and the contiguous rural centers. Each of these could be linked to the same data banks and computers that the urban planning and governing agencies tie into. The laws could be so written that it would be illegal to deny these "citizen terminals" access to any of the data that the agencies use.[7] Since agencies cannot use data legally defined as private or privileged without special permission, misuse of such data may be discovered if the computational results the citizens obtain differ from those of the agencies, even though both are supposedly using the same data and computer programs. The law could further require that the computer programs for manipulating data and the conceptual schemes that the programs presumably reflect also be public information. And all ancillary information that the planners may not store in the computer, such as maps, must be displayable for the citizens' use. Thus, all the information and methods for manipulating information available to the planners and decision-makers would also be available to the citizen. If information was privileged or proprietary, this would have to be indicated when a citizen requested that information. Means would have to be established allowing the citizen to determine the significance of that information for the proposed plan or related project. Since such information is sometimes critical for choosing among options, confrontation procedures would have to be developed.

The hunches, biases, and political sense that usually influence the planner's preferences and the politician's choices probably could not be detected or evaluated by such means. The citizen *would* know, however, what there was to know about the data-based and theoretical relationships of the issue to the options. He could then apply his own hunches, preferences, and biases and push for one option or goal rather than another. Thus, this approach would not eliminate nor reduce the political or emotional factors in the pursuit of urban goals.

This approach seems to carry with it more than just a new means for maintaining an uneasy balance between the citizen and the urban government. Because we must cope with urban complexity by long-range planning, citizen participation responsive to the same methods and types of data the planners use can help produce citizen attitudes oriented to the future and preferring the long-range planning approach to the *ad hoc* and spasmodic styles that have typified the American way of dealing with urban problems.[8] Because long-range planning must be flexible and responsive to changes in the human and material environment as the plan works its way out over the years, the government must be alert to and responsive to feedback about the general environment as well as the specific environment the plan is intended to effect. With access to all the data the government agencies will have about what is happening to their areas of responsibility, it can be expected that the citizens' various interests will result in one or another group scanning each pertinent situation, alert for new data revealing unexpected gains or losses that can be attributed to the working out of one or another plan. These continuing monitoring efforts could force the agencies not only to appropriate programmatic responses to what the citizens discover, but also to collect new types of data needed for improved evaluation of the programs.

Most important of all, the extraordinary degree of openness required to operate this way could mean that, over time, the political system, including the citizen, could come to recognize error and failure as natural products of trying to cope with a complex urban environment. No longer would the government have the need to cover up: The degree of ignorance about the feasibility and implications of any program would be evident to the recipients of the program at the time it was initiated as well as all along thereafter. Knowing that some error and failure are inevitable, both government and citizen would be able to accept social experiments more easily for what they are, making changes candidly and quickly when needed, without pretending or expecting that the initial plans were more certain to succeed than realistic estimates would suggest. And no one doubts that we will have to experiment socially if we are deliberately to invent a better urban world.

Even after one discounts the large majority of citizens who will be uninterested in such sophisticated participation in the conduct of the community, most of those who do want to take part will be unable to do so directly, being untrained in the statistical, social, and technological concepts involved in querying and interpreting the computer outputs. Specialists will be needed to do this, people who see the issue writ large, who can play with data, who see what is and is not in a computer program, who can invent alternative programs, who can sense the ethical and social problems and opportunities implicit in the planning options. Although the individual citizen can usefully contribute to the elucidation of some of these issues on the basis of his own circumstances, much of what he will need to transform his concerns into decisive queries to the information system will have to be provided by specialists. Analogous roles are filled today by lawyers, crusaders like Nader and Carson, some theologians, advocate planners, and even an occasional systems analyst, technologist, or scientist caught up in an urban issue that impinges directly on him. But the present roles are not refined enough to provide a readily accessible resource for linking citizens with computers.

A more specific delineation of specialties will be needed to implement the proposed system. These would provide the functional equivalent of the "shadow" planning, policy-making, and program-evaluation agencies of urban government. These specialists, retained by citizen groups, could be individuals or consulting firms that do not take government contracts and thus avoid conflicts of interest. The affluent ought to be able to pay for some services. As mobility and affluence increase, their interests in overlapping issues in nonoverlapping geographic locals should also increase.[9]

The poor or the less affluent will need subsidization in this area much as we are beginning to provide them with legal services and other professional aid services. Perhaps foundations will help; the U.G.F., for example, might include such services among its worthy causes. Perhaps specialists could contribute their services part time as some do now in other activities. Universities might find some answers to their presently fumbling search for relevancy by providing such services on a nonpartisan basis. Their faculty members could raise the questions, pose alternative conceptual models and computer programs, and interpret findings in the light of their expertise. Just as universities encourage faculty members to consult in conventional ways, they might also encourage this sort of service, compensating their faculty members accordingly. Political parties might find ways of matching the interests of citizens and party by supporting particular efforts, publicizing the results, and using political leverage to get the alternatives attended to.

For those who want to participate in the political process, the opportunity to challenge the system or to support it on the basis of knowledge *as* the government develops its own position and then to monitor and criticize *continuously* the implementation of whatever policy prevails should be a heady incentive for extensive use of such computer facilities. But the approach proposed here involves no casual laying-on of minor modifications in the conduct of urban government. Opening up the information base of political decision-making would be one of the most painful wrenches conceivable for conventional styles of governing. Those now involved who have devised over their political lifetimes elaborate strategies for maintaining operational power and a complimentary personal self-image would find themselves naked, having to armor themselves anew and in new ways. Many simply could not do this, and many will fight such an approach with the cunning and commitment elicited by threats to survival. As a result, the scheme proposed here would hardly be in fully effective use in any urban area by 1976. Political and dollar costs and the technical complexity of installing citizen terminals might be too great for more than a few experimental terminals to be operating. Moreover, the numbers and types of experts available to aid citizens might be too small to man more than a few terminals. Perhaps the most that can be done is to ensure that citizens have access to the computer in the offices of the planners so that they can query the computer there during periods when the planners are legally obligated to free it for citizen use.

Indeed, it is not at all clear that this scheme would, in fact, realize its goal: more vigorous and knowledgeable participation by even a small percentage of the population. Citizens doing the same sorts of professional-political thinking and feeling as those legally empowered to run the government full time may turn out to be as destructive of a workable democracy as citizens not participating meaningfully. We shall have to experiment over many years to discover if we can have *both* long-range planning and democracy—that is, if we can have a viable, complex, huge, and dignifying urban condition. Thus, an approach such as this to inventing mutual urban and democratic viability must be attempted, and we had better have made a good start in this direction by 1976. We really have no choice in the matter if we wish to maintain the reality of democracy. If one expects that the conventional political system will fight computer-based long-range planning or exploit it in order to preserve conventional political power, then one must expect that those who plan and decide for urban government will try to do so ever more protected behind impenetrable barriers of complexity. In that case, the citizen would be less and less able to assess the implications of what the government proposes in his best interest. Being unable to assess his interest, he would be forced either to abdicate political participation based on a knowledgeable assessment of the situation or to accept out of ignorance what the planners and politicians offer him. And in the urban world of 1976 these alternatives would, I hope, be unacceptable.[10]

REFERENCES

1. The concept of long-range planning used here subsumes both the formulation of desired end states and the design and implementation of the means for getting from here to there. It thus includes procedures for revising the means and for re-evaluating the ends as the program evolves over time. It is, thereby, responsive rather than rigid and, as such, is much harder to formulate, but more likely to be socially justifiable and feasible.

2. Let me immediately make clear I do not mean on-call, "push-button" voting. This simpleminded updating of the mythology of the golden age of the town meeting or the Greek forum could only limit the range of options and the time to deliberate needed by the policy-maker and planner, and restrict them to the inadequate understanding of the "voting" masses. In the absence of a truly sophisticated and enlightened citizenry—which absence will be amply evident in 1976—such voting would result in a tyranny of the masses, destructive of the very processes it was intended to preserve.

3. Throughout, "citizen" means concerned citizen: the citizen who is politically active and knowledgeable about the objects of his attention. Also, "citizen" is to be understood as shorthand for the citizen either as individual or as represented by a group (or a spokesman or newspaper), the latter being the likely mode of expression in the kind of situation to which this article attends. The purpose of the analysis and recommendation herein is not particularly to enlarge the portion of concerned citizens as such. Rather, it is to preserve and extend the capability of such citizens to be meaningfully concerned and usefully potent politically.

4. By city government I mean all those offices, agencies, and activities empowered by the city to conduct its affairs. It includes the mayor or manager, the welfare agencies, the planning commission, and the port authority, to single out a few such entities. By 1976, there will probably be some new forms of urban government in response to the geographical and functional overlapping of some cities that now are still separate, and there will be new relationships with the federal government. But whatever forms these take, I assume political motivations will persist.

5. Numerous studies attest to this. A recent study of the interaction between planning and politics concludes that "on the basis of these five [studies of the implementation of urban redevelopment plans] it seems reasonably clear that the realization of any of the democratic values incorporated in the procedural requirements of public law were fortuitous. The extent to which these values are reflected in the decision-making process will depend on the lineup of economic and political forces outside the legal system. This seems particularly true of the goal of disinterested planning. In all of the situations discussed, including the public housing of Chicago, the planning experts were sought and used as tactical support for the political decisions. The governmental planning units were distressingly ineffective in performing the role envisaged by the law. Planning was essential to achieve the redevelopment goals, but it was strictly partisan." J. Sheldon Plager, "The Politics of Planning for Urban Redevelopment: Strategies in the Manipulation of Public Law," *Wisconsin Law Review* (Summer, 1966), pp. 724-75.

6. A sense of what is looming in pertinent urban issues is to be found in the controversy over the Moynihan report. The data, the conceptual model for interpreting them, and the program options following from the interpretation have all been subject to controversy and confusion. See Lee Rainwater and W. L. Yancey, *The Moynihan Report and the Politics of Controversy* (Cambridge, 1967). And see D. Schneider's review of the book

in which he criticizes both the political and social science premises assumed by Rainwater and Yancey: *Bulletin of the Atomic Scientists,* Vol. 24, No. 3 (March, 1968), p. 20.

That the report produced controversy among experts is scant comfort when we look to the future. The controversy produced as much confusion as clarification, although it was based on relatively simple and accessible data and social-science models concerning the meaning of the data. What will the situation be when the data and models are as complex as we are anticipating them to become here?

7. The new "Freedom of Information Act" may set the precedent here. The persistent distrust of government—not a new response in American life, but one likely to remain exacerbated in this and the next generation of concerned citizens as a result of Vietnam—should add incentives too.

8. While it is not obvious to all planners—and this is another reason for the approach proposed here—most of us would agree that there is much more to the human and urban condition than can be encompassed in computer-assisted long-range planning. But unless *this* planning activity succeeds, it is hard to see how the more ineffable and, quite possibly, more important aspects of living can be realized in the world of 1976.

9. Consider the nationwide membership of the Sierra Club as a prototype response. The growing number of people who spend substantial time in more than one city may come to see proposals for pollution control and crime reduction as important for them to judge in one place as in another. They will not be able to vote in both places, but they may well be able to influence policy and programs—and votes—by helping to defray the costs of citizen computer terminal services.

10. The author is presently a Special Research Fellow of the National Institute of Mental Health, Center for Studies of Metropolitan and Regional Mental Health Problems. Preparation of this paper was facilitated by this fellowship.

103

ALEXANDER L. GEORGE

Political Leadership and Social Change in American Cities

I

THE NATURE of the poverty problem and the tasks of social change
we face today differ sharply from those that confronted the United
States in the era of the New Deal. In the thirties, poverty and unemployment were pervasive and the economy was stagnant, reflecting fundamental flaws in the workings of the free enterprise system.
In contrast, the poverty of the sixties is "confined, limited, isolated
and oftentimes hidden; it does not seem to threaten directly the
whole of society. It is locked up in the inner-city neighborhoods,
the Negro ghettos, the remote and economically depressed areas
of the nation."[1] Moreover, it is interlaced with the task of assimi-
lating the Negro and other minority groups.

Whereas the Great Depression could be dealt with by action at
the national level, today's poverty problem poses critical requirements for leadership at the local level. Effective leadership from
Washington and ample federal funds are needed. It is doubtful,
however, that they alone will be sufficient, for federal initiatives and
resources can be frustrated in many ways and eventually defeated
by inadequate performance at the local level. Certainly there is an
urgent need for adapting new management tools, such as program
budgeting and operations analysis, to decision-making at the city
level, and for additional scholarly research on the cluster of interrelated urban problems. These efforts can have their full impact only
if the special constraints that affect leadership, planning, policy
formation, and administration at the local level are taken into account.

The optimistic expectations associated with the older middle-
class ideal of "good government" have gradually given way in the
past twenty years before the realization that this model of local

government conflicts with deeply ingrained features of the urban political environment, particularly in larger cities, and cannot cope with demands for social change. An alternative model associated with new "politician-type" mayors, such as Richard Lee and Richard Daley, has emerged in practice and deals somewhat better with these constraints.

The incumbent of the mayor's office must be capable of harnessing for purposes of reform the highly pluralistic, fragmented distribution of authority characteristic of the political system in most American cities. He must be capable of inspiring city planning and administrative practices that are sensitive to political considerations and a variety of socio-economic interests. Even when the other necessary resources are available, the quality of leadership in these respects often makes the difference between achieving outstanding success, mediocre or uneven results, or miserable failure in urban renewal. Thus, in New Haven "very little happened until redevelopment became attached to the political fortunes of an ambitious politician," Mayor Lee, who possessed political skills of a high order.[2] In Chicago, though Mayor Daley did not always take the initiative as Lee did, he has nonetheless personally identified himself with the many urban redevelopment improvements in that city since he took office in 1957 and has usually managed to take credit for them.[3] In Cleveland, on the other hand, ineffectual mayoral leadership contributed to the failure of a program of urban renewal that was overly ambitious, inadequately planned, and poorly implemented. The Department of Housing and Urban Development, which channels federal funds into renewal projects, was finally forced in 1967 temporarily to cut off support to Cleveland.[4]

The strategy of urban renewal can no longer be defined narrowly, as in the fifties, in terms of slum clearance and rebuilding of downtown areas. For some years now it has been increasingly evident that urban renewal was not achieving the broader aims associated with it. In too many places it failed to relocate the poor slum dwellers in "decent, safe, and sanitary" housing. Nor was the earlier approach successful in raising the new tax revenues the cities badly needed. Urban renewal did not curb the exodus of middle-class whites to the suburbs nor lure many of them back to the city.[5]

The early successes in urban renewal achieved by the energetic mayors of the fifties and early-sixties are dated in some respects and do not provide firm patterns and guidelines for dealing with today's deepening urban crisis. The mayor's priority task in urban reform is no longer merely one of altering and renovating the physical topography of the city, but of participating in and providing encouragement for efforts to preserve and extend democratic values.

II

The nature of the urban political environment makes intense demands on the mayor for special leadership skills of a high order if the need for social change is to be met; at the same time, however, the realities of urban political life make it difficult for him to perform these role requirements effectively and consistently. The root of this paradox lies in the considerable fragmentation of authority and dispersal of power characteristic of the formal governmental structure of American urban areas. In the larger cities, governmental authority is divided and dispersed among federal, state, county, and city jurisdictions; among mayor, council, and various independent officials, boards, and commissions designated by the electorate to deal with specific services and functions.[6]

In an earlier era, the dispersal of formal governmental power was often counteracted—though typically for private advantage rather than for social reform—by powerful political machines. The rising urban middle class rebelled against flagrant political corruption, and the ensuing movement for "good government" led to important gains in the honesty, impartiality, and efficiency of city administrations. This was accompanied by weakening of political parties, stronger emphasis on nonpartisan elections, and a somewhat greater centralization of formal authority in the hands of the executive. As the position of the middle class was strengthened, the urban community became more willing to see decisions made on the basis of criteria broader than narrow private advantage or group interest.

In few cities today, however, does the mayor have *formal* authority and resources commensurate with the responsibilities and tasks which face him. Local government of the city-manager type has performed reasonably well in smaller cities that have a more homogeneous population and are not afflicted with acute social-political tensions. Most of the bigger cities, however, have opted for "strong mayor" government. Nonetheless, the concept of a strong executive, prevalent elsewhere in our society, has not taken hold in the cities.

Although the modern management-oriented mayor is likely to handle the routine business of the city adequately, he may lack the force and vision needed to deal with the city's largest, most difficult, and longer-run problems.

It is precisely in this respect that the realities of urban political systems challenge the appropriateness and utility of the leadership model implicit in the old "good government" ideal. That approach envisaged a strong independent executive who would ignore special interests and assert his own impartial conception of the "public interest" of the community as a whole. Such an executive need not possess the interests and skills of a politician; rather, he should be a technically-oriented expert proficient in business-like management.

This vision of government without politics has gradually faded. The proliferation of effectively organized interest groups has imparted a more complex pluralistic character to urban political systems. New forms of informal functional representation and influence have emerged in local government. Important changes have taken place in the relation between parties and local government that, in turn, have altered the composition of the urban policy-making elite as well as the environment in which it operates.[7] As a result, recent years have seen a rather full turning of the circle in the attitude toward "politician-type" leaders in city hall. There is growing awareness that the executive of the big city must be a gifted politician to cope with the tasks of renewal and social change in the urban setting. The pluralistic structure of dispersed, decentralized power requires a political leader who can accumulate personal influence to supplement his limited formal authority.

Richard Neustadt's thesis that power and influence in the office of the President are highly unstable commodities applies in even greater measure at the city level.[8] Studies of successful leaders in urban systems have led to the formulation of a simple, but incisive model of the "political entrepreneur"—a political activist adept at accumulating a variety of political resources and using them to gain influence and additional resources. To the political entrepreneur who possesses skill and drive, the pluralistic dispersion and fragmentation of power in democratic systems offer unusual opportunities for pyramiding limited initial resources into a substantial political holding.[9]

Even though an individual leader possesses the skills of a political entrepreneur, he may not choose to employ them in furnishing the creative leadership that urban social change requires. Carmine

De Sapio, for example, was not interested in using his power resources aggressively on behalf of social reform. Others view social policy issues as essentially divisive and potentially dangerous for their power position and, therefore, seek to avoid or minimize involvement in them. As is perhaps illustrated by the case of Mayor Yorty, certainly a gifted politician, personal involvement in reform projects may also be viewed cautiously and instrumentally because of ambitions for higher political office.

It seems unlikely, therefore, that the leadership needed to deal with the contemporary problems of poverty, equality, and social change in American cities will be offered by astute politicians who are motivated only by an interest in the mechanics of power and in power for personal gain. Such a leader must possess, in addition, a "sense of direction" and an affinity for moving society forward. He must be interested in government, not merely in politics. Thus, Mayor Daley indeed resembles some of his predecessors ("Big Bill" Thompson and Ed Kelly) in being the undisputed boss of a powerful political machine and in exercising political skills of a high order. Nonetheless, he differs from them in his dedication to making Chicago a better place. He has made slum clearance and urban renewal his priority programs. Daley regards himself as a new type of city boss, one who identifies with the goals of the "good government" movement, but uses certain of the traditional means associated with machine politics to realize these objectives.

The job of mayor, however, evidently has not attracted men of outstanding political talent or, for that matter, of strong political ambition. Men who possess the leadership skills of a Daley or a Lee do not often direct their careers toward the mayor's office.[10] The question arises whether, as the urban crisis deepens, the office of mayor will become more or even less attractive to talented political leaders.

III

The task of urban revitalization poses another important requirement for the role of mayoral leadership. A broad and relatively long-range perspective must be provided by city hall in order to temper the otherwise incremental, fragmented, uncoordinated nature of government decision-making.

For many decades students of local government in the United States have been perplexed by the fundamental "tension" that exists between the nature of urban political culture and political systems, on the one hand, and the requirements of comprehensive, "rational" city planning on the other.[11] This "tension" has handicapped efforts to promote urban renewal on a broad scale. Different approaches to overcoming or moderating the discrepancy have emerged. Efforts have been made to alter the political structure of the metropolitan area so that it lends itself more readily to efficient central planning and administration. The fragmentation of authority, the multiplicity of jurisdictions, and the attitudes and practices embedded in urban political culture that adversely affect efforts to promote the welfare of urban communities have been attacked. There has been an attempt to inculcate the ideals of "good government," to achieve "home rule," to charter revision, to create specialized metropolitan authorities, and to strengthen the mayor's office. These efforts have fallen short of creating the "rational" social-political environment in which traditional textbook models of comprehensive city planning and administration can flourish. More recently, therefore, the problem has been attacked from the opposite direction on the assumption that urban political systems cannot be changed sufficiently to permit fruitful use of the preferred theoretical models of city planning, and that *traditional planning concepts need to be revamped* to suit the nature of pluralistic democratic politics in the cities.

Professional planners traditionally defined the boundaries of planning to exclude the "action system" and considered planning in technical, rationalistic, apolitical terms. As a result, city planning offices often withered on the vine or enjoyed little meaningful contact with the mayor's office.

If master planning in a political vacuum is utopian and ineffectual, how can long-range comprehensive planning and policy be brought together? Martin Meyerson suggests that the gap might be bridged by preparing comprehensive middle-range plans linking individual projects with the aspirations and goals embodied in the typical long-range plan.[12] Thus, the major function of the long-range plan would be to map out a desired but feasible state of affairs, without specifying the courses of action needed to achieve that desired state. The middle-range development plan covering five to ten years would indicate specific changes for each year, their costs and expected sources of funding.

Others have redefined the planning function more radically, urging that it be brought directly into the mayor's office where it can be related more closely to policy formation and to budget preparation.

Alan Altshuler, on the other hand, argues that a city planning commission independent of the mayor's office may be distinctly preferable to one under his control in cities with weak mayor governments, such as Minneapolis and St. Paul. Altshuler also contends that independence does not necessarily prevent city planners from developing close liaison with political officials and other governmental offices. The city planner can, in fact, assume the role of an independent political actor in community affairs. Thus, in the Twin Cities, the independent city planners have occasionally filled the "vacuum" of political leadership in this policy sphere; they have utilized their independence to initiate and pursue planning projects more successfully than might have been the case had they been accountable to and controlled by mayors who have typically, but with a few notable exceptions, been reluctant to become identified with controversial issues that might cost them votes in the next election.[13]

From these various emphases there has emerged a *politicized* concept of city planning which stresses that planning must be linked with a better understanding of the community's social structure and political processes. This concept emphasizes that planners must realize that adequate political support has to be mobilized within the community to attain the changes desired. Thus, planning activities must devote considerable attention to devising strategies for consensus-building, coalition-formation, persuasion, and bargaining.[14]

Thus, to be a successful "achiever" of the likes of Lee and Daley, a mayor must have the ability to ascertain which of the interests and power-holders in the community, county, state, and federal governments can become political resources, suppliers, and allies on behalf of alternative goals and programs. Such a leader also benefits from being able to foresee those interests and groups likely to oppose different programs in varying degrees and with various instrumentalities. Political actors and interests in the community who offer obstacles to renewal have to be "won over," "neutralized," or effectively "bypassed." Thus, if nothing can be done immediately to neutralize the recalcitrant head of an organization, an interest group, or an administrative office, the mayor's plan must be re-examined or altered to reduce its vulnerability to this particular impediment. Politically sophisticated city planning, therefore, leaves the executive free later to "improvise ways of moving forward with essential change despite entrenched obstructionism."[15]

In any field of endeavor, a good plan anticipates the constraints on the *user's* freedom of action and attempts to meet his criteria of how the plan can be employed effectively in the situations that are expected to arise. Insofar as the mayor will be the chief "user" of a plan for urban renewal, he must satisfy himself that it will work *for him* in the various political contingencies that can be anticipated. His understanding of the nature of politics and social processes in his community should alert him to the danger of accepting a plan that depends heavily upon an ability to predict and control future political-social developments or one too inflexible to permit adaptation on the basis of learning, feedback, new information, or unexpected political developments.

Renewal programs often affect the interests of different social-political groups within the community in quite different ways. Consideration must be given to these potential social-political constraints in the design phase of planning; such consideration cannot be deferred until the so-called "technical" planning has been completed. To ensure adequate attention to the relevant political factors, the mayor or his alter egos may have to participate early and often in the planning process.

To assure political feasibility and realism in planning, Lee and Daley have often resorted to the expedient of formal or informal participation by interested parties and community power-holders in the planning and decision-making process. Thus, both Mayor Lee with his Citizens Action Commission and Mayor Daley with his practice of cooperating with civic leaders for purposes of policy-making have supplemented in an important sense the existing formal governmental institutions for representation and decision-making. Daley has employed this practice to such an extent that on occasion he has relied largely on private business and civic organizations to prepare initial plans, which his own planning officials later adapt. In the Exhibition Hall and Fort Dearborn cases, Edward Banfield notes, "Mayor Daley passed on proposals that came from unofficial sources, and when he finally ordered a plan made, it was to a large extent a collection of decisions that private bodies had already made or were expected to make."[16]

In these and other ways, informal mechanisms of representation may be deliberately created and existing ones strengthened and mobilized on behalf of urban change. At the same time, devices for bringing influential groups and interests into the planning and decision-making process can set the stage for utilizing their organizations and organizational power as an informal, albeit effective, "political infrastructure" within the community not only to gain agreement and support for reform programs, but also to maintain the momentum needed for implementation.

In December 1966, Mayor Daley released an ambitious fifteen-year master plan for Chicago, which commits the city to a policy of full integration in housing, education, employment, and opportunity. Reportedly to overcome expected objections, Chicago's city planners have broken down the master plan into plans for sixteen areas of the city. It is significant that these are being made public at the rate of one a month. The city leadership and the business community have undertaken the task of discussing the plans with civic and church groups, political and small business leaders in each of the areas.

The plan provides considerable flexibility by distinguishing between "strategic objectives," general policies, and the more detailed project and neighborhood planning that will be determined later on a decentralized basis in each of the sixteen areas. In this respect, it explicitly departs from the traditional "block-by-block" blueprint plan that has engendered negative citizen reaction in the past. Rather, as the introduction to the plan states, "the policies planning approach is being used to present information and preliminary recommendations for the city and then to refine this material through the joint efforts of citizens and public officials."

The Daley administration will most probably follow its usual practice of seeking agreement on as many aspects of the plan as possible and then out-waiting the opposition. As implementation of the plan unfolds, it is expected that the initial steps taken will create incentives and pressures that will generate additional support for its subsequent phases. The planners expect opposition to important elements of the plan from the suburbs outside Chicago, but are reported as saying that they will go ahead with those parts of the plan that do not require cooperation from the suburbs. They are counting on the assistance of major financial forces eventually to persuade industries and businesses outside the city to relocate or develop their plants along the lines laid down by the master plan.[17]

IV

Daley and Lee appear to be distinguished from less noteworthy mayors in possessing a strong personal need for achievement which has been transferred to the political arena. Such an individual is personally challenged by and attracted to difficult political tasks because he finds in them an opportunity to employ his political skills and resources, to exert mastery, and to achieve something socially worthwhile. He is sensitive to the power dimension of a whole range of situations and activities and adept at accumulating and pyramiding resources. Unlike other individuals who attain positions of leadership, such a "political man" does not regard "politics" as being immoral or distasteful.

In addition to a strong need for achievement and a distinctive entrepreneurial approach to power, politician-type leaders like Daley and Lee also possess a marked sense of personal efficacy. They believe that what they do often makes an important difference, that the individual leader can indeed help to move events in a desired direction. Such a belief shapes a leader's behavior in ways that contribute importantly to his political success if, in addition, he acquires the ability to assess the balance of opportunity and constraint present in the situations with which he must cope. In the latter respect, Lee and Daley have demonstrated an unusual motivation and knack in dealing with the often complex tension between what is desirable and what is feasible, without unduly diluting the content of renewal programs or slowing the tempo of change.

In contrast to mayors who have compiled less distinguished records, successful politician-type mayors do not confine themselves to overly cautious, passive leadership. When the situation offers an opportunity and the stakes warrant it, they employ their leadership skills and resources in order to convert into a high probability what would otherwise remain only an uncertain possibility.

Leaders such as Lee and Daley do not function merely as political barometers in assessing the prospects for desirable change; nor do they define their leadership role as that of a passive broker. The activities of a political broker are indeed often essential for developing sufficient consensus on behalf of a specific change. The much maligned, often misunderstood role of political broker can be played either passively and conservatively (as Mayor Robert Wagner, to name but one example, tended to do[18]); or it can be performed energetically and imaginatively (as Lee and perhaps only to a lesser extent Daley have done).

In the complex political setting of Chicago, successful performance of the mayor's broker role has seemingly required greater patience and caution than it has in New Haven. Some observers, noting this, have tended to downgrade Daley's leadership as being essentially passive or at least too opportunistic. Daley's initiatives have indeed been more guarded and less spectacular than Lee's, whose leadership is of a more heroic stamp. On more than one occasion, Lee has given the impression of orchestrating the political coalition he created as if he were not only the conductor of the symphony, but also the composer of the music it plays and the leading soloist.[19] In contrast, Daley's performance has been that of a "signal giver" rather than "orchestrator." As the term "signal giver" conveys, his leadership in expediting urban renewal has been selective and specialized. He has intervened in controversies in order to establish priorities to which underfinanced and undermanned administrative units could then turn for a clearer definition of immediate goals. Daley has also stepped in, preferably at moments of his own choosing, to "impose solutions" when controversy among other political actors has led to stalemate. Thus, while the "signal giver" does not attempt to make so comprehensive a contribution as the "orchestrator," the tasks he pursues are nonetheless essential in a complex, pluralistic political system.

Daley's strategic contribution to renewal efforts, then, has taken the form of facilitating the decision-making process by making city hall "available." In clearing the way politically for the Hyde Park-Kenwood redevelopment in 1957-58, Daley directed his administration to work with the community without immediately or explicitly committing himself to all-out support. Having delimited his role to that of "signal giver," he remained "ready at all times to gallop or dismount."[20]

A coalition of Negro tenants and homeowners, small businessmen, and local Catholic and Protestant clergy was formed in the Woodlawn section of the city in 1960 when its residents saw what redevelopment meant for the residents of a neighboring area, the Hyde Park-Kenwood section. Fearing that Woodlawn, too, would wake one morning to find bulldozers in the streets, the residents organized The Woodlawn Organization (T.W.O.) in order to establish the principle that no similar redevelopment plan would be adopted by city hall for Woodlawn without their active participation in planning and policy-formation to ensure that their interests would be protected. The struggle of T.W.O. took several dramatic turns before achieving success. Mayor Daley eventually recognized the legitimacy of T.W.O.'s demands when it mustered and demonstrated sufficient power to back its claims. Representatives of T.W.O. were finally brought into negotiations to revise the city's plans for redeveloping Woodlawn and won significant concessions. It was agreed that Woodlawn would be renewed in stages, that only houses beyond salvage would be torn down, that people displaced by demolition would have new homes waiting for them in the same neighborhood. Of particular interest was Daley's decision giving T.W.O. majority representation on the citizens' planning committee that was to draw up more detailed plans and supervise their execution.[21]

At about the same time (January 1963), Mayor Daley extended the same principle to another slum area of the city which had organized an effective community association, the Northwest Community Organization. It, too, was granted majority control over the Conservation Commission established for this section of the city.[22]

It is possible to view the flexible, if not opportunistic, quality of Daley's commitments as his way of protecting the role he has defined for himself. Given the political context in which he operates, Daley feels it prudent to time and to control his initiatives and the taking of positions. Banfield regards Daley's habit of "watchful waiting" not merely as a rational strategy in situations in which there is disagreement within the "good government" forces, but also as a response to role requirements shaped by the local urban political culture. According to prevailing expectations in Chicago, "a policy ought to be framed by the interests affected, not by the political head or his agents. In this view, the affected interests should work out for themselves the 'best' solution of the matter (usually a compromise). The political head should see that all principally affected interests are represented, that residual interests (i.e. 'the general public') are not entirely disregarded, and that no interest suffers unduly in the outcome. He is not expected to have decided views of his own."[23]

Under the circumstances of urban politics, it is not surprising that a shrewd leader calculates the requirements both of the situation and his self-interest and attempts to balance them in deciding whether and when to take initiatives, and whether to make them visible. Daley is sometimes thought to play a more passive role than has actually been the case, an impression that is abetted by his tactical preference for nonvisible initiatives and for avoiding premature commitments. Closer and more detailed examination of the politics of urban renewal in Chicago, however, shows that he

115

has played a decisive role. Exhibiting versatility and good judgment, he has acted at times behind the scenes and at times openly to amplify the influence of citizens organized on behalf of redevelopment.[24] In this respect, Daley's leadership may be favorably contrasted with that of his predecessor, Mayor Kennelly. Though he strongly endorsed policies favoring expansion of housing and renewal, Kennelly, unlike Daley, espoused the role of a "weak mayor" and fostered full decentralization of authority during his regime.[25]

A "political man" often seeks to maximize the weight of his leadership for expediting social change also by reshaping the political process in some way. Once in office, such political personalities make it the first order of business to recast political institutions by reinterpreting and expanding the functions of existing political roles or by creating new ones that better fit their needs, political style, and aspirations. Being "power-oriented," they seek opportunities for maximizing their influence and impact.[26] Thus, Lee recognized at the outset that the considerable latent support for urban renewal in New Haven would not materialize in response to a simple announcement that he was ready to lead in that direction. Lee understood that political and administrative support would have to be organized, structured, given specific purpose and direction, and made subject to his mobilization, command, and use.[27]

To this end, Lee converted the political system of New Haven, as Robert Dahl has described it, from a "pattern of petty sovereignties" to an "executive-centered coalition."[28] More specifically, Lee reshaped to his own advantage the mayor's relations with three other major political forces in the community: the bureaucratic departments and agencies, the politicians, and business. Willing, in order to clear the way for redevelopment, to pay a price to the Democratic political machine that had elected him, Lee sought an accommodation with its two leading figures on the basic question of who would control what.[29] His task with business interests in New Haven was one not of overcoming strong business opposition to redevelopment, but of winning their confidence and mobilizing them. When he entered office, the New Haven business community was no longer strong nor unified. To give the business community an image of unity and power, Lee created a new organization of business leaders, the Citizens Action Commission (C.A.C.), and used it to gain respectability, prestige, and support for his initial renewal programs. Not only did Lee co-opt business leaders in this fashion, but he attached the new organization informally to his command post and took precautions against the possibility that the C.A.C. could be captured and led to oppose his leadership and programs.[30]

Lee's creation of an executive-centered coalition with the Democratic machine and the business community is better known than the story of his conquest of the city bureaucracy. The successful assault of the urban reform movement on corruption and inefficiency over the decades has led to the rise in many cities of professionally-oriented career bureaucracies organized in individual departments and agencies along narrow functional lines of specialization. While this bureaucratization had not proceeded so far in New Haven when Lee became mayor in 1953 as it has in New York, Lee was sensitive to the potential obstacles that the departments and agencies of the city government could place in the way of his plans for large-scale municipal reconstruction. He moved quickly to establish his authority over the departments and to neutralize the obstacles they might create to thwart his purposes. Given Lee's political personality and the knowledge of the city government he had previously acquired, his insight into the power requirements of his role is not surprising.

Lee's first two years in office were devoted largely to reshaping and controlling the city bureaucracy and to reorganizing and staffing agencies with competent, dedicated, loyal people. Lee found an early occasion to employ shock tactics against one department in order to demonstrate to it—and others—that he had the power and would not hesitate to exercise it to punish and reward. He also made it a point to exercise vigorously all his formal powers (even those seldom used in the past) in order to multiply his influence within the city administration; thereby he put the departments on notice that all available powers and influence would be used in one way or another on behalf of his larger purposes. On other occasions, Lee made use of consultants he appointed to a department to weaken its head, to manipulate policy advice from that department, and to "take over" the department. He dealt with other recalcitrant agency directors by usurping key persons on their staffs.[31]

In this respect and in his relations with business and civic organizations, the pattern of power and leadership that Daley worked out differs in some respects from Lee's.[32] Daley revived the Democratic political machine, made himself its head, and then used it as a personal instrument for dominating the city council.

More generally, he has maintained the party machine as a stable informal power base that can be put at the disposal of "good government" measures and development programs.[33]

V

"Citizen participation," initially viewed by city officials in Chicago and elsewhere as a means of winning popular middle-class support for urban renewal, has had to be extended and broadened. Even in the absence of organized action by slum dwellers, city officials have at times involved them in urban planning out of a realization that slum clearance was uncovering and creating more problems than it solved.[34]

Some interesting administrative and planning techniques to broaden public involvement in urban social change have been introduced which may possibly lead to a new style of municipal politics, if not also to a new philosophy of local government. Thus, in some urban centers, officials charged with city planning have been sent into local communities and neighborhoods to persuade slum landlords and house-owners to renovate and have assisted them in doing so.

Some mayors, like Lee of New Haven, have initiated broader citizen participation "from above." As these mayors have turned attention and resources to the task of revitalizing life in the depressed neighborhoods, they have seen that the traditional social-welfare approach was grossly inadequate. They are drawing, instead, upon new approaches to the problem of delinquency that see it fundamentally as a response to the lack of opportunities available to many slum youth for achieving normal working-class and middle-class goals. According to this diagnosis, the remedy lies in increasing opportunities to the inhabitants of slum areas through community organization and community-action programs. Influential in this respect have been the New York City program for delinquency prevention called Mobilization for Youth and the related activities of the Ford Foundation and of the President's Committee on Juvenile Delinquency and Youth Crime.[35]

These novel social-welfare approaches to delinquency have combined with the broadening emphasis in urban renewal to produce new concepts and programs for strengthening neighborhood institutions and making them a focal point for renewal. To this end some cities have taken steps to ensure that the many separate programs designed to deal with the need for housing, jobs, health, family services, and better education are no longer carried out in isolation. Arrangements have been made to coordinate these programs at the neighborhood level in order to enhance and reinforce their impact on the recipients. A new leadership cadre has been created—the neighborhood worker. Recruited from the slum neighborhood itself, he serves as a link between the various welfare programs and the people in need of assistance. The objective of such organizational devices is to bring available opportunity programs more effectively to underprivileged people in the slum neighborhoods and, more generally, to make local institutions more relevant to their needs.[36] Finally, cities experimenting in this direction have also attempted to stimulate citizen interest and participation in the process of government, to encourage and help residents of slum areas to articulate their problems and organize for action. These are, indeed, the major goals set for Community Progress, Inc., the private anti-poverty organization developed by Mayor Lee's administration in 1962, which Mitchell Sviridoff headed.[37]

The emergence of Mobilization for Youth in New York City, Community Progress, Inc., in New Haven, and similar programs elsewhere reflect growing discontent with existing approaches to urban poverty. The traditional social-welfare approach to the needy has been criticized not only because it smacks of a bureaucratized "welfare colonialism," but also because it deals with individual symptoms rather than root causes. Its critics favor the alternative of working with the poor in the ghettos in such a way as to get them to help themselves, overcome their apathy, and develop their own community organizations and leadership. It is felt that the urban poor and underprivileged (particularly, but not exclusively, the Negro) should seek not merely voting power, but also the broad influence resources that would be appropriate for attaining their needs and aspirations.

There are ample precedents for these developments. It is indeed in the American political tradition for dissatisfied groups to organize in order to further their desire for a larger share of political power and economic resources. The tragedy of ghetto riots should not be allowed to obscure this fact. Conflict has often preceded accommodation and the eventual adjustment, however imperfect, of the pluralistic political system to the emergence of newly organized, hitherto-fore under-represented groups of citizens. Further, it has been the historic role of the federal government to assist underprivileged, under-represented strata to acquire a more equitable position and to participate more effectively in the processes of the pluralistic political system.

The federal "anti-poverty" program has to be viewed from this perspective. The Economic Opportunity Act of 1964 established a Community Action Program that drew upon some of the ideas of the President's Committee on Juvenile Delinquency and Youth Crime, and some of the practical experience of New York City's Mobilization for Youth and New Haven's Community Progress, Inc. In developing its programs in various cities, however, the Office of Economic Opportunity has often bypassed the mayor's office and reached directly into neighborhoods. In contrast, New Haven's C.P.I. established an organizational network in the neighborhoods, but also worked closely with city agencies and departments. The same harmony of objectives, close coordination, and communication between C.P.I. and the New Haven administration has not been replicated in many urban areas in which O.E.O. has set up programs. In addition, whereas New Haven's C.P.I. emphasizes strong executive control of its programs, O.E.O. has stressed maximum participation of the poor in local anti-poverty boards and their involvement in program planning. This has led to considerable friction with mayors who have seen in O.E.O.'s local community-action programs a source of political power that can be used either by themselves to buttress their own position or by their political opponents.[38] Generally speaking, it appears that efforts to organize low-income slum dwellers politically have not been very successful. The impact and autonomy of community-action agencies have been eroded as a result of counter-pressures asserted by city hall and other agencies and interests who felt threatened thereby.[39]

The Department of Housing and Urban Development has attempted to take some of this experience into account in designing its new "Model Neighborhoods" program. With this initiative, the federal government attempts to overcome some of the worst consequences of the dispersal and fragmentation of urban governmental authority and to secure the modicum of comprehensive planning and coordination needed to improve the quality and results of various programs for urban revitalization. Thus, federal grants in the "Model Neighborhoods" program are to be contingent on the ability of city administrations to provide assurances and plans for local coordination.

Some observers take a pessimistic view of the efficacy of the federal government's effort to encourage and to require coordinated metropolitan planning. They believe that the mismatch between the character of local government and the metropolitan-regional nature of urbanization problems is too great to be overcome by such devices. They emphasize that the social and economic aspects of urban problems do not fit the geographic boundaries that prescribe and limit local governmental organizations. Moreover, they doubt whether the various governmental bodies and agencies in a locality can be made to behave as an integral urban unit and urge consideration of alternative approaches—such as some form of federally guaranteed annual income—that would bypass the fragmentation of governmental power in urban areas.

Implicit in this position, too, is the belief that federal programs such as "Model Neighborhoods" require a greater capacity for mayoral leadership than exists in most cities. This issue is difficult to judge. Programs and strategies that minimize further the requirement for vigorous leadership at the local government level may be necessary, but it is doubtful whether the need for enlightened and courageous local leadership of this kind can be reduced altogether.[40]

We have reviewed in this essay some of the special constraints that affect mayoral leadership, planning, policy formation, and administration at the city level. These constraints stem from deeply ingrained characteristics of American urban political systems and from the traditional, but still vigorous political culture in which they are embedded. Experience indicates that a particular kind of mayoral leadership is needed to harness for purposes of social change the highly pluralistic, fragmented distribution of authority typical of most urban areas. A mayor must be capable of inspiring new kinds of city planning and administrative practices that are sensitive to political considerations and the variety of often conflicting socio-economic interests affected by programs for social change.

In order to learn more about how relatively successful mayors have coped with these tasks in the past, we have reviewed the careers and political styles of Lee of New Haven and Daley of Chicago. These men have been continuously in office since 1954 and 1957 respectively. Their experience spans much of the history of urban renewal and the successive phases through which it passed— from public housing to slum clearance, then to urban redevelopment and community revitalization, and now to the "war on poverty" and "Model Neighborhoods." Lee and Daley have not only managed to stay in office during this period of rapid urban social change, but have done reasonably well with various urban renewal programs. This suggests that they have been able to adapt their leadership style and practices to the increasingly complex problems of the city. It remains to be seen, of course, whether Lee and Daley can cope constructively with the acute tensions of the ghetto, with increased Negro militancy, and with white blacklash. Both New Haven and Chicago have now experienced ghetto riots, but it is questionable whether this in itself can be taken as a sign of irrevocable failure in coping with the problems of social change.

Finally, it must be recognized that conditions differ from one city to another. Leadership patterns and programs that prove reasonably effective in one urban area may not be applicable or easily transferable to others. While American cities share many features of a common political culture, important differences in this respect and in their political systems cannot be ignored in appraising the prospects for social change and in designing programs to this end.

REFERENCES

1. Mitchell Sviridoff, "Dynamics of Change," Keynote Speech, Training Seminar, Mayor's Committee on Human Resources, Inc., Pittsburgh, September 8, 1965. Sviridoff, formerly executive director of Community Progress, New Haven, became director, Human Resources Administration, in New York City under Mayor Lindsay. He joined the Ford Foundation in late 1967.

2. Robert Dahl, *Who Governs?* (New Haven, 1961), p. 115. This book will be supplemented by a companion volume, soon to be published by Raymond E. Wolfinger, *The Politics of Progress*. The story of New Haven's experience in urban renewal is brought up to date by Jeanne R. Lowe, *Cities in a Race with Time* (New York, 1967), Chapter 9; and particularly by Allan R. Talbot, *The Mayor's Game* (New York, 1967).

3. James Q. Wilson, in *The Amateur Democrat* (Chicago, 1962), observes: "Indeed, the credit was often well-deserved for with Chicago's badly fragmented formal government, a boss like Daley was required to clear away the political obstacles to these changes (p. 72)." For detailed case studies of redevelopment in Chicago, see Peter H. Rossi and Robert A. Dentler, *The Politics of Urban Renewal* (New York, 1961), and Edward C. Banfield, *Political Influence* (New York, 1961). There is, unfortunately, no up-to-date study of Daley's career.

4. Wallace C. Chapla underscored the failure of leadership by pointing to the city administration's basic "lack of understanding" of its role as "expeditor of all related departmental activities." The mayor's office had failed to ensure proper planning and coordination of the activities of the various departments—recreation, parks, public service, police, social services, capital improvement as well as urban redevelopment—all of which must contribute integrally to a successful over-all program of urban renewal. The mayor's office had also failed to coordinate public activities with those of many private agencies capable of contributing to urban renewal in one way or another. "The Chapla Report on Urban Renewal City of Cleveland," Cleveland Little Hoover Commission, November 16, 1966. See also article by D. J. R. Bruckner, *Los Angeles Times*, March 5, 1967.

5. For summaries and evaluations of these matters, see, for example, Herbert J. Gans, "The Failure of Urban Renewal," *Commentary* (April, 1965); Martin Anderson, *The Federal Bulldozer: A Critical Analysis of Urban Renewal, 1949-1962* (Cambridge, 1964); Scott Greer, *Urban Renewal and American Cities* (New York, 1965).

6. There are many detailed descriptive accounts of the distribution of governmental powers and responsibilities affecting different cities. For a general over-all summary, see Edward C. Banfield and James Q. Wilson, *City Politics* (New York, 1963), Ch. 6.

7. Interesting from this standpoint is the systematic study of the political system of New York City by Theodore J. Lowi, *At the Pleasure of the Mayor* (New York, 1964).

8. Richard E. Neustadt, *Presidential Power* (New York, 1960).

9. Dahl, *Who Governs?*, pp. 225-27, 308; Banfield, *Political Influence*, Ch. 8 and pp. 17, 309, 312-13, 320-21; Aaron Wildavsky, *Leadership in a Small Town* (Totowa, N. J., 1964), pp. 244-45, 248; Hugh Douglas Price, *The Metropolis and Its Problems* (Syracuse, N. Y., 1960), pp. 27-28. Also see Max Weber's brief description of the political entrepreneur in "Politics as a Vocation," *From Max Weber: Essays in Sociology*, eds. H. H. Gerth and C. Wright Mills (New York, 1946), p. 109.

10. Relevant here is the study by Marilyn Gittell of the careers of ninety-six mayors, "selected at random," who held that office in the last twenty years. Only ten of the ninety-six were ever elected to any higher office after serving as mayor. "Metropolitan Mayors: Dead End," *Public Administration Review*, Vol. 23 (March, 1963).

11. For a good summary of this and related themes, see the historical-analytic survey by Wallace S. Sayre and Nelson W. Polsby, "American Political Science and the Study of Urbanization," *The Study of Urbanization*, eds. Philip M. Hauser and Leo F. Schnore (New York, 1965).

12. Martin Meyerson, "Building the Middle-Range Bridge for Comprehensive Planning," *Journal of the American Institute of Planners* (Spring, 1956), reprinted in Edward C. Banfield (ed.), *Urban Government* (New

York, 1961). See also Martin Meyerson and Edward C. Banfield, *Politics, Planning, and the Public Interest: The Case of Public Housing in Chicago* (New York, 1955). Robert Walker was one of the first to point out the disadvantages of entrusting the city planning function to an independent commission and to urge a much closer relationship of city planners to the mayor's office. See his *The Planning Function in Urban Government* (Chicago, 1941).

13. Alan Altshuler, *The City Planning Process* (Ithaca, 1965), especially Ch. 7. The theme of Altshuler's book is that the political culture of Minneapolis and St. Paul has tended to inhibit the development of comprehensive city planning.

14. See, for example, James Q. Wilson, "An Overview of Theories of Planned Change," in *Centrally Planned Change: Prospects and Concepts,* ed. Robert Morris (New York, 1964), p. 39; Dahl, *Who Governs?,* p. 116; Banfield, *Political Influence,* pp. 250-51; Norton E. Long, "Political Science and the City," *Urban Research and Policy Planning,* eds. Leo F. Schnore and Henry Fagin (Beverly Hills, 1967), Vol. 1, p. 257; Irwin T. Sanders, "Professional Roles," in *Centrally Planned Change: Prospects and Concepts,* p. 110; John C. Bollens and Henry J. Schmandt, *The Metropolis* (New York, 1965), p. 281.

15. Mitchell Sviridoff emphasizes this point in his analysis of "The Strategy of Change in New Haven," an address to the American Orthopsychiatric Association, New York, March 18, 1965.

16. Banfield, *Political Influence,* pp. 251-52, 271, 300, 302.

17. Article by D. J. R. Bruckner, *Los Angeles Times,* January 16, 1967.

18. See, for example, Warren Moscow, *What Have You Done for Me Lately?* (Englewood Cliffs, 1967), pp. 38-40; and Barry Gottehrer, "Urban Conditions: New York City," *The Annals* (May, 1967), pp. 143-44, 151.

19. This image of the political broker as a virtuoso who orchestrates the political process almost singlehandedly emerges also from some accounts of Lyndon B. Johnson's exploits as Senate minority and majority leader. See, for example, the account of Johnson's management of the civil rights bill of 1957, in Rowland Evans and Robert Novak, *Lyndon B. Johnson: The Exercise of Power* (New York, 1966), Ch. 8.

20. Rossi and Dentler, *The Politics of Urban Renewal,* pp. 249-52, 261.

21. For a sympathetic account of the controversial Woodlawn Organization written by a member of the Board of Editors of *Fortune,* see Charles E. Silberman, *Crisis in Black and White* (New York, 1964), and the same author's "Up from Apathy—The Woodlawn Experiment," *Commentary* (May, 1964).

22. For an account of the development which emphasizes Saul Alinsky's role, see Hillel Black, "This Is War," *Saturday Evening Post* (January 25, 1964). Alinsky pioneered in developing community organization and techniques of direct action as weapons of the poor in slum areas in the

late-thirties when he organized the successful Back of the Yards Neighborhood Council in Chicago. Alinsky outlined his approach in an early book, *Reveille for Radicals,* in 1946. See also the two-part account of conversations with Alinsky in *Harper's* (June and July, 1965). Alinsky's critical views of the approach taken by the Johnson Administration's "War on Poverty" are presented in his "The War on Poverty—Political Pornography," *Journal of Social Issues* (January, 1965).

23. Banfield, *Political Influence,* pp. 252-53, 270-71.

24. Rossi and Dentler, *The Politics of Urban Renewal,* pp. 241, 248-66. See also the account of Daley's strategy for dealing with race relations issues, in which he often allowed his Commission on Human Relations to act both as his agent and as a source of pressure on him, in J. Q. Wilson, *Negro Politics* (New York, 1960), pp. 90-91. Material on Mayor Lee's approach to racial issues is to be found in Talbot, *The Mayor's Game,* Chs. 12-14, and in Bernard Asbell, "Dick Lee Discovers How Much Is Not Enough," *New York Times Magazine* (September 3, 1967).

25. Meyerson and Banfield, *Politics, Planning, and the Public Interest,* pp. 61-88; Rossi and Dentler, *The Politics of Urban Renewal,* pp. 248-49.

26. The creation or reinterpretation of leadership roles, of course, cannot be understood in narrow personality terms, but requires reference to interactions between personality, social-historical dynamics, and the institutional setting. Erik Erikson's emphasis of this point reinforces and amplifies earlier observations along these lines by sociologists and others who, like Hans Gerth and C. Wright Mills for example, hold that the "great leader" has often been a man who successfully managed such institutional dynamics and created new roles of leadership. Gerth and Mills, *Character and Social Structure* (New York, 1953), Ch. 14.

27. "The elements of a comprehensive program were there when I became Mayor," Lee explained later. "Someone had to fuse them, and give the program direction and purpose. . . . The town seemed ready for change if I could show that concrete progress was possible." (Quoted in Talbot, *The Mayor's Game,* p. 20.)

28. Dahl, *Who Governs?,* Ch. 17.

29. For an account of some of the techniques and strategies Lee used in order to maintain an advantageous position vis-à-vis the other two leaders of the local Democratic Party, see Talbot, *The Mayor's Game,* Ch. 4.

30. *Ibid.,* Ch. 5; Dahl, *Who Governs?,* pp. 129-37.

31. Talbot, *The Mayor's Game,* Ch. 3. For a succinct elaboration of the thesis that the professionalized bureaucratic departments in city governments have become "relatively irresponsible structures of power," not readily subject to the controls and broader perspectives of any higher authority, and that as a result we now have efficiently run but "ungoverned" cities, see Theodore J. Lowi, "Machine Politics—Old and New," *The Public Interest* (Fall, 1967).

32. There is, surprisingly, no rounded study of Daley's political style and, so far as I have been able to discover, no full-length political biography or study of his political career. Banfield's *Political Influence* is particularly useful on some aspects of Daley's use of the Democratic political machine and on his relations with business and civic organizations. I have been unable to find much material on the way in which Daley structured his relations with city departments and agencies. James Q. Wilson provides an informative analysis of the ways in which Daley regulated his relations with organized Negro political groups during the first years of his long tenure as mayor (*Negro Politics*, pp. 81-93). Insightful observations about Daley's political personality are contained also in Keith Wheeler, "Last Big Boss on U.S. Scene," *Life* (February 8, 1960); "Clouter with Conscience," *Time* (March 15, 1963); Hal Higdon, "A Minority Objects, but Daley Is Chicago," *New York Times Magazine* (September 11, 1966).

33. The importance of a dominant party (Republican in this case) for the task of informally coordinating government powers at various levels—city, suburban, county, and state—is also emphasized by Roscoe C. Martin, Frank J. Munger *et al.*, *Decisions in Syracuse* (Bloomington, 1961), pp. 326-28.

34. J. Q. Wilson, "Planning and Politics: Citizen Participation in Urban Renewal," *American Institute of Planners Journal*, Vol. 24, No. 4 (November, 1963). See also Robert C. Weaver, "New Directions in Urban Renewal," reprinted in *Urban Renewal*, ed. James Q. Wilson (Cambridge, 1966); Greer, *Urban Renewal and American Cities*.

35. For a useful review of developments leading to establishment of community-action programs in U.S. cities, see Herbert J. Gans, "Urban Poverty and Social Planning," *The Uses of Sociology*, eds. Paul F. Lazarsfeld, William H. Sewell, and Harold L. Wilensky (New York, 1967), pp. 437-76. A more detailed and recent analysis is provided by Peter Marris and Martin Rein, *Dilemmas of Social Reform: Poverty and Community Action in the United States* (New York, 1967).

36. The trend in social welfare work toward using carefully selected and partly trained neighbors of the intended clients to serve as sub-professionals in opportunity programs is discussed by Frank Riessman, "The Revolution in Social Work," *Transaction* (November-December, 1964), and Arthur Pearl and Frank Riessman, *New Careers for the Poor* (New York, 1965).

37. Talbot, *The Mayor's Game*, Ch. 15; Lowe, *Cities in a Race with Time*, pp. 522-46. Similar concepts were articulated by Sviridoff in the 1966 study which he headed for Mayor Lindsay: see *Developing New York City's Human Resources* (June, 1966), Vol. 1.

38. See, for example, the observations of the former assistant director and inspector general of the O.E.O., William F. Haddad, "Mr. Shriver and the Savage Politics of Poverty," *Harper's* (December, 1965); and Talbot's account of the clash between New Haven's C.P.I. and O.E.O. (*The Mayor's Game*, pp. 219-21).

39. For a sober, balanced appraisal of the impact of community-action programs up to mid-1965, see Herbert Gans, "Urban Poverty Social Planning," *The Uses of Sociology*, pp. 457-60; and Marris and Rein, *Dilemmas of Social Reform*.

40. The author expresses his appreciation to Alton Frye, Ira S. Lowry, Nelson W. Polsby, James Q. Wilson, and Raymond E. Wolfinger for comments and suggestions, and to the Foundations' Fund for Research in Psychiatry for a grant some years ago that provided an opportunity for some of the research on which this article is based.

FRANKLIN A. LINDSAY

Managerial Innovation and the Cities

THE IRONY of the urban crisis in America is that it exists in a society that has accumulated the greatest economic, technological, and physical resources the world has seen. No country has faced a greater challenge than that confronting our urban complexes, but neither has any been so uniquely equipped to solve its major problems. The resources are there: the power to heat, light, and transport; the economic strength to house and feed; the technological understanding to lessen labor and free the intellect. Yet, with all this, the problems of the cities multiply.

What is lacking is a sense of direction and urgency. The most critical "missing factors" are an understanding and acceptance of what is required to make headway on the complex interrelated social and economic problems, and the will to mobilize the necessary human and physical resources with the urgency that the problems demand.

The country has before been face to face with impending calamity. Each time it has mustered its available resources, identified key points of leverage, and brought its resources to bear swiftly and accurately. For example, an Axis victory in World War II was prevented, in part, because we were able to marshal our total resources quickly and efficiently. Between 1939 and 1944, the United States military establishment was expanded from three hundred thousand men and women to more than ten million. The managerial skills of the tiny professional military cadre made it possible to train and organize these combat forces. In parallel, the managerial skills of industry were applied to the monumental requirements for new and different kinds of products and to the logistical problems inherent in organizing, deploying, and supplying the Allied armies, the largest military force the world had ever seen. The scientific and

128

engineering talents of our universities and research establishments were harnessed to develop new weapons systems and new logistics systems.

The situation today is no less critical. We stand at the threshold of a society deteriorating from years of neglect—a crazy-quilt of wealth and poverty, efficiency and waste. But, unlike the situation in the early forties, our present crisis lacks the compelling sense of urgency and direction that leaves no reasonable alternative. In World War II, society was forced to act by a clear external threat and by a very simple goal—victory. Today we have a terrible foreboding, but we do not yet have a clear picture of our objectives or of the route to achieve them.

Much of the blame for our urban problem lies in the society's demonstrated inability to use efficiently the country's knowledge and organizational skills. The depth and urgency of the problem are only now beginning to be understood. Very large sums are at last being provided to solve some of the most pressing urban problems, and only the Vietnam war prevents even larger expenditures. The size of the economic problem alone is huge. Only twenty years ago, for example, the entire annual operating budget of New York City was $1 billion. Today, that would just about pay the city's welfare bill for assisting eight hundred thousand people—slightly more than 10 per cent of its residents.

Money is necessary, but not sufficient to solve the problem. Appropriations provide only the right to acquire resources *if* they are available. Priorities on funds can be shifted overnight, but the depth of knowledge and the managerial resources to use these funds effectively cannot be created simply by budget shifts. Lead time is required for research, for program development, for the creation of a corps of economic managers to direct the programs, and—most important—for the establishment of new institutions and new ways of doing our urban business that will allow and encourage an innovative, creative, solution-oriented urban society. We have already squandered a large part of the lead time available. The time left to us is our scarcest resource, because time is the only resource that cannot be expanded by our own efforts.

In addition to necessary funding, other steps are prerequisites for full use of the little lead time that remains. They are all related to obtaining the knowledge to solve our problems and to using this knowledge effectively. These activities are all being undertaken now, but the present level of effort is far too low. We need:

Greatly increased research on urban problems: technical, managerial, social, and economic;

Development of broad capabilities to analyze, as systems, the complex interactions of the elements of the urban social and economic structure;

A massive education and training program for managers of the urban organizations of today and for those of the future;

Overhaul of existing government organizations, with the objectives of providing for greater innovation and creativity, greater freedom for effecting change, and greater incentives to attract and hold the best possible talent;

The creation of new forms of government and public or private organizations oriented specifically toward the solution of major urban problems.

Problems as complex and urgent as those of the cities will be solved in time only by a systematic attack at many levels; they require rapid innovation at many points. Some areas for innovation are immediately clear, and these in turn will lead to a broad and continuing capability for constructive creativity in the execution of future programs.

Increasing the Level of Urban Research

A spectrum of institutions for the conduct of research and development should be created or expanded and funded as rapidly as money can wisely be spent. An important step is the new Urban Institute, established to serve the federal government for research into urban problems. The Institute will study problems shared by the cities—such as poverty, housing, education, and transportation—and propose solutions to them. It will provide a central gathering point for knowledge and research about urban problems and will act independently to evaluate the effectiveness of federal, state, and local urban programs. The Institute, patterned on the Rand Corporation, will receive support from government contracts and grants, as well as from private foundations.

The research programs of university faculties and university-sponsored urban research centers are also important and should be expanded. But the cities also need R & D organizations under their own control for two reasons. First, the city knows its own problems and priorities, and this should be reflected in the research programs undertaken. Second, and even more important, the transfer of new knowledge and new solutions from R & D organizations to operating organizations is the most difficult part of any R & D program. The closer an R & D program can be to the operating organizations it serves, the easier and quicker will be the transfer of the results. A single large city might have more than one research organization, each working directly with a major department, such as education or sanitation.

Some other research organizations can be established (or expanded) by cities in close cooperation with local universities. Public funds will clearly be required to support these research organizations, but core funds must be provided without strings of any sort, either from public or private sources, and on the basis of long-term commitments. Only in this way can the organization achieve the security and independence needed to attract the best personnel and to explore new problems on its own initiative. Public funds for specific program studies should, if possible, come from more than one source, again to help preserve the autonomy and creativity of the research. Undue interference by government bureaucrats has often been the price of funding from a single source. And such interference can seriously impair the quality of research and its application to problems.

In many areas, especially technical ones, existing corporate R & D facilities can be used on a contract basis, as is now true of military R & D programs. It is important to recognize, however, that most corporations are reluctant to sell their R & D capabilities on a "time and materials" basis, unless there is a real possibility of a continuing involvement in the products of research and an opportunity for continued earnings from this involvement.

Research activities will have to be built up gradually as professional staffs are assembled and as key research problems are identified more precisely. A minimum goal to be reached ten years from now should be a level of R & D funding equal to 1 per cent of the operating budgets of the nation's cities. The inadequacy of current spending on research is pointed out by a recent report of the Arden House Conference on Public Welfare, which notes that "solid research is virtually unknown in public welfare. Less than 1/10 of 1 per cent of welfare funds are spent for that purpose. Rarely has so costly a program operated with so little knowledge."

131

The 1 per cent figure is a minimum when viewed in comparison with an average research budget for larger American corporations of more than 5 per cent of sales. For the twenty-five largest cities alone, 1 per cent would total $100 million per year.

Analyzing the Cities as Systems

A second set of prerequisites for the successful solution of our urban problems is the identification of key factors affecting the city's major problems and an awareness of the complex ways in which they interact. Only with a reasonably accurate understanding of such interactions can solutions be found that will have over-all validity and not, inadvertently, do more harm than good.

One particularly useful tool for understanding is systems analysis, increasingly used by planners and by research-oriented companies to project the environment in which their future equipment must operate and to provide interfaces with other equipment in the same system. Systems analysis is the systematic study of all the complex elements of any given problem as an entity seen in its total perspective. It enables management to identify and describe the problem accurately, to determine quantitatively the major trade-offs, to evaluate all the real alternatives, and to compare the usefulness of alternative solutions when measured against alternative criteria of value.

Major urban processes lending themselves particularly to systems analysis today are physical activities, such as transportation, waste disposal, and land use. The most important areas for future development will increasingly involve the human aspects of broad "systems."

Systems analysis, as an approach to complex problems, has on occasion aroused a great deal of fear and antagonism. Part of this criticism is justified, but part results from a misunderstanding and misuse of systems analysis. Some members of Congress have criticized its use by the Defense Department and attacked "computer decision-making," "the whiz kids" and their product, "cost-effectiveness analysis," as an attempt to substitute machine calculations for the judgment of generals. Systems analysis is, of course, no substitute for human judgment. When used properly, however, it provides a means of assessing the implications of alternative courses of action. The products of such analysis will be no better than the data on which they are based, and no better than the judgment of the analysts as to which factors are to be included and which omitted. The great capacity of computers and our expanding understanding of how to use them have now reached a point where computer models of large systems can be of great effectiveness in testing alternative courses of action and in planning and operating complex systems.

New York City provides an example of a growing tendency among municipal departments to view themselves in the framework of interrelated systems, rather than as self-contained bailiwicks. Early in 1969, the City Commissioner of Air Pollution Control delivered a paper entitled "Metropolitan New York Pollution Problems as a System." He spoke of the city as an "organic unit" and discussed refuse disposal as it affects the "interrelationship of solid, liquid, and gaseous pollution of the environment." His comments reveal a keen appreciation of the varied trade-offs, including both cost-effectiveness and aesthetic considerations, that must be weighed in evaluating courses of action.

One potentially useful application of systems analysis is the creation of a model or series of models from which one can draw information useful in generating or modifying urban programs. For example, a population model of a city would include a statistical sample of all the families in the city, incorporating such factors as age, number of children, type and location of housing, income characteristics, type and location of employment, expenditure patterns, and probable medical requirements. Such information can be made dynamic in the sense that future projections can be formulated as each individual grows older, leaves the family and school, marries, starts a family, changes location of living, or progresses upward on the employment ladder. A variety of alternative assumptions can be fed into the model and tested for effects on the community. Changes in education level, for example, will subsequently result in employment and upgraded economic status. Assumptions can be made regarding the effects of education or lack of it on future crime levels and costs of crime control. Alternative employment levels can be specified, and from this welfare demands can be generated.

In considering such a model, it is important to distinguish what it can and cannot do. It cannot, by itself, make predictions for the future, such as the relationship between education and crime rate. It can, however, show quantitatively the implications of alternative assumptions and help distinguish those factors whose effect is important from those factors that are of less significance.

Training Qualified Managers

A third line of attack on the urban problem is to provide the cities with numbers of qualified managers at all levels and to open city administrations to the recruiting of competent, well-trained, innovative, and motivated individuals. A series of specific actions is required to provide them with the opportunities and incentives to make major contributions to pressing problems. The nation's universities must provide graduate training programs for future managers by broadening their present curricula, by expanding some of the graduate business schools to provide economic management training for both public and private organizations, and by including in law school curricula course work specifically oriented toward pragmatic economic management. Equally important, the universities must draw upon graduate humanities programs—such as history and anthropology—for the kind of human-relations perspective necessary in managing an urban organization made up of diverse ethnic and historical substructures. Finally, new schools and institutes must be established. Major federal and state funds will be required to finance these management training programs. The combined programs should aim at making available to the cities at least five thousand graduates per year by the end of the decade. For comparison, the nation's universities are now providing business with more than 7,500 men a year from two-year graduate (MBA) programs alone.

Although many kinds of schools should be called upon to accept the added responsibility of training economic managers, the business schools can make a special contribution. Other than the military command and staff schools, business schools are the only institutions set up to train future general (and generalist) managers for large economic activities. Moreover, we will increasingly need economic managers broadly trained in the management of both public and private sectors and in their combined operation as public-private systems. It will be of little use to try to involve corporations more closely in the solutions of urban problems if those in government are unaware of how business operates and what incentives will be most effective in making possible a greater business contribution.

It is also clear that increased participation by Negroes and other minority groups in urban management at all levels is of great importance, both to the Negro community and to the metropolitan community as a whole. The proposed rapid expansion of professional training programs will provide a significant opportunity to members of minorities to move rapidly into key posts in urban management. Unless sufficient numbers from minority groups are given the full professional training that will enable them to carry out managerial functions, either the minority communities will be denied their rightful participation or the key positions will be filled by people inadequately trained to benefit the particular groups from which they come and the city population as a whole.

Parallel to these programs, middle-management training courses of six months' to a year's duration should be required for present managers as soon as institutions and curricula can be developed. They should be considered as permanent establishments so that managers can be given refresher courses and advanced training every five to ten years as they progress in their careers.

Opening Up Government Organizations

A fourth key point of leverage is the opening up of city and regional government departments to more creative, innovative, and efficient management, which in time can become more responsive to the needs of the people. City management requires the highest level of skill and enthusiasm. In size of operating budget alone, for example, New York City outranks all industrial corporations except General Motors, Ford, Standard Oil of New Jersey, General Electric, Chrysler, and Mobil Oil. The ten largest cities rank along with the three hundred top industrial corporations. Even size of budgets, however, does not adequately reflect the complexity of the problems with which city management must deal. Unlike the corporation, the city has no market place to measure the value of municipal services or to determine how much of each service the city's inhabitants are willing to buy. Furthermore, there is no competitive scale against which to measure the costs and values of such services. Corporation managements are usually allowed a wide degree of managerial freedom by their stockholders, but city managements must thread their way through a maze of conflicting pressures from informed (and often uninformed) interest groups. Moreover, the top management of a corporation is normally re-elected year after year, provided it has done a reasonably good job; top city management, on the other hand, has to fight for its life at least every four years and often every two years, no matter how good a job it has done. In short, I believe that the management of a city is a much more difficult and exacting task than the management of a corporation.

The career hierarchies in city governments are often severely restricted by state law, city ordinance, or civil service regulations that unduly limit the upward and lateral career movements of able managers. In many cities, civil service regulations, union rules, or traditional practices provide no entry into management ranks for well-trained persons except at the bottom—and the trip upward depends upon seniority rather than performance. These practices must be replaced by policies that provide both for career advancement from within and for lateral transfers from other departments, other city governments, universities, research centers, and corporations; and finally for a judicious balance of seniority advancement and merit advancement.

Because the services that cities provide are not subject to competitive markets, substitute means must be found to measure cost performance and quality of service. Although the ultimate evaluation of quality and cost of city services is at the polls, this is a gross, unreliable, and often irrational measure of actual performance. Comparative costs for varying levels of service under varying environmental conditions can be developed that give a measure of the *relative* efficiency of each city in providing the major services. For example, the costs of refuse removal can vary with the city's density or means of disposal, and the differences from city to city can be adjusted to give true comparative costs.

The general application of such standards would give elected officials, as well as department heads, a relatively objective indication of their performance and their progress in improving that performance. Moreover, the electorate would thereby have some measure of the costs of various services so that more informed public decisions could be made on the levels of service desired in relation to the added cost or savings.

Creating New Institutions

A fifth principal line of attack on urban problems is the creation of new institutions. There seems to be a predictable life cycle in most public and private organizations. A new organization, created to solve an urgent problem, tends to attract aggressive, entrepreneurially-oriented people. It has no ongoing responsibilities inherited from the past, no encrustations of past bureaucracy, no organizational ladder crowded with "play-it-safers" who have advanced by seniority and by keeping out of trouble. A new institution may be able to set a new pattern more easily and efficiently, although given time it, too, can age and fall into the trap of "business as usual" and excessive bureaucracy.

Not only must new institutions be created, but existing organizational boundaries must be regrouped to correspond more closely to the natural boundaries of the problems and the constituencies. Transportation, water supply, waste disposal, and pollution are, for example, becoming regional rather than local problems. In contrast, school districts or slum-clearance areas may need to be reduced in order to give the local residents a meaningful opportunity to share in decisions and opportunities.

Greater use of private corporations to provide public services can also stimulate organizational innovation. An example of success in this area is the telephone system in the United States, which, unlike that in nearly every other country, is in private hands. Its service is incomparably better than that of most government-owned telephone systems in other countries. AT&T and other telephone companies have not only delivered better service, but have provided billions of dollars in new funds (not including reinvestment of internally generated earnings) that otherwise would have had to be provided through public channels. In the post-World War II years alone, AT&T has spent close to $50 billion on plant construction. Remarkably, the company seems to have been able to avoid the worst of the aging process that stultifies so many government agencies, nonprofit government-chartered authorities, and profit-making corporations. Perhaps the principal reason is that the management of AT&T has long recognized that it can only survive if it consistently provides a higher quality of service than do its government counterparts.

The condition of most American railroads, however, demonstrates the other side of the coin. In this case, the competition between the railroads and other forms of transportation has been so altered by excessive regulation and by inequitable taxes and subsidies to competing forms of transportation that true economic competition has been badly distorted. Because the railroads were limited years ago by the government to operating in a declining area of transportation, they were unable to grow into new areas and thus lost the most important incentives necessary to attract and reward creative management.

Private corporations, acting as regulated monopolies, can perform important services to the community only if they are provided with an economic environment that promotes rather than kills true economic competition; with a reasonable freedom from administrative regulation; and finally with the opportunity to grow into new areas and the incentives to improve their services which, together, provide growth careers for able young management.

Corporations are successful in attracting enthusiastic, innovative management in part because they are able to spend billions of dollars on research and development, whereas cities spend almost nothing. Corporations are also more and more concerned about the organizational dry rot that tends to infect any organization, while city administrations, on the other hand, are increasingly hamstrung by frustrating rules, regulations, and practices. Cities remain far less well-equipped for their management tasks than are corporations. All the funds in the world will be inadequate unless the cities can simultaneously provide for a commensurate level of innovation, creativity, and management skills to administer those funds.

The records of private telephone companies demonstrate that public services can be provided efficiently and without capital cost to the community as long as the urban "community" supports an economic and regulatory environment in which a private company has a real chance and a real incentive to make it go. The state of many railroads indicates what can happen without this support.

Many corporations have announced in the last two or three years that they were launching major programs to provide many of the services so urgently needed by the cities, including education, transportation, low-cost housing, urban renewal, and job training. If these efforts do not succeed, and there are already signs of disillusionment on the part of some of the companies involved, it will probably be due to the failure of the companies to understand the markets and the economic environment, and to the government's failure to create the economic incentives and the environment in which private companies can succeed in making a solid and continuing contribution. Unless an activity is of continuing and central importance to a corporation, it will not receive the managerial attention and "push" needed for success. It is up to business to find ways to serve better the new needs of society, such as the reconstruction of the cities. But it is also up to government to make it possible for business to continue to provide these services.

Private organizations can be used advantageously to carry out major operating functions of the city's business in part because the city is freed of the whole range of personnel management responsibilities and instead looks only to the specific public authority or company to provide a specified level of service at a specified cost. The operating responsibility is thus decentralized and delegated. Moreover, an attitude of monopoly, with all the attendant weaknesses, can be avoided only if the private profit-making or nonprofit organization knows the city is free to make other arrangements in the event it becomes dissatisfied with the service or the cost.

A good example is the difference in relationships between private corporations serving the Defense Department and government arsenals. The Defense Department generally procures from private contractors as a result of competition for both the design and the cost of new weapons systems. In the case of the government arsenal, however, such competition seldom exists, and the arsenal is assumed to have a permanent monopoly—particularly by the city in which it is located. The difficulties encountered by the Defense Department in closing the Brooklyn Navy Yard and the Springfield Arsenal illustrate the problems of relationship. While the shifting of government business from one aerospace company to another is not without its political complexities as well, the Defense Department has much greater flexibility in achieving better products through competitive designs and proposals.

A word is in order about the competitive advantages of profit-making corporations and nonprofit corporations to supply the services required by the cities. Profit—although by no means an end in itself—is probably the best measure of performance of public services over the long run, provided reasonably true economic competition exists. If the organization is by charter nonprofit, no such measure exists, and the government must subsidize any managerial inefficiencies. The possibility of profits also provides a means of raising private capital which otherwise would have to be provided through public channels, such as bond issues. This is especially important when the city's requirements for capital are large and growing even larger. Moreover, a profit-making corporation stands on its own feet. If it fails to make profits long enough, it goes out of business, and the government has no continuing responsibility.

There are, of course, major obstacles in moving the cities in the direction of greater use of private organizations. Labor unions tend to regard the city as an employer from which they can more easily win wage increases. Civil service organizations are often determined to prevent change and have become powerful lobbies in the city and state legislatures. Nevertheless, the role of management in creating a competitive operating organization in which some of the services are provided on an economically competitive basis appears to be a principal point of leverage in the control of costs and the improvement of service.

The key to the urban problems will be in finding critical points of leverage for effecting political change. The obstacles to change—ignorance, apathy, entrenched bureaucracies, special-interest groups—must be attacked primarily through the political process. Nevertheless, expanded research will open up new areas of knowledge and inevitably contribute to effecting change, especially if research organizations are in direct communication with potential political leadership. The training of an adequate corps of innovative and skilled administrators will become as powerful a force for change in the cities as it has been in the corporation. Knowledge of the complex interrelations in the physical and human "system" of urban life will give well-motivated political leadership the ammunition it needs to demonstrate the dangers of resisting change. Further involvement of corporations in urban affairs will also contribute to a better informed electorate and thus to more effective constituencies for change. Finally, strengthened research and well-trained management will ensure the probability that the federal government's leverage in effecting urban change will be used wisely and constructively.

EDWARD C. BANFIELD

Why Government Cannot Solve the Urban Problem

*The city as it exists is very largely the product of
tendencies of which we have as yet little knowledge
and less control.* —Robert E. Park, 1928

I SHALL argue, first, that all of the serious problems of the cities are
largely insoluble now and will be for the foreseeable future and,
second, that insofar as it is open to government (federal, state, and
local) to affect the situation, it tends to behave perversely—that is,
not to do the things that would make it better, but instead to do
those that will make it worse. These two arguments prepare the way
for the question with which I shall be mainly concerned: What is
there about our politics that accounts for this perversity?

I

By the serious problems of the cities I mean those that affect,
or may affect, the essential welfare (as opposed to the comfort,
convenience, and business advantage) of large numbers of people
or the ability of the society to maintain itself as a "going concern,"
to be in some sense free and democratic, and to produce desirable
human types. As examples of serious problems I will cite chronic
unemployment, poverty, ignorance, crime, racial and other injustice,
and civil disorder. To my mind, these problems are of a different
order of importance than, say, the journey to work, urban sprawl,
or the decline of department store sales.

What I am calling serious problems exist mainly in the inner
parts of the central cities and of the older larger suburbs. The
large majority of city dwellers do not live in these places and have
little or no firsthand knowledge of these problems; most city dwellers have housing, schools, transportation, and community facilities

141

that are excellent and getting better all the time. If there is an urban crisis, it is in the inner city. The lowest-skilled, lowest-paid, and lowest-status members of the urban work force have always lived in the highest-density districts of the inner city, that being where most of the jobs for the low-skilled have always been. Improvements in transportation have in the last thirty years or so hastened a process of outward growth that has always been going on. Most of those who could afford to do so have moved from the central city to the suburbs and from inlying suburbs to outlying ones. Much manufacturing and commerce has done the same thing. The inner city still employs most of the unskilled, but the number (and proportion) that it employs is declining, and considerable numbers of the unskilled are in a sense stranded in the inner city. The presence there of large concentrations of people who have relatively little education and income accounts for—perhaps I should say constitutes—the so-called urban crisis. Most of these people are black. From an objective standpoint, this is of less importance than most people suppose: If all Negroes turned white overnight, the serious problems of the city would still exist and in about the same form and degree; it is the presence of a large lower class, not of Negroes as such, that is the real source of the trouble.

Government can change the situation that I have just described only marginally; it cannot change it fundamentally. No matter what we do, we are bound to have large concentrations of the unskilled, of the poor, and—what is by no means the same thing—of the lower class in the inner parts of the central cities and the larger older suburbs for at least another twenty years. Rich as we are, we cannot afford to throw the existing cities away and build new ones from scratch. The decentralization of industry and commerce and of residential land use is bound to continue, leaving ever larger semi-abandoned and blighted areas behind.

If government cannot change fundamentally the pattern of metropolitan growth, neither can it solve any of the serious problems associated with it. To be specific, it cannot eliminate slums, educate the slum child, train the unskilled worker, end chronic poverty, stop crime and delinquency, or prevent riots. Of course, I do not mean that it cannot eliminate a single slum, educate a single slum child, or prevent a single riot. What I mean is that it cannot put a sizable dent in the problem as a whole. These problems may all become much less serious, but if they do, it will not be because of the direct efforts of government to bring about reforms.

142

Why Government Cannot Solve the Urban Problem

We cannot solve these problems or even make much headway against them by means of government action not because, as many seem to suppose, we are selfish, callous, or stupid, but rather because they are in the main not susceptible to solution. For one reason or another, solving them is beyond the bounds of possibility. In the largest class of cases, solution depends upon knowledge that we do not and perhaps cannot possess. Consider, for example, the problem of educating the lower-class child. In recent years, there has been a vast outpouring of effort on this, and a great many well-thought-out and plausible ideas have been tried, some of them, like Operation Head Start, on a very large scale. So far none of these efforts can be said to have succeeded, and most of them have clearly failed. After surveying the various efforts at compensatory education, the U.S. Commission on Civil Rights said in *Racial Isolation in the Public Schools* that "none of the programs appear to have raised significantly the achievement of participating pupils, as a group, within the period evaluated by the Commission."[1] It is probably safe to say that if the leading educators of this country were given first call on all of the nation's resources and told that they could do whatever they liked, they would not succeed in giving what any of us would consider an adequate education to a substantial number of slum children.

The nature of some problems is such that even if we knew how to solve them, we probably could not make use of the knowledge because the cure would be worse than the disease. However attractive they may otherwise be, all "solutions" that are incompatible with the basic principles of our political system must be considered unavailable—that is, beyond the bounds of possibility. If, for example, it were found to be possible to educate the lower-class child by taking him from his family shortly after birth and in no other way, we should have to give up the idea of educating those lower-class children whose parents refused to give them up; a free society cannot even consider taking children from their parents on the mere presumption—indeed not even on the certainty—that otherwise they will grow up ignorant, dependent, lower class.

Incompatibility with the basic principles of the political system is by no means the only ground on which a "solution" may be judged worse than the disease. Consider, for example, the police "crackdown" as a method of reducing crime on the streets. I do not know how well this method really works, but suppose for the sake of argument that it works very well. Even so, it is not a solution because, rightly or wrongly, a "crackdown" would be regarded by Negroes as an affront to the race. What is accomplished if crime is reduced slightly at the cost of deepening the cleavage between the Negro and the rest of society?

It is only because we seldom pay any attention to the indirect, unintended, and unwanted consequences of government actions that we fail to see that they are often worse than the diseases that the actions are supposed to cure. The usual assumption seems to be that a desirable consequence in hand offsets two undesirable ones in the bush. This may be reasonable. But what if the bush is full of extremely undesirable consequences?

II

Although government cannot cure the serious ills of the city, it might make the patient more comfortable and enable it to lead a somewhat more useful life despite its ills. I will list what I think are the more important things that it might do to improve the situation. In general, these are not the things that one would most like to have done (those being in most cases beyond the bounds of possibility for the reasons indicated), but they are all ones that it is possible in principle for government to do and that would make a more than trivial contribution to the improvement of the situation. Some of the items on the list may strike the reader as highly implausible, but this is not the place to try to justify them.

The list is as follows:

1. Use fiscal policy to keep unemployment below 3 per cent even though this would entail undesirable inflation. (The possibility of this for more than a few years was denied by Milton Friedman in his Presidential Address to the American Economics Association in 1967. Other leading economists assert it, however, and the question must be considered unsettled.)

2. Eliminate impediments to the free working of the labor market, particularly that for low-skilled labor. This implies removing legal and other barriers to the employment of the young, the unschooled, women, and Negroes. It implies repeal of minimum wage laws and of laws that enable unions to exercise monopolistic powers. It also implies im-

proving the information available to workers about job opportunities in other places.

3. If the second recommendation is not carried into effect, suspend immigration of the unskilled. Also, by bringing about expansion of the rural southern and Puerto Rican economies and by setting welfare allowances so as to favor rural and small-town residence, discourage migration of unskilled Americans to the large cities.

4. Pay the poor to send infants and small children to nursery and pre-schools. Create a competitive school system by giving vouchers for use in any private (including parochial) school to parents of children who do not go to public school. Lower the compulsory attendance age to twelve and the normal school-leaving age to fourteen (grade twelve). Give boys and girls who leave school the choice between taking a job and going into a youth corps. Make it possible for all who qualify to get higher education subject to later repayment.

5. Define poverty in terms of "hardship" (as opposed to "inconvenience" or "relative deprivation") and bring all incomes up to this nearly fixed level. With respect to those competent to manage their own affairs (that is, all but the insane, the severely retarded, the senile, and unprotected children), make the income transfer by means of a negative income tax, leaving the recipients free to spend their money as they please. Public housing, public hospital care, "rehabilitation," and other welfare services in kind rather than in cash should go only to those requiring institutional or semi-institutional care.

6. Allow police officers wider latitude to deal out "curbstone justice" to petty offenders, especially juveniles. Repeal laws against gambling and usury. Change insurance and police practices (for example, free recovery of stolen cars) so that potential victims of crime will not be deprived of incentive to take precautions to prevent loss.

7. Eliminate impediments to the free working of the housing market. Establish building codes, uniform for the whole of a metropolitan area, that will permit the widest latitude for innovation and economizing consistent with safety. As-

sure that some part of every suburb is zoned in a manner that does not prevent low-income occupancy.

8. Prohibit "live" television coverage of riots.

9. Avoid rhetoric tending to create demands and expectations that cannot possibly be fulfilled or to excite alarm about nonexistent crises. Above all, stop attributing more importance to racial factors, including discrimination, than the facts warrant. Explain nothing on racial grounds that can be explained as well or better on income or class grounds.

I trust I do not need to say again that this is not a list of "consummations devoutly to be wished." Rather it is one of things that government could do and the doing of which would contribute more than trivially to the amelioration of the serious problems of the city. But even if all of these things were done, the situation would not be fundamentally changed; the improvements would be ones of degree rather than of kind.

III

Although the measures listed are possible, they are not politically feasible. It is safe to say that none of them will be tried in the near future. A politician with a heterogeneous constituency probably could not support any of them vigorously. Indeed, with respect to most of the items on the list, the politically feasible thing is the exact opposite of what has been recommended: for example, to raise the minimum wage, to raise the normal school-leaving age, to encourage immigration of the unskilled, to define poverty as relative deprivation rather than as hardship, to emphasize racial factors while denying the existence of class ones, and so on.

Why this perversity in the choice of policies? Before offering an answer to this question, I should acknowledge that its premises are questionable. Perhaps the recommendations made above are unsound; perhaps, too, the things that I said were beyond the bounds of possibility are not beyond them. Even if the recommendations are sound, the system may not be perverse in rejecting them for their opposites. It may be that "problems" arise only in those instances—which may be a very small proportion of the whole— where the system fails to select a right policy and by so doing fails to prevent a problem from arising. To explain an occasional visible failure on the grounds that the system is perverse is like explaining the presence of a few men in death row on grounds that the threat of capital punishment is not a deterrent. For all we know tens of thousands of men may *not* be in death row precisely because they *were* deterred. Space does not permit me to deal with these objections. All I can do is say that I am aware of them.

Perhaps the most palpable reason for the political infeasibility of most of the items on the list is that they would be instantly squashed by some interest group (or groups) if they were ever put forward. The founding fathers went to great pains to distribute power so widely that "factions" would check one another and prevent the growth of tyranny. This arrangement has the defects of its virtues, of course; one of the defects is that a very small group can often veto a measure that would be of great benefit to a large public. It is laughable, for example, to talk about eliminating impediments to the free working of the labor market so long as labor unions are politically powerful. New York City cannot employ unskilled laborers to repair the slum housing that they live in because to do so it would first have to get them into the building trades unions and then pay them union wages.

There are well-armed and strategically placed "veto groups" (as David Riesman calls them in *The Lonely Crowd*) for almost every item on the list. The organized teachers would veto a proposal to lower the school-leaving age. The organized social workers would veto the substitution of a negative income tax for the traditional arrangements. Civil rights organizations would veto giving policemen more latitude to deal out "curbstone justice." The television industry would veto the prohibition of "live" TV coverage of riots. And so on.

Although interest groups most often exercise their power by vetoing measures that might be injurious to them, they sometimes initiate ones that they think will benefit them. Why, it may be asked, do not the putative beneficiaries of the measures on the list above organize and apply pressure counter to that of the veto groups? The answer (as Mancur Olsen has explained in *The Logic of Collective Action*) is that in most instances the benefits are in the nature of what economists call "public goods"—that is, they are such that if anyone benefits, all must benefit. This being the case, no individual has any incentive to support an organization to bring them into existence. TV stations find it to their advantage to maintain an organization that can influence the F.C.C. not to prohibit "live" coverage of riots, but the ordinary citizen, even if he were very much in favor of prohibiting it, would not pay much of anything to have his view urged upon the F.C.C. because he would be sure that his small contribution would not affect the outcome. In a certain sense, therefore, it would be irrational for him to contribute, since he would have the same chance of getting the benefit (prohibition of "live" coverage) if he kept his money in his pocket. For most of the items on the list, the logic of collective action is of this sort.

In the last analysis, however, what makes the items on the list politically infeasible is that promising them would not help anyone to get elected. To some extent this is because public opinion does not favor them. (It is not for this reason entirely, however. As Anthony Downs has explained, candidates and parties offer combinations of measures—"budgets"—that confer on voters large benefits in terms of their primary interests and, at worst, small costs in terms of their secondary and tertiary interests. Thus, in principle, a winning coalition may be built around a "budget" no single item of which is favored by more than a few voters.)

It is pertinent to inquire, therefore, why *public opinion* is perverse. An answer sometimes given is that in matters such as these it is generally dominated by the opinion of the well educated and well off. These people (so the argument runs) are indifferent or downright hostile to the interest of the less well off and the poor. In short, the "masses" are against the recommended measures because they have been misled by an elite that is looking after its own interests.

This explanation does not fit the facts. The perversity of policy does not benefit the well off; on the contrary, it injures them. The well off are not benefited by the minimum wage or by other laws and practices that price low-value labor out of the market and onto the welfare rolls. They are not benefited by laws that keep hundreds of thousands of children who cannot or will not learn anything in schools that they (the well off) must support. They are not benefited by an official rhetoric tending to persuade everyone that the society is fundamentally unjust.

I want to argue that public opinion (which I agree is decisively influenced in many matters by the opinion of the relatively well off) tends to be altruistic and that it is precisely because of its altruism that it opposes the recommendations on the list and favors instead ones that are the reverse of those recommended as well as ones that are beyond the bounds of possibility.

Why Government Cannot Solve the Urban Problem

The American cultural ideal, which is most fully exemplified in the upper-middle and upper classes (and within those classes in people of dissenting—Protestant and Jewish—traditions), is oriented toward the future and toward progress. It sees the individual as perfectible by his own effort and society as perfectible by collective effort. Accordingly, it feels a strong obligation to engage in efforts at improvement of self and community. Americans tend to believe that all problems can be solved if only one tries hard enough, and they acknowledge a responsibility to improve not only themselves, but everything else—community, society, the whole world. Ever since the days of Cotton Mather, whose *Bonifacius* was a "how to do it" book on the doing of good, service has been our motto. I do not mean to say that our practice has corresponded to our principles. The principles, however, have always been influential and often decisive. For present purposes they can be summarized in two very simple rules: first, DON'T JUST SIT THERE. DO SOMETHING; and, second, DO GOOD.

It is the application of these two rules that produces most of the perversity that I claim characterizes our choice of policies. Believing that any problem can be solved if only we try hard enough, we do not hesitate to attempt what we do not have the least idea how to do and what may even be impossible in principle. Not recognizing any bounds to what is possible, we are not reconciled to, indeed we do not even perceive, the necessity for choosing among courses of action all of which are unsatisfactory, but some of which are less unsatisfactory than others. That some children simply cannot or will not learn anything in school and that we do not know how to change this are facts that the American mind will not entertain. Our cultural ideal demands that we give everyone a good education whether or not he wants it and whether or not he is capable of receiving it. This ideal also tells us that if at first we don't succeed, we must try, try again. To suggest lowering the normal school-leaving age is, in terms of this secular religion, out-and-out heresy.

The recommendations listed above are unacceptable—indeed, downright repellent—to public opinion because what they call for does not appear to be morally improving either to the doer or to the object of his doing. It does not appear to be improving to the child to send him to work rather than to school, especially as that is what it is to one's interest as a taxpayer to do. It does not appear to be improving to the delinquent to let the policeman "slap him around a little," especially as that accords with one's feelings of hostility toward the juvenile. It does not appear to be improving to the slum dweller to tell him that if his income is adequate and if he prefers to spend it for other things than housing, that is his affair, especially as that is in one's "selfish" interest. From the standpoint of the cultural ideal, the doing of good is not so much for the sake of those to whom the good is done as it is for that of the doers, whose moral faculties are activated and invigorated by the doing of it, and also for that of the community, the shared values of which are ritually asserted and vindicated by the doing of it. For this reason good done otherwise than by intention, especially good done in the pursuance of motives that are selfish or even "non-tuistic," is not really "good" at all. For this reason, too, actions taken from good motives count as good even when, in fact, they do harm. By far the most effective way of helping the poor is to maintain high levels of employment. This, however, is not a method that affords upper-middle- and upper-class people the chance to flex their moral muscles or the community the chance to dramatize its commitment to the values that hold it together. The way to do these things is by a War on Poverty. Even if the War should turn out to have precious little effect on the incomes of the poor—indeed, even if it should *lower* their incomes—the undertaking would be justified as a sort of secular religious revival that affords the altruistic classes opportunities to bear witness to the cultural ideal and, by so doing, to strengthen society's adherence to it. One recalls the wisecrack about the attitude of the English Puritans toward bear-baiting: that they opposed the sport not for the suffering it caused the bear, but for the pleasure that it gave the spectators. Perhaps it is not farfetched to say that the present-day outlook is similar: The reformer wants to reform the city not so much to make the poor better off materially as to make himself and the society as a whole better off morally.

There is something to be said for this attitude. The old Puritans were certainly right in thinking it worse that people should enjoy the sufferings of animals than that animals should suffer. And the reformers are certainly right in thinking it more important that society display a concern for what is right and just than that the material level of living of the poor (which is already well above the level of physical hardship) be raised somewhat higher. There are problems here however. One is to keep the impulse for doing good from gushing incontinently into mass extravaganzas (Domestic Marshall Plans, for example) in which billions are pledged for no one knows what or how; surely if it is to be morally significant, good must be done from motives that are not contrived for the individual by people with big organizations to maintain and foisted upon him by the mass media. Another is to find ways of doing good that are relatively harmless—that do not unduly injure those to whom the good is done (as, for example, children who cannot or will not learn are injured by long confinement in a school), that are not unfair to third parties (taxpayers), and that do not tend to destroy the consensual basis of the society (as headline-catching official declarations about "white racism" may).

Looking toward the future, it is impossible not to be apprehensive. The frightening fact is that vast numbers of people are being rapidly assimilated to the ethos of the altruistic classes and are coming to have incomes—time as well as money—that permit them to indulge their taste for "serving" and "doing good." Television, even more than the newspapers, tends to turn the discussion of public policy questions into a branch of the mass entertainment industry. "Doing good" is becoming—has already become—a growth industry, like other forms of mass entertainment. This is the way it is in the affluent society. How will it be in the super-affluent one? How preoccupied can a society be with reform without thereby loosening the bonds that hold it together? If there is an urban crisis, perhaps this is its real basis.

REFERENCES

1. U. S. Commission on Civil Rights, *Racial Isolation in the Public Schools* (Washington, 1967), p. 138.

Part III:

New Functions in
Urban Communities

PETER F. DRUCKER

Worker and Work in the Metropolis

WORK, EMINENT doctors tell us, is on its death bed. By the year 2000, according to their prognosis, Americans will work only twenty minutes a week to enjoy a standard of living several times as high as the present one.

This report of the demise of work is not only premature; it is false. Indeed the trends run the other way: Work is growing faster than the work force and is likely to continue to grow faster. There are indeed great changes going on, but they are qualitative: a change in the relationship between biological age, chronological age, and the working-life span; a rapid conversion from organized experience to systematic knowledge as the foundation of performance. These changes do, of course, have major impacts and are raising major challenges. But the impacts, the challenges, and the resulting problems are quite different from the things one hears and reads in both popular and scholarly discussions—and, on the whole, they are more serious.

Instead of "automation unemployment" we will, for instance, need in the next eight or ten years around one million new workers in computer programming; this is basically semiskilled work within the reach of junior high school graduates after a short—three to six months—period of training. We will need one to two million additional workers in health-care professions—physical therapists, dieticians, medical technologists, and the like doing typically skilled work. We will probably need more additional skilled mechanics and maintenance men to service jet freighters by 1980 than we now employ in the entire railroad industry—again skilled workers in the fullest sense of the word. And we will need a very large additional number of college teachers—"skilled workers"

153

again (though so far we know neither what the skill of teaching is nor how to convey or acquire it).

At the same time, in the fast-growing categories of employment—skilled, but especially the technical, professional, and managerial—people work longer hours, it seems. Our statistics are pretty poor, for we keep figures only for rank-and-file people covered by the Fair Labor Standards Acts. There is little doubt, however, that the majority in our nonfarm work force—that is, technical, professional, and managerial people—work longer hours today than they did in the twenties, perhaps even longer hours than they worked during World War II. The factory worker goes home when the shift changes. The typist or the shopgirl goes home at five. But the engineer or the accountant or the young lawyer either stays on or takes work home. And there is no letting up of this trend in sight.

After looking at the evidence, economists are almost certain to conclude that nothing, but absolutely nothing is going on.[1] Quantitatively there is only one conclusion: Nothing has happened to work and jobs, and nothing is about to happen. Blue-collar workers do work shorter hours and professional and managerial people longer hours, but most economists would tend—with considerable force—to ascribe this phenomenon to the fact that we have to pay overtime to the former and not to the latter. The economists would not, however, convince the rest of us, whether unskilled laborer, company president, or chairman of a graduate philosophy department. We *know* that something *is* going on.

The popular explanations ("automation," for instance) are indeed wrong, dangerously wrong. They misdiagnose the problem. I very much doubt, for instance, that the popular "problem of leisure" is much more than a guilt-feeling of middle-aged academicians who have become bored with teaching. The popular explanations also lead to wrong treatment which can only make things worse. (Some of the widely supported proposals for handling the "Negro ghetto" may belong here as will be discussed later.)

Major qualitative changes are taking place; but these are entirely different from the romantic fiction that is the patient's own explanation of what ails him. One of these changes—and in the short run the one with greatest impact—is the *lengthening of the life span* of modern man in the modern city and the resulting change in the patterns and rhythms of *working-life span*. This, in turn, has been leading to a steady pushing up of the age of entrance into adulthood and the work force and to the unemployability of young people who, while chronologically adults, are culturally "too young." With this, jobs have had to be changed to make labor demand match the available labor supply.

The second of these long-run trends, one of even greater importance, is the *application of knowledge to work*.

Extended Schooling and Working-Life Span

At the beginning of this century, few people in the working population could expect to be able to work full time and with unimpaired productivity and income beyond the age of forty-five. Today most people reach retirement age—sixty-five or sixty-eight—still capable of full-time work.

Better public health and medicine were only minor factors in extending working-life span. The main cause was the shift from agriculture as the occupation of the majority. Farming is physically exhausting work that ages early. Crippling and disabling accidents are also many times more common in farm work than in the most hazardous industrial employments. In addition, physically destructive toil has largely been taken out of industrial work. We tend to forget that a century ago, at the time the transcontinental railroads were being built, the working life of a navvy, whether Irish or Chinese, was around five and at most ten years; after that, if not crippled by accident, he was worked out and physically spent. (The same was true of the laundress or the early-twentieth-century seamstress with her twin occupational hazards of tuberculosis and blindness.)

In other words, working-life span has increased by at least 50 per cent. The boy who went to work at age fourteen in 1900 or 1910 could not normally expect to be capable of full-time work past age forty, certainly not past age forty-five. The young man who goes to work today at age eighteen or twenty can expect to be capable of doing most available jobs at age sixty-five—an extension of working life from fewer than thirty to more than forty-five years: If we had not raised the age of entrance into full-time work, working life today would be almost twice what it was fifty years ago.

The extension of working life is being counteracted by social pressures leading to a continuous pushing up of the age at which a person enters the work force. A fifty-year working life is obviously considered as too long, whether individually or socially. In the great majority of jobs and occupations there has been no increase in requirements. There is no reason in the work itself why a fourteen-year-old girl was old enough to sell behind a counter in 1914 and why today the salesgirl has to have a high school degree (and preferably a year or two of college). There is nothing to being a typist in a typing pool or being a file clerk that requires high school or college education or particular "maturity." The foreman's job in the automobile assembly plant has not changed one whit in forty years. Yet the men who held such jobs in the late 1920's normally had gone to work before they were fifteen. By 1940 they normally had gone to work after finishing high school. Now there is great pressure for candidates for foremanship to have a college degree— and two years of college are really the absolute minimum.

Seen in this context, the "educational explosion" is not primarily concerned with more knowledge—for little of it is needed so far. It is concerned with postponing the age of entry into the labor force—and, as such, it has been very successful. The extension of the years of preparation through the lengthening of the years of formal schooling has forced on us a *wide-ranging shift in jobs*. It has changed the supply of labor, and, to a very large extent, the demand—the jobs offered—has had to accommodate itself to this change in the supply.

Sitting in school four or eight years longer produces a marked change in the *expectations* of the young man or woman entering the labor force at the end of formal schooling. People who have completed high school—let alone college—expect to be employed in "white-collar" jobs, to work as technical, professional, and managerial people, and to have opportunities corresponding to their level of schooling. They are, normally, not available for manual work and even less for long years of skill-training through apprenticeships.

Extension of the years of formal schooling, therefore, presented a formidable challenge to American society and economy. Jobs had to be created that satisfied the expectations of people who considered themselves endowed with superior education because they had spent more years in school. (Whether these assumptions were or are justified is well beyond my topic and largely irrelevant to it.) At the least, jobs that were unchanged in every respect had to be paid as if they had become different and much more demanding.

One example I know has been the "labor squeeze" in the Midwest during the last few years. Next to the South, the Midwest has the shortest years of schooling and the smallest proportion of youngsters in college—which, by the way, is the old tradition. Until recently, therefore, the manufacturing industry in the Midwest could keep on hiring the way it had been hiring all along, with main emphasis on semiskilled mass-production jobs. As a result, of course, the Midwest has for decades been suffering from a "brain drain" with a substantial proportion of its most highly educated manpower moving off to the East or the West. Since 1963 or so things have been changing rather fast, for the "educational explosion" is engulfing the Midwest too. When the Vietnam war made sudden demands on midwestern industries, the additional labor needed for the traditional jobs simply could not be found. Statistically the Midwest was still a "labor surplus area," but in actuality jobs—well-paying factory jobs of the kind that spell "prosperity" to labor economist and banker alike—could not be filled. Midwestern manufacturers had to change their job pattern and manning policies in a hurry—and at great expense. The sharp drop in the earnings of so many midwestern companies in 1965 and 1966 was brought on by the combined costs of working the available manpower overtime and of rapidly changing jobs from manual to knowledge work. In one company, for instance, there were about sixty engineers in a factory of 2,400 men, and management was convinced that the engineering department was overstaffed. Today there are one hundred and fifty, but the work of the plant had to be changed rather drastically. By contrast the 2,400 men in the plant do work now, albeit with a considerable overtime charge, that under the traditional manning practices would have required at least 10 per cent more men. But young men with engineering degrees were available—at engineers' wages, of course. Costs—whether measured as total costs, as costs per hour, or as costs per piece—are quite a bit higher, even after taking out the effects of increases in wage rates and raw material prices. In other words, the shift—and it has only begun—could not have been justified as "labor saving." But at least the work gets done.

Within two decades the center of gravity in the American labor force has shifted to the jobs the census calls "technical, professional, and managerial." The *major* problem in the American labor force in the last twenty years was never the lack of traditional manual jobs. It was always the threat of a shortage of the new—the knowledge—jobs for the ever increasing number of high school and college graduates with their ever increasing expectations regarding position, pay, and opportunities. If the American economy had not been able to satisfy these expectations, we would have been confronted with the largest and most alienated intellectual proletariat conceivable—and with an infinitely more explosive situation than even the Negro ghetto presents.

The American economy—and especially its free-enterprise sector—not only managed to provide the job opportunities for these aspirations of the graduates of extended schooling. It did so without decrease in over-all productivity such as might have been expected when large numbers of knowledge positions were being created without much experience with this kind of worker and work; and when large numbers of jobs were sharply upped in pay to satisfy people with extended schooling even though there was no corresponding increase in productivity.[2]

This shift in the structure and composition of the jobs and, with it, of the labor force that was imposed on us by the extension of formal schooling—in turn, provoked by the extension of working-life span—is the central "event" of the last twenty years in respect to work and worker in America. It is a remarkable achievement; indeed, any labor economist twenty years ago would have considered it impossible.

The Coming Knowledge Jobs

It is not the much-vaunted "complexity" of today's jobs that has pushed up the years of schooling. This is shown by the experience of those advanced countries, Germany for instance, where the extension of the years in school is lagging behind that in the United States (though it is beginning to move in the same direction every place). In Germany jobs for which college degrees are required in this country are filled with high school graduates and even with what corresponds to our junior high school graduates (*Ober-Sekunda Reife*). Yet there is no discernible difference in job performance or productivity.[3]

But filling these jobs with people with advanced schooling also forces us to change the jobs. It forces us to apply knowledge to work. And this, in the long run, is going to be a great deal more important and is going to have a much greater impact than the extension of the years of schooling itself.

The extension of the working-life span and the response to it in the form of longer years of schooling are, of course, both directly traceable to the impact of knowledge on work. The great shift from agriculture is the result of the application of knowledge to farming, which has resulted in the tripling and quadrupling of farm productivity over the last fifty years. We would not have been able to finance the very expensive additional years of schooling for everybody without the tremendous increase in productivity brought about by the increase in farm yield and by the application of "scientific management" to manual work—that is, by the application of knowledge.

Taylor's "scientific management" did not take the skill out of work. He applied knowledge to work that had no skill to begin with. Wherever we have applied knowledge to skilled work, however, *knowledge has become the foundation of skill.* It has made possible higher skill. It has made it possible to acquire skill faster and to acquire many more skills. Knowledge, in other words, is proving to be the most effective means of making skill truly productive.

Skill was first applied to work seven thousand years ago or more. In the irrigation civilizations of early neolithic times, all present skills were developed, and with them practically all occupations. In those remote times we also developed what is up to this day the most effective (and some of us might say "so far the only effective") educational technique—namely, apprenticeship. Apprenticeship organizes exposure to experience under the supervision of a master. It provides standards of workmanship and performance leading to a "masterpiece."

But now knowledge is taking over the function which, through the ages, apprenticeship has fulfilled. Indeed there is no craft, from bricklayer to physician, where the application of knowledge could not telescope the learning period from the many years of apprenticeship to a few months or so—as the experience of World War II amply proved. At the same time, the man whose skill is founded on knowledge is capable of learning new skills very fast. Examples abound especially in the armed services where apprenticeship is simply not possible—the enlisted man does not stay long enough.

People use concepts and theory in their long years of schooling. They learn, in other words, to acquire knowledge in a systematic manner. Knowledge-trained men, even if otherwise without education, are capable of acquiring a completely different skill in a minimum of time, again through systematic knowledge-training. (For example, barely literate southern Negro electricians in the armed services can learn missile maintenance.)

People who are hired for knowledge jobs because of their long formal schooling expect to put knowledge to work. Indeed this is all they really know how to put to work. This pressure is rapidly transforming our work structure. "Automation" is nothing but the application of knowledge to work—an extension of "scientific management" from the operation of the manual worker to a whole productive process. It results, above all, in a tremendous increase in the number of people who do skilled work, but skilled work based on knowledge. This is the work of computer programmers and systems engineers, of production planners, quality-control men, and process analysts—the skilled occupations for which demand is insatiable. None of these jobs requires advanced knowledge. In fact, none of them really requires a college education. But they all base skills on a foundation of systematic knowledge acquired not through exposure to experience, but through program—that is, through an organized conceptual process.

The application of knowledge to work is only in its infancy today, even in this country and even in our most advanced employments. But it has gone far enough to enable us to predict results as great—and as lasting—as the earlier application of skilled work thousands of years ago. It is likely to be a permanent and enduring change in work and in the way one acquires skill. "Scientific management" which first conceived of it is, therefore, one of the great philosophical events of man's intellectual and social history.[4]

When I was a youngster, a scant generation ago, opportunities to apply education and knowledge to one's life work were still limited to the traditional professions: the law, the ministry, medicine, and teaching. Today, the choices before a young man who has learned a little bit are practically limitless.

The shift to knowledge has opened opportunities for the individual such as never existed before. Because knowledge can be acquired systematically and fast, and because, once acquired, it can be extended in almost any direction, basing job and skill on knowledge means making all jobs available to everybody. It creates a society with opportunities for the individual to make a good living doing what he likes to do. Never before has this been possible. The reason is not that an affluent society can afford the luxury of knowledge, but that a knowledge society generates affluence. In other words, the application of knowledge to work creates productivity, incomes, and comfort.

For the economy, the shift to knowledge creates the opportunity to be productive—to be able to generate whatever satisfactions society wants, material and immaterial. This opportunity requires, of course, that knowledge and the knowledge worker be managed productively. This is both the great opportunity and the great challenge for our economy.

For society in general, the central opportunity is that of diversity and mobility. In knowledge work, there is essentially no "superior" and no "subordinate." There is only a "senior" and a "junior." Moreover, there is almost infinite flexibility—people can work as individuals, in organizations, in teams, or in any configuration they choose. In fact, the organizational freedom is so great as to be frightening to a great many.[5] There is abundant evidence that it is not organizations that impose the "organization man" on the individual. On the contrary, individuals scared stiff of their new autonomy and freedom of movement impose conformity on organizations.

The Social Impacts

A change of this impact and magnitude also creates problems. The first major one to be considered is the impact on *social structure*.

For the first time in American history, there is a threat that society will be split in two by a "diploma curtain." The 50 per cent of the population who have "only" a high school education (or a junior college degree, which is rapidly taking the place of the high school diploma) will not be considered eligible for meaningful opportunities. And the 15 to 20 per cent or so who have not finished high school are in danger of being considered unemployable altogether. This is stupid in the extreme. There is no correlation between academic accomplishment and capacity to perform (except perhaps in academic pursuits). There is, in other words, little reason to believe that the 50 per cent with "higher education" represent a significantly greater reservoir of ability, maturity, and integrity than the other 50 per cent.

Historically, it has always been one of the strengths of American society that it did not arbitrarily limit its human resources. It was willing to use strengths productively—the one exception, of course, being the black man. Now for the first time we are imposing on ourselves restrictions that will make it difficult, if not impossible, to put to productive use the talents and strengths of half our population. But above all, the "diploma curtain" violates every basic belief of the American nation. I expect within ten years—at the most—to see a proposal on the ballot in one of the major states to ban questions on educational status on application forms for employment—just as today asking for race, sex, or age is forbidden in many states. I, for one, if I have the chance, will gladly vote for such a proposal. Intellectual ability, especially verbal facility, is after all also an "accident of birth."

But I hope that we shall not wait until then before we begin to take action. Every institution, whether business, university, hospital, government agency, or armed service, owes it to itself as well as to American society to organize for the systematic identification of people without the proper degrees who prove their ability through performance. Every institution owes it to them, to itself, and to American society to provide opportunities for those people, including the opportunity, if necessary, to acquire the lacking sheepskin easily and fast. And it would be very intelligent if educational institutions set up soon an "earned" degree to be awarded for performance rather than for sitting the required time on school benches. Such a degree would have to be considered the full equal of one acquired in the more traditional and easier way.

Maybe the places to start such a program are small or medium-sized industrial cities with strong local business leadership—places like Columbus, Indiana, with its Cummins Engine Company; Corning, New York, with Corning Glass; or the Jersey Meadows around Bloomfield, Nutley, and Clifton with their pharmaceutical companies. In these areas business and the school system already work closely together—on continuing education, on offering specialized courses to the technical and professional people in the companies, and, lately, on upgrading the functional illiterate and making him capable of being employed. It would take neither much money nor much organization to have an automatic review of all employees in the companies in these areas (or at least of the larger ones) once a year during the first ten years of their employment to identify the "over-achievers" who perform above the level of their formal education. It would not be hard to award a degree for such performance—most school systems have enough discretion to do this. I have tried to identify such men in a medium-sized company in the Jersey suburbs. I did not have to dig very hard; their names were known to the personnel director anyhow. Although the list was not a very long one—about twenty men out of a total employment of three hundred—it represented a considerable proportion of the younger men. Of course, some of those should have picked up on the side the formal education they lacked and a good many were doing this with some encouragement from the company. But most of these men actually knew more—in many cases much more—than they could possible have learned in the courses they failed to take in their teens. Yet the lack of formal credentials made the personnel people most reluctant to give them the jobs they had actually earned through their performance. "But he didn't go to college" or "But he has no high school diploma" was their automatic rejoinder when one of these men was proposed for promotion into a supervisory or managerial position.

This, I admit, is gross stupidity, but it is the stupidity that rules our society, and chairmen of university departments suffer from it even worse than industrial personnel managers.

The extension of schooling inevitably makes anyone who has not reached age eighteen or twenty "unemployable." It somehow is not proper to give a job to a "mere child." And even if someone below the accepted age has a job, it cannot be a "real" job and be meaningful to him. A "public service" advertisement in the New York subways summed it up neatly: "'Boy'—That's what they'll be calling you all your life if you drop out of school now."

Bluntly, there is no remedy for this. In a society in which entrance into the labor force has been pushed above the age of eighteen—whether the reasons be good or bad—anyone below this age is "unemployable." We had better accept this as a fact and think through what it means.

But there are also impacts on the *worker*. The shift to knowledge jobs and to knowledge as a foundation of skill has had a paradoxical impact on the *unskilled manual worker*. He was the first beneficiary of this shift. Indeed, no occupational group has ever changed position faster than the unskilled machine operator did in the first half of the twentieth century. Traditionally, the unskilled worker has always been at the bottom, barely able to eke out a subsistence, and without job security. He was the "casual" worker. As a result of "scientific management," the unskilled

163

worker acquired, almost overnight, income and (for him) very high job security. With the coming of the mass-production union in the thirties, the unskilled worker acquired also political power and social standing.

This is now seen as a quirk of history, a freak accident. The next step in the process is changing the position—above all, the psychological position—of the unskilled worker back to where it has always been historically. There is no likelihood of his losing his newly found affluence—"scientific management" makes him productive enough so that an affluent society can pay him well. There is also no danger that there will be a sharp and rapid shrinkage of jobs for him. Indeed, "scientific management" has yet to be extended to quite a few manual unskilled occupations in the economy. When it is, such jobs will both increase in numbers and be sharply upgraded in income.

But the psychic position of unskilled work has again changed completely; we now see it as an "engineering imperfection." We may never get around to eliminating it—not only for economic reasons, but also, more importantly, because we are unlikely ever to understand most of the processes well enough to replace them by machines.[6]

But this does not alter the fact that the unskilled worker knows that the *real* work is not done by him. It has been done by the industrial engineer who laid out the job or by the machine designer. No matter how difficult it is to get rid of him in practice, in theory the machine operator is not truly necessary and is certainly not central.

This is going to be one of the major political issues—a particularly bitter and difficult one because it is an emotional problem. To point out that "automation" does not have any economic effects is not relevant. What causes the problem is loss of power and, above all, loss of pride and self-respect.

The only way out, bluntly, is *not* to try to preserve unskilled jobs but to speed their disappearance. The unskilled worker will remain frightened and insecure whatever we do; he will be conscious of this all the more as knowledge workers become confident and secure. At the same time, mass-production unions can no longer act as initiators of policy and as agents of constructive developments. They must increasingly become reactionary, able only to say "No"—similar to the way the traditional farm organizations have turned from progressive and energetic forces into palsied reactionaries who are opposed to any change and always hark back to yesterday.

A great deal can be done with respect to the *skilled worker* and the impact of the changes on him. Although we need more and more skilled men, we need different skills and, above all, different organizations of skills. The traditional craft is obsolete, both in the way it prepares for a skill and in its definition of a skill. With universal schooling lasting until age eighteen or twenty, apprenticeships have ceased to be viable. With the application of knowledge to learning, apprenticeship is rapidly becoming the wrong way to acquire a skill.

Skills, moreover, become flexible the moment they are based on knowledge. A craft is by definition ultra-conservative. What was done yesterday is hallowed; indeed it is usually embedded in ritual. Knowledge by definition is always inquisitive and innovative. It knows no boundaries and pokes its nose everywhere. Knowledge, in other words, constantly changes skills. In addition, once a man has a knowledge foundation, he can easily acquire a new skill.

With this change, the traditional craft, the traditional idea that one has learned everything one will ever use when one finishes an apprenticeship, the traditional idea that certain work "belongs" to a craft and has to be done in a certain way forever—all these become meaningless. This, in turn, makes untenable the traditional labor organization of skilled work: the craft union.

How to liquidate the craft union will more and more become a central question. Increasingly, the craft union will be a bar to economic and technical growth and development, and a threat to its own members. As the American maritime or newspaper industries show, the traditional craft union with its "jurisdiction" and its ritualistic definition of jobs and of craft skills exposes the member to unemployment and loss of job without obtaining for him job security or the opportunity to learn new skills.

What we need is to make the skilled man the carrier of change and development, a person capable of applying the new skills based on knowledge and its growth. We need to do this in such a way that his flexibility and his capacity to grow and learn become the basis for maintaining his income and for giving him job security.

This may seem utopian—but it is actually being done with conspicuous success in Europe's greatest "success story"—Sweden. Sweden emerged from World War II prosperous and unscathed, but still essentially a producer of primary materials—lumber, pulp, iron, and steel. Today Sweden has the second highest per-capita income in the world and has become, above all, a producer and exporter of high-technology products (for example, the new high-voltage transmission of direct current which has made atomic energy competitive with fossil fuels). No small part of this success is due to a labor leader, Goesta Rehn, who persuaded his constituents in the early-fifties not to fight change, but to speed it up. Mobility —in skill, work, and place of employment—has become the special concern of the Swedish unions. They started and then persuaded the government to take over a nationwide agency for identifying new opportunities, finding the employees for it, training and relocating them. This agency undertakes to find a job for anyone whose present employment is likely to terminate—which means that employers are willing to plan their manpower and to inform their men of layoffs and plant closings in advance. Instead of trying to prevent the closing down of an old plant or the phasing out of an old process, this government agency works with the employer and the workers to speed it up. If the worker needs retraining, it is being made available. If he needs to travel to look at other places to live, this, too, is being made available. If no job is available for him immediately, he is being carried. The total cost has been amazingly low, perhaps less than half of what unemployment insurance for these men would have cost. As a result, a rather old-fashioned labor force, heavily concentrated in low-skill, low-pay occupations twenty years ago, is now the highest-skill, highest-pay labor force in Europe. Of course, Sweden is a small country—but then this only means that the U.S. would need a dozen such agencies rather than one.

The impacts on the *knowledge worker* also deserve a few comments. By and large, the knowledge worker is the main beneficiary of the shift to knowledge. Yet there are clearly some problem areas. The first of these is the productivity of knowledge work, which is still very low. We do not know how to manage knowledge work or the knowledge worker. Nor do we truly know how to use knowledge jobs to create personal satisfaction and accomplishment. We are learning—but the level of performance is, on the whole, understandably still very low. Indeed, the productivity of knowledge work is clearly the *major economic and managerial challenge* of today's advanced economy.

Then there is the problem of the status and function of the

knowledge worker in modern society. Here is something essentially new; an employed professional who is not management, let alone "capital," and yet who is not "labor," let alone a "proletarian."

Lastly, even the reduced working-life of today's knowledge worker is still too long. The existing job structures are inappropriate to a working-life span of forty years or more.

This is not a problem of the knowledge worker alone. The manual worker, whether skilled or unskilled, also clearly regards a forty-five- to fifty-year working-life span as being very long indeed, as witness his receptivity to the various plans for earlier retirement such as that of the steel workers or the rubber workers. But the manual worker who takes advantage of such a plan does not, it seems, encounter any "problem of leisure." He adjusts to retirement easily and without any trauma even though he may physically and mentally still be healthy and vigorous. If there is a problem of "leisure," it is not going to be a problem of the manual worker.

But the knowledge worker has a very different problem: He tends to get bored with a job after twenty or twenty-five years—that is, before he reaches fifty. Physically and mentally he is likely to be in perfect condition and not ready to retire. The men who reach the top are seldom afflicted with this disease. But the men who reach the "sound" middle-level positions as heads of a department or a function—for example, the director of market research in a business, the senior economist in a government agency, the pathologist in the hospital, or the competent professor in a university—tend to be prone to a modern version of the medieval "accidie," the mental disintegration of the *clerc*.

This is one reason why we need continuing education for the knowledge worker. Above all, however, we will have to think seriously about a *second career* for the successful knowledge worker who has reached the limit of his accomplishment in a certain area while he is still physically and mentally vigorous. I believe strongly that we will come to look upon a good many occupations as ideally suited for men of riper years—occupations such as minister, teacher, and perhaps even physician. I consider this one of the most urgent, but also one of the most difficult tasks ahead.

The Impact on the Negro

A few words need to be said about the impact of these developments in work on the Negro. The Negro is affected by these changes not because of "race," but primarily because he is the latest immigrant into the city. And for this reason, a solution to these problems would not also solve the race issue in America. Every group immigrating to the urban society during the last century or so has had to jump an educational gap. This gap, however, has become wider with every generation. Where the gap was only a few weeks of schooling when the Irish arrived in the 1840's from a background of total rural illiteracy, it has now become a matter of twelve to sixteen years of schooling. This distance is more than any one generation—regardless of its skin color or of its acceptance by the majority—can possible jump in one or even in two generations.

The Negro, because he is the most recent immigrant into American urban society, is hit particularly hard by the exclusion of those under eighteen or twenty from meaningful employment. Nothing in his background or tradition makes him accept, let alone want, a long artificial adolescence or value staying in school forever. Indeed, only recently the life expectancy of the Negro was still so short as to make the extension of schooling meaningless to him.

The Negro is also particularly affected by the reversal in the standing and power of the unskilled mass-production worker. The short-lived upgrading of the mass-production worker's social status and political power was, above all, an upsurge in the socio-economic status and political power for the Negro American. In mass-production work, the Negro American was accepted simply because the demand for men to fill such positions was so great. In such work he first achieved, in one important social group, equality of income and, after unionization, equality of job security with the white man. Through the union, he first achieved self-respect, social cohesion, and access to power in American society. In fact, the civil rights victories, beginning with the Supreme Court decision of 1954 which outlawed segregated schools, were largely a consequence of the tremendous gains the Negro had made socially, economically, and politically as a mass-production worker in the thirty years between World War I and the Korean War. The psychological downgrading of mass-production work is, therefore, a sharp and crushing setback to the Negro American—coming just at the time when the promise of equality and advancement through membership in the mass-production group has lured a majority of the younger Negroes from the rural South into the big city.

What is needed now, therefore, is a jump rather than amelioration—not because this latest immigrant generation is discriminated against on racial grounds, though that is serious enough, but because work has shifted to a knowledge foundation. The preparation for adult work is no longer experience and apprenticeship, but formal education.

Of course, there is need to find jobs for the Negro and especially for the male Negro. But the only jobs that can be found fast are unskilled mass-production jobs. Thus, there is the danger that the Negro American will be pushed, with the best of intentions, into a new ghetto, which, though economically comfortable, will be as confining and as segregated as the present one. There is the further danger that the Negro will become confined to the mass-production jobs while the whites increasingly move out of these jobs as they lose social acceptability, prestige, and power. This has already happened in meat packing and is happening in the rubber industry. Signs indicate that it is also happening in the automotive industry. Such a development can only lead to an escalation of bitterness and frustration and would also create a major dilemma for American social and economic policy. On the one hand, policies to speed the demise of unskilled mass-production jobs would at once come to be considered as being directed against the Negro. On the other, any policy that tries to protect these jobs, let alone increase their numbers, will only create frustration, friction, and fear.

The much needed efforts to open up the traditional crafts to the Negro are equally unlikely to do the job for more than a short period ahead. They, too, can only end up by creating a conflict between the need to liquidate the traditional crafts and to replace them by flexible knowledge-based technologies and the necessity of protecting the Negro minority and its hard-gained positions of opportunity, income, and prestige.

A massive effort is required to find and develop the Negro knowledge worker for the job opportunities of tomorrow. It is always easiest to find room where there are more opportunities than there are people to fill them. Social habits always originate at the top of the social hierarchy; thus, if we want Negro equality, it can only come through acceptance of the Negro by the new leading group—that is, the knowledge worker. Acceptance of the Negro in the mass-production unions, as the events of the last few years have made abundantly clear, has not created the social habit of acceptance, for social habits never move up the social scale.

We need to identify early the young Negro likely to become a knowledge worker, especially the male, to encourage him and his family, and to start career planning for this youngster very early—perhaps in the first years of elementary school. This job is being done here and there by individuals, often under local church auspices. A successful Negro scientist, for example, in one of the big research centers spends his weekends talking to teachers, parents, and youngsters in the local Negro community. He is willing, if need be, to spend a whole weekend with one boy—or, more often with his family. He has roped in all his friends and acquaintances to serve as "references" to whom he can send a bright youngster or his family for advice and, above all, for encouragement. He works both in the fairly well-to-do Negro suburbs and in one of the worst Negro slums. He does not always succeed, but I know personally about two dozen young people who are now in professional work—as computer programmers, market researchers, city planners, and teachers—who would have been "dropouts" without his counsel. Once one youngster in a family has been encouraged to keep on, has been stimulated, given aspirations, self-confidence, and the expectation of success, the younger children in the family tend to follow. It is the family rather than the youngster who does not believe in the possibility of achievement.

The most rapid rise in Negro occupations in the last decade has taken place in the professional and technical category—almost 6 per cent of this category is now Negro as against 3½ per cent only ten years ago. At that, this proportion is still way below the Negro's share in the population. And far too many of these "professional" jobs tend to be in teaching or for women. But it has been demonstrated, I believe, that the job opportunities exist or can be made to exist with a little effort. The Negro in a knowledge job is not home free, of course; he is still discriminated against socially, in his career, let alone in housing. In many ways the ambiguity of his position in America is greater than it was before—and it is felt with much greater poignancy by him. He is much more likely, I would say, to be a "radical" than the Negro fireman, or the Negro policeman, or the corner shopkeeper. But he is also capable of giving leadership and of being accepted as a leader both by his own community and by white society.

The topic of this paper is "Worker and Work in the City." But it must have been obvious to the reader that education and educators are central to the topic if only because school has been replacing experience to such a large extent, and knowledge is rapidly becoming the foundation of work and especially of skill, high impact, high value. Education rather than work is central not only because education is increasingly going to be the major "industry," the major "investment," and the major "factor" of production in the economy of the city.

The work of the educator, its performance, its standards, its quality, and its results are the decisive and determining work in the knowledge society. This is probably the greatest and most important change in the making today. The educator, especially the college and university educator, had better accept that his position cannot be one of privilege, but must be one of responsibility; that he is not entitled to monopoly power, but holds a public trust. What was good enough yesterday, when education was an ornament and essentially unnecessary, is wrong today when education is a basic necessity and our major capital cost and investment. Arrogant self-righteousness ill becomes us when we have as yet no performance standards for doing the teaching job on which our society has increasingly come to depend and is increasingly placing its bets.

REFERENCES

1. It should be said that economists, whatever their persuasion, were conspicuously absent all along from the "automation" chorus. While their boss, the Secretary, predicted horrendous "automation unemployment," the exceedingly able economists of the Bureau of Labor Statistics kept their mouths shut, but published study after study showing a total absence of any such phenomenon.

2. At least the salesgirl of 1967 did not sell proportionately more per hour or per customer than did the one of 1937, considering the change in the purchasing power of the dollar. But her real income is much higher, and, thanks to rising social security, pensions, and other fringe benefits, her real cost to the economy is higher still.

3. An even better example can be found in Canada. In Toronto, where years of schooling are on a par with those of the neighboring U. S. Midwest, entrance requirements for job candidates are, by and large, the same as in Buffalo or Detroit, with high school considered as practical minimum for any job. In Quebec, on the other hand, where going to high school is only now becoming general, the same jobs are being filled by the same employers—the supermarket chains, for instance, the commercial banks, or manufacturers—with candidates who have two to four years less schooling, with little difference in the demands on the employee, in his or her performance, or in productivity.

4. Incidentally, contrary to what most people believe, Taylor was motivated primarily by social considerations—that is, by an ardent desire to improve the lot of the working man and, at the same time, to create harmony in industrial society; efficiency and profits were quite secondary in his mind.

5. On this, Abraham Maslow has had some very wise things to say.

6. On the limitations on "automation," see especially Charles E. Silberman, *The Myths of Automation* (New York, 1967).

ADAM YARMOLINSKY

The Service Society

THE CITY has always welcomed man in search of services. In the country, service arrangements are matters of status. People have their services the way Boston ladies have their hats.

This is not to assert that the country man leads a life of Thoreauvian self-sufficiency. Some services come to you even out in the country—the mailman, the milkman, and (not always) the trashman. Some you can find in the nearest crossroads hamlet. The service station is omnipresent—but what the average service station can do for your car is strictly limited, as are the selections at the neighborhood grocery store. The new shopping center offers great volume and somewhat greater variety. It may include headquarters for service tradesmen, the druggist, the dry cleaner, the TV repairman—and even for service professionals, the local doctor and the local dentist.

More and more services we do for ourselves with the help of the machines that live with us in city and country—washers, dryers, garbage disposals. We use Polaroid cameras with which we can develop and print our own pictures on the spot, and we buy readimix desserts to go with TV dinners out of our home freezers, while we watch prepackaged entertainment or listen to a stereophonic sound cartridge.

But we still depend on the city as the ultimate source of the services that invade our houses, and the direct source of the most valuable and most complex services that we need. The druggist will still usually deliver. The doctor expects you to come to him— no matter how you feel about it—and the specialist expects you to come to the city.

The TV set may be manufactured in Rolling Acres Industrial Park and sold in the shopping center down the street, but TV programming is done in the city. The TV script writer may live in the exurbs, but he has to go to the city to see his agent, who has to work in the city so he can meet face to face with the packager, who has to meet face to face with the ad agency, who has to meet face to face with the advertiser—and all of them meet in the city.

Men first came together in cities to exchange services of greater complexity and specialization than the village or the manor could afford. The city was the first place where specialized human labor achieved special value—apart from the specialized labor of the fighting man.

But the character of services in our society has changed in three major aspects, and these changes must change the cities themselves.

The provision of services rather than the production of goods is becoming the dominant sector of the economy.

The range of services has increased enormously, despite the increase in the range of what we can do for ourselves with the help of mechanical and electronic servants.

The increasing complexity and interrelatedness of services have made it a necessity that many different services be organized into some kind of system in order to be used most effectively by the individual (or the group) who needs them.

The increasing importance of services is an index both of the increasingly urban character of our society and of the increasing need to orient cities toward their service functions. Because we need services, we need cities. If cities are no longer essential as centers of production or trading or as entrepôts, they are increasingly important as multiservice centers where individuals and organizations can find the services that they need and that are too specialized or too complex to be obtainable outside the city. Some of these services may not be particularly specialized or complex in themselves, but they are intimately involved with the functioning of the central headquarters of a large organization (like the central office typing pool), and the central headquarters must be in the city so that its officers can deal with their opposite numbers in other headquarters.

The increasing range of services that individuals and organizations call for is presumably a function of the increasing proportion of disposable income and the expansion of human organization to take advantage of expanding technology. But the relevant question for the student of cities is how the city should organize itself to make this wider range of services better available—or even better known—to the citizens or visitors who need them. Doctors recognize the scarcity of the general practitioner. Lawyers recognize the competitive advantage of the lawyer whose name shows up in the Yellow Pages as "Aaronson" or "Abbot." In fact, the Yellow Pages are still the average urban citizen's information storage and retrieval system. When the Rockefeller study commission published its first report, on "International Security—The Military Aspect," an enormous public demand for copies was stimulated by a TV news commentator. The demand turned out to be less than effective, however, because newsstand and drugstore distributors were not equipped to handle a "one-shot" publication, and few people in the television audience could find their way to a bookstore.

Even the experts are stumped. When the O.E.O. attempted to compile a catalogue of federal programs available to cities, for use by mayors and city officials, they found that a mere listing of programs ran to several hundred pages. At the same time, the record of existing social services in reaching the urban citizens who need them most is increasingly under fire, and the watchword of progress in the poverty arena is "outreach."

If the range of services is multiplying, so is their complexity. The example of the open-heart surgery team is particularly striking. So, in its own way, is team teaching in the public schools and the development of educational parks. The principle of community action assumes that helping people to emerge from poverty requires a coordinated effort to transform the entire environment in which they live. A pleasant urban environment is something that even the rich man cannot purchase from a single willing seller, as he could build a Fifth Avenue or Back Bay townhouse in an earlier era. Instead he depends on the combined efforts of urban planners and politicians in combing zoning controls, transportation planning, antipollution measures, and so forth.

Indeed, some of the most elementary urban services can only be obtained as the end result of the most elaborate systems planning. In the country, you can get in your car and drive into the sunset, provided only that you have stopped off recently at an open gas station. In the city, you cannot move by car, even at foot pace, without a system that will control traffic lights electronically, send out foot patrolmen to bad intersections, and tow away illegally parked cars, as well as construct freeways and provide storm sewers, street lights, and off-street parking spaces. Even then you are helping to choke your neighbors to death in the process.

The service function of urban society, then, is becoming more important, more varied, and more complex. Yet the organization of services is no new task for the city. The first principle of organization is geographical. Like attracts like, whether on the Street of the Goldsmiths or in the garment district. And coincidence of interest often results in collocation. Around the banks, the business lawyers find their offices. Around the courthouse congregate the criminal lawyers, the bail bondsmen, and the process servers. But new linkages develop, and geography becomes a problem. Corporate offices of national corporations cluster in midtown Manhattan. Banks and brokerage houses cling to Wall Street. Law firms serving both are schizophrenic, and the dark subway tunnels between them are a daily reminder of man's inhumanity to man. In Los Angeles, the law firms that represent the big movie companies occupy the solid old office buildings "downtown," while the lawyers who represent the talent have moved out to Beverly Hills. When the need to confer face to face arises, someone must take to the freeways.

The growth of suburbs complicates the distribution and accessibility of services. Department stores develop suburban branches to reach out for the expanding suburban market. Suburban customers discover the convenience of local shopping, and the frequency of their downtown excursions drops off. The downtown shopping area loses business, and the greater variety it offers must become more expensive or disappear altogether. This easier accessibility tends to mean greater homogeneity of product, particularly as economic segregation operates in a more effective—not to say deadly—fashion in the suburbs than in the city. And in the inner city, the ghetto dweller, who may live almost in the shadow of the downtown shopping district, finds his own local shopping district at least as limiting an experience as the rest of his environment.

Sometimes geographical separation underlines functional separation—form really following function. "Off-Broadway" theater has to be far enough off geographically to distinguish itself, and it is.

A fundamental characteristic of geographic organization is that by and large it puts the convenience of the serving agency above the convenience of the person being served. Not only is it a mark of status for the professional to receive his clients rather than to visit them, but the client must travel to the professional's neighborhood. Particularly is this true of services to the poor. Welfare offices are in the civic center. Public employment offices are there also, or in the business district. Clinics are in the hospitals. Parks and playgrounds are in other people's neighborhoods.

Plainly, the geographic organization of services is not enough by itself to make them readily available to users.

Another traditional principle of organization for urban service is by economic class. The rich go into the hospital's private pavilion, the middle class go into semiprivate rooms, and the poor go into the charity wards. Rich children go to private preparatory schools, middle-class children go to "academic" high schools (Boston Latin, New Trier Township), and the poor go to trade schools. Railroads, steamships, and airlines offer first-, second-, and (sometimes) third-class accommodations. Some services have been thought of as only for the rich—investment advice, psychoanalysis—and some for the rich and the middle class, but not, except under special circumstances and restrictions, for the poor (lawyers and higher education). But these distinctions have largely broken down, and those that still exist are crumbling under the impact of the omnipresent television screen, Medicare, and the Economic Opportunity Program. The result has been confusion: confusion of identity on the part of the recipients of services and confusion of standards on the part of the producers of services.

Egalitarian principles suggest that everyone should be entitled to the same level of service, but these principles are contradicted by the continued existence of institutionalized service differentials. When Pentagon officials reacted with near-neurotic resentment to rules curbing first-class air travel, their anxieties were temporarily assuaged by a rule permitting them to travel first-class whenever they chose to, provided that for each trip they filed a piece of paper explaining why they believed they were entitled to first-class accommodations. The new rule survived until the next economy wave washed it out.

Confusion of standards is particularly a problem in providing legal services for those who cannot afford to pay for them—which means most potential recipients of lawyers' help, except for those fortunate enough to have accident claims or other problems that a lawyer can accept on a contingent fee basis. Legal Aid offices have traditionally treated their services as a privilege rather than a right for their clients. Legal Aid clients can get separations, but divorces are for the paying clients. Legal Aid clients can get arrangements to pay off their accumulated debts, but bankruptcy or Chapter XI proceedings are for the paying clients. Legal Aid clients brought up on criminal charges are encouraged to accept the plea bargain offered by the prosecutor. There just is not time to try every case. The problem is not one of lazy lawyers, but rather of impossible caseloads.

The new legal assistance offices financed by the Office of Economic Opportunity have recognized that the size of the caseloads is their number-one problem, and they have agreed that, whatever the principle of choice, they simply cannot afford to handle more clients and cases than can be dealt with in the same professional manner that the Wall Street law office provides for its clients. Some will have to be turned away, but those who are accepted as clients will be treated with full respect for the complexity of their problems and the dignity of their persons. It is not at all clear, however, what will happen to the standards of these new organizations when the flood of clients really begins to pound at the doors, or when the first flush of enthusiasm abates that now brings some of the best young lawyers into these offices.

Confusion of standards dogs other professions as well. Investment advisers once served only the rich, who could judge the quality of the service—or could afford to pay the penalty for misjudgment. With the advent of mass-merchandised mutual funds, however, sheer salesmanship means more than professional judgment, and professional success is divorced from professional competence.

The problem is particularly acute where the fixed costs of services are high and the variable costs low, so that high sales volume is essential in order to survive in competition. Television programming is perhaps the extreme case, and the struggle over pay-TV is one indication of the difficulty in re-establishing a hierarchy of values for mass media services. The notion that a small audience may be willing to pay a premium for entertainment that is only caviar to the general public is resisted by the high priests of mass entertainment. The problem is less obvious but equally troublesome in the small world of book publishing. (A book has been described as the only item of durable goods that has to be bought in order to use it once; I prefer to treat it as a service for which one pays by purchasing a copy.) Here, at least, a partial technological solution may be in sight, with the development of new copying techniques. But even the most flexible new techniques are more likely to work for a limited circulation technical manual than for a new Little Magazine.

The problem of maintaining the profitability of high-quality services in a professedly egalitarian society suggests a third principle for the organization of services: Some services are offered for sale (either directly or through some kind of insurance scheme). Others are made generally available by the state. Still others are available at a price to those who are willing to pay and gratis, by the state or by private charity, to those who are willing to submit to a means test. But it is difficult, if not impossible, to separate the first two categories into watertight compartments. Most private services can be found to receive some form of public subsidy. Even entertainment has benefited by subsidies, from the Roman circuses to the National Foundation on the Arts and the Humanities. Most public services depend in part on some kind of user charge—except perhaps for national defense (unless one conceives of Selective Service as a randomized user charge). Even in the case of police and fire services and public schools, the local tax base for the services approximates, with rough justice, a kind of user charge. In fact, the trend is now toward more specific allocation of real costs to actual users. The Postmaster General has even proposed turning over his job to a quasi-private entity, in part to ease the problem of eliminating present subsidies in the system.

The third category, services subject to a means test, overlaps the first two and embraces most essential services (perhaps even including, if one thinks of progressive taxation as a kind of means test, education and the basic protective services).

The traditional example of means test services is in medicine. But here again the distinction is breaking down. Most of the population of the United States has to be defined as medically indigent if faced with a major illness. And most of the medical service system (including medicine and all the related professions) is simply not organized to provide medical care in the most efficient fashion. Whether medical services are provided by direct fee, insurance, subsidy, or some combination of all three, there is a pervasive need for more effective service in relating patient needs to available resources—and increasingly so as the range and complexity of available resources increase.

The problems of availability and pertinence of medical services

179

are only a special case of the problems of all urban services, as they become more important, more various, and more complex. Perhaps the single most difficult problem is to avoid fragmentation of services. Although the Yellow Pages may locate one specialist, they cannot tell you how to use the services of even two related specialists.

Recent changes in medical education reflect increasing acceptance of the proposition that medicine must treat the whole man, at the same time that treatment of the whole man involves the coordination of more and more services and people and institutions. Developments like the new organization of medical student volunteers to help patients who are unable to cope with the system by themselves—because they are too poor or too old or too sick—suggest that medicine is reaching out for new ways to serve its patients more effectively.

Other service industries attack the problem in other ways. A major airline recently instituted the extraordinary practice of detailing an employee to walk about in the passenger area at each airport that it serves—not to stand behind the barrier of the counter, sell tickets, handle baggage, or announce flights, but just to be helpful. The results, in the experience of this air traveler, have been to smooth out a host of minor difficulties—from a last-minute ticket switch to a prematurely exhausted supply of telephone change—that can make the difference between a harassed trip and a relaxed one.

The lesson of the free-floating airlines representative is perhaps easier to note because her role is a minor one in a series of very minor dramas. But the lesson is clear, and it is a threefold one. She is uniquely useful because she has no specific limiting function. She is uniquely useful because she is not separated from her clientele by a broad counter or a shiny desk top; rather she is the embodiment of the new concept of outreach. And she is uniquely useful because her services are not bought and sold; they are absorbed into something called general overhead.

She might be even more useful if she did not work for the airlines at all, so that instead of whispering that it was "policy" not to serve dinner on a dinner-time flight between Washington and Boston, she could lead the embattled travelers in a waiting-room demonstration. Ideally, she might even be a volunteer, putting in a year of national service in a chosen occupation.

But airline passengers are by and large affluent, knowledgeable, and worldly, and most people in an urban society are none of these. The core of our largest cities is inhabited by people so poor in resources and capacities that they are simply not reached by the range and complexity of services that the city affords, and the small minority precariously enjoys. They can hear the planes taking off, but have no idea of how to reach the departure gates. If periodically they explode in rage and frustration, it is scarcely surprising.

It may seem like an inverted argument to suggest that poverty and civil unrest are caused by the failure of urban society to organize the services that are its greatest accomplishment so that they reach the residents of its slums and ghettos. But the argument is circular and can be entered at any point. People are poor because they themselves (or the individuals to whom they look for support) cannot get and hold decent jobs. Their breadwinners are ineffectual (or absent) because they lack the education and the other kinds of services that go to make up an environment that makes them feel society has a productive role for them. Jobs are essential, but they must be decent jobs, and decent jobs are a result of the interaction between the job and the job holder. If the potential job holder finds the services he needs and wants—decent schools, decent housing, decent streets, decent police protection— he will be motivated to meet the demands and to reach for the rewards of a decent job. Thus improving the quality of services for the poor may be one way of breaking the cycle of poverty.

Even for those who can afford them, urban services are increasingly difficult to adapt to human needs. The happy thought that the Sabbath may be made for man is contradicted by the daily experience of the citizen in the urban society. Surely better planning can improve the quality of services. But the problem of finding and choosing the particular services one needs remains overwhelming. So does the problem of putting together all the parts of the system to meet the individual circumstances of a specific individual. No one method of organizing or financing services provides a panacea. But the whole process of rendering services needs to be informed with a more acute awareness of human needs. This is particularly so for the poor, but it is true also for the computerized student in the urban university, the gray flannel man from the bedroom suburb, or the elderly couple confined to a city apartment.

There is no inconsistency between the idea of analyzing and organizing urban service as a complex system and the idea of making separate provision to adapt the system to individual needs and demands. Systems analysis can vastly improve the organization of urban medical services. But the more complex the resulting system, the greater the need for unspecialized human intervention to guide people through it. Systems analysis can reduce the time it takes to get a policeman to the scene of trouble. (Or conversely, it can reduce the cost of getting the policeman there in a given amount of time, so that more policemen or more money is available for other services.) But once he is on the scene, he must be able and willing to deal with what is likely to be at least in part a human problem.

One of the consequences of the application of systems analysis is that established routines are changed, and not once and for all, but from time to time as other factors in the situation change. Ordinary citizens, on the other hand, become accustomed to routines, even unreasonable ones, and need to be informed, guarded, and helped to adjust to change. When the New York subway system made a number of shifts in its train schedule recently in order to improve the efficiency and convenience of its service, the one factor for which it apparently had not made sufficient allowance was the unreadiness of its passengers to adapt to the changes.

Another consequence of the application of systems analysis is likely to be increased mechanization. What can be routinized is more efficient, and what can be routinized can also, at least to some extent, be mechanized. People are more expensive than machines. But there is a natural human desire to produce a reaction in any encounter, and machines are not satisfactory reactors. The most sophisticated vending devices can only say "thank you" in a recording, and you cannot pass the time of day with a recorded announcement. Here, too, human intervention is needed.

Lastly, systems analysis permits the system to make finer discriminations over a wider range of cases than human beings, unaided, could manage. An electronic traffic control system can adjust the timing of traffic lights to maximize the flow of traffic. It can even cut off access to a freeway when additional vehicles would choke it and actually reduce the car-miles covered per minute. At the same time, the system creates the possibility of more effective use of the freeways if people are told about the advantage of alternative routes at particularly crowded times.

The mix of systematic organization of services and voluntary intervention is itself not susceptible of systematic analysis. It depends on the particular situation. But, in an increasingly systematized urban society, it is reasonable to suppose that voluntarism will not be overplayed, and its advocates need not fear that they will have an unfair advantage over the systems people.

The proposition that people need help in order to find and use the enormous range of complex and interrelated services available to them today, and that providing this help is a major part of the job of providing services in an urban society may be so simple that it is, in fact, revolutionary. A corollary of this proposition is that while everyone engaged in providing services must undertake some of the responsibility for sorting out the needs of the people or the organizations he is serving, as every doctor should serve the whole patient, there is a special need for service generalists, whose focus is not on particular services, but on those who are being served. The uncommitted intervener, whatever his starting point—as neighborhood lawyer, general practitioner, medical student volunteer, community-action worker, roving airline passenger agent— can adapt services to needs, by heightening awareness of those needs among the purveyors of services.

The volunteer can help with every age group, but perhaps most dramatically with the young and the old. Volunteers in the schools can be more than teachers' aides—although that, too, is an important function, particularly where teachers themselves are in such short supply. Volunteers can help to make the school as a system less formidable for the new pupil or the disadvantaged pupil. They can visit children and their parents at home, before the school year begins, to explain what will be required of child and parent. They can, even without extensive professional training, act as tutors for children who need encouragement or who march to the music of a different drum. They can organize trips into new parts of the city, making the city itself a school for children whose worlds have narrow horizons, and they can serve as counselors for children whose hopes and ambitions need to be expanded.

For old people, who also may find themselves in a narrowing world, volunteers can make physical movement in and out of the city or within the city less burdensome. They can encourage old people to seek new kinds of participation and responsibility appropriate to their physical energies and handicaps. And they can press for changes in the physical and social arrangements of urban society that presently add to the burdens of old age.

Even the most active members of urban society need help. Consider the problem of urban sports. Any city child can still play

183

stickball or shoot baskets when he is not watching other people play games on television. The more fortunate, or the better off, may find a tennis court or a ballfield. But one must generally leave the city to find a place to learn sailing or skiing or mountain-climbing; although more and more young people are taking up these activities, the effort and expense required just to get there is not insignificant. Yet these sports are by and large more challenging and more rewarding, as training for all the human faculties. They involve the development of higher skills, which is presumably why they were traditionally part of the education of the privileged few. And some of them could be organized and carried on within city limits, if they were not "too much trouble," if they did not require a paid staff and all kinds of arrangements. Why couldn't volunteers, then, help to clean up urban rivers and lakes at least enough to open sailing marinas and staff them with volunteer instructors? Why couldn't they open ski tows (with snow-machines) in city parks? Why couldn't they generally make a greater variety of sports available with less effort for the participant within the city?

Indeed, volunteers can do all kinds of things to help people break out of the bounds of a particular urban system. If the central human advantages of the city are the increased variety and freedom that it offers, then as the urban environment is increasingly systematized, these advantages are inevitably to some degree diminished. Voluntary intervention can mitigate the intractably systematic quality of the system by helping people to get outside its boundaries, whether geographic or economic or professional, physical or spiritual.

Who should be volunteers? There is a natural assumption that the volunteer role is one primarily for young people. Certainly young people are appropriate candidates for a wide variety of volunteer roles. But certain roles require a greater degree of maturity and human understanding than young people can muster, and for these roles retired people or women who have finished with child-rearing may be better qualified.

A number of elements in the population are underemployed, and hence under-rewarded with any sense of participation. Perhaps the most wastefully underemployed group are the poor. If they were able to make a contribution to society that society was willing to recognize as such, they would find their way out of poverty. One way to begin may be with voluntary service. The mother on welfare, the high school dropout, the occasional laborer may be able not only to find their way back into the main stream of society, but to help others with least difficulty by engaging in voluntary work, part time, in their own community. Involving poor people in voluntary work will not be easy, but it may be less difficult initially than achieving the proper fit between a good full-time job and an untrained worker who has no experience of regular paid work. Asking a poor man (or woman) to work for no pay may seem a cruel paradox, but if the alternative is no work for no pay, and if the volunteer job may lead to a paid job, the suggestion becomes less unreasonable. And from the point of view of the person being helped, assuming that he, too, is a member of the same under class, there are two real advantages: The volunteer knows something of the problems of the person he is helping, and he has a minimal commitment to the system that produces the need for help and a minimal vested interest in his volunteer status, which he must be inclined to regard as temporary.

The status of an uncommitted intervener is a difficult one to keep up without becoming a defender of the system—hence the virtue in being a volunteer and a short-timer. The VISTA Volunteers, Mayor Lindsay's Urban Service Corps, and the American Friends Service Committee suggest models of volunteer activity. Shriver's principle of the "five-year flush" for Peace Corps staff reflects the essentially temporary nature of the volunteer's work. Because volunteer work ought to be a temporary assignment, the need for an enormous expansion in the number of volunteers to serve the urban society is even more urgent. This expansion must be accomplished, however, in a sufficiently pluralistic way to preserve the voluntary character of the service. Perhaps a system of federal matching grants to qualified public and private organizations, primarily at the local level, is the way to keep large-scale voluntarism really voluntary.

If a primary purpose of voluntarism is to help people to transcend the system, to break out of its bounds, voluntarism itself must remain uncommitted to any particular system of organizing itself. Support ought to be made available for a wide variety of forms of voluntary organization that can compete with one another, some in the same locality, others in different localities. And whenever a particular form appears to have proved itself, it should be re-examined periodically to raise the question of whether it has the spirit as well as the form of voluntarism.

But even the volunteer is in danger of becoming only another social worker (a useful but limited occupation) unless he can bring his clients to participate in the process of remolding the service society to their needs. The service society requires not only maximum feasible participation of the poor, but maximum feasible participation of the human beings served.

This participation can be encouraged by the volunteer in the schools, when he helps parents to take an active interest in their children's schooling. He may even recruit mothers as additional volunteers in the classroom, on the playground, and in visiting other children's homes to bring the parents closer to the school. He can involve the entire community when he helps to make the lighted schoolhouse a beacon of community activity after regular school hours. The volunteer can help older people to participate too, by finding ways to bring them out of retirement into second careers—an opportunity that will increasingly be available in urban society.

That the principle of participation is easily subject to abuse does not make it any less valid. A college student (or a ghetto parent) need not participate in the selection of the school officials in order to participate actively in his own (or his children's) education. On the other hand, if a slum dweller sees the city police as a hostile occupying force, violence in his community may have to be dealt with by organizing indigenous security forces. An elderly patient can become an object of nursing care for his remaining years or an instrument of his own recovery.

The person who is being served may not be the best judge of the efficiency or effectiveness of service arrangements. He may be unwilling to exercise his imagination on new ways of doing things. Or he may overlook the disadvantages that go along with an apparent change for the better. But he does know when the shoe pinches, and at least he ought to be encouraged to speak up about it.

There is something more, however, to the service relationship. It is at the opposite pole from the Lady Bountiful role of the social service volunteer of a previous generation. That role was an expression of privilege and inequality. The future service role is at best an expression of mutuality, of mutual recognition of human capacities and human needs. As urban society makes possible greater mutuality of service among its citizens, it enables them to fulfill their possibilities as men.

STEPHEN CARR AND KEVIN LYNCH

Where Learning Happens

THE BEST learning happens by surprise; it is very different from the normal process of deliberate education. By watching young children happening to learn, it is still possible to sense what learning might be.

Surprising things happen in cities, although frequently their people, places, and events are predictable. The routine business of life demands some regularity and enforces it through selective attention to what supports our efforts. But often, when we have "nothing better to do," when we are waiting, in transit, on vacation, just hanging around—or even occasionally when we are busy with our tasks—cities surprise us. A particular scene—a place, the people in it, what they are up to—suddenly comes into focus. We see it as if for the first time.

When a "new" scene is related to our interests, we may learn something. When it is compelling, we may enter it to change it by our actions or to join with others. At such times, we teach ourselves: The learning is integral with the experience, a by-product of some perception or activity engaging in itself. Most likely this informal learning will be relevant to our needs, to finding or making our place in the world. The occasions for such incidents can be dramatically increased by urban policy.

Ideally, learning begins when we awake and ends when we go to sleep. If we are fortunate enough to learn how to learn from our experiences, education extends over a lifetime. Schools, on the other hand, are conservative institutions normally closed to the world around them and obsessed with the training of "skills." Formal education looks to the filling of career slots, certifying performance by a succession of numbers, grades, and diplomas. For the poor, and

187

especially the black poor, schools fail to do even this much. For many, as Peter Drucker points out elsewhere in this volume, schooling has become a way of filling time, sometimes a way of staying alive, more often a way of postponing entry into work. In a more reasonable society, time has other uses.

Our failure to help people to learn how to learn is not only due to the resistance of the educational establishment; the environment itself is growth-denying in the suburb as well as the slum. Too often the city fences us away from other kinds of people. By the scale, impersonality, and even hostility of its places and institutions, the city tends to discourage independence of action and to encourage fear and feelings of powerlessness. The white mother and child in the suburb are kept from new experiences almost as effectively as their black counterparts in a ghetto housing project.

The growth of individuals into rich and competent human beings is a fundamental value, directly satisfying in itself. It is also instrumental to other social goals, such as survival and economic development. Development of the individual will be a future focus of social action in this country, both by choice and by necessity. Education is shifting from being preparation for work to being a continuing part of life. When more routine work becomes automated, learning and working may become indistinguishable in the same way that the boundaries between education and play are dissolving as leisure is devoted to learning. Education is already an expensive public concern, but only in the context of traditional institutions and conventional measures of academic performance. The development of the individual other than in these stereotyped ways has never been a matter of conscious public policy, neither in our society nor in any other.

By development, we mean that an individual becomes more competent in some way, more highly organized yet more responsive, more engaged in a significant interchange with the environment and yet more independent of it. We think of growth in its broadest senses: physical, emotional, intellectual, and social. We include development both to known and unknown ends; creating a new poetic style as well as learning to read. Development is whatever increases the individual's involvement in self-motivated choice and action, whatever increases his power to formulate and execute personal intentions, whether delighting in the moment or planning a course of life. In our view, development is not limited to the forms sanctioned by culture and class (by which weight-lifting is vulgar, and the growth of Black Power bad). The aim is not to produce well-adjusted people who will operate competently without making waves. Development in this radical sense is a disturbing and dangerous pursuit, one that sometimes must be subject to constraints to assure the stability of society and the continued development of others. What is developmental depends on the individual's unrealized potentialities, his situation, and his purposes. We refer to the process—growing well—rather than to any specific ends for growth.

If development is to be an aim of public policy, some criteria for selection will be needed. We choose to favor developmental experiences that are self-motivating and self-rewarding, absorbing and committing rather than momentary and whimsical. This kind of experience gives the most promise of further development. We would emphasize development that aids the development of others: for example, skill in teaching rather than in the art of domination. Finally, we would encourage development that has socially useful by-products, even if such a judgment may be hard to make.

Vague as they are, even these criteria may be too narrowly focused on the individual. In many cases, society will (or should) give higher priority to group development: the growth of community identity, pride, purpose, and competence. This may be the case for the poor nations of the world as well as the critical issue for the Negro American. Perhaps in a saner society, individuals would naturally develop best as members of a developing community. As things are, individual development and group development will often be in conflict.

How can the urban environment promote development? The city has been a center for acculturation in the past—even if it has not been the melting pot once assumed. For the present rural migrants, however, urban society is not performing well. Any improvement in this performance will involve the urban school and urban politics, as well as patterns of work and leisure. We will confine our speculations to the influence of city form—the distribution in space and the scheduling in time of people, their activities, and the spaces that contain them.

The urban environment, in this specific sense, already serves many functions in supporting the development of individuals. It is a medium for transmitting the form and content of contemporary society, a territory to be explored, and a setting for the testing of identity. With the attrition of family function and the waning influence of tradition and authority, the individual seeks identity through his own experience. He must make himself in choice and action, and he must do so, by and large, in the urban environment.

Growing Up in the Future City

The present city offers a wide range of opportunity and stimulus, if mostly for the mobile and well-to-do. The trend of city growth, however, is toward increasing the apparent standardization and masking the available choices. Although physical mobility is increasing, exposure to diversity is sharply decreasing, especially for women and children. The decentralization of cities is bringing about a coarser spatial segregation of life styles and environmental qualities, although over-all variety continues to increase. There has been a general shift from participation to observation, which increasing electronic communications will most likely accelerate. There are "do it yourself" compensations (if that is what they are), but the processes of production, distribution, government, and even daily servicing become more impersonal, invisible, and remote.

A substantial minority is shut out or disaffected by urban society. Many people go from exclusion to disaffection without any transitional engagement. Given the fear and blindness of the majority, there is little reason to suppose that frustrated and disaffected people will disappear in the near future. Such minorities will increase, along with those who simply find affluence boring. There will no doubt be a corresponding increase in such "counter-insurgency" efforts as the Peace Corps and Vista. For those fortunate young people who have not lost the faith, these experiences can have great educational depth, despite re-entry problems. Reports of the death of the hippie, however, are probably premature —at least in the sense that young people, whatever they may call themselves, will continue their search for involving experiences "outside the system."

The *laissez-faire* alternative to societal support for individual growth does not mean disaster (except for a minority). It does, however, represent a serious loss of potential. No set of policies dealing with city form can be a panacea for such problems. Yet cities are where we live. Their form shapes our experience and consequent growth. To our minds, the single most important endeavor for city planning and design is to understand the developmental function of environment and to find ways to improve it.

Access and Diversity

An urban region is an immense storehouse of information. Its stimuli, diverse ways of life, events, and facilities are a prime occasion for learning. Developmental policy should aim at making this information accessible. One straightforward way is to provide a free public-transportation system, bringing all parts of a metropolitan region within some reasonable time-distance. The system must be workable at low densities, so that nondrivers are not caught within suburban areas nor central city residents excluded. Young children, as well as handicapped persons, should be able to use it with safety. If it proved impossible for an affluent country to provide basic transportation as a free public utility, then public transit might be subsidized so that children and adults of low income ride free. A more limited policy would subsidize educational trips where the destination was a school, museum, or another specifically educational locale. It might even be possible to subsidize "first-time" trips by distributing free tickets to random destinations.

The transportation system should be easy to use, as well as cheap and ubiquitous. It should be designed to be completely legible—the system of routes and transfers easy to follow and the destinations clear. Symbolic maps should be displayed, and direction-giving devices installed at all critical points. Public transit vehicles and routes should visually correlate with their destinations not only by using route and destination symbols, but by giving a circumferential route or vehicle a typically different form than a radial route or vehicle. The location of moving vehicles in the system and especially their imminent arrival should be displayed at waiting points. There should also be a network of paths along which young children can move safely by the means under their control: by foot, bicycle, cart, pony, or otherwise. Even the prosaic walk to school might be an educational device.

All vehicles and routes should give a clear view of the region being traversed—of its most important activities and particularly of its changes. The environment itself might be designed to be "transparent," wherever possible without intruding on individual privacy. The form of structures and of land, as well as signs and electronic devices, can communicate the activity and function of a place, express its history or ecology, reveal the flow and presence of people, or signal the social and environmental changes that are occurring. In an industrial area, factories would be encouraged to let

191

their machines be seen in action, to label raw materials and their origin, to distinguish the different kinds of operatives and explain what they do, to exhibit finished products, to make their transportation containers transparent. Thus the city, like a good museum, would be designed to increase the physical and perceptual accessibility of its contents.

To some extent, city trips are already used for educational purposes: sight-seeing buses, historic trails, and the rather stereotyped excursions of schoolchildren to museums. The environment could be exploited much more systematically and imaginatively. A complete network of educational tours, clearly marked and adequately manned, would explain the city's history, its technical functioning, its system of production, its politics, its ecology, its diversity of social groups. Tours would be organized particularly for the young, the physically handicapped, or the socially disadvantaged. They would be available within the tourist's own region, in other cities or rural areas, or abroad. The promotion and subsidy of travel for those now unable to do so would be a matter of public policy. Temporary exchanges of groups of children between families or different institutions might insure that these new experiences were not superficial. In Boston's METCO, children from inner Roxbury attend suburban schools; in summer travel camps in Europe, children live temporarily with foreign families.

There are also ways to amplify environmental information. One step would be to prevent and reverse the growing spatial segregation of the population by socio-economic status. As larger areas of our cities are occupied by similar groups of people or shelter similar productive activities, the child and the housewife have fewer opportunities to see at least the outward show of other ways of life. To have diverse people and different ways of making a living within walking distance is a basis for a young child's education. In our ideal city, no one would be constrained to live or work in any very large and substantially homogeneous area. Each activity requires a certain threshold of extent to maintain its special character, but these thresholds are far smaller than the gross separations that our cities exhibit. The fine-grain diversity and interlude to be found in some of the more favored old inner suburbs would be characteristic of the metropolitan area as a whole.

In a similar vein, every intense center of urban activity would be easily accessible. The outward extension of metropolitan regions requires a well-distributed constellation of points of intense economic, institutional, and residential activity, each of sufficient size to offer a diversity of people and action, chance encounters and unsought information. Some of these centers must be small enough or be controllable on a small enough scale to be responsive to the individual, as town centers often are and regional shopping centers are not. Temporal diversity can also be encouraged: Opportunities can be provided for celebration and for the rescheduling of the daily and weekly routine of urban events.

Since growth thrives on the alternation between intake and meditation, these centers might be associated with places and facilities that are completely calm, safe, and quiet—gardens, cloisters, public cells. The withdrawal available in wilderness and institutionalized in some cultures might thus be introduced into the heart of the city.

Openness and Responsiveness

Making people and information accessible is one way of using the environment for learning. Another is to see that environmental form is responsive to individual and small group effort. To act experimentally and to see the results of that action are the most effective ways to learn. This can be done in the spatial environment in a way often denied us in our social world of complex and remote institutions. High-density housing, for example, could be designed to provide the relative autonomy of the single-family dwelling. Allotment gardens and sites for owner-built vacation homes might be provided. A new technology of house maintenance and rehabilitation would increase the ability of the tenant to "do it himself." Features in the environment could be responsive to individual manipulation: arrangeable lighting, "pop-out" shelters, controllable micro-climate. The present trend toward homeostatic constancy—the caretaker environment—might be superseded by sensing and control devices by which environments would react visually, aurally, or tangibly to manipulation, or to the motion of the observer—just as artists are now inviting the active engagement of the spectator in their works. We might train for environmental management —for development, building, gardening, interior and exterior decorating, and other socially useful skills that allow unlimited use of individual sensibilities.

As experiments in radical decentralization, it should be possible for the inhabitants of small city areas to shape and maintain them themselves. Communal institutions might assume some functions of planning, building, repairing, servicing, and policing in their own environments. Neighborhood teenagers, for example, might install and manage their own recreation facilities. Long-term changes in environment through new development or renewal can be growth enhancing, if effective roles can be found for individuals in shaping such change. Greater decentralization of change management will also be more productive of diversity. Our developmental city must include responsive local institutions for environmental control, as well as responsive physical features. Widespread political engagement would be its characteristic.

We would provide an ubiquitous network of open space throughout the urban region—"open" not always because it is free of buildings and covered with plants, but in the sense that it is uncommitted to prescribed users. Dumps and vacant lands would be in this inventory, as well as woods, fields, waterways, and marshes. In these open areas, actions and explorations are permissible that would be intolerable on developed sites. Anything might be constructed from the materials available—temporary sculptures (as on the mudflats of San Francisco Bay) or tree houses. Open lands would be widely distributed so that some are safely accessible to the young child exploring on his own. Open space could be interior space as well—for instance, large barn-like structures, whose volume would be temporarily allotted for spontaneously organized projects and constructions. Raw materials and technical advice might be available on call, much as in the junk playgrounds of Scandinavia. But since these uncommitted open areas are vulnerable to abuse and neglect, we must either provide enough of them to keep the density of use low or be prepared to police them regularly.

Environment as a Base for Special Programs

The environment may also be a base for special educational actions. We would, for example, attempt to increase the availability of symbolic information. Our policies would include a wide regional distribution of computer consoles (probably with reproduction capabilities drawing on large central libraries), museums, tutors, directories, local newspapers, local TV and radio programs, and other such information outlets. Moreover, this flow of information would be made responsive to the user in many ways: Observers would be able to shut off or turn on environmental displays, make simple inquiries of visible signs, or find places to put up their own public signs. Local newspapers and broadcasts should be open to the announcements, plays, and stories of their listeners, so that groups can speak to one another, rather than be spoken to. Community TV will facilitate this. Would ham TV be a future possibility?

Particular areas in the city would be devoted to self-testing. Adolescents or adults might try themselves against a graded series of challenges and difficulties—cognitive, physical, or artistic. Teenagers might scale buildings or drive in obstacle races. Others might compete in the skill with which they rearrange a landscape. Many of these activities can emphasize mutual dependence and trust on the model of Outward Bound. Areas of this kind would have ambiguous border zones, where the unsure could watch and consider whether to take the plunge.

Other temporary communities might be places where it was permissible to break the habitual mold of action and to try out new roles: child-rearing or marriage, different kinds of productive work, or new and unfamiliar ways of life. These groups would be like participatory theater or continuous happenings, the tentative gesture would for a time be the substitute for the competent committed act. Such a policy implies our judgment that vicarious experience—watching others, reading novels, seeing movies, learning by identification, processes already institutionalized in our culture— is no substitute for real experience. Obsolete parts of central cities will be apt locations because of their accessible, cheap, and anonymous space. These temporary communities could also be used for special celebrations or for the coming-together of strangers for some common purpose or interest like surfing, socialism, or yoga. They would be ephemeral, voluntary ghettos. This will be a touchy policy to implement since many of the strange activities in such places will be seen as threats to society. They will have to be monitored, yet the monitoring must not be impatient interference.

The school, the institution formally devoted to education, could make much greater use of the city environment not simply by field trips, but by dispersing its scholarly activities more widely in time and space. Children would then be drawn into contact with other kinds of children and adults, and learning would not be sealed off, but intimately mixed with other activities. The best teaching is mutual. Parents and local specialists can be drawn into the educative process—simultaneously being the teacher and the taught. Anyone may drop in, even if only to observe. Informal classes and workshops might be organized wherever people do not have other overriding purposes (while in transit, in open areas, vacation spots, in bars and hangouts, for example). There might be brief apprenticeships in work processes, recreation skills, politics, or the use of the city. Working and learning might be combined, as they sometimes are in research institutions or cooperative colleges, and not be a series of irrelevant lessons interspersed with drudgery. The school would be affirmed as a crucial institution, whereas it is likely to wither away as a separate physical plant.

Implementation

Since we are not recommending a single coordinated strategy, we can only indicate some means of implementing our main policy suggestions. The policies for accessibility and for encouragement of travel could be carried out by present transport agencies with new criteria that go beyond optimizing economy of use. Such performance standards can be built into the federal program on which local transport is increasingly dependent. Educational agencies devoted to exposing and amplifying environmental information and increasing the outlets for information could be established on a regional basis. To avoid creating a new monopoly with concomitant distortion and suppression, the function of opening additional channels must be kept apart from any attempt at over-all regulation of environmental information.

We will also need new institutions to increase environmental openness and responsiveness. One possibility might be to establish an agency charged with assuring that various city regions are open to access, that the kind of open space we have described and the means to use it are widely distributed. Such an agency might evolve from existing open-space programs. It would most certainly encourage experimental uses and responsive environments. Due to the failures of urban renewal, new attitudes toward city building are already in the wind. New criteria are needed for the design and management of urban development. Block grants for local self-help and for new community institutions can emphasize local control and decision-making. Such programs already exist for farmers' cooperatives. Activities like Head Start, Upward Bound, and More Effective Schools may possibly presage developments *within* the schools (within in the sense of Trojan Horses) that will bring children out of the institutional shell into the kind of environment we have described. The new Leicestershire schools in England already demonstrate how a rich environment within the school may be used to stimulate freely chosen learning. Nevertheless, the educational establishment in the United States is well organized to resist such innovation in the near future, and thus we face the necessity of increasing educational opportunity outside the school.

Where might support be generated for these programs? John Seeley foresees a broad social movement, at least partially in this direction, for which the hippies are the early martyrs. Less optimistically, we can point to excluded and disaffected minorities. Others are left out as well—housewives, the elderly—for whom a more engaging environment might prove attractive indeed. There are the enlightened conservatives, for whom the individual is already the cause. Finally, a large group on the fringe of the education coalition is concerned with the growing problems of youth and may find such policies more compelling than the present one of suppression.

Difficulties and Issues

An environment for growth would be more exposed, accessible, and diverse, more open both physically and psychologically, more responsive to individual initiative and control. It would invite exploration and reward it; it would encourage manipulation, renovation, and self-initiated changes of many kinds. It would contain surprises and novel experiences, challenges to cognition and action. It would not be the most efficient and safe environment. Nor would it offer maximum stability and security. It would certainly not be extremely comfortable, nor even very beautiful, unless we look for beauty in the process of interaction rather than in static form.

We know a good deal about the developmental effects of environment in extreme situations, but less about the more normal case. Deprivation in environmental stimulus is particularly serious for early growth. Human babies brought up under sensorily deprived conditions do not flower so quickly or so fully as those growing under enriched conditions. In later life, sensory deprivation has negative consequences even for short periods. The McGill experiments have demonstrated that emotional discomfort and hallucinations follow quickly after the sensory isolation of human subjects. At the other extreme, there is considerable evidence to show that overload causes breakdowns in normal functioning. Besides experiencing confusion and stress, the individual becomes closed to all but the essential perceptions. In between, there is some optimum condition where the individual is stimulated sufficiently to maintain interest and alertness, but is not overloaded.

Most environments, however, no matter how stimulating initially, become dull and even "invisible" with repeated experience. Either the environment must continually change to maintain interest, or the individual must be motivated to search for new levels of experience and meaning in an environment that offers successive levels of complexity. Only when aspects of the familiar environment seem relevant to him will he attend to them, be they other people, indications of status, occupancy, or territory, signs of human activity, or symbols of strong cultural significance. Individuals may become sensitive to the aesthetic significance of the environment, because of its vivid, sensuous form or because they have been instructed by artists to see certain characteristics. (The romantic landscape painters once taught people to see the previously utilitarian or hostile countryside, and Pop artists are now doing the same with the utilitarian or hostile products of our urban society.) The organization of the environment can facilitate or inhibit a person in experiencing these several levels of meaning and the learning by discovery that accompanies it.

By current evidence, the preschool years are the most critical. Young children are still learning about the environment as a matter of necessity, organizing their impressions of it through direct action and sharp, vivid perceptual imagery. Less word-bound than adults, their sensibilities are not so attenuated by the categories and concepts of conventional wisdom. If brought up in a stimulating environment, the child is naturally a poet, painter, sculptor, builder, storyteller, and actor of great expressiveness, if limited skill. Such interests are not fostered by our schools.

The years of adolescence are another critical period for growth. The teenager begins to explore the wider city. What does he know of the opportunities it offers? Where does he go and what does he do there? Does he find places where he can feel "at home"? The city is a stage for testing his identity and for playing various roles. How does it function? Beyond childhood and adolescence, there are specific moments in the individual's life when he is most open to new possibilities. These are not task-oriented periods, but times of leisure, holidays, commuting, waiting. They are opportunities for providing access to information or chances to engage one's self.

There are particular adult groups for whom development is crucial: the poor in general and Negroes in particular; those with the most time to engage in developmental activities (mothers of school-age children, retired people); and those desiring to change their life or facing an enforced change (the misfits, malcontents, and potential discards). We should also like to include those most likely to influence the development of others—the teachers, political leaders, executives—but we will have more difficulty with them. The environment should encourage involvement outside the realm of career. Task-orientation narrows the range of relevant perceptual information, and it may be necessary to shock individuals to new levels of awareness. Yet environmental shock can hardly be imposed upon a city population.

What would be the benefits of our policies, as against the *laissez-faire* alternative? Poverty is not solely a question of income. We hope for a richer culture, legitimizing new styles of behavior. We look for the spreading of opportunities of achieving fulfillment, for the inclusion of excluded groups, perhaps for the downgrading of diplomas. Our city would build the competence to act as individuals or in small groups. In the process, the leadership now generally lacking would develop. We might even hope that the ethic of active mutual responsibility would come to replace the establishment ideal of service. We would also hope that in time social emphasis might shift from certification to performance; but we risk overselling our product.

What are the dangers of success? If completely open-ended development is encouraged, we may fail to train people for the tasks that must be done. Will we raise a generation of developed incompetents? Regular, perhaps even coercive, training might be a necessity for learning such skills as child-rearing, group cooperation, verbal and other communication, and various vocational abilities. Exposure to social diversity is not necessarily growth-enhancing unless it occurs under an institutional framework that requires cooperation on common problems. In our schools today, it may often reinforce stereotypes and distrust. The skills that result from an open-ended environment may be dangerous, rather than just unneeded. They may include the ability to coerce or harm others, to damage property, or to destroy one's self. One can learn arson, knife-wielding, and the use of drugs. The open world can be abused and neglected. Social controls will have to be exercised to suppress or divert dangerous developments.

This is the dilemma of developmental policy. Simply because new activities disturb custom or are similar to real dangers, they often seem dangerous without being so. Marihuana is classified with heroin rather than alcohol; sexual experimentation seems to undermine the family and the raising of children. In some cases, the implication of new development may be highly uncertain. In others, a new way of doing things will run against the interest of a special group or threaten them psychologically without being of serious concern to society as a whole. More developed, participating individuals may make surprising changes, not always benign. If we encourage a developmental world, we must exercise greater social control and also be able to restrain that control, pending the appearance of real dangers. There will be protests and reactions. Education, except for limited and sanctioned ends, is a controversial affair.

In a world oriented to learning and development, we must allow for an escape from it. There must be retreats to which people can retire temporarily to digest what they have learned or permanently if they do not wish to change. If our policies are successful, it will be necessary to conserve places of stable, even archaic, ways of life. Many people may become increasingly impatient and dissatisfied with the mundane work of the world. Such a reaction would cause serious reverberations throughout the economy. The emphasis on an integrated life runs counter to the view that Western man has developed precisely because he has been able to abstract experience, reducing it to bare symbols. Some would suggest that the "highest values of man" are best developed in a judiciously impoverished environment. Although we disagree, there is no doubt that an environment as rich as we have envisioned would put a heavy load on the individual's ability to select and discard.

If we focus our efforts on individual development, we risk encouraging a wholly self-regarding attitude, a belief that the growth of self is the single central value or that the world is made for "fun" and novel experience. We intend, rather, that environmental novelty be primarily a device for encouraging long-term committed development. Growth of this kind is not always fun; it can be hard and protracted, exhausting and sometimes agonizing, even if deeply satisfying.

We would like to encourage skills that advance the development of others or require group interaction. Just how these features of commitment and a regard for others might be encouraged in each case is not always clear. Many side effects of the policies we advocate cannot be foreseen. Society will have to reappraise what is permissible. We see the city as a purposefully designed "school," a place for learning and growing throughout life. In our eyes, that is the brightest possibility for the future city, and there are definite public actions that might bring it about.

JAMES S. COLEMAN

Education in Cities

ONE OF the major focal points of urban turbulence in recent years
has been education. The directions of movement in education have
shifted so rapidly that it has been difficult to gain any sense of the
future shape of urban education in America. Augmenting this
difficulty is the fact that there is no national policy in education.
Consequently, any conjectures about the future of education in
American cities must be based on the interplay of various forces
at the local level, together with possible supplementary policies at
state and national levels. Similarly, any conscious attempts to shape
the future of education in American cities must depend upon local
policies, as modified through the directed use of state and federal
resources.

The turbulence that has characterized urban education in recent
years has arisen from several sources. First, given barriers to Negroes
in employment, American Negroes have invested much of their
hopes and aspirations for social mobility in education. Indeed,
despite the high level of interest in education among whites in
America, the interest of Negroes is even higher, at every social level,
as a number of surveys of both parents and children have shown.
Secondly, the schools have been seen by Negroes as a way into the
larger society, a locale in which Negro children could mix with
whites on an equal basis, despite the barriers to residential integration. In short, schools have been seen by Negroes as a governmental institution that could overcome the barriers created by
actions of whites in two private sectors of life: employment and
residence.

202

Both these hopes have met with a high amount of frustration. Schools in the city have been far less successful in teaching Negro children than they have been in teaching whites. Thus, Negro achievement is low, and the likelihood of dropping out is high, in effect making the school, for many Negroes, another barrier to social mobility rather than a vehicle for such mobility. The hope that schools will serve as a means for entering the larger society through school integration has also been frustrated, with few exceptions. The residential segregation in existence in American cities means that a policy of inaction results in segregated schools focused around the neighborhood, and the resistance by whites to widespread integration has prevented positive action.

It is true that there have been a few small cities in which system-wide school integration has been instituted: White Plains, New York; Evanston, Illinois; Berkeley, California; and others. And in many larger cities, there are small efforts at integration. These, however, affect a tiny minority of Negro children.

Another source of the school's centrality in urban turbulence of recent years lies in the residential invasion of Negroes into white areas, as the ghetto expands from the city center. This invasion is most fully a threat to whites when it is an invasion of the school along with the neighborhood. For, since education remains largely tied to neighborhood, a black neighborhood means a black school. Thus, some whites, threatened with the loss of neighborhood and school, have reacted by pressing for explicit policies of school integration, to spread the black population to other predominantly white schools. In general, such explicit policies have not occurred, and both the "preservationist" aims of whites and the integration aims of Negroes have been frustrated, with integration merely a transitory phase through which a school passes on its way to becoming all Negro.

The dual frustration of Negroes with schools as a path to occupational mobility and as a path to social integration has made Negro communities responsive to a new set of goals enunciated by an emerging set of leaders: goals of racial identity, black control of black schools, and maintenance of segregated schools. Thus, in those cities where Negroes are numerous enough to make black control feasible, these goals have begun to replace the older goals of integration. This has shifted the struggle in many places from a fight over positive action to integrate schools to a fight over control of the schools. In cities where Negro children are in a minority, as in New York City, this becomes a fight over decentralization and local control; in cities where Negro children are in a majority, as in Washington, D.C., it becomes a fight over black vs. white control of the central school apparatus. In the latter case, the Washington experience suggests that it will not be a bitterly contested fight. In Washington, before the struggle for control of the school apparatus occurred, white children had almost entirely evacuated the city schools, leaving a public-school population of about 95 per cent Negro. More generally, the ease of leaving the city for most whites, who need suffer little or no economic loss to do so, means that once they are effectively in a political minority, they will evacuate the city rather than fight for control of the schools—just as they have done in particular school districts as the school has become predominantly Negro. Washington, D.C., provides some evidence that the rapidity of flight of whites to suburbs depends upon economics rather than degree of ideology or prejudice. First of all, Washington had a higher proportion of middle-class professionals among its whites than other cities, with less prejudice but more money than working-class whites. Secondly, Washington has experienced a very high demand and rapidly rising prices for housing in the city. Both of these facts provided an economic facilitation for the flight; and Washington's school population shifted from half white to nearly all black with greater speed than comparable border-state cities— even though Washington is not experiencing a flight of white *adults* from the city comparable to other cities.

The turbulence surrounding the schools has, in large part, been the combined result of undirected individual actions, each householder attempting to solve *his* problem, whether it is a Negro family moving to a better neighborhood, or a white family moving away from a newly Negro neighborhood. At the same time, there have been policies directed toward implementing some of the interests of Negroes described above. A review of these policies will give some indication of directions that future policies might take. These policies have been aimed in three directions: toward increasing school integration, toward increasing school achievement of Negro children, and toward increasing Negroes' degree of control of schools their children attend. These policies have been relatively distinct, and can be examined separately.

Policies Designed to Implement Integration (and thus create social mobility through assimilation)

There have been numerous policies in cities instituted to facilitate integration, largely depending on the ecological patterns presented by the degree of residential segregation, the relative sizes of the white and Negro population, and the absolute size of Negro population concentrations.

a. Expanding catchment areas and reducing the grade span of schools.

Where two elementary schools exist in contiguous districts, one largely white and the other largely Negro, a possible mode of school integration is cutting the grade span of each in half, and merging the two districts or catchment areas so that each school draws from the total area. This pattern, known as the "Princeton Plan" from the city of its first usage, is a special case of the general use of expanded school districts and contracted grade spans to bring about integration. The success of the plan in bringing about stable school integration depends, of course, on a stable population, and it is feasible only where the concentration of Negroes is very small, covering at most a few schools. It is feasible for small cities with a small proportion of Negroes. It has been attempted in various places, with differential success. Probably the least successful was in New York City, where it encountered organized reaction from white parents, resistance which probably led to its lack of widespread use in New York in areas at the fringe of ghettos.

b. Greatly expanded catchment areas with new large physical plants.

One device for school integration that generated much interest in the mid-sixties with very little implementation, is the educational park. Although there were proposals for educational parks in many cities, there appear to have been few, if any, actually implemented. Pittsburgh may be a single exception; it constructed a plant which has many aspects of an educational park.

Educational parks are designed to carry out a wider range of functions than current schools, such as a longer school day, a more diversified set of activities, and even residential facilities for a small number of children. From the point of view of racial integration, however, which was one of their principal aims, the difference between an educational park and an ordinary school lay in the much wider district covered by such a park, since the number of children included is much greater than in current schools. Educational parks could be used as means for integration in even the largest cities, if the proportion of whites in the city is large enough for integration, for the districting possible (and ordinarily proposed) for such parks is that of a pie-shaped wedge, from the center of the city outward, including a wide range of economic levels, and both races. In Philadelphia, for example, a proposal to the school board from an educational consulting firm would have divided the city into a set of such wedges, each with one or more such parks at different grade levels.

c. *Dispersing Negroes concentrated in one or two schools in the city, with equalization of racial composition in the city's schools.*

In a few small cities where the proportion of Negroes is less than 30 per cent, such as White Plains, New York, and Evanston, Illinois, school integration has been achieved through reassignment of children among schools. This has ordinarily been done through redistricting, and thus depends on both a small proportion of Negroes in the system, and a small absolute size of the Negro population. In a few places, such as Berkeley, California, which has about 50 per cent Negroes in its schools, a combination of redistricting and cutting the grade span of school has been carried out to accomplish equality of racial composition. In some cities, such as Ann Arbor, attempts at redistricting to achieve integration have run into opposition from Negroes because of the loss of a predominantly black school; and because of the increase in pressures toward black local control, such a procedure is probably not feasible in most parts of the North today. Even in the South, where guidelines from the Department of Health, Education, and Welfare prohibit continuation of such schools which are residues of a dual system, resistance to the explicit integration of all-black schools is beginning among Negroes.

d. *Bussing within a system or across system boundaries.*

Bussing of students is one of the simplest means of creating school integration, and has been carried out both within systems and between systems (most often from central city to a suburban district). A few cities, like Buffalo, have engaged in a rather wide-spread bussing plan within the city. In other cities, a token bussing program is operated by groups outside the school system.

The problems bussing has encountered between systems show, formally, the nature of the informal forces that have kept it relatively small within systems. Between systems, such a plan requires assent by both the sending system and the receiving one; and the characteristic obstacle has been the receiving system in the suburbs. Small amounts of bussing have taken place from some city systems to suburban ones, but many more attempts have been blocked by the suburban veto. Within the city, something of the same process occurs, but with less force, since it is only the poorly organized parents in the host schools who can protest, and consequently most bussing has been within-city. Nearly all bussing is a movement of Negro students to predominantly white schools; and most of this is done on a voluntary basis.

e. Merging of school systems.

One means to make integration possible when school systems themselves have become largely of a single race which is increasingly characteristic of some of the larger metropolitan areas (and best exemplified by the Washington, D.C., metropolitan area), is to merge the systems. Such a merger will not in itself create school integration, but it will prevent the veto power that now exists in the separate systems. Apart from metropolitan government plans that have occurred in Nashville and Miami, only one example of an attempt at such a merger exists: an attempt by the NAACP to force the merger of a small, predominantly Negro district in Wyandanch, Long Island, with the surrounding predominantly white districts. This attempt was a failure, opposed by the Wyandanch district itself, whose black leaders saw themselves losing control of the system.

f. Free choice.

In a number of school systems in the South, integration has been implemented by abolishing not only the dual districting that maintained segregation, but all districting whatsoever. The child's parents were thus to make a choice of school, ordinarily between the previously all-Negro school and the previously all-white school.

The plan has worked well in some localities to move a large proportion of Negroes into previously white schools, and has not worked well in others. Because the free-choice plan has sometimes been abused in Southern communities, the Department of Health, Education, and Welfare has never accorded it full acceptance as a desegregation plan in those communities. In some larger cities of the North, free choice is and has been widely used at the high-school level, sometimes in conjunction with a system of specialized high schools, as in New York City. While such plans reduce the dependence of school integration on residence, they have never functioned in large cities to bring about widespread integration. In one city, Baltimore, free choice at the junior-high and high-school levels has functioned to bring many Negroes into previously predominantly white schools, along with severe overcrowding, which has led in some cases to two-shift integrated schools, along with under-utilized schools in the ghetto. The crowding and double shifts have then left whites with the alternatives of moving out or sending their children to private schools, thereby reducing the overcrowding but leaving the school occupied by Negroes. Thus the free-choice plan appears to have hastened the resegregation of schools, by adding to the incentive of whites to leave, through the overcrowding it creates in the most desired schools.

Policies Designed To Directly Augment Achievement

Policies designed to bring racial integration to schools have sometimes been justified in terms of achievement benefits they bring to lower-class Negro children and to lower-class children in general. Apart from these policies, there have been numerous programs wholly to augment achievement. These programs, which are often termed "compensatory education," have usually constituted a general enrichment of the program, through an increase in numbers of teachers and time in kinds of activities. No clear-cut results from these programs have been obtained which can serve as a basis for such future programs. Indeed, the major experience has been negative—as exemplified by probably the most massive such experiment: the More Effective Schools program in New York City, which showed little or no effect from a large input of additional resources, amounting to about double the per-pupil expenditures. What evidence exists, in fact, indicates that the side effects of school integration on Negro achievement are greater than the effects of compensatory programs designed directly to increase achievement.

But for general policy purposes, the most important aspect of the compensatory programs is that no general strategies for bringing about increased achievement have emerged for widespread use in policy. This is not to say that there are not successful programs, but rather that no general policies have been found that could be instituted on a widespread basis and be expected to have effects.

Policies Designed To Increase Black Control or Community Control

The most recent source of turbulence in urban education has been the increasing pressure among many Negroes for community control of their schools. Initially enunciated by black militants, pressure toward local control has coincided with the interests of, and thus has found a response from, Negro professional educators, who are seldom at the head of whole systems, but are, instead, principals or assistant superintendents in large systems. In a few systems where Negro students are in the vast majority (the most notable being Washington, D.C.), the militant pressure for black control of black schools has been translated into pressure not for local control, but for black control of the system as a whole. Indeed, the recent reappointment in Philadelphia of the white superintendent who is widely regarded as one of the most successful of big-city superintendents was very problematic because of the pressures for a black superintendent.

a. Decentralization within the school administration.

Local control could logically be realized in any of several ways, within the present administrative structure of city school systems. One general mode is decentralization by delegation of greater authority to intermediate positions in the school administrative structure. This could take place at either of two levels: at the level of district superintendents, as is the case in St. Louis, or at the level of school principals, as is currently being attempted in Philadelphia. Such decentralization gives greater authority over policy questions, such as budget allocations, curriculum, and school organization, to the district superintendent or principals. The degree to which the superintendents or principals make use of community members through advisory boards or parents' organizations depends on the superintendent or principal himself, since the delegated authority rests with him.

b. Community control.

A second mode of local control, deriving in large part from the ideological proposition of "participation of the poor," delegates authority directly from the central school board to local community boards. This is the pattern attempted in New York City in three areas of the city, with disastrous results in one (Ocean Hill-Brownsville) and serious problems in a second (Harlem). The general potential of this mode of instituting community control is obscured by this example, because in these cases there was an absence of clear definition of the scope of delegated powers before the local groups were established. The failure of these attempts does show, however, the necessity for extreme clarity in the delegation of authority from a central system to the local level, a necessity that is probably greater when the delegation lies outside the professional bureaucracy, as in the case of the New York attempts.[2]

c. Locally controlled partial schools and supplementary schools.

Apart from these modes of decentralizing control within the public school system, the pressures toward community control of education have in effect burst the bounds of public education through the establishment of local schools, part-schools, and storefront classrooms outside the public system. The Harlem Street academies sponsored by the Urban League are the most prominent example. These activities have occurred in a number of cities, but on a very small scale, because they are privately financed and because they must operate as supplements to the public school, after school hours, or for dropouts (since they have not attempted to compete directly with the public school).

d. Community-industry collaboration in supplementary education.

In a few instances, there has developed still another mode of increased local control of education. This is collaboration between an education branch of a business firm and the local community, offering educational programs either within the school or outside it. In San Jose, California, for example, the Education Division of Lockheed Aircraft, in collaboration with school leaders, took over the curricular program for a group of San Jose school children—an activity funded through the state Department of Education. There has been a minor breach in the solid front of the public-education system through a few such experiments with publicly-funded, privately-operated educational activities.

Although these modes of community control are ordinarily seen as quite outside the system, they provide useful prototypes, for they make clear that decentralization of function, and local control over certain educational functions, can be accomplished without shifting control of the school as an entity from the city to the local community.

Demands by Teachers and Demands by Students

Besides the turbulence in urban education that has arisen from racial composition of schools and the frustrations of lower-class Negroes in schools, turbulence has arisen from two other principal sources as well: the organization of teachers, and most recently, the organization of students. The unionization of teachers and the teachers' use of the strike as a collective-bargaining weapon have escalated the strains that exist in the system: strains between teachers and administrators, and strains between teachers and the community. Teacher organization has also had the effect of shifting the power balance in schools in the direction of teachers. Thus, curriculum changes and changes in school organization must, to a much greater extent than a few years ago, take into account the interests and demands of teachers. For example, moves to make education less labor-intensive, or even to introduce lower-paid teachers' aides, may be opposed by teachers because of the reduced demand for teachers such moves imply.

The source of turbulence that is just beginning in urban education is the organization of students. In a number of cities, underground student newspapers have arisen; and in some cities "student unions"—sometimes black student unions, sometimes general student unions—have formed and made demands on school administrators. It is difficult to anticipate the amount and kind of change this development will bring about. Yet it constitutes a force of the greatest potential.

JAMES S. COLEMAN

The Future of Education in Cities

There have been, currently and in the recent past, the three general policy goals for education in cities stated above: policies primarily designed to increase racial integration, policies primarily designed to increase Negro achievement, and policies primarily designed to increase local control or community control or black control of black schools. At the same time, there has been a massive movement, on the part of the middle-class population, out of the central city and toward schools that are racially and socially homogeneous. This too can be viewed as a movement toward decentralization, since it is a movement of population from large central-city systems to smaller systems which reflect the character of the local (suburban) community. Some of this movement has been the result of policies for increasing racial integration, and much of it has resulted from the racial invasion of neighborhoods by Negroes, which has meant a simultaneous invasion of the schools.

This middle-class-white movement to the suburbs (and more recently, a middle-class-black movement to the suburbs) stands as a reminder that school administrators and government officials have only partial control over school organization. Individual families, with increasing financial resources to allow for free choice of residence and school, have a greater measure of control through their actions than at any time in the past. Thus, any school policies must be adopted in cognizance of this freedom of choice, and should be so designed that the individual actions will aid rather than thwart (as they have in the past) the goals of school policy.

From this mixture of collective goals and individual actions, a variety of patterns for urban education could develop in America. I will examine each of these, with an indication of how such patterns might be attained.

A Metropolitan-Area System, with Strong Central Powers, and Integrated Schools Separate from the Neighborhood

One pattern of control of education for urban areas is a metropolitan system, covering the suburbs as well as the central city. There are some movements in the direction of such metropolitan-area control, stemming partly from the inequities of financing (and the tax base on which financing depends) between the central city and the suburban areas, and partly from the growing racial separation between some central cities and suburbs. There have, in fact, been lawsuits filed recently, and others are in the process of being filed, on both these grounds, with the state as defendant, based on the equal-protection clause of the Constitution.

It is clear that the adequate financing of central-city education requires either such metropolitan-wide action, or a larger share of school financing from state or federal sources. Similarly, it is evident that in many cities, there can be no central-city mechanism to reduce the racial separation in education, due to the growing segregation by school system.

The clear necessity for a broader tax base for central-city schools indicates the possibility of metropolitan systems. Yet metropolitan governments, school or otherwise, have nearly without exception failed to be adopted, largely due to the veto power of the suburban voters. In addition, there are some central cities in which Negroes constitute a proportion of the population large enough to take over the political structure. In those cities, the veto of the suburbs would likely be paralleled by a veto from the central city, for the merging of school systems on a metropolitan basis stands in direct conflict with community or local control. Because of all these sources of a veto, it is likely that the necessary financial resources for central-city education will come not from amalgamation with wealthier suburbs, but from state or federal support, leaving control largely in the hands of the local system.

If a centrally-controlled metropolitan school system did occur, the administrative apparatus would be present for bringing about full racial integration in schools. However, there are indications of two sorts that this would not occur, whatever the strength of the metropolitan system. First, this would do away with all-black schools which now exist in central cities. These schools have recently come to be seen by Negroes as black territory to be kept intact and in the hands of blacks. It is unlikely that even if the black staff and black control were kept intact, the transformation of the student body to include a large proportion of whites would be accepted in many cities.

Second, the experience of bussing within cities has shown the resistance of whites to large-scale transfer of children to achieve racial balance. Much of this resistance would remain if the bussing did not involve Negroes at all. For white communities, particularly in ethnically homogeneous neighborhoods, have the same perspective toward their ethnically or socially homogeneous schools that Negroes have recently come to acquire toward their schools. Beyond this, the same force that has impelled many whites to flee the central city will act to thwart any moves that seriously change the character of middle-class suburban schools. The response cannot be to move residence, if the system is metropolitan-wide, but it would be naïve to expect that there would be no response.

These forces from blacks and whites are strong enough in most urban areas to prevent a massive redistribution of children to overcome residential segregation, but it is possible that in some areas, they might be overcome. Berkeley, California, has recently instituted exactly such a redistribution system, indicating that it can, under certain conditions, be carried out in a small central city. It is too early to see if this will result in stable integration, or if residential mobility will mean that it merely leads to black Berkeley schools within a few years.

For the reasons described above, it appears to me unlikely that metropolitan-area school systems, with widespread bussing to achieve racial and social integration, could muster the political support necessary to come into being. Whatever the societal benefits of such systems as a means for reducing the racial separation and educational inequalities that currently exist, it is not attractive enough to individuals, white or black, to lead to its existence.

Systems as Currently Organized, with Financial Aid from State and National Governments

A major source of instability and strain in the present organization of schools into school systems is the financial problems of most central cities and some suburbs. If this stress is removed by state or federal aid, a viable set of school systems will result. In some systems, where the Negro population is not large enough to gain black control of the system itself, a somewhat larger amount of autonomy at the local school level may be necessary in order to have a viable system; but with such modifications, the present systems could continue with little organizational change. This pattern is probably the one which would result from a continuation of present policies; thus it has political feasibility to recommend it.

The consequences of such a policy in terms of racial segregation of education and resulting inequalities of opportunities depend very largely on residential patterns. At present, both racial discrimination in housing and the greater economic resources of whites mean that the present policies lead toward increasing racial segregation between central-city systems and suburban ones.

What is less clear is the future patterns of residential migration of Negroes. If housing discrimination in suburban areas is sharply reduced, and if the economic resources of Negroes continue to increase at a rate comparable to the past few years, then the white exodus will be accompanied by a black exodus as well. The desire of blacks to leave the ghetto, strengthened by the riots and the rising ghetto crime rates, can lead to a more integrated residential pattern than at present. This depends greatly, however, upon the reduction of racial discrimination in low-cost suburban housing, because most of the current movement from the ghetto merely results in an expansion of its perimeter.

Thus, if the present organization of schools is to be maintained, the consequences for social and racial segregation and for equality of educational opportunity depend largely on housing policies. If anti-discrimination laws are effective, and if there is a continuing supply of low-cost housing in suburban areas, then school equalization and integration will be achieved through residential changes—leaving a declining and transient population in the ghetto. If these conditions are not met, the geographic expansion of the ghetto will result in an increasing number of all-black school systems and a maintenance of socially and racially homogeneous white schools in the suburbs.

Explicit Decentralization of Large Systems

In the largest urban school systems, the demands of blacks take the form of demands for local control. A policy of system decentralization can be carried out, as indicated earlier, either through placing power in the hands of local boards, or through placing more power in the hands of local administrative officers, such as district superintendents or principals. If such decentralization does indeed delegate most of the power to smaller units, several consequences will emerge. Education will be tied even more fully to residence than at present; local subsystems, both black and white, will have more ability to prevent bussing children in or out as well as other policies to achieve racial integration, such as those described earlier. Variation between schools in their ability to bring about achievement will increase. It is very likely that such variation will be in the direction of relative improvement of predominantly white schools first because of the greater educational, organizational, and financial resources of whites, and second, because teachers will have greater option to teach in "desirable" schools, once there is no authority of the central system to assign teachers to schools.

The presence of a number of young idealistic teachers, mostly white, who desire to teach in difficult central-city schools, would appear to represent a new ability of these schools to attract teachers. However, the staying power of these teachers is extremely low, their idealism not matched by an ability to manage poorly socialized children in a setting that provides little support. Their own socialization has largely been through a sweet and yielding reasonableness, and they are unaccustomed to conflict—a pattern almost diametrically opposed to the experience of the children they come to teach. They are, thus, quickly defeated by these children.

In short, it appears likely that decentralization will result in an increase in inequality of education between Negroes and whites. Negro professionals may benefit, because of their greater degree of authority, just as Negro professionals in the South benefited from the dual systems there.[3] Negro children, however, appear likely to suffer in both the short and long run.

Separating the Functions of Education

One policy that is suggested by the existence of part-schools and supplementary educational activities such as reading clinics, street academies, and tutorials is a separation of educational functions. This implies decentralization of a different sort than that described above: decentralization from the school of the activities of education. With such decentralization, different groups and organizations would have control over different educational functions—subject to authorization by the central school administration, whether city, metropolitan area, or state. The school, as presently constituted, would remain the home base for children from the neighborhood or district, but some of their educational activities would be carried out under local community control, while others would cut across district lines and even system lines.

In this fashion, both local control and racial integration would be achieved, for there would be local control of *activities* rather than *school*, and racial integration of *activities*, rather than *school*. (It is useful to recall that racial integration of schools often does not mean racial integration of activities, because of a tracking system that largely separates the races.) In addition, the structuring of these activities, organized by different groups, could be carried out in such a way that any family had the choice of at least two such contexts within which the activities are carried out. One of these could well be the home-base school, which could continue to offer the same range of activities as at present, as a standing alternative to an external competitor. Thus a larger portion of control over the child's education than at present would rest in the hands of the parent and child.

Such separation or decentralization of school functions has a number of other possible benefits as well. It would constitute a means by which various organizations, ranging from art museums to business firms, could participate directly in public education. There are many such organizations, some profit-making and some nonprofit, which could greatly augment the resources of public education, if educational activities could be carried on outside the school on a contract basis. The benefits to the school system itself of having external competitors should be great, though they would not be seen as benefits by the school authorities or teachers who had lost their monopoly over the child's time. The external competitors would serve as a stimulus for innovation to the school itself, a stimulus that it now badly needs.

Closer integration of education with the rest of the community would result from the external contracting of activities as would the development of additional activities that are not now the province of the school, but are an appropriate form of education activity. For example, organizations could contract to operate public educational camps (summer or winter) which could provide both a more important interracial experience and a more important educational experience than a white or Negro might ever have in an ordinary school.

The principal difficulty that such a policy faces is the political opposition of established school authorities. This pressure, for example, has insured that all funds for federal aid to education under the Elementary and Secondary Education Act go directly to the state education agencies and cannot be used in innovative ways that would involve other means. More generally, there is a broad political sentiment against "private education" and in favor of "public education," which has come to be interpreted as a single administrative unit operating schools. However, along with this political support for the *status quo* in schools, there is strong political opposition to the *status quo*: pressure for local control of schools, the pressure for school integration, and the pressure of agencies outside the educational system to participate in public education. All three of these forces could be mobilized in support of such a decentralization of school function—and this policy is probably the only one that could simultaneously mobilize these forces.

These are possible futures for education in urban areas. Which of these comes to occur in America's cities depends upon a variety of factors. All but the second policy, which is largely the maintenance of present organization, require mobilization of strong political support. Yet, it appears to me that the first alternative, metropolitan systems with broad redistribution of children, cannot possibly obtain the political support necessary for success, while the third, decentralization, will lead to increasingly inferior education for the poor and the blacks of America. The consequences of the second alternative, the *status quo*, depend very much on future residential mobility of Negroes, and could either lead to a natural, though slow, social integration of Negroes, or to a polarization between the two territorial domains of blacks and whites. The fourth alternative, decentralization of educational function, I see as clearly the most attractive alternative. It has as well, I believe, the basis for broad political support, despite the long-established sentiment in America for keeping public education insular.

NOTES

1. The term "district" is ambiguously used in education, sometimes referring to the area from which a particular school draws its pupils, and sometimes referring to the total area covered by a school taxation district, with more than one school, and governed by a superintendent and school board. I will use the term district here to refer to a single school's catchment area, and the term system to refer to the entity that levies taxes, has a school board

and superintendent, and contains a number of schools. The school system of a city is ordinarily coincident with the city itself, while those in suburban areas may be county-wide (as is characteristic of the South) or municipality-wide or township-wide or may have still another basis.

2. It is likely that the very process of obtaining the "participation of the poor" increases the likelihood of delusion about the extent of community control. For, to obtain participation, organizers must promise power, and the greater the power they promise, the more likely they are to obtain participation. They thus have a strong incentive to promise a great deal of power.

3. In the North, the ratio of Negro teachers to white is much lower than the ratio of Negro students to white, with many Negro students taught by white teachers. In the dual systems of the South, Negro students were taught by Negro teachers.

RICHARD L. MEIER

The Metropolis as a
Transaction-Maximizing System

A METROPOLIS is where the real action is. New people come to participate, and most present residents stay despite their complaints. The urban environment writ large represents both an escape from boredom and an opportunity to get ahead. A great city and its immediate satellites make up a social engine that mobilizes action and powers progress unless it is brought to a shuddering halt by the failure of an essential part or an accumulation of internal frictions. How are higher performance engines built? Answers to this question are to be found in the attempts to measure action and to get the greatest value from it.

In America we see all around us the first transition from the advanced industrial society to an affluent *post-industrial* one.[1] Money means less than before, because it takes only a small amount of effort to acquire enough to get by. This shift suggests that the most effective metropolis may no longer be the one that produces the most income per resident. The concepts of efficiency as applied to cities acquire some new connotations. We must rethink the reasons for living in cities, and the not-quite-explicit concept of *action* appears to take into account the important non-economic factors as well as the economic ones in reaching a balanced assessment.

When repeated often enough, an action can be reduced to a custom or a routine. Institutions arise to provide public arenas and otherwise to support the continuation of specialized action. The market place is one of the oldest of these institutions and has elaborated many variants, some of them approaching the limits of cybernation. The newer kinds of bargaining, however, demand extensive human participation. Politics swirl around city hall; training is expedited in schools and gymnasia; jobs are obtained at the employment exchanges; trips are undertaken with self-operated vehicles; messages flow through communications networks; contacts with popular culture are offered by cinemas and night spots; and ritual is reproduced in churches for the parishioners. Such voluntarily initiated action is generally presumed to be healthy, so we may use it to judge the relative success of various urban environments: The greater the action, the better the metropolis. The universality of this assertion will be examined later.

Extraordinary tools for measuring various interactions are now appearing on the scene as an outgrowth of the new electronic data-processing systems, with the same kind of software often employed in both the public and the corporate sector. Moreover, the compatibility between data-storage and data-processing programs is steadily increasing. Already the records of an insurance firm are being linked to the accident-reporting system created by the police, and both are based upon the federal census. Thus, the salient *transactions* in urban society are soon to be reported with all pertinent data—*who, when, where, what,* how much *money* transferred, *linkages,* and so forth. The counting and classifying of these voluntarily initiated transactions completed in all phases of public life provide a foundation for simple quantitative measurement. The post-industrial society insists upon quantification whenever the transactions can be isolated and enumerated, because one or another of the knowledge-based institutions will need the numbers to apply its art with precision.

When speaking of quality, however, we are disposed to start from the planner's self-imposed directive: The design of a city must promote the harmonious interaction of a population. Until recently, harmony had been considered to be a matter of expert judgment that was ultimately subject also to the planner's own taste for form, pace, elegance, complexity, ambiguity, and so forth. Harmony in urban life takes on added meaning as we develop new capabilities in data processing; it implies the minimization of clashing *error* and thereby reduces the confusion so induced. Error includes miscalculations, accidents, illness, and crime. Conflict is not included in this list, because to minimize conflict is to take much of the spice out of life. Managed conflict can generate much constructive action at the same time that it produces friction. This difference is exceedingly important. Yet, at the other extreme, violent unmanageable conflict can halt the growth of a metropolitan community and reduce its action-packed future to ashes—a prospect

221

TABLE 1

The Pace of Social Transactions

(Population Average Estimates: United States, 1965)

		per day per capita
Checks and Credit Card Payments	0.4	~5
Purchases (by item)		
Trips (vehicular)	2	
Telephone Calls	1.9	
Mail	1.0	
Shipments	0.2	
Newspapers read (at 3 readers per copy)	1.0	
News items read (including advertising)		~10
Magazines read	0.3	
Classes attended	0.6	
Library circulation (including schools)	0.03	
Television viewing (hours)	1.9	
TV ("exposures" to messages)		~30
Radio (hours)	0.6	
Radio ("exposures")		~10
Face-to-face exchanges		~20
Physical environment (items consciously noted)		~10

The average employed person will be operating at twice this rate, except for television and classes. The typical professional will be engaged at perhaps three times this rate with much greater emphasis upon written materials. Human capacity is at least tenfold greater when well organized. (Sources for this information are Statistical Abstracts of the United States, *Business Week*, and other trade journals.)

that is faced by Watts and Newark, to mention two headliners, but by a dozen other cities as well. Planning for peaceful, productive, personally rewarding social action will require fundamental, systematic analysis before the challenges to harmony posed by the current "underclass" and the future pace-setting class can be reviewed. Thereafter policies for the metropolitan area as a whole can be outlined and tested for consistency.

Identifying Atoms of Action

A set of accounts based upon *the aggregate of transactions per unit of time* yields the kind of gross index that seems to be needed to guide future urban policy. The metropolises that discover the changing nature of the competition among urban areas can employ such measures of action to seize the initiative and convert their head start into power and influence on the regional and national scene. If the city fathers refuse to recognize these criteria for urban self-development, they inadvertently condemn their community to genteel decline into a relative state of depression.

Such a set of accounts is to be used primarily as a basis for estimating costs and consequences of alternative projects proposed for social and economic development. Projects are presently chosen after unit costs have been minimized and the level of public benefits maximized. Except in the area of health, the calculations are made in terms of dollars. This approach to welfare maximization notably understates the nonmonetized (mainly social and cultural) values of the most modern urban regions. Specifically, a metropolis maximizing the services produced for residents from a limited tax base cannot provide very much for the young, vigorous, educated component of the affluent society who are interested in the amenities—not even if this group insists that a rich, varied environment enhances their opportunities to make innovating, organizational contributions. Competition for talent has begun, however, and the manner in which it is expected to affect urban plans requires as complete an explanation as can be put forward at this time. The new accounts must be sensitive to the consequences of competition.[2]

Another characteristic is the extreme emphasis upon careful system description. Anyone who wishes to make sense out of the investment decisions of cities over the next decade will recognize that urbanism, although the most complex of living systems, is subject to the general laws regarding life.[3] We shall regard a city to be an adaptive community comprising many subspecies living together in harmony within a specific locale. An unmistakable characteristic of the city population, as contrasted to the noncity one, is the highly constructed environment in which it lives—nature has been greatly improved upon in order to reduce the risks facing members of the community. Moreover, a much less intense level of interaction exists in the territory between urban communities than within them. Somehow the population density, aided by walls, streets, power-houses, and other urban equipment, stimulates transactions between individual actors. A predominant share of the action serves, mostly indirectly rather than directly, to keep the physical apparatus in repair and to maintain the urban institutions at a steady state.

An aggressive metropolis on the American scene would accelerate the formation of the new public-utility network based upon the sharing of computer time while simultaneously constructing estimates of daily transaction rates from the still incomplete records. It would identify the kinds of individuals who make the greatest marginal contribution to the action. The support these individuals need would be studied, and then the scarcest services would be assigned a high priority in the budgets. Contacts would then be made with geographically mobile, educated individuals with the aim of getting them to come to the city in order to demonstrate to them that their life would be more exciting in this metropolis than where they were.[4]

Simultaneous studies of the least active components of the population need to be undertaken. What constraints do they experience? Cannot some of the bottlenecks be removed? What internal conflicts are likely to be produced by a rapidly expanding volume of social transactions among the formerly lethargic components? What kinds of negotiations (complex transactions) should be initiated to moderate the explosiveness of the threatened conflicts? Are there nonmarket situations that have excluded universal participation assuring that benefits will be distributed to "members"?[5] For example, residents of a ghetto are rarely in a position to play golf because they are excluded from membership in country clubs and are generally distant from municipal courses.

Mentioning both an advantaged and disadvantaged group within the urban population focuses our attention upon the *power* of each of the parties completing a transaction. Both enter into the transaction voluntarily because they hope to gain from this atomic social event, but the most powerful party is expected to appropriate the bulk of the surplus values created, if that is at all possible. Thus, although the poor do not get poorer, the rich do become richer, so the disparity increases. The unequal nature of transactions eventually discourages enthusiastic participation of the weak, and their withdrawal detracts from the over-all action in the metropolis. Alfred Kuhn has carefully analyzed the place of power in social transactions in his systematic synthesis of models describing social interaction.[6] Neither Kuhn nor his predecessors realize, however, that social accounts based upon transactions can be aggregated meaningfully, thus becoming helpful for making public decisions in the metropolis.

In the adaptive metropolis of the middle 1970's, we must expect to see all persons, firms, organizations, departments, and other public actors represented by one or more entries in the data-processing records. Parcels of property (addresses) and licensed vehicles would be similarly recorded. Important transactions, such as telephone calls, mail delivery, or advertising would not be counted individually, but by sampling techniques. What does not get recorded now are the face-to-face communications carried out in offices, classrooms, and other public places where the "bids" and the "offers" are introduced in the course of conversations that can eventually connect to produce a nonroutine transaction. Sometimes the transaction is with the environment, as in planting seeds to get a crop or pounding a nail to steady a rail. Again in such cases some ambiguities arise concerning what shall be counted, but the clear aim is to maximize satisfactions in public contacts.

The importance of a transaction is that neither party is rewarded for his effort until it is completed. Each participates in the hope that he will be better off afterward than before. Completion brings about a shift from anticipation to experience. The same behavior may be assigned to two or even three different transactions, but such double counting says something important about the richness of life and the compression of action in certain environments. Because each transaction also represents a micro-adaptation to changing conditions, the frequency of completion also measures the adaptability of the population, particularly its capability for meeting challenges that demand large-scale adjustments.

Organization in the Ghetto

A few years ago, when visiting at the University of North Carolina, I was reviewing origin-destination plots that students had mapped depicting "action in urban space." The basic data were obtained from the nearby manufacturing city of Durham, which happened also to be endowed with a good university.

Three patterns emerged clearly from the background blur of miscellaneous motion. One of these generated complex trip-making with multiple stops in various parts of the city, suburbs, and environs. The urban actors in that case were the managers, the business class, and the professionals. Another pattern, originating in the most recently built tracts, trailer courts, and rooming-house areas, contained a predominantly in-out movement, either to strings of highway services or back to the village and farm. The people behaving in this way were relatively recent migrants who frequently went "home" for weekends or engaged in such rural recreation as hunting, fishing, or moonshining. Parallel studies in the less-developed metropolis of Athens, Greece, yielded what appeared to be the same movement patterns discernible in nonrefugee communities that had been settled in the past generation. A third pattern stood out in Durham. A tightly knit crisscross of sociable visits, meetings, movements to school, and shopping excursions characterized one quarter of the city; this, I was told, was the Negro ghetto. Comparable interaction intensity was found in Athens, but only for long-established communities with upper-middle-class representation.

The last comparison is significant because the Durham ghetto segregates middle-class people along with the blue-collar and the lower-class population, so that the over-all income level was higher than the Greek example and the years of education per adult was roughly equivalent. Thus, the resources underlying urban spatial movements were certainly comparable. Recognizing Athens' position among the metropolises of the world today, one might describe the Negro ghetto in Durham as operating at an advanced stage of semi-development.

About the same time, planners alert to the dynamics of great cities were noting that the underworld—a part of the metropolitan system over which they had no control, but which nevertheless could make a difference in the implementation of plans—was likely to undergo reorganization. The Mafia Syndicate (Cosa Nostra is the popular appellation on the East Coast) was beginning to have more at stake in its legitimate business than in the underworld. Many of the sons in these tightly interrelated families were going to college and becoming doctors, priests, lawyers, and accountants, thus committing the new generation even more strongly to legitimate operations. Such a transformation surely would leave a power vacuum in the underworld. Who would move in to take over the gambling and the narcotics rackets? Might it not be the most desperate and unscrupulous, yet highly organized elements in the ghetto, as had happened earlier in Polish, Jewish, and Italian urban communities? If so, we had to consider the possibility that some Negro youth gangs would be transformed into an underworld organization, skilled in the use of violence and terror, but still sensitive to the kinds of information useful for the expansion of the vice market. Perhaps planners should look for a policy approach that would deflect the gangs from an involvement in organized crime. At any rate, a careful watch over progress in the organization of youth gangs in the ghetto needed to be maintained.

The Metropolis as a Transaction-Maximizing System

The best guess was that effective, quick-action, and adaptive organizations would be created wherever the models were visible within the metropolis itself. Concepts of organization diffuse across ghetto barriers via the mass media and through night-school courses. They are mobilized by some natural genius who sees an opportunity to build an organization. Los Angeles, a city that the Mafia failed to crack, was most likely to be in the vanguard, with its government contractors, television and movie industries operating with a minimum of corporate loyalty in a risk-laden environment. New York, Chicago, and Washington were the other nominees for early trouble.

A hostile outburst with epidemic-like qualities, the "Watts rebellion," destroyed much of the commercial and cultural center of the Los Angeles ghetto. The organization of desperation was slowed down and perhaps shifted in direction. Simultaneously, the Office of Economic Opportunity directed sizable funds into Harlem and Washington in a way that resulted in at least a postponement of extremism merely by promoting an efflorescence of legitimate organizations. Chicago became the first to witness the forging of a disciplined, armed organization—The Mighty Blackstone Rangers, Inc.—a coalition of gangs, some with a long history, that began to receive attention outside Chicago early in 1966.

Unexpectedly, the Blackstone Rangers did not escalate alienation in order to bind the organization together. They decided instead to run some of the most blatant hustlers off their turf and to create a communications network so fast-acting they could put as many of their men on an intersection after a disturbance as the police could mobilize with their vaunted computer system. They organized dances and excursions for themselves and began to press for anti-poverty and other grants to speed up the action. Their opposition to the vice rackets supported by the corrupt elements in the police and their conflicts with other intruders resulted in pressures on the ruling political machine that forced a veto on the expenditure of such monies for activities sponsored by the Blackstone Rangers. For more than a year there were no visible rewards granted by the society at large to this group as repayment for having cast their lot with the "good guys." Indeed, what they earned was almost continuous police harassment and entrapment along with a bad press.[7]

Some anti-riot measures taken by the Rangers were novel and exceedingly effective. In the course of an incident when a miscel-

227

laneous crowd of youths boiled over and began to heave bricks through store windows in the Woodlawn area, for example, one Ranger jumped out into the middle of the street and shouted that anyone who wanted to die in the streets should be there in five minutes. The disturbance broke up immediately, because individual rioters do not fancy themselves playing a "High Noon" scenario. Again, when Chicago's race relations became particularly tense in 1966, the Rangers kept their members off the streets by calling a "mandatory" dance every night the West Side "blow" lasted. For a while they enforced a "voluntary curfew" for anyone under twenty-five years of age. Formal treaties have also been negotiated with the neighboring Disciples gang. The motivation of this behavior has apparently been that of demonstrating control over the situation.

The promotion of peace and order will provide plenty of action during a crisis, but when the heat is off, doldrums set in. During quiet times, the Organization is hard put to generate new, yet legitimate, kinds of action. Then it may listen to the two white professional group workers who have contrived to maintain tenuous contacts with them. Whites are used primarily for "technical assistance." Together they have prepared applications for grants from foundations for any projects that looked fundable. The Rangers produced a topical musical, "Opportunity Please Knock," successful enough to go on the road. The Rangers are now interested in launching several business enterprises. None of these has to do with narcotics, even marijuana, since members were long ago ordered to lay off.

Somewhat similar organizations are being formed in the ghettos elsewhere. A few take old names, such as the Rangers and Satans, but others have an odd flavor that seems to beg for legitimacy: "The Young Adults" in Cleveland, "Youth for Service" in San Francisco, "Sons of Watts" in Los Angeles, "The Real Great Society" in New York, and "Rebels with a Cause" in Washington. Most of the members are high school dropouts, with experiences of extreme poverty and police records that make them difficult to employ. They are suspicious of whites, talk a Black Power line, and are personally acquainted with violence, as the urban underclass has always been in the past. The dangers inherent in these supergangs, should they become pathological, are very great indeed, but I have chosen to underscore the more agreeable surprises.

Henceforth the ghetto will be judged by the action that can

be produced for its residents. Two categories are particularly scarce: economic transactions and cultural messages with real meaning. The first of these requires jobs that are on some kind of promotion ladder, so that a stake exists in the total society. The second is most likely to be based upon the faces one knows or expects some day to meet, so that a community culture develops. It could be based, in part, on music and the performing arts as a vehicle for self-expression. Corrective measures to eliminate illiteracy (and the parallel innumeracy) should have a strong redistributive effect upon both the economic transactions (since ability to read enhances employability) and the social transactions that can be completed in and around the ghetto. Neighborhood television productions can stimulate cultural participation at very low cost, using the new equipment together with the new cable television outlets. These potentials are currently being explored in more than one metropolitan area in America. The metropolis that discovers how to exploit them successfully will become an immensely attractive area for educated persons who seek an "urban place compatible with liveliness." It would simultaneously become a place where new enterprise investment faces fewer risks.

A Generation of Space Consumers

Success in the competition among metropolitan areas in the post-industrial era will depend mainly upon an ability to attract persons capable of instigating action. What are the special values of people possessing skills, ideas, and other assets enabling them to differentiate between one urban area and another? For the North American society, we must focus upon the better-grade professional and graduate schools that have found a way of sifting a cohort for the promising talent and of attracting individuals from a great distance. After the new professionals complete their training, they rarely go back home, preferring instead to drift for a while in the society in search of opportunity. Military service, apprenticeships, and other commitments are met one way or another during a period of job-changing and environment-testing. Appealing institutional, urban, climatic, and cultural environments are sought that are compatible with internally formulated ideals.

Early in 1965 I asked a class drawn from several of the graduate and professional schools at the University of Michigan to describe the living arrangement they would prefer, including housing characteristics that would fit their life style. These prospective professionals are expected to set the pattern for incremental growth of the mobile cosmopolitan contingent of the 1970's.

To my surprise, prospects of affluence had caused an abrupt shift in outlook. A strong majority of these students rejected both suburbs and central cities and opted instead for a kind of urban environment that is hardly ever analyzed or discussed. Indeed it is so seldom treated that no term has been coined and accepted universally for the pattern. They wanted good-quality public schools for the children, an acre of space for themselves, and the kind of convenience provided by having a vehicle for everyone in the household over ten years of age, and motorized ones for those over fifteen. Those students who grew up in the central city might still accept the best suburbs as a compromise, but former suburbanites, town dwellers, and rural inhabitants held firmly to this extraordinary low-density ideal. More than that, their prospective incomes as gauged by economists were more than sufficient to meet the extra expense.

A quick survey of the university revealed that their opinion was representative of their peers and that succeeding classes all the way down to incoming freshmen (the professionals of the 1980's) had already developed values so similar they could not be distinguished. Subsequent spot-checking among prospective professionals educated at the University of California uncovered the same rejection of present-day planned urbanization. Here, then, is a culturally potent subgroup, a leading sector in the future society, that produces models and fashions likely to be widely imitated in their more physical and superficial aspects by the bulk of the middle class ("organization men"), the clerical workers ("white collar"), and the technicians; these leaders should understand the consequences, but they stubbornly choose life styles in conflict with planning doctrine. They seem to be willing to try out what urban designers believe would provide "the good life in cities," but only as a way station to something they are quite sure would be much better.[8]

Is it really possible to create a dispersed urbanism far less dense than anything known before and still have an effective, productive city able to earn its affluence?[9] Instead of collecting more data to establish this change in outlook as a fact, it was accepted as a hypothesis, and extra information was sought to discover how such additions to cities might be organized. We looked around to see who already lived that way, most of them being lumped into the "rural nonfarm" census category. It was then possible to identify a variety of more idiosyncratic life styles. Several hundreds of families, for example, had already moved out of town to live with their horses. Others developed land and stock to the point that they could hang a pedigree sign out front. Quite a few produced children in numbers that forced them out of suburban tracts, while others found that the accumulation of sporting equipment was equally demanding of space. An increasing demand was noted for year-long contact with a bit of wilderness. (A small bog was rapidly becoming a real-estate asset.) Interspersed with these space consumers were urbanites from quite different walks of life who were rarely willing to pay for open space indirectly through taxation, but consumed it nevertheless. Among them were retirees from railroads and government offices, construction workers with rural backgrounds (often living in mobile homes), and technicians or handymen from Appalachia and the Ozarks.

A pattern can be discerned in almost all of these groups. Breadwinners engage for brief periods of time in intense interaction where high levels of performance are demanded of them; thereafter, they withdraw to an environment where the pace of events is usually under their own control. Space is used as a buffer that each household employs to suit its own privacy requirements. Extra time and effort are required to maintain one's own land and that of the neighborhood, but these settlers apparently do not consider the overhead cost for occupying extra space exorbitant. The market for such plots, particularly those with some extra natural amenity, is brisk already, well before the new professionals enter as bidders. Design exercises show that it is possible to support good schools without condemning students to extra time on buses, that waste disposal and water supply can be adequate, that the traffic and parking problems involved in participation and withdrawal are severe but soluble, that community services at urban standards can be supplied (although conflicts in life style sometime lead to embittered impasses), and that sufficient space is available around most metropolitan areas to meet the demand likely to be experienced between now and the year 2000. The technical and economic feasibility of the new outlook forces us to analyze social process at a more fundamental level in order to understand how cities need to be reconstructed.

Properties of the Accounts

This picture of the metropolis as a stream of action maintained by a human population requires that the system be something more than self-maintaining and self-repairing. It must also be self-propelling, self-directing, and continually learning. Inevitably, the most revolutionary ideas for the control of error and the stimulation of development of cities come from findings at the micro-level because they use information out of the realm of general observation and common sense. The strategies for intervention to readjust the urban system may then call for a change in diet or some potent pills rather than for painful surgery. These possibilities force us to look more closely at the properties of transactions, because they hold clues to the taming of metropolitan excesses.

The city is made up of cells—households and other small groups —that insist on privacy. Strangers, even behavioral scientists, are excluded from observing all the action that goes on inside these cells. Some of it, such as use of the mass media, is readily reported, but monitoring the content of telephone calls involves a breach of privacy in many instances. A practical reporting system would therefore include action that involves arenas outside the household and the tightly bound small group. The word *public*, used in the sense of nonprivate, encompasses the full range of observable action. The limitation is not a serious one, because the forthcoming data-gathering apparatus needs to be designed as a public service and the inferences from the accounts it makes possible are intended to guide public policy.

Social transactions also link up to form chains, clumps, or large aggregates. Names are often given to these sets, such as *task, custom, role, patronage, constituency*, and so forth. The aggregates have already been studied in sociology, political science, industrial engineering, business organization, and many other fields of research. The body of knowledge accumulated by these disciplines can readily be restated as interrelations between assemblages of transactions. The strength of the linkages between transactions provides the best foundation for forecasting trends and long-range developments, since new transactions are brought into existence and the degree of organization is enhanced when links increase over time. Life in the ghetto would most probably show significantly smaller conglomerates in virtually all aspects of public transaction. For example, the merchant-customer relationship would have fewer purchases per visit and perhaps fewer visits per year; the teacher-student interaction is similarly impoverished. The clustering properties of transactions can be useful for diagnosing why certain sectors are lagging. They should also produce special indicators for judging effects of policy changes.

Balancing one category of transactions against another requires some fundamental conceptualizations of the social system. We must expect the full complement of transactions to contain:

1. Many that extract materials and information from the environment;

2. Many more that involve the preparation of artifacts;

3. Even greater numbers involving transitions in spatial coordinates (transport and communication);

4. Others that maintain social structure (reassignment of roles);

5. Many that involve changes in ownership or attachment;

6. A few that represent the synthesis of new relationships or combinations to replace those lost inadvertently through accident or death.

These can be subdivided into a number of other subcategories that may be required, but only in minor frequencies—for example, legislative votes. Wherever extremely critical transactions are involved, we are likely to find huge multipliers associated with them that generate much subsequent behavior. Institutions, governmental and otherwise, serve as multistage amplifying systems for the central decision transaction sufficient to restore balance to the unwieldy metropolitan juggernaut.

Any outline of the properties of a set of social accounts suited to urban settlements must relieve the doubts that arise in the mind of the potential user. Why add up completed transactions when everyone knows that some transactions are vastly more important than others? Will this not create a possibility that the aggregate will be inflated by inducing a large number of small transactions, thus discrediting the set of accounts? Suppose a number of small transactions were to be replaced by one large transaction: Would this not be efficient in reality, but still cause a net loss in the number that is used as a proxy for urban welfare?

Persons who raise such questions forget the properties of money as a measure of value, one that is indispensable in the preparation of GNP-type aggregates. Some dollars are spent on essentials; more on strongly felt wants; and the remainder on luxuries. A part of the funds spent has much higher utility than the remainder, but through the trick of marginal analysis that assigns the value of the dollar at the level of the last one spent, the economists have been able to standardize their measures and evade these imponderables. Analogously, people complete the transactions required to survive and then pay attention to those bids that promise lesser rewards. They continue until their resources of time, income, effort, information, or intellectual interest are expended. The marginal transaction has properties for an urban population that a marginal dollar would for a household.

A related question concerning social resources and resource scarcity is fundamental. This showed up in the description of many of the most desirable future urban immigrants as "space consumers." Fortunately the supply of *space* has been adequately surveyed and its allocation quantified; thus feasibility tests could be carried out immediately. We are just now learning how people choose to allocate their *time* to various activities. Typical time budgets for urban communities are being prepared, but the practice is still far from routine. The *energy* available to firms and households has ceased to become a constraint in American cities, and much the same can be said of *income*, except in places like the ghetto. The gravest deficiencies in the ghetto are those of *information* and *motivation* since a prior investment in education, organization, and the construction of communications networks is required before a channeling of such resources to deprived sectors can be effective.

Pathologies in Transacting

Not every transaction comes out well. Some have unexpected consequences that inhibit follow-up transactions by the parties concerned; and others have constraining spillover effects on the environment. Moreover, a few situations stimulate a frenzy of transacting that exhausts the available resources, material and psychic, that are transformed and transferred in social processes. In a few instances, the destruction of such resources is intentionally aimed at eliminating a rival community from the competition. Everyone agrees that these faulty transactions should be prevented;

the natural reaction of the members of the community is to pass a law, establish a rule, or promulgate a regulation that prevents the completion of such mistaken transactions. An illegitimate transaction, should it still occur, is rendered less fertile and less likely to be repeated. Affluent societies are those that have succeeded far better than the average in reducing the frequency of erring transactions.

Pathologies in public behavior must be examined closely because on the surface they provide local contradictions to the principle enunciated in the title. Fostering transactions with a negative yield will quickly eliminate a city from inter-urban competition. It is not difficult to detect a number of sick transactions, but quite a few are elusive and require identification by sophisticated investigators. Any "law" that alters the circumstances or shifts the behavior responsible for the pathology operates as a preventive measure. The proper prevention strategy resembles that of public health.

When an outcome is different from what was anticipated, an *accident* is said to have occurred. Cities with high accident rates waste scarce resources. Some people, especially women, shun them. Fire departments, inspection systems, traffic patrols, and many other agencies are organized therefore to prevent expensive accidents. The physical environment is redesigned to minimize the effects of natural catastrophes. As many as 1 per cent of all transactions may be initiated as measures to prevent loss.

Closely related to accidents and often overlapping in etiology is *illness*. It may be defined as a reduced capability of an actor to carry out transactions that were otherwise expected of him. His rate of completion goes down significantly. Prevention of illness requires control of the environment (water, housing, food, patterns of association among individuals, and so forth) that eliminates deleterious man-nature transactions.

Another category difficult to segregate from these is *crime*. A criminal appropriates material and psychic benefits to himself at the expense of the other actors. Crime prevention, if it could be achieved to a large degree with small cost, would make a city highly attractive to those mobile households that bring their assets with them. They react strongly against situations that breed violent crime, but are more tolerant on the whole of what is termed on the international scene as "intellectual offenses," such as fraud or perjury.

Behavioral traps are now known to exist. They stimulate transactions by tricking the actors about the likelihood and the character of the outcomes. "Gold fever" and other *mirages* make up a good share of this class. *Addiction* to gambling and other repetitive and nonproductive behavioral sequences add a large component. Studies of the "prisoner's dilemma" in the laboratory indicate that the "beat the opposition even if it hurts" tactic persists in transaction-poor environments, but is displaced by the cooperative "continuous small-gains" tactic when communications channels are open and used.[10] In this, as well as in the other categories, we see that a transaction-rich community is able to discover sick situations quickly and allocate some effort to rectify them. A high rate of transaction completion seems to quench much of the obsessive unproductive behavior engaged in by groups.

One class of situations produces a speed-up of transactions and stimulates innovations, but is still destructive over the long run. Feuds and other forms of *cutthroat competition* that may be enlarged to open warfare stubbornly resist restraining endeavors. Strong emotions are built up that block out the signals produced by intermediaries. A reading of the rules that apply to market behavior suggests that much has been accomplished toward inhibiting cutthroat competition and other destructive activity so long as the use of coercion is unimportant. When competing parties resort to war, they are involved in the ultimate behavioral trap—the pressure to escalate destructive transactions.

From a social-system point of view, all of these can be called *errors*. A community, to be successful, must consciously minimize errors at the same time that it attempts to maximize transactions. The first leads to the second, but usually only in the long run, so that at a given point in time each serves as an independent criterion for rule-making and environmental design.

The Search for the Space Consumer's Utopia

The moves that people made during the 1960-65 period in the United States were primarily attempts to optimize their own chances in life. They were not *pushed* by distress and poverty, but were *pulled* by opportunity.[11] This was a period when space-consuming life styles began to flourish, but were still unimportant when compared to the aggregate of all migrations. Which cities were found to be attractive and which were being abandoned? Table 2 aggregates urban population shifts brought about according to the "images of locale" maintained in the minds of strangers.[12] Los Angeles was the great gainer, despite the publicity about smog, while Pittsburgh was the most noteworthy loser. The most interesting members of the attractive group are those that offer specialized action—the near pathological emphasis upon entertainment in Las Vegas and the space technology frontier of Huntsville, Alabama.

TABLE 2

Net Migration for Metropolitan Areas of the United States: 1960–65

	Net Gain (000's)
Greater Los Angeles (Riverside to Ventura to Orange County)	865
New York (Bridgeport to Princeton)	332
San Francisco–San Jose	271
Washington (with adjoining Maryland and Virginia)	222
Miami–Palm Beach	204
Houston	139
Atlanta	106
Dallas	104
Phoenix	90
Las Vegas	85
Tampa–St. Petersburg	77
Denver	61
Philadelphia	60
Sacramento	56
Huntsville	50

	Net Loss
Pittsburgh	143
Boston–Lawrence–Haverhill–Lowell	82
Buffalo	65
Detroit	55
Milwaukee	53

Source: U. S. Census Estimates. Statistical Abstracts of the United States (1967).

Let us escape for a time from the preliminaries for accounting and illustrate these principles by applying them to the future competition among cities in an affluent society. How, for example, may a city get more than its proportionate share of the highly educated contingent and use their contributions to advantage? How might it enrich the ghetto so as to greatly reduce error frequency?

The proper ploys seem to be quite obvious, and one set has already been introduced, but they are, alas, most difficult to implement.

A metropolis can, for example, go out as much as 100 to 150 minutes in travel time from its center during rush hour and obtain some kind of leverage upon the development of high-amenity land. This distance permits an employer to locate halfway in-between and allows his employees the maximum opportunity to find the landscape that suits them best. The city is forced to behave in a devious fashion (except in Texas, where city-initiated annexation is legal) to gain this control because the respective county, town, and suburban realty-development cliques are presently in control of land development in the outer fringe areas and will use every trick they know to preserve this control. Yet somehow the amenities must be preserved and at the same time prevented from being controlled by the large estate owner. They should be allocated to the settlers who use space and natural environments as a shield to manage the stresses of the fast-acting affluent society.

The extraordinary importance of high-quality public education has already been emphasized. Due to the school-district mode of control over local school standards, the "young professionals" group must quickly dominate a school district or be limited to the aspirations of small-town people for the education of the next generation. An insistence upon school quality rather than racial segregation forces the space consumers into a low-density, single-class community that concentrates people with very similar and highly compatible values into the same neighborhood and their children into the same schools. A means of evading school-district constraints would give a metropolis competitive advantage because access to good schools could then be fitted to scattered high-amenity sites.

Education carries through in the modern metropolis to the university with a full range of graduate and professional schools. A university recognized as a "center of excellence" serves to attract top professionals and to foster innovations in technology and the arts. Metropolises that have yet to create their leading university operate under a severe handicap. A center of excellence is a tender sprout that is easily bruised by short-run attempts to save money; thus, protection by a stable urban power structure is needed to sustain it.

The metropolis must also work out a better-than-average solution to its traffic problems. In the next few decades, these seem likely to include arteries, radiating from the center, that do not congest either the center or circulation on the periphery, and greatly improve service for inter-urban trips. Calculations show that the low-density one-vehicle-to-the-adult life styles can be fitted to the present proposals for the 150-400 m.p.h. inter-center transport, although this may mean enclosing a station with high-rise parking structures as well as the introduction of radio-controlled and computer-managed integration of buses, taxis, jitneys, rented cars, and so forth. The greatest hindrance encountered here is the existence of a series of antiquated franchises that have created vested interests opposing modernization.

A final feature is that of "error minimization," a quality that is highly appreciated when the mass media headline urban riots, automobile accidents, air crashes, and crime rates. A city that gains a reputation for cleanliness and safety without being dull has little trouble attracting the people it wants. Institutions for the distribution of social and cultural opportunities must be expanded to the point where the effects of cultural deprivation begin to disappear.

The new professionals are expected to be primarily responsible for launching the new transactions-generating promotions in business, public service, and the arts. Will their predilection for spacious living reduce the contribution that is made by the next generation? Does it signify a retreat? Almost certainly not, because the new professionals seem to be opting for a pattern already popular with the most intense, high-speed actors on the urban scene—one address in the thick of things and another away from it all. The added transactions will contain a much stronger communications component than before, and electronic techniques can be employed to reduce the cost of overcoming space. The city that watches carefully how well it is doing in the generation of transactions will discover its constraints early. If these blocks are removed, the generation of surplus value—in non-monetized as well as the financial sectors—will bring in more of the ambitious, organization-building component of the younger generation.

Conclusions

The task of the urban planner is quite clear in this assessment of conditions in an era of affluence. He and his agencies are the troubleshooters removing bottlenecks in urban social process. His success is measured by the over-all growth in transactions. If the plans do not achieve this objective, opportunities diminish, population shrinks, and institutions rigidify.

Special attention must be paid to the lagging and leading sectors—the ghetto slums and the territory to be occupied by the new professionals. The former generate friction, doubt, insecurity, and therefore a reluctance to participate. The latter must accommodate a proliferation of new action-oriented life styles. The prospective urban information systems should allow a careful calculation of aggregate cultural and social consequences of alternative proposals in terms that can be compared with the economic results.

REFERENCES

1. The term "post-industrial" is used to indicate a period when intellectual institutions achieve central significance in the social structure: See Daniel Bell, "Notes on the Post-Industrial Society," *The Public Interest*, Nos. 6 & 7 (1967). A quantitative description is found in Herman Kahn and Anthony J. Wiener, *The Year 2000* (New York, 1967).

2. By now it is apparent to the few who have followed the efforts to prepare a basis for a Social Report on the State of the Nation that I am in pursuit of a "social indicator" with properties like that of gross product. Marginal analysis should be possible and trade-offs between sectors should be calculable, if compromise policies are to be found. The human-time budgets have these properties, if treated properly, but the repeated interview and the diary are techniques with low levels of sensitivity to changes in welfare. See R. L. Meier, *A Communication Theory of Urban Growth* (Cambridge, 1962); *American Behavioral Scientist* (special issue; December, 1966); John P. Robinson, "Social Change as Measured by Time Budgets," paper presented at the American Sociological Association (San Francisco; August, 1967). A review of the contents of Department of Health, Education, and Welfare's *Indicators* (monthly) and the *Trends* (yearly) revealed data of great interest to a variety of special-interest groups, but nothing (not even really suitable demographic information) for the metropolis. The recent volume *Social Indicators*, edited by Raymond A. Bauer (Cambridge, 1966), is largely programmatic, but useful in illuminating the problems of reporting social pathology. Manuscripts on social accounting by Philip M. Hauser and indicators of environmental quality by Harvey S. Perloff are available and quite helpful in providing background to the measurement problem that faces us today in planning for the metropolis. On the other hand, the earlier theoretical work on action, which provided an intellectual base for so many contemporary social scientists, is rarely helpful. Talcott Parsons and Edward A. Shils *et al.* in *Toward a General Theory of Action* (Cambridge, 1951) were concerned with general equilibrium, which is not conducive to measurements of growth, the use of synoptic data, or concepts of transaction.

3. I am guided by the body of coherent thinking regarding systematic analysis of the phenomena of life, allowing the city to be fitted into the larger framework as a special case. See, for example, James G. Miller,

The Metropolis as a Transaction-Maximizing System

"Living Systems," *Behavioral Science*, Vol. 10 (1965), pp. 193-237, 337-411.

4. The only instance in which I have seen these strategies consciously applied in a precomputer version is the locationally disadvantaged metropolis of Seattle, where the university and the leading technology-based firm collaborated, starting about 1964. Perhaps it was not all good fortune that converted the region into the fastest-paced growth area in the country as an outgrowth of successful competitive bids. Some well-formulated plans seem to have made a significant contribution.

5. Rigorous analysis of the economics for this category of social organization was first applied to the development of water resources, but has now been extended to recreation and neighborhood organizations. The arguments have been updated by A. Allen Schmidt, "Non-Market Values and Efficiency of Public Investments in Water Resources," *American Economic Review*, Vol. 56 (1967), pp. 159-68.

6. Alfred Kuhn, *The Study of Society: A Unified Approach* (Homewood, Illinois, 1963).

7. The latest word (July 1968) is that the leaders of almost all groups like the Rangers have been in jail on a murder charge, which the members claim was "framed," but most have now been freed.

8. R. L. Meier, *Megalopolis Formation in the Midwest*, Regional Planning Studies V, Department of Resources Planning and Conservation, School of Natural Resources, University of Michigan (1965).

9. See the contribution of Melvin M. Webber to this volume, where further implications of this question are explored.

10. The "prisoner's dilemma" situation has been characterized by Kenneth Boulding as the "fruit fly" of organization studies. See also A. Rapoport, *Fights, Games, and Debates* (Ann Arbor, 1961).

11. Everet S. Lee, "A Theory of Migration," *Demography*, Vol. 3 (1967), pp. 47-57.

12. An ingenious economical technique for measuring the relative attractiveness of geographic locales along with some information about the factors incorporated in these judgments is introduced by Peter Gould, "Structuring Information on Spacio-Temporal Preferences," *Journal of Regional Science*, Vol. 7 (1967), pp. 259-74. Unfortunately, however, the data he chose to treat were not representative of the mobile contingent in American population.

Part IV:

Ways Out of the Ghetto

ROBERT COLES

Like It Is in the Alley

"*In the alley it's mostly dark, even if the sun is out. But if you look around, you can find things. I know how to get into every building, except that it's like night once you're inside them, because they don't have lights. So, I stay here. You're better off. It's no good on the street. You can get hurt all the time, one way or the other. And in buildings, like I told you, it's bad in them, too. But here it's o.k. You can find your own corner, and if someone tries to move in you fight him off. We meet here all the time, and figure out what we'll do next. It might be a game, or over for some pool, or a coke or something. You need to have a place to start out from, and that's like it is in the alley; you can always know your buddy will be there, provided it's the right time. So you go there, and you're on your way, man.*"

Like all children of nine, Peter is always on his way—to a person, a place, a "thing" he wants to do. "*There's this here thing we thought we'd try tomorrow,*" he'll say; and eventually I'll find out that he means there's to be a race. He and his friends will compete with another gang to see who can wash a car faster and better. The cars belong to four youths who make their money taking bets, and selling liquor that I don't believe was ever purchased, and pushing a few of those pills that "*go classy with beer.*" I am not completely sure, but I think they also have something to do with other drugs; and again, I can't quite be sure what their connection is with a "residence" I've seen not too far from the alley Peter describes so possessively. The women come and go—from that residence and along the street Peter's alley leaves.

Peter lives in the heart of what we in contemporary America have chosen (ironically, so far as history goes) to call an "urban ghetto." The area was a slum before it became a ghetto, and there still are some very poor white people on its edges and increasing

243

numbers of Puerto Ricans in several of its blocks. Peter was not born in the ghetto, nor was his family told to go there. They are Americans and have been here *"since way back before anyone can remember."* That is the way Peter's mother talks about Alabama, about the length of time she and her ancestors have lived there. She and Peter's father came north *"for freedom."* They did not seek out a ghetto, an old quarter of Boston where they were expected to live and where they would be confined, yet at least some of the time solidly at rest, with kin, and reasonably safe.

No, they sought freedom. Americans, they moved on when the going got *"real bad,"* and Americans, they expected something better someplace, some other place. They left Alabama on impulse. They found Peter's alley by accident. And they do not fear pogroms. They are Americans, and in Peter's words: *"There's likely to be another riot here soon. That's what I heard today. You hear it a lot, but one day you know it'll happen."*

Peter's mother fears riots too—among other things. The Jews of Eastern Europe huddled together in their ghettos, afraid of the barbarians, afraid of the *Goyim*, but always sure of one thing, their God-given destiny. Peter's mother has no such faith. She believes that *"something will work out one of these days."* She believes that *"you have to keep on going, and things can get better, but don't ask me how."* She believes that *"God wants us to have a bad spell here, and so maybe it'll get better the next time—you know in Heaven, and I hope that's where we'll be going."* Peter's mother, in other words, is a pragmatist, an optimist, and a Christian. Above all she is American: *"Yes, I hear them talk about Africa, but it don't mean anything to us. All I know is Alabama and now it's in Massachusetts that we are. It was a long trip coming up here, and sometimes I wish we were back there, and sometimes I'd just as soon be here, for all that's no good about it. But I'm not going to take any more trips, no sir. And like Peter said, this is the only country we've got. If you come from a country, you come from it, and we're from it, I'd say, and there isn't much we can do but try to live as best we can. I mean, live here."*

What is "life" like for her over there, where she lives, in the neighborhood she refers to as "here"? A question like that cannot be answered by the likes of me, and even her answer provides only the beginning of a reply: *"Well, we does o.k., I guess. Peter here, he has it better than I did, or his daddy. I can say that. I tell myself that a lot. He can turn on the faucet over there, and a lot of the* time, he just gets the water, right away. And when I tell him what it was like for us, to go fetch that water—we'd walk three miles, yes sir, and we'd be lucky it wasn't ten—well, Peter, it doesn't register on him. He thinks I'm trying to fool him, and the more serious I get, the more he laughs, so I've stopped.

"Of course it's not all so good, I have to admit. We're still where we were, so far as knowing where your next meal is coming from. When I go to bed at night I tell myself I've done good, to stay alive and keep the kids alive, and if they'll just wake up in the morning, and me too, well then, we can worry about that, all the rest, come tomorrow. So there you go. We do our best, and that's all you can do."

She may sound fatalistic, but she appears to be a nervous, hard-working, even hard-driven woman—thin, short, constantly on the move. I may not know what she "really" thinks and believes, because like the rest of us she has her contradictions and her mixed feelings. I think it is fair to say that there are some things that she can't say to me—or to herself. She is a Negro, and I am white. She is poor, and I am fairly well off. She is very near to illiterate, and I put in a lot of time worrying about how to say things. But she and I are both human beings, and we both have trouble—to use that word—"communicating," not only with each other, but with ourselves. Sometimes she doesn't tell me something she really wants me to know. She has forgotten, pure and simple. More is on her mind than information I might want. And sometimes I forget too: "Remember you asked the other day about Peter, if he was ever real sick. And I told you he was a weak child, and I feared for his life, and I've lost five children, three that was born and two that wasn't. Well, I forgot to tell you that he got real sick up here, just after we came. He was three, and I didn't know what to do. You see, I didn't have my mother to help out. She always knew what to do. She could hold a child and get him to stop crying, no matter how sick he was, and no matter how much he wanted food, and we didn't have it. But she was gone—and that's when we left to come up here, and I never would have left her, not for anything in the world. But suddenly she took a seizure of something and went in a half hour, I'd say. And Peter, he was so hot and sick, I thought he had the same thing his grandmother did and he was going to die. I thought maybe she's calling him. She always liked Peter. She helped him be born, she and my cousin, they did."

Actually, Peter's mother remembers quite a lot of things. She remembers the "old days" back South, sometimes with a shudder, but sometimes with the same nostalgia that the region is famous for generating in its white exiles. She also notices a lot of things. She notices, and from time to time will remark upon, the various changes in her life. She has moved from the country to the city. Her father was a sharecropper and her son wants to be a pilot (sometimes), a policeman (sometimes), a racing-car driver (sometimes), and a baseball player (most of the time). Her husband is not alive. He died one year after they all came to Boston. He woke up vomiting in the middle of the night—vomiting blood. He bled and bled and vomited and vomited and then he died. The doctor does not have to press very hard for "the facts." Whatever is known gets spoken vividly and (still) emotionally: *"I didn't know what to do. I was beside myself. I prayed and I prayed, and in between I held his head and wiped his forehead. It was the middle of the night. I woke up my oldest girl and I told her to go knocking on the doors. But no one would answer. They must have been scared, or have suspected something bad. I thought if only he'd be able to last into the morning, then we could get some help. I was caught between things. I couldn't leave him to go get a policeman. And my girl, she was afraid to go out. And besides, there was no one outside, and I thought we'd just stay at his side, and somehow he'd be o.k., because he was a strong man, you know. His muscles, they were big all his life. Even with the blood coming up, he looked too big and strong to die, I thought. But I knew he was sick. He was real bad sick. There wasn't anything else, no sir, to do. We didn't have no phone and even if there was a car, I never could have used it. Nor my daughter. And then he took a big breath and that was his last one."*

When I first met Peter and his mother, I wanted to know how they lived, what they did with their time, what they liked to do or disliked doing, what they believed. In the back of my mind were large subjects like "the connection between a person's moods and the environment in which he lives." Once I was told I was studying "the psychology of the ghetto," and another time the subject of "urban poverty and mental health." It is hoped that at some point large issues like those submit themselves to lives; and when that is done, when particular but not unrepresentative or unusual human beings are called in witness, their concrete medical history becomes extremely revealing. I cannot think of a better way to begin knowing what life is like for Peter and his mother than to hear the following and hear it again and think about its implications: *"No sir, Peter has never been to a doctor, not unless you count the one at school, and she's a nurse I believe. He was his sickest back home before we came here, and you know there was no doctor for us in the county. In Alabama you have to pay a white doctor first, before he'll go near you. And we don't have but a few colored ones. (I've never seen a one.) There was this woman we'd go to, and she had gotten some nursing education in Mobile. (No, I don't know if she was a nurse or not, or a helper to the nurses, maybe.) Well, she would come to help us. With the convulsions, she'd show you how to hold the child, and make sure he doesn't hurt himself. They can bite their tongues real, real bad.*

"Here, I don't know what to do. There's the city hospital, but it's no good for us. I went there with my husband, no sooner than a month or so after we came up here. We waited and waited, and finally the day was almost over. We left the kids with a neighbor, and we barely knew her. I said it would take the morning, but I never thought we'd get home near suppertime. And they wanted us to come back and come back, because it was something they couldn't do all at once—though for most of the time we just sat there and did nothing. And my husband, he said his stomach was the worse for going there, and he'd take care of himself from now on, rather than go there.

"Maybe they could have saved him. But they're far away, and I didn't have money to get a cab, even if there was one around here, and I thought to myself it'll make him worse, to take him there.

"My kids, they get sick. The welfare worker, she sends a nurse here, and she tells me we should be on vitamins and the kids need all kinds of check-ups. Once she took my daughter and told her she had to have her teeth looked at, and the same with Peter. So, I went with my daughter, and they didn't see me that day, but said they could in a couple of weeks. And I had to pay the woman next door to mind the little ones, and there was the carfare, and we sat and sat, like before. So, I figured, it would take more than we've got to see that dentist. And when the nurse told us we'd have to come back a few times—that's how many, a few—I thought that no one ever looked at my teeth, and they're not good, I'll admit, but you can't have everything, that's what I say, and that's what my kids have to know, I guess."

What *does* she have? And what belongs to Peter? For one

thing, there is the apartment, three rooms for six people, a mother and five children. Peter is a middle child with two older girls on one side and a younger sister and still younger brother on the other side. The smallest child was born in Boston: *"It's the only time I ever spent time in a hospital. He's the only one to be born there. My neighbor got the police. I was in the hall, crying I guess. We almost didn't make it. They told me I had bad blood pressure, and I should have been on pills, and I should come back, but I didn't. It was the worst time I've ever had, because I was alone. My husband had to stay with the kids, and no one was there to visit me."*

Peter sleeps with his brother in one bedroom. The three girls sleep in the living room, which is a bedroom. And, of course, there is a small kitchen. There is not very much furniture about. The kitchen has a table with four chairs, only two of which are sturdy. The girls sleep in one big bed. Peter shares his bed with his brother. The mother sleeps on a couch. There is one more chair and a table in the living room. Jesus looks down from the living room wall, and an undertaker's calendar hangs on the kitchen wall. The apartment has no books, no records. There is a television set in the living room, and I have never seen it off.

Peter in many respects is his father's successor. His mother talks things over with him. She even defers to him at times. She will say something; he will disagree; she will nod and let him have the last word. He knows the city. She still feels a stranger to the city. *"If you want to know about anything around here, just ask Peter,"* she once said to me. That was three years ago, when Peter was six. Peter continues to do very poorly at school, but I find him a very good teacher. He notices a lot, makes a lot of sense when he talks, and has a shrewd eye for the ironic detail. He is very intelligent, for all the trouble he gives his teachers. He recently summed up a lot of American history for me: *"I wasn't made for that school, and that school wasn't made for me."* It is an old school, filled with memories. The name of the school evokes Boston's Puritan past. Pictures and statues adorn the corridors—reminders of the soldiers and statesmen and writers who made New England so influential in the nineteenth century. And naturally one finds slogans on the walls, about freedom and democracy and the rights of the people. Peter can be surly and cynical when he points all that out to the visitor. If he is asked what kind of school he would *like*, he laughs incredulously. *"Are you kidding?*

No school would be my first choice. They should leave us alone, and let us help out at home, and maybe let some of our own people teach us. The other day the teacher admitted she was no good. She said maybe a Negro should come in and give us the discipline, because she was scared. She said all she wanted from us was that we keep quiet and stop wearing her nerves down, and she'd be grateful, because she would retire soon. She said we were becoming too much for her, and she didn't understand why. But when one kid wanted to say something, tell her why, she told us to keep still, and write something. You know what? She whipped out a book and told us to copy a whole page from it, so we'd learn it. A stupid waste of time. I didn't even try; and she didn't care. She just wanted an excuse not to talk with us. They're all alike."

Actually, they're all *not* alike, and Peter knows it. He has met up with two fine teachers, and in mellow moments he can say so: *"They're trying hard, but me and my friends, I don't think we're cut out for school. To tell the truth, that's what I think. My mother says we should try, anyway, but it doesn't seem to help, trying. The teacher can't understand a lot of us, but he does all these new things, and you can see he's excited. Some kids are really with him, and I am, too. But I can't take all his stuff very serious. He's a nice man, and he says he wants to come and visit every one of our homes; but my mother says no, she wouldn't know what to do with him, when he came here. We'd just stand and have nothing to talk about. So she said tell him not to come; and I don't think he will, anyway. I think he's getting to know."*

What is that teacher getting to know? What *is* there to know about Peter and all the others like him in our American cities? Of course Peter and his friends who play in the alley need better schools, schools they can feel to be theirs, and better teachers, like the ones they *have* in fact met on occasion. But I do not feel that a reasonably good teacher in the finest school building in America would reach and affect Peter in quite the way, I suppose, people like me would expect and desire. At nine Peter is both young and quite old. At nine he is much wiser about many things than my sons will be at nine, and maybe nineteen. Peter has in fact taught me a lot about his neighborhood, about life on the streets, about survival: *"I get up when I get up, no special time. My mother has Alabama in her. She gets up with the sun, and she wants to go to bed when it gets dark. I try to tell her that up here things just get started in the night. But she gets mad. She wakes me up. If it weren't for her shaking me, I might sleep until noon. Sometimes we have a good breakfast, when the check comes. Later on, though,* before *it comes, it might just be some coffee and a slice of bread. She worries about food. She says we should eat what she gives us, but sometimes I'd rather go hungry. I was sick a long time ago, my stomach or something—maybe like my father, she says. So I don't like all the potatoes she pushes on us and cereal, all the time cereal. We're supposed to be lucky, because we get some food every day. Down South they can't be sure. That's what she says, and I guess she's right.*

"Then I go to school. I eat what I can, and leave. I have two changes of clothes, one for everyday and one for Sunday. I wait on my friend Billy, and we're off by 8:15. He's from around here, and he's a year older. He knows everything. He can tell you if a woman is high on some stuff, or if she's been drinking, or she's off her mind about something. He knows. His brother has a convertible, a Buick. He pays off the police, but Billy won't say no more than that.

"In school we waste time until it's over. I do what I have to. I don't like the place. I feel like falling off all day, just putting my head down and saying good-bye to everyone until three. We're out then, and we sure wake up. I don't have to stop home first, not now. I go with Billy. We'll be in the alley, or we'll go to see them play pool. Then you know when it's time to go home. You hear someone say six o'clock, and you go in. I eat and I watch television. It must be around ten or eleven I'm in bed."

Peter sees rats all the time. He has been bitten by them. He has a big stick by his bed to use against them. They also claim the alley, even in the daytime. They are not large enough to be compared with cats, as some observers have insisted; they are simply large, confident, well-fed, unafraid rats. The garbage is theirs; the land is theirs; the tenement is theirs; human flesh is theirs. When I first started visiting Peter's family, I wondered why they didn't do something to rid themselves of those rats, and the cockroaches, and the mosquitoes, and the flies, and the maggots, and the ants, and especially the garbage in the alley which attracts so much of all that "lower life." Eventually I began to see some of the reasons why. A large apartment building with many families has exactly two barrels in its basement. The halls of the building go unlighted. Many windows have no screens, and some windows are broken and boarded up. The stairs are dangerous;

some of them have missing timber. ("*We just jump over them,*" says Peter cheerfully.) And the landowner is no one in particular. Rent is collected by an agent, in the name of a "realty trust." Somewhere in City Hall there is a bureaucrat who unquestionably might be persuaded to prod someone in the "trust"; and one day I went with three of the tenants, including Peter's mother, to try that "approach." We waited and waited at City Hall. (I drove us there, clear across town, naturally.) Finally we met up with a man, a not very encouraging or inspiring or generous or friendly man. He told us we would have to try yet another department and swear out a complaint; and that the "case" would have to be "studied," and that we would then be "notified of a decision." We went to the department down the hall, and waited some more, another hour and ten minutes. By then it was three o'clock, and the mothers wanted to go home. They weren't thinking of rats anymore, or poorly heated apartments, or garbage that had nowhere to go and often went uncollected for two weeks, not one. They were thinking of their children, who would be home from school and, in the case of two women, their husbands who would also soon be home. "*Maybe we should come back some other day,*" Peter's mother said. I noted she didn't say *tomorrow,* and I realized that I had read someplace that people like her aren't precisely "future-oriented."

Actually, both Peter and his mother have a very clear idea of what is ahead. For the mother it is "*more of the same.*" One evening she was tired but unusually talkative, perhaps because a daughter of hers was sick: "*I'm glad to be speaking about all these things tonight. My little girl has a bad fever. I've been trying to cool her off all day. Maybe if there was a place near here, that we could go to, maybe I would have gone. But like it is, I have to do the best I can and pray she'll be o.k.*"

I asked whether she thought her children would find things different, and that's when she said it would be "*more of the same*" for them. Then she added a long afterthought: "*Maybe it'll be a little better for them. A mother has to have hope for her children, I guess. But I'm not too sure, I'll admit. Up here you know there's a lot more jobs around than in Alabama. We don't get them, but you know they're someplace near, and they tell you that if you go train for them, then you'll be eligible. So maybe Peter might someday have some real good steady work, and that would be something, yes sir it would. I keep telling him he should pay more* attention to school, and put more of himself into the lessons they give there. But he says no, it's no good; it's a waste of time; they don't care what happens there, only if the kids don't keep quiet and mind themselves. Well, Peter has got to learn to mind himself, and not be fresh. He speaks back to me, these days. There'll be a time he won't even speak to me at all, I suppose. I used to blame it all on the city up here, city living. Back home we were always together, and there wasn't no place you could go, unless to Birmingham, and you couldn't do much for yourself there, we all knew. Of course, my momma, she knew how to make us behave. But I was thinking the other night, it wasn't so good back there either. Colored people, they'd beat on one another, and we had lot of people that liquor was eating away at them; they'd use wine by the gallon. All they'd do was work on the land, and then go back and kill themselves with wine. And then there'd be the next day—until they'd one evening go to sleep and never wake up. And we'd get the Bossman and he'd see to it they got buried.

"Up here I think it's better, but don't ask me to tell you why. There's the welfare, that's for sure. And we get our water and if there isn't good heat, at least there's some. Yes, it's cold up here, but we had cold down there, too, only then we didn't have any heat, and we'd just die, some of us would, every winter with one of those freezing spells.

"And I do believe things are changing. On the television they talk to you, the colored man and all the others who aren't doing so good. My boy Peter, he says they're putting you on. That's all he sees, people 'putting on' other people. But I think they all mean it, the white people. I never see them, except on television, when they say the white man wants good for the colored people. I think Peter could go and do better for himself later on, when he gets older, except for the fact that he just doesn't believe. He don't believe what they say, the teacher, or the man who says it's getting better for us—on television. I guess it's my fault. I never taught my children, any of them, to believe that kind of thing; because I never thought we'd ever have it any different, not in this life. So maybe I've failed Peter. I told him the other day, he should work hard, because of all the 'opportunity' they say is coming for us, and he said I was talking good, but where was my proof. So I went next door with him, to my neighbor's, and we asked her husband, and you know he sided with Peter. He said they were taking in a few here and a few there, and putting them in the *front windows of all the big companies, but that all you have to do is look around at our block and you'd see all the young men, and they just haven't got a thing to do. Nothing."*

Her son also looks to the future. Sometimes he talks—in his own words—"big." He'll one day be a bombadier or "*something like that.*" At other times he is less sure of things: "*I don't know what I'll be. Maybe nothing. I see the men sitting around, hiding from the welfare lady. They fool her. Maybe I'll fool her, too. I don't know what you can do. The teacher the other day said that if just one of us turned out o.k. she'd congratulate herself and call herself lucky."*

A while back a riot excited Peter and his mother, excited them and frightened them. The spectacle of the police being fought, of white-owned property being assaulted, stirred the boy a great deal: "*I figured the whole world might get changed around. I figured people would treat us better from now on. Only I don't think they will.*" As for his mother, she was less hopeful, but even more apocalyptic: "*I told Peter we were going to pay for this good. I told him they wouldn't let us get away with it, not later on.*" And in the midst of the trouble she was frightened as she had never before been: "*I saw them running around on the streets, the men and women, and they were talking about burning things down, and how there'd be nothing left when they got through. I sat there with my children and I thought we might die the way things are going, die right here. I didn't know what to do: if I should leave, in case they burn down the building, or if I should stay, so that the police don't arrest us, or we get mixed up with the crowd of people. I've never seen so many people, going in so many different directions. They were running and shouting and they didn't know what to do. They were so excited. My neighbor, she said they'd burn us all up, and then the white man would have himself one less of a headache. The colored man is a worse enemy to himself than the white. I mean, it's hard to know which is the worst."*

I find it as hard as she does to sort things out. When I think of her and the mothers like her I have worked with for years, when I think of Peter and his friends, I find myself caught between the contradictory observations I have made. Peter already seems a grim and unhappy child. He trusts no one white, not his white teacher, not the white policeman he sees, not the white welfare worker, not the white storekeeper, and not, I might add, me. There we are, the five of us from the 180,000,000 Americans who surround him and of course 20,000,000 others. Yet, Peter doesn't really trust his friends and neighbors, either. At nine he has learned to be careful, wary, guarded, doubtful, and calculating. His teacher may not know it, but Peter is a good sociologist, and a good political scientist, a good student of urban affairs. With devastating accuracy he can reveal how much of the "score" he knows; yes, and how fearful and sad and angry he is: *"This here city isn't for us. It's for the people downtown. We're here because, like my mother said, we had to come. If they could lock us up or sweep us away, they would. That's why I figure the only way you can stay ahead is get some kind of deal for yourself. If I had a choice I'd live someplace else, but I don't know where. It would be a place where they treated you right, and they didn't think you were some nuisance. But the only thing you can do is be careful of yourself; if not, you'll get killed somehow, like it happened to my father."*

His father died prematurely, and most probably, unnecessarily. Among the poor of our cities the grim medical statistics we all know about become terrible daily experiences. Among the black and white families I work with—in nearby but separate slums— disease and the pain that goes with it are taken for granted. When my children complain of an earache or demonstrate a skin rash I rush them to the doctor. When I have a headache, I take an aspirin; and if the headache is persistent, I can always get a medical check-up. Not so with Peter's mother and Peter; they have learned to live with sores and infections and poorly mended fractures and bad teeth and eyes that need but don't have the help of glasses. Yes, they can go to a city hospital and get free care; but again and again they don't. They come to the city without any previous experience as patients. They have never had the money to purchase a doctor's time. They have never had free medical care available. (I am speaking now of Appalachian whites as well as southern blacks.) It may comfort me to know that every American city provides some free medical services for its "indigent," but Peter's mother and thousands like her have quite a different view of things: *"I said to you the other time, I've tried there. It's like at City Hall, you wait and wait, and they pushes you and shove you and call your name, only to tell you to wait some more, and if you tell them you can't stay there all day, they'll say 'lady, go home, then.' You get sick just trying to get there. You have to give your children over to people or take them all with you; and the carfare is expensive. Why if we had a doctor around here, I could almost pay him with the carfare it takes to get there and back for all of us. And you know, they keep on having you come back and back, and they don't know what each other says. Each time they starts from scratch."*

It so happens that recently I took Peter to a children's hospital and arranged for a series of evaluations which led to the following: a pair of glasses; a prolonged bout of dental work; antibiotic treatment for skin lesions; a thorough cardiac work-up, with the subsequent diagnosis of rheumatic heart disease; a conference between Peter's mother and a nutritionist, because the boy has been on a high-starch, low-protein, and low-vitamin diet all his life. He suffers from one attack of sinus trouble after another, from a succession of sore throats and earaches, from cold upon cold, even in the summer. A running nose is unsurprising to him— and so is chest pain and shortness of breath, due to a heart ailment, we now know.

At the same time Peter is tough. I have to emphasize again *how* tough and, yes, how "politic, cautious and meticulous," not in Prufrock's way, but in another way and for other reasons. Peter has learned to be wary as well as angry; tentative as well as extravagant; at times controlled and only under certain circumstances defiant: *"Most of the time, I think you have to watch your step. That's what I think. That's the difference between up here and down in the South. That's what my mother says, and she's right. I don't remember it down there, but I know she must be right. Here, you measure the next guy first and then make your move when you think it's a good time to."*

He was talking about *"how you get along"* when you leave school and go *"mix with the guys"* and start *"getting your deal."* He was telling me what an outrageous and unsafe world he has inherited and how very carefully he has made his appraisal of the future. Were I afflicted with some of his physical complaints, I would be fretful, annoyed, petulant, angry—and moved to do something, see someone, get a remedy, a pill, a promise of help. He has made his "adjustment" to the body's pain, and he has also learned to contend with the alley and the neighborhood and us, the world beyond: *"The cops come by here all the time. They drive up and down the street. They want to make sure everything is o.k. to look at. They don't bother you, so long as you don't get in their way."*

So, it is live and let live—except that families like Peter's have a tough time living, and of late have been troubling those cops, among others. Our cities have become not only battlegrounds, but places where all sorts of American problems and historical ironies have converged. Ailing, poorly fed, and proud Appalachian families have reluctantly left the hollows of eastern Kentucky and West Virginia for Chicago and Dayton and Cincinnati and Cleveland and Detroit, and even, I have found, Boston. They stick close together in all-white neighborhoods—or enclaves or sections or slums or ghettos or whatever. They wish to go home but can't, unless they are willing to be idle and hungry all the time. They confuse social workers and public officials of all kinds because they both want and reject the city. Black families also have sought out cities and learned to feel frightened and disappointed.

I am a physician, and over the past ten years I have been asking myself how people like Peter and his mother survive in mind and body and spirit. And I have wanted to know what a twentieth-century American city "means" to them or "does" to them. People cannot be handed questionnaires and asked to answer such questions. They cannot be "interviewed" a few times and told to come across with a statement, a reply. But inside Peter and his brother and his sisters and his mother, and inside a number of Appalachian mothers and fathers and children I know, are feelings and thoughts and ideas—which, in my experience, come out casually or suddenly, by accident almost. After a year or two of talking, after experiences such as I have briefly described in a city hall, in a children's hospital, a lifetime of pent-up tensions and observation comes to blunt expression: *"Down in Alabama we had to be careful about ourselves with the white man, but we had plenty of things we could do by ourselves. There was our side of town, and you could walk and run all over, and we had a garden you know. Up here they have you in a cage. There's no place to go, and all I do is stay in the building all day long and the night, too. I don't use my legs no more, hardly at all. I never see those trees, and my oldest girl, she misses planting time. It was bad down there. We had to leave. But it's no good here, too, I'll tell you. Once I woke up and I thought all the buildings on the block were falling down on me. And I was trying to climb out, but I couldn't. And then the next thing I knew, we were all back South, and I was standing near some sunflowers—you know, the tall ones that can shade you if you sit down.*

"*No, I don't dream much. I fall into a heavy sleep as soon as I touch the bed. The next thing I know I'm stirring myself to start in all over in the morning. It used to be the sun would wake me up, but now it's up in my head, I guess. I know I've got to get the house going and off to school.*"

Her wistful, conscientious, law-abiding, devoutly Christian spirit hasn't completely escaped the notice of Peter, for all his hard-headed, cynical protestations: "*If I had a chance, I'd like to get enough money to bring us all back to Alabama for a visit. Then I could prove it that it may be good down there, a little bit, even if it's no good, either. Like she says, we had to get out of there or we'd be dead by now. I hear say we all may get killed soon, it's so bad here; but I think we did right to get up here, and if we make them listen to us, the white man, maybe he will.*"

To which Peter's mother adds: "*We've carried a lot of trouble in us, from way back in the beginning. I have these pains, and so does everyone around here. But you can't just die until you're ready to. And I do believe something is happening. I do believe I see that.*"

To which Peter adds: "*Maybe it won't be that we'll win, but if we get killed, everyone will hear about it. Like the minister said, before we used to die real quiet, and no one stopped to pay notice.*"

Two years before Peter spoke those words he drew a picture for me, one of many he has done. When he was younger, and when I didn't know him so well as I think I do now, it was easier for us to have something tangible to do and then talk about. I used to visit the alley with him, as I still do, and one day I asked him to draw the alley. That was a good idea, he thought. (Not all of my suggestions were, however.) He started in, then stopped, and finally worked rather longer and harder than usual at the job. I busied myself with my own sketches, which from the start he insisted I do. Suddenly from across the table I heard him say he was through. Ordinarily he would slowly turn the drawing around for me to see; and I would get up and walk over to his side of the table, to see even better. But he didn't move his paper, and I didn't move myself. I saw what he had drawn, and he saw me looking. I was surprised and a bit stunned and more than a bit upset, and surely he saw my face and heard my utter silence. Often I would break the awkward moments when neither of us seemed to have anything to say, but this time it was his turn to do so: "*You know

257

what it is?" He knew that I liked us to talk about our work. I said no, I didn't—though in fact the vivid power of his black crayon had come right across to me. *"It's that hole we dug in the alley. I made it bigger here. If you fall into it, you can't get out. You die."*

He had drawn circles within circles, all of them black, and then a center, also black. He had imposed an X on the center. Nearby, strewn across the circles, were fragments of the human body—two faces, an arm, five legs. And after I had taken the scene in, I could only think to myself that I had been shown *"like it is in the alley"*—by an intelligent boy who knew what he saw around him, could give it expression, and, I am convinced, would respond to a different city, a city that is alive and breathing, one that is not for many of its citizens a virtual morgue.

ANTHONY DOWNS

Alternative Futures for the American Ghetto

IN THE past few years, the so-called "ghetto" areas of large American cities have emerged as one of the major focal points of national and local concern. Yet there have been very few attempts to develop a comprehensive, long-run strategy for dealing with the complex forces that have created our explosive ghetto problems.

Historically, the word "ghetto" meant an area in which a certain identifiable group was compelled to live. The word retains this meaning of geographic constraint, but now refers to two different kinds of constraining forces. In its *racial* sense, a ghetto is an area to which members of an ethnic minority, particularly Negroes, are residentially restricted by social, economic, and physical pressures from the rest of society. In this meaning, a ghetto can contain wealthy and middle-income residents as well as poor ones. In its *economic* sense, a ghetto is an area in which poor people are compelled to live because they cannot afford better accommodations. In this meaning, a ghetto contains mainly poor people, regardless of race or color.

Considerable confusion arises from failure to distinguish clearly between these different meanings of the word "ghetto." In the remainder of this analysis, I will use the word in its racial sense unless otherwise noted.[1]

The Population of Ghettos

In March 1966, there were 12.5 million nonwhites living in all U.S. central cities, of whom 12.1 million were Negroes. Since the Negroes were highly segregated residentially, this number serves as a good estimate of the 1966 ghetto population in the racial sense. Approximately 39 per cent of these racial ghetto residents had incomes below the "poverty level" (the equivalent of $3,300 per year for a four-person household), based upon data for 1964 (the latest available).[2]

On the other hand, in 1964 the total number of persons with incomes below the "poverty level" in all U.S. central cities was about 10.1 million. Approximately 56 per cent of these persons were white and 44 per cent were nonwhite.[3] Since there were about 11.3 million nonwhites altogether in central cities in 1964, the ghetto in its purely economic sense contained about 11 per cent fewer people than in its racial sense. Moreover, about 4.4 million persons were doubly ghetto residents in 1964—they were central-city citizens who were both poor and nonwhite.[4]

No matter which ghetto definition is used, it is clear that the population of ghettos is a small fraction of total U.S. population— less than 7 per cent. Moreover, future growth in the ghetto population will be dwarfed by future growth in the suburbs of metropolitan areas, which are predominantly white. From 1960 through 1980, those suburbs will gain about 40.9 million persons.[5] Thus the *growth* of suburban population in this period will be almost twice as large as the *total size* of all U.S. ghettos by 1980.

Any policies designed to cope with the ghetto must recognize that the concentrations of Negro population in our central cities are growing rapidly. In 1950, there were 6.5 million Negroes in central cities. In 1960, there were 9.7 million. This represents an increase of 49.2 per cent, or an average of 320,000 persons per year. In the same decade, the white population of central cities went from 45.5 million to 47.7 million, an increase of 2.2 million, or 4.8 per cent. However, in the largest central cities, the white population actually declined while the Negro population rose sharply.[6]

Since 1960, the growth of nonwhite population in central cities has continued unabated. White population growth in all those cities taken together has, however, ceased entirely. In 1966 the total Negro population of all central cities was about 12.1 million. This is a gain of 2.4 million since 1960, or about 400,000 persons per year. Thus the *absolute* rate of growth of ghettos per year has gone up to its highest level in history. In contrast, the white population of central cities in 1965 was 46.4 million, or 1.3 million *less* than in 1960. So for all 224 central cities considered as a whole, all population growth now consists of gains in Negro population.[7]

Moreover, nearly all Negro population growth is now occurring in ghettos, rather than in suburbs or rural areas. From 1960 to 1966,

Alternative Futures for the American Ghetto

89 per cent of all nonwhite population growth was in central cities, and 11 per cent was in suburbs. Nonmetropolitan areas (including the rural South) actually *lost* nonwhite population. This indicates that heavy out-migration from rural areas to cities is still going on.[8]

Future Ghetto Growth If Present Policies Continue

All evidence points to the conclusion that future nonwhite population growth will continue to be concentrated in central cities unless major changes in public policies are made. Not one single significant program of any federal, state, or local government is aimed at altering this tendency or is likely to have the unintended effect of doing so.[9] Moreover, although nonwhite fertility rates have declined since 1957 along with white fertility rates, ghetto growth is likely to remain rapid because of continued in-migration, as well as natural increase.

Recent estimates made by the National Advisory Commission on Civil Disorders indicate that the central-city Negro population for the whole U.S. will be about 13.6 million in 1970 and could rise to as high as 20.3 million by 1985. These estimates assume continued nonwhite in-migration at about the same rate as prevailed from 1960 to 1966. But even if net in-migration is reduced to zero, the 1985 central-city Negro population would be about 17.3 million.[10]

Within individual cities, rapid expansion of segregated ghetto areas will undoubtedly continue. Our 1967 field surveys in Chicago show that about 2.9 city blocks *per week* are shifting from predominantly white to nonwhite occupancy, mainly on the edge of already nonwhite areas. This is somewhat lower than the 3.5 blocks-per-week average from 1960 to 1966, but above the average of 2.6 from 1950 to 1960.[11] If such "peripheral spread" of central-city ghettos continues at nearly the same rate—and there is no present reason to believe it will not—then a number of major central cities will become over 50 per cent Negro in total population by 1985. These cities include Chicago, Philadelphia, St. Louis, Detroit, Cleveland, Oakland, Baltimore, New Orleans, Richmond, and Jacksonville. Washington, D.C., Newark, and Gary are already over 50 per cent Negro. The proportion of nonwhites in the public school systems in most of these cities now exceeds 50 per cent. It will probably be approaching 90 per cent by 1983—unless major changes in school programs and districting are adopted before then.[12]

This future growth has critical implications for a great many policy objectives connected with ghettos. For example, it has been suggested that school district boundaries within central cities should be manipulated so as to counteract *de facto* segregation by creating districts in which many Negroes and many whites will jointly reside. This solution is practical over the long run only when there is reasonable stability in the total size of these two groups. But when one group is rapidly expanding in a city where there is no vacant land to build additional housing, then the other group must contract. The only alternative is sharp rises in density which are not occurring. Therefore, as the Negro population expands in such cities, the white population inevitably falls. So possibilities for ending *de facto* segregation in this manner inexorably shrink as time passes. For this and other reasons, no policy toward ghettos can afford to ignore this rapid expansion of the Negro population.

The Complexity of the Ghetto Population and Ghetto Problems

To be accurate, every analysis of ghettos and their problems must avoid two tempting oversimplifications. The first is conceiving of the ghetto population as a single homogeneous group, all of whose members have similar characteristics, attitudes, and desires. Thus, because many ghetto residents are unemployed or "underemployed" in low-paying, transient jobs, it is easy—but false— to think of all ghetto households as plagued by unemployment. Similarly, because some ghetto residents have carried out riots and looting, whites frequently talk as though *all* ghetto dwellers hate whites, are prone to violence, or are likely to behave irresponsibly. Yet all careful studies of recent riots show that only a small minority of ghetto residents participated in any way, a majority disapprove of such activity, and most would like to have more contact with whites and more integration.[13]

In reality, each racial ghetto contains a tremendous variety of persons who exhibit widely differing attitudes toward almost every question. Many are very poor, but just as many are not. Many have radical views—especially young people; many others are quite conservative—especially the older people. Many are "on welfare," but many more are steadily employed.

262

This diversity means that public policy concerning any given ghetto problem cannot be successful if it is aimed at or based upon the attitudes and desires of only one group of persons affected by that problem. For example, take unemployment. Programs providing job training for young people could, if expanded enough, affect a large proportion of ghetto dwellers. But the inability of many adult ghetto men to obtain and keep steady, well-paying jobs is also a critical ghetto problem.[14] Also, many women with children cannot work because no adequate day-care facilities are available. Thus, public policy concerning every ghetto problem must have many complex facets in order to work well.

A second widely prevalent oversimplification of ghetto problems is concentration of remedial action upon a single substandard condition. For instance, improving the deplorable housing conditions in many slums would not in itself eliminate most of the de-humanizing forces which operate there. In fact, no single category of programs can possibly be adequate to cope with the tangled problems that exist in ghettos. Any effective ghetto-improvement strategy must concern itself with at least jobs and employment, education, housing, health, personal safety, crime prevention, and income maintenance for dependent persons. A number of other programs could be added, but I believe these are the most critical.[15]

The Location of New Jobs

Most new employment opportunities are being created in the suburban portions of our metropolitan areas, not anywhere near central-city ghettos.[16] Furthermore, this trend is likely to continue indefinitely into the future. It is true that downtown office-space concentrations in a few large cities have created additional jobs near ghettos. But the out-flow of manufacturing and retailing jobs has normally offset this addition significantly—and in many cases has caused a net loss of jobs in central cities.

If we are going to provide jobs for the rapidly expanding ghetto population, particularly jobs that do not call for high levels of skills, we must somehow bring these potential workers closer to the locations of new employment opportunities. This can be done in three ways: by moving job locations so new jobs are created in the ghetto, by moving ghetto residents so they live nearer the new jobs, or by creating better transportation between the ghetto

263

and the locations of new jobs. The first alternative—creating new jobs in the ghetto—will not occur in the future under normal free-market conditions, in my opinion.

That nearly all *new* job opportunities will be located in suburbs does not mean that central cities cannot provide *any* employment to their Negro residents. There are still millions of jobs located in central cities. Just the turnover in workers regarding those jobs will open up a great many potential positions for Negro central-city residents in the future—if employers and other workers cease racial discrimination in their hiring and promotion practices. Nevertheless, as the total number of Negro central-city job-seekers steadily rises, the need to link them with emerging sources of new employment in the suburbs will become more and more urgent as a means of reducing unemployment in Negro neighborhoods.

Recently, a number of proposals have been advanced to create public subsidies or guaranteed profits encouraging free enterprise to locate new jobs in ghettos.[17] It is possible that they might work to some extent if the promised profits are high enough to offset the risks and disadvantages involved. Any ghetto improvement strategy must, however, face the problem of linking up persons who need employment with those firms which can provide it or those public agencies assigned to create it.

The Future "Cost Squeeze" on Local Governments

Traditionally, individual productivity has risen faster in the manufacturing, mining, construction, and agricultural sectors of our economy than in sectors where personal services are dominant —such as finance, insurance, and real estate; retailing; services; and government. The ability to employ larger amounts of capital per worker, coupled with technological change, has caused much larger increases in hourly output-per-worker in the former sectors than in the latter.

All sectors compete with one another for talent and personnel, and all use many of the same products as basic inputs. This means that wages and salaries in the service-dominated sectors must generally keep up with those in the capital-dominated sectors. This tends to place a "squeeze" on the cost of those activities for which individual productivity is hard to increase.

A recent analysis of the performing arts by economists William

Baumol and William Bowen highlighted this type of "cost squeeze" as the major reason why it is so difficult to sustain theaters, opera, symphonies, and ballet companies on a self-supporting basis.[18] A pianist cannot perform Chopin's Minute Waltz in 30 seconds, or spend half as much time learning how to play it, to improve efficiency. Yet his salary and the salaries of all the electricians, accompanists, administrators, and others needed for the performing arts are constantly raised to keep their living standards comparable with those of people in the sectors where wage gains can be offset by productivity increases.

Baumol has argued that a similar "cost squeeze" is one of the reasons why state and local expenditures have risen so fast in the postwar period. They increased 257 per cent from 1950 to 1966, as compared to 159 per cent for Gross National Product and 206 per cent for federal expenditures.[19] Moreover, Baumol believes that this pressure to increase service-oriented wages and salaries faster than real output-per-man-hour in the service-oriented sectors will generate an even bigger "explosion" of local and state government costs in the future. For one thing, a higher fraction of society is now and will be employed in public activities than ever before. So there is a steady increase in the proportion of persons whose compensation tends to rise faster than their real output. This reflects both rapid automation in non-service-oriented sectors and an increasing shift of consumer demand toward such services as education, entertainment, and government activities of all types.

The resulting upward pressure on local and state government costs—and tax needs—will undoubtedly be offset to some extent by two forces. The first is greater automation of services themselves through use of computers, closed-circuit TV, duplicating machines, and other devices. The second is the partial substitution of semiskilled and low-skilled assistants for highly-skilled professionals. For example, teachers' aids could relieve professional teachers of immense amounts of administration and paperwork, thereby freeing the latter for more effective use of their time.

Nevertheless, the huge future growth of suburban population will almost certainly force a continuance of the trend toward rising local and state taxes that has now gone on for twenty years. Similar upward pressure on revenue needs will be felt even more strongly by central-city governments. Center cities will contain ever higher proportions of low-income residents who need more services per capita than wealthier suburbanites.

This future "cost squeeze" is important to our analysis because of its impact upon the willingness of suburban taxpayers to help finance any large-scale programs aimed at improving ghetto conditions. Such programs would almost certainly require significant income redistribution from the relatively wealthy suburban population to the relatively poor central-city population. Yet suburbanites will be experiencing steadily rising local and state tax burdens to pay for the services they need themselves.

The "Law of Dominance"

The achievement of stable racial integration of both whites and nonwhites in housing or public schools is a rare phenomenon in large American cities. Contrary to the views of many, this is *not* because whites are unwilling to share schools or residential neighborhoods with nonwhites. A vast majority of whites of all income groups would be willing to send their children to integrated schools or live in integrated neighborhoods, *as long as they were sure that the white group concerned would remain in the majority* in those facilities or areas.

The residential and educational objectives of these whites are not dependent upon their maintaining any kind of "ethnic purity" in their neighborhoods or schools. Rather, those objectives depend upon their maintaining a certain degree of "cultural dominance" therein.[20] These whites—like most other middle-class citizens of any race—want to be sure that the social, cultural, and economic milieu and values of their own group dominate their own residential environment and the educational environment of their children. This desire in turn springs from the typical middle-class belief of all racial groups that everyday life should be primarily a *value-reinforcing* experience for both adults and children, rather than primarily a *value-altering* one. The best way to insure that this will happen is to isolate somewhat oneself and one's children in an everyday environment dominated by—but not necessarily exclusively comprised of—other families and children whose social, economic, cultural, and even religious views and attitudes are approximately the same as one's own.

There is no intrinsic reason why race or color should be perceived as a factor relevant to attaining such relative homogeneity. Clearly, race and color have no necessary linkage with the kinds of social, cultural, economic, or religious characteristics and values that can have a true functional impact upon adults and children. Yet I believe a majority of middle-class white Americans still perceive race and color as relevant factors in their assessment of the kind of homogeneity they seek to attain. Moreover, this false perception is reinforced by their lack of everyday experience and contact with Negroes who are, in fact, like them in all important respects. Therefore, in deciding whether a given neighborhood or a given school exhibits the kind of environment in which "their own" traits are and will remain dominant, they consider Negroes as members of "another" group.

It is true that some people want themselves and their children to be immersed in a wide variety of viewpoints, values, and types of people, rather than a relatively homogeneous group.[21] This desire is particularly strong among the intellectuals who dominate the urban planning profession. They are also the strongest supporters of big-city life and the most vitriolic critics of suburbia. Yet I believe their viewpoint—though dominant in recent public discussions of urban problems—is actually shared by only a tiny minority of Americans of any racial group. Almost everyone favors at least some exposure to a wide variety of viewpoints. But experience in our own society and most others shows that the overwhelming majority of middle-class families choose residential locations and schools precisely in order to provide the kind of value-reinforcing experience described above. This is why most Jews live in predominantly Jewish neighborhoods, even in suburbs; why Catholic parents continue to support separate school systems; and partly why so few middle-class Negro families have been willing to risk moving to all-white suburbs even where there is almost no threat of any harassment.

However demeaning this phenomenon may be to Negroes, it must be recognized if we are to understand why residential segregation has persisted so strongly in the United States, and what conditions are necessary to create viable racial integration. The expansion of nonwhite residential areas has led to "massive transition" from white to nonwhite occupancy mainly because there has been no mechanism that could assure the whites in any given area that they would remain in the majority after nonwhites once began entering. Normal population turnover causes about 20 per cent of the residents of the average U.S. neighborhood to move out every year because of income changes, job transfers, shifts in life-cycle position, or deaths. In order for a neighborhood to retain any given character, the persons who move in to occupy the resulting vacancies must be similar to those who have departed.

But once Negroes begin entering an all-white neighborhood near the ghetto, most other white families become convinced that the area will eventually become all Negro, mainly because this has happened so often before. Hence it is difficult to persuade whites not now living there to move in and occupy vacancies. They are only willing to move into neighborhoods where whites are now the dominant majority and seem likely to remain so. Hence the whites who would otherwise have moved in from elsewhere stop doing so.[22] This means that almost all vacancies are eventually occupied by nonwhites, and the neighborhood inexorably shifts toward a heavy nonwhite majority. Once this happens, the remaining whites also seek to leave, since they do not wish to remain in an area where they have lost their culturally dominant position.

As a result, whites who would be quite satisfied—even delighted —to live in an integrated neighborhood *as members of the majority* are never given the opportunity to do so. Instead, for reasons beyond the control of each individual, they are forced to choose between complete segregation or living in an area heavily dominated by members of what they consider "another group." Given their values, they choose the former.

Many—especially Negroes—may deplore the racially prejudiced desire of most white middle-class citizens to live in neighborhoods and use schools where other white middle-class households are dominant. Nevertheless, this desire seems to be firmly entrenched among most whites at present. Hence public policy cannot ignore this desire if it hopes to be effective. Moreover, this attitude does not preclude the development of racial integration, as long as whites are in the majority and believe they will remain so. The problem is convincing them that their majority status will persist in mixed areas in the face of past experience to the contrary. Even more difficult, the people who must be persuaded are not those now living in a mixed area, but those who must keep moving in from elsewhere to maintain racial balance as vacancies occur through normal population turnover.

Clearly, the dynamic processes related to this "Law of Dominance" are critical to any strategy concerning the future of American ghettos. They are especially relevant to strategies which seek to achieve stable residential or educational integration of whites and nonwhites, instead of the "massive transition" and "massive segregation" which have dominated the spatial patterns of nonwhite population growth in the past twenty years. Such stable integration will occur in most areas only if there is some way to guarantee the white majority that it will remain the "dominant" majority. This implies some form of "quotas" concerning the proportion of nonwhites in the facility or area concerned—even legally supported "quotas."

Unless some such "balancing devices" are *explicitly* used and reinforced by public policies and laws to establish their credibility, whites will continue to withdraw from—or, more crucially, fail to keep entering—any facility or area into which significant numbers of nonwhites are entering. This means a continuation of *de facto* segregation and a reinforcement of the white belief that any nonwhite entry inevitably leads to "massive transition." Even more importantly, it means continued failure to eliminate white perception of race as a critical factor by encouraging whites and nonwhites to live together in conditions of stability. Thus, in my opinion, the only way to destroy the racial prejudice at the root of the "Law of Cultural Dominance" is to shape current public policy in recognition of that "Law" so as to encourage widespread experience that will undermine it.[23]

The Concept of Social Strategy

Americans typically do not attempt to solve social problems by means of behavior patterns that could reasonably be considered "strategies." The concept of strategy implies development of a single comprehensive, long-range plan to cope with some significant social problem. But U.S. decision-making concerning domestic issues is too fragmented and diffused to permit the formulation of any such long-range plan regarding a given problem. Instead, we approach most social problems through a process which has been aptly labeled "disjointed incrementalism."[24] Each decision-maker or actor makes whatever choices seem to him to be most appropriate at that moment, in light of his own interests and his own view of the public welfare. For two reasons, he pays little attention to most of the consequences of his action upon others—especially the long-run consequences. First, no one has the detailed knowledge and foresight necessary to comprehend all those consequences. Second, no one has the time nor the energy to negotiate in advance with all others likely to be affected by his actions. So instead he acts "blindly" and waits for those who are hurt to complain or those who are benefited to applaud.

A process of mutual adjustment ensues. Those who are unduly harmed by each decision supposedly recoup their losses by exercising whatever economic, moral, or political powers are available to them. Those who benefit use their powers to encourage more of the same. Presiding over this melee is a set of mainly "reactive" governments and other public agencies. They keep altering the "rules of the game" and their own programs and behavior so as to correct any grievous imbalances that appear.

There is no guarantee that the checks and balances built into this uncoordinated process will effectively counteract every destructive condition or trend that emerges from it. It is certainly possible that each individual will be motivated by the incentives facing him to take actions that, when combined with those taken by others acting in a similar individualistic fashion, will lead to collective disaster.

So far in history, the system has been remarkably effective at avoiding such outcomes. Part of this success undoubtedly results from society's ability to generate in most of its citizens a single set of basic values and even broad policy objectives that exert a cohesive influence on their supposedly individualistic decisions. But another important ingredient in the system's success is the ability of enough significant actors in it to perceive threatening trends in time to formulate and carry out ameliorating policies.

This means they must accurately forecast any potentially dire outcome of current trends. They must also visualize alternative outcomes that would be preferable and are within the capabilities of society. Finally, they must devise policies and programs that will shift individual incentives so one of those alternatives will occur. In some cases, the ongoing trends that threaten society are strongly entrenched in its institutional structure. If so, alternatives that avoid the pending threats may not be attainable without fundamental changes in institutions. Those changes in turn may be possible only if a preponderance of powerful people in society share at least a broad concept of the need for change and the kinds of objectives motivating it. This concept closely resembles a social strategy. It visualizes a certain desired outcome, implies a wide range of policies by various actors necessary to attain that outcome, and serves as a "hidden coordinator" of seemingly individualistic behavior.

The above reasoning implies two conclusions crucial to this analysis. First, strategic thinking about social problems can play a vital role in stimulating social change even where decision-making is dominated by disjointed incrementalism. Second, the alternative outcomes conceived in such thinking can usefully include some which could not be achieved without major changes in existing institutions or values. For example, some of the strategies discussed herein require a highly coordinated set of policy decisions. Such coordination is unlikely to occur in the presently fragmentalized governmental structures of our metropolitan areas unless major changes in the incentives facing these governments are created.

I will therefore formulate several alternative strategies for coping with the problems posed by future ghetto growth, even though carrying out some of them would require a far more consciously coordinated development of social change than has been typical of America in the past.

Formulation of Major Alternative Strategies

Because of the immense complexity of our society, an infinite number of alternative future strategies regarding ghettos could conceivably be designed. But for purposes of practical consideration, this number must be narrowed drastically to a few that highlight the major choices facing us. Selecting these few is inescapably arbitrary—there is no "scientific" way to do it. I believe, however, that the narrowing of alternative ghetto futures can best be accomplished by focusing upon the major choices relating to the following three questions:

To what extent should future nonwhite population growth be concentrated within the central cities, as it has been in the past twenty years?

To what extent should our white and nonwhite populations be residentially segregated from each other in the future?

To what extent should society redistribute income to relatively depressed urban areas or population groups in society in a process of "enrichment"?

Each of these questions can be answered with any one of a whole spectrum of responses from one extreme to the other. But for purposes of analysis, I believe we can usefully narrow these

271

answers down to just two points on the spectrum for each question. This allows us to reduce the alternatives to the following:

Degree-of-Concentration Alternatives

1. Continue to concentrate nonwhite population growth in central cities or perhaps in a few older suburbs next to central cities. *(Concentration)*
2. Disperse nonwhite population growth widely throughout all parts of metropolitan areas. *(Dispersal)*

Degree-of-Segregation Alternatives

1. Continue to cluster whites and nonwhites in residentially segregated neighborhoods, regardless of where they are within the metropolitan area. *(Segregation)*
2. Scatter the nonwhite population, or at least a significant fraction of it, "randomly" among white residential areas to achieve at least partial residential integration. *(Integration)*

Degree-of-Enrichment Alternatives

1. Continue to provide relatively low-level welfare, educational, housing, job training, and other support to the most deprived groups in the population—both those who are incapable of working, such as the vast majority of public-aid recipients, and those who might possibly work, but are unemployed because of lack of skills, discrimination, lack of desire, or any other reason. *(Non-enrichment)*
2. Greatly raise the level of support to welfare, educational, housing, job-training, and other programs for the most deprived groups, largely through federally aided programs. *(Enrichment)*

Even narrowing the alternatives in this fashion leaves a logical possibility of eight different combinations. A number of these can, however, be ruled out as internally inconsistent in practice. For example, I believe it is extremely unlikely that any strategy of dispersing the nonwhite population throughout metropolitan areas could be accomplished without provision of substantially greater incentives to both nonwhites (to get them to move) and whites (to increase their willingness to accept large numbers of nonwhite in-migrants without strong resistance). Thus no combination of both dispersal and non-enrichment need be considered.

Similarly, in the very long run, concentration of future non-white population growth within central cities is probably inconsistent with integration. Many of those cities will become so preponderantly nonwhite that integration within their borders will be impossible. Admittedly, it may take two or more decades for this to occur in some central cities, and it might never occur in others. Nevertheless, some types of integration (such as in the public schools) will become impossible long before that if a concentration policy is followed. For these reasons, I will consider only one special combination containing both concentration and integration. This consists of continued concentration, but a build-up of a gradually expanding inner-city core of fully integrated housing and public facilities created through massive urban renewal. For reasons explained below, this strategy would require a significant enrichment program too.

This whole process of elimination leaves five basic alternative strategies relevant to future development of ghettos. For convenience, each has been assigned a short name to be used throughout the remainder of this article. These strategies can be summarized as follows:

1. *Present Policies:* concentration, segregation, non-enrichment.

2. *Enrichment Only:* concentration, segregation, enrichment.

3. *Integrated Core:* concentration, integration (in the center only), enrichment.

4. *Segregated Dispersal:* dispersal, segregation, enrichment.

5. *Integrated Dispersal:* dispersal, integration, enrichment.

Before these strategies are examined in detail, two things about them should be emphasized.

First, they apply to individual metropolitan areas. Therefore, it would be at least theoretically possible to adopt different strategies toward the ghetto in different metropolitan areas. There are, in fact, some convincing reasons why this would be an excellent idea.

Second, these strategies are formed from relatively extreme points on the relevant ranges of possibilities. Hence they could actually be adopted in various mixtures, rather than in the "pure" forms set forth above. This further strengthens the case for using a variety of approaches across the country. For purposes of analysis, however, it is fruitful to examine each of these strategies initially as though it were to be the sole instrument for coping with ghetto problems in all metropolitan areas.

The Present-Policies Strategy

In order to carry out this strategy, we need merely do nothing more than we do now. Even existing federal programs aimed at aiding cities—such as the Model Cities Program—will continue or accelerate concentration, segregation, and non-enrichment, unless those programs are colossally expanded.

I do not wish to imply that present federal and local efforts in the anti-poverty program, the public housing program, the urban renewal program, health programs, educational programs, and many others are not of significant benefit to residents of ghettos. They are. Nevertheless, as both recent investigations and recent violence have emphasized, existing programs have succeeded neither in stemming the various adverse trends operating in ghetto areas nor in substantially eliminating the deplorable conditions there. Therefore, the strategy of continuing our present policies and our present level of effort is essentially not going to alter current conditions in ghettos.

This may make it seem silly to label continuation of present policies as a specific anti-ghetto strategy. Yet failure to adopt effective policies is still a strategy. It may not be a successful one, but it nevertheless is an expression of society's current commitment and attitude toward the ghetto.

Thus, if we maintain our current programs and policies, segregated areas of residence in our central cities will continue to expand rapidly and to suffer from all the difficult problems inherent in both racial and economic ghettos.

The Enrichment-Only Strategy

The second fundamental ghetto future strategy I call "enrichment only." This approach is aimed at dramatically improving the quality of life within the confines of present ghetto areas and those nearby areas into which ghettos will expand in the future if concentration continues. I presume that any such policy would apply to the poverty meaning of ghetto more than the racial one— that is, any enrichment strategy would aim at upgrading the lowest-income and most disadvantaged citizens of our central cities, re-

274

gardless of race. Nevertheless, a sizable proportion of such persons are nonwhites. Moreover, programs aimed at reducing racial discrimination in employment and in the quality of public services would form an important part of any strategy aimed at upgrading the most deprived groups. So the enrichment-only strategy would still concentrate upon the same areas as if it were to follow a racial policy.

The basic idea underlying the enrichment-only strategy (and part of every other strategy involving enrichment) is to develop federally financed programs that would greatly improve the education, housing, incomes, employment and job-training, and social services received by ghetto residents. This would involve vastly expanding the scale of present programs, changing the nature of many of them because they are now ineffective or would be if operated at a much larger scale, and creating incentives for a much greater participation of private capital in ghetto activities. Such incentives could include tax credits for investments made in designated ghetto areas, wage subsidies (connected with on-the-job training but lasting longer than such training so as to induce employers to hire unskilled ghetto residents), rent or ownership supplements for poor families, enabling them to rent or buy housing created by private capital, and others.[25]

It is important to realize that the enrichment-only strategy would end neither racial segregation nor the concentration of nonwhites in central cities (and some older adjoining suburbs). It would help many Negroes attain middle-class status and thus make it easier for them to leave the ghetto if they wanted to. Undoubtedly many would. But, by making life in central-city ghettos more attractive without creating any strong pressures for integration or dispersal of the nonwhite population, such a policy would increase the in-migration of nonwhites into central cities. This would speed up the expansion of racially segregated areas in central cities, thereby accelerating the process of "massive transition" of whole neighborhoods from white to nonwhite occupancy.

The Integrated-Core Strategy

This strategy is similar to the enrichment-only strategy because both would attempt to upgrade the quality of life in central-city ghettos through massive federally assisted programs. The integrated-core strategy would also seek, however, to eliminate racial segregation in an ever expanding core of the city by creating a socially, economically, and racially integrated community there. This integrated core would be built up through large-scale urban renewal programs, with the land re-uses including scattered-site public housing, middle-income housing suitable for families with children, and high-quality public services—especially schools.

All of these re-uses would be based upon "managed integration" —that is, deliberate achievement of a racial balance containing a majority of whites but a significant minority of Negroes. Thus, the integrated-core strategy could be carried out only if deliberate racial discrimination aimed at avoiding *de facto* segregation becomes recognized by the Supreme Court as a legitimate tactic for public agencies. In fact, such recognition will probably be a necessity for any strategy involving a significant degree of integration in public schools, public housing, or even private residential areas. This conclusion was recently recognized by the Chicago Board of Education, its staff, and its consultants, who all recommended the use of quotas in schools located in racially changing neighborhoods to promote stable integration.[26]

The integrated-core strategy essentially represents a compromise between an ideal condition and two harsh realities. The ideal condition is development of a fully integrated society in which whites and Negroes live together harmoniously and the race of each individual is not recognized by anyone as a significant factor in any public or private decisions.

The first harsh reality is that the present desire of most whites to dominate their own environment means that integration can only be achieved through deliberate management and through the willingness of some Negroes to share schools and residences as a minority. The second harsh reality is the assumption that it will be impossible to disperse the massive Negro ghettos of major central cities fast enough to prevent many of those cities from eventually becoming predominantly, or even almost exclusively, Negro in population. The development of predominantly Negro central cities, with high proportions of low-income residents, ringed by predominantly white suburbs with much wealthier residents, might lead to a shattering polarization that would split society along both racial and spatial lines.

This strategy seeks to avoid any such polarization by building an integrated core of white and nonwhites in central cities, including many leaders of both races in politics, business, and civic affairs. Negro leadership will properly assume the dominant position in central-city politics in many major cities after Negroes have become a majority of the municipal electorates there. By that time, integration of leadership within those cities will, it is to be hoped, have become a sufficient reality so that leaders of both races can work together in utilizing the central city's great economic assets, rather than fighting one another for control over them.

Thus, the integrated-core strategy postulates that a significant movement toward racial integration is essential to keep American society from "exploding" as a result of a combined racial-spatial confrontation of central cities vs. suburbs in many large metropolitan areas. It also postulates that development of integration in the suburbs through massive dispersal cannot occur fast enough to avoid such a confrontation. Therefore, integration must be developed on an "inside-out" basis, starting in the core of the central city, rather than in the suburbs.

The Concept of Dispersal

The two dispersal strategies concerning the future of ghettos are both based upon a single key assumption: that the problems of ghettos cannot be solved so long as millions of Negroes, particularly those with low incomes and other significant disadvantages, are required or persuaded to live together in segregated ghetto areas within our central cities. These strategies contend that large numbers of Negroes should be given strong incentives to move voluntarily from central cities into suburban areas, including those in which no Negroes presently reside.

To illustrate what "large numbers" really means, let us postulate one version of dispersal which I call the "constant-size ghetto strategy." This strictly hypothetical strategy aims at stopping the growth of existing central-city ghettos by dispersing enough Negroes from central cities to the suburbs (or to peripheral central-city areas) to offset potential future increases in that growth. Taking the period from 1970 through 1975, estimates made by the National Advisory Commission on Civil Disorders show that the nonwhite population of all U.S. central cities taken as a whole would, in the absence of any dispersal strategy, expand from about 13.6 million to about 15.5 million.[27] Thus, if dispersal of nonwhites were to take place at a scale large enough to keep central-city racial ghettos at their 1970 level during the five subsequent years, there would have to be an out-movement of 1.9 million Negroes into the suburbs. This amounts to 380,000 per year.

From 1950 to 1960, the suburban Negro population of all U.S. metropolitan areas grew a total of only 60,000 per year. In that decade, the white population of suburban portions of our metropolitan areas (the so-called "urban fringe") increased by about 1,720,000 persons per year. Thus, 96.6 per cent of all suburban population growth consisted of whites. From 1960 to 1966, the Negro population growth in all suburban areas declined sharply to a rate of 33,300 per year. In fact, there was actually in-migration of Negroes from suburbs to central cities. But the white population in all suburbs went up an average of 1,750,000 per year. Thus the proportion of suburban growth made up of whites climbed to 98.1 per cent—an even higher fraction than in the decade from 1950 to 1960.[28] Undoubtedly, some of this white population increase was caused by an exodus of whites from central cities in response to the growth therein. If future Negro population growth in central cities were stopped by a large-scale dispersion policy, then white population growth in the suburbs would be definitely smaller than it was from 1950 through 1966. The size of the resulting decline would depend upon the fraction of white exodus from central cities that occurs in response to Negro growth, as opposed to such other factors as rising incomes, the aging central-city housing stock, and shifts in life-cycle position. If whites leave central cities in a one-to-one ratio with the expansion of Negro population therein, then a cessation of Negro ghetto growth would result in a large drop in white suburban growth. In that case, future suburban population increases would consist of about 23 per cent Negroes (based on very rough calculations). This contrasts with proportions of less than 5 per cent from 1950 through 1960 and less than 3 per cent from 1960 through 1966.

Clearly, such dispersal would represent a radical change in existing trends. Not only would it stop the expansion of Negro ghettos in central cities, but it would also inject a significant Negro population into many presently all-white suburban areas. It is true that policies of dispersal would not necessarily have to be at this large a scale. Dispersal aimed not at stopping ghetto growth, but merely at slowing it down somewhat could be carried out at a much lower scale. Yet even such policies would represent a marked departure from past U.S. practice.

Such a sharp break with the past would be necessary for any significant dispersal of Negroes. Merely providing the *opportunity* for Negroes to move out of ghettos would, at least in the short run, not result in many moving. Even adoption of a vigorously enforced nationwide open-occupancy law applying to *all* residences would not greatly speed up the present snail's-pace rate of dispersion. Experience in those states that have open-occupancy ordinances decisively proves this conclusion.

Hence, positive incentives for dispersal would have to be created in order to speed up the rate at which Negroes voluntarily move from central cities and settle in suburban areas. (Certainly no policy involving *involuntary* movement of either whites or Negroes should ever be considered.) Such incentives could include rent supplements, ownership supplements, special school-support bonus payments linked to the education of children moving out from ghettos, and other devices which essentially attach a subsidy to a person. Then, when the person moves, he and the community into which he goes get credit for that subsidy. This creates incentives both for him to move and for the community to accept him gladly. Both of the strategies involving dispersal would thus represent radical changes in existing practices.

Segregated vs. Integrated Dispersal

One of the fundamental purposes of any dispersal strategy is providing Negro Americans with real freedom of choice concerning housing and school accommodations. The experience of other ethnic groups indicates that Negroes would exercise that choice in suburban areas in a combination of two ways. Some individual Negro households would become scattered "randomly" in largely white residential areas. But other Negro households—probably a larger number—would voluntarily cluster together. This would create primarily Negro neighborhoods, or even primarily Negro suburban communities. Such a combination of both *scattering* and *clustering* would occur even if Negro households had absolutely no fears of hostility or antagonism from white neighbors. It is unrealistic to suppose, however, that *all* prejudice against Negro neighbors can be eliminated from presently all-white suburbs in the immediate future. As a result, even if a dispersal strategy is carried out, there will still be some external pressure against Negro newcomers. This will encourage an even higher proportion of in-coming Negro households to cluster together than would do so in the absence of all fears and antagonism. Moreover, public policies to accomplish dispersion might include deliberate creation of some moderate-sized clusters of Negro families, as in scattered-site public housing developments.

Once all-Negro clusters appear in previously all-white suburbs, there is a high probability that they will turn into "ghetto-lets" or "mini-ghettos." The same forces that produced ghettos in central cities are likely to repeat themselves in suburbs, though in a much less pathological form. Those pressures are a rapidly expanding Negro population, the "Law of Cultural Dominance" among whites, and at least some restriction of Negro choice in areas far removed from existing all-Negro neighborhoods. Therefore, once a Negro cluster becomes large enough so that Negro children dominate a local elementary school, the typical phenomenon of white withdrawal from the local residential real-estate market is likely to occur. This has already taken place regarding Jews and gentiles in many suburban areas. Thus, any dispersal strategy that does not explicitly aim at preventing segregation, too, will probably create new segregated neighborhoods in the suburbs.

This new form of *de facto* segregation will, however, have far less damaging effects upon Negroes than existing segregation concentrated in central cities. In the first place, if Negro clusters are deliberately created in almost all parts of the metropolitan area at once, whites will be unable to flee to "completely safe" suburbs without accepting impractically long commuting journeys. This will strongly reduce the white propensity to abandon an area after Negroes begin entering it. Moreover, the presence of some Negroes in all parts of suburbia will also make it far easier for individual Negro families to move into all-white neighborhoods on a scattered basis. Thus any dispersal policy that really disperses Negroes in the suburbs will immediately create an enormous improvement in the real freedom of residential choice enjoyed by individual Negro families. This will be true even if most of those families actually choose to remain in Negro clusters.

Second, any dispersal strategy would presumably be accompanied by strongly enforced open-occupancy laws applying to all housing. At present, these laws do not lead to scattering, but they would in the climate of a dispersal strategy. Then Negro willingness to move into all-white areas would rise sharply, and white antagonism toward such move-ins would drop.

Third, *de facto* residential segregation need not lead to segregated suburban schools. In relatively small communities, such as most suburbs, it is easy to bus students to achieve stable racial balance. Thus, the formation of clustered Negro housing would not have to cause the quality-of-education problems that now exist in central-city ghettos. True, if a given suburb became predominantly Negro, its schools might become quite segregated. In that case, school systems in adjoining suburbs might have to merge or at least work out student exchange procedures with the segregated community in order to counteract segregation. This may be difficult to accomplish (though in the climate of a dispersal strategy, it would be at least thinkable). Hence it is possible that some segregated school systems might appear in suburban areas. But Negro families would still have far more opportunities than they do now to move to areas with integrated schools.

A dispersal strategy that did not succeed in initially placing Negro households in almost all parts of the metropolitan area would be more likely to generate "ghetto-lets." Hence, if dispersal tactics call for initially concentrating on dispersion only to a few suburbs, it is quite possible that segregated dispersal would result. This implies that integrated dispersal could be attained in only two ways. Either the initial dispersal strategy must place Negroes in almost all suburban communities, or specific integration-furthering mechanisms—such as school and residential quotas—must be adopted.

The speculative nature of the above discussion illustrates that society needs to do much more thinking about what dispersal really means, how it might be achieved, what alternative forms it might take, and what its consequences would be.

In an essay of this length, it is impossible to present an adequate analysis of each of the strategies described above. Certain factors will, however, have a crucial influence on which strategy actually prevails. These factors should be at least briefly mentioned here.

The Possibility of a Spatial-Racial "Confrontation"

Society's existing policies toward the ghetto are, by definition, those called for by the present-policies strategy. Yet there are strong reasons to believe that maintenance of these policies in ghettos is not possible. The striking increase in violence in big-city ghettos is probably related to a combination of higher aspirations, reduced sanctions against the use of violence, and continued deplorable slum conditions. If so, persistence of the present-policies strategy may continue to spawn incidents, riots, and perhaps guerrilla warfare. Then existing local police forces might have to be supplemented with para-military forces on continuous alert. Thus, the present-policies strategy might lead to further polarization of whites and Negroes and even to the creation of semi-martial law in big cities.

Moreover, when Negroes become the dominant political force in many large central cities, they may understandably demand radical changes in present policies. At the same time, major private capital investment in those cities might virtually cease if white-dominated firms and industries decided the risks of involvement there were too great. In light of recent disorders, this seems very likely. Such withdrawal of private capital has already occurred in almost every single ghetto area in the U.S. Even if private investment continues, big cities containing high proportions of low-income Negroes would need substantial income transfers from the federal government to meet the demands of their electorates for improved services and living conditions.

But by that time, Congress will be more heavily influenced by representatives of the suburban electorate. The suburbs will comprise 41 per cent of our total population by 1985, as opposed to 33 per cent in 1960. Central cities will decline from 31 per cent to 27 per cent.[29] Under a present-policies strategy, this influential suburban electorate will be over 95 per cent white, whereas the central-city population in all metropolitan areas together will be slightly over 60 per cent white. The suburban electorate will be much wealthier than the central-city population, which will consist mainly of Negroes and older whites. Yet even the suburbs will be feeling the squeeze of higher local government costs generated by rising service salaries. Hence the federal government may refuse to approve the massive income transfers from suburbs to central cities that the mayors of the latter will desperately need in order to placate their relatively deprived electorates. After all, many big-city mayors are already beseeching the federal government for massive aid—including Republicans like John Lindsay—and their electorates are not yet dominated by low-income Negroes.

Thus the present-policies strategy, if pursued for any long period of time, might lead to a simultaneous political and economic "confrontation" in many metropolitan areas. Such a "confrontation" would involve mainly Negro, mainly poor, and fiscally bankrupt larger central cities on the one hand, and mainly white, much wealthier, but highly taxed suburbs on the other hand. Some older suburbs will also have become Negro by that time, but the vast majority of suburbs will still be "lily white." A few metropolitan areas may seek to avoid the political aspects of such a confrontation by shifting to some form of metropolitan government designed to prevent Negroes from gaining political control of central cities. Yet such a move will hardly eliminate the basic segregation and relative poverty generating hostility in the urban Negro population. In fact, it might increase that population's sense of frustration and alienation.

In my opinion, there is a serious question whether American society in its present form could survive such a confrontation. If the Negro population felt itself wrongly "penned in" and discriminated against, as seems likely, many of its members might be driven to supporting the kind of irrational rebellion now being preached by a tiny minority. Considering the level of violence we have encountered already, it is hard to believe that the conditions that might emanate from a prolonged present-policies strategy would not generate much more. Yet the Negro community cannot hope to defeat the white community in a pitched battle. It is outnumbered 9 to 1 in population and vastly more than that in resources. Thus any massive resort to violence by Negroes would probably bring even more massive retaliation by whites. This could lead to a kind of urban *apartheid,* with martial law in cities, enforced residence of Negroes in segregated areas, and a drastic reduction in personal freedom for both groups, especially Negroes.

Such an outcome would obviously violate all American traditions of individual liberty and Constitutional law. It would destroy "the American dream" of freedom and equal opportunity for all. Therefore, to many observers this result is unthinkable. They believe that we would somehow "change things" before they occurred. This must mean that either the present-policies strategy would not lead to the kind of confrontation I have described, or we would abandon that strategy before the confrontation occurred.

Can the Present-Policies Strategy Avoid "Confrontation"?

What outcomes from a present-policies strategy might prevent this kind of confrontation? For one thing, if incomes in the Negro community rise rapidly without any additional programs, the Negro population of central cities may enter the middle class at a fast rate. If so, the Negro electorate that comes to dominate many major central cities politically by 1985 under the present-policies strategy may consist largely of stable, well-to-do citizens capable of supporting an effective local government.

To test this possibility, we have done some projections of incomes in the nonwhite population on a rough basis through 1983, assuming a present-policies strategy. These indicate that about two thirds of the nonwhite population at that time will have incomes *above* the existing poverty level—about the same fraction as at present. Since nonwhites will then form a much larger share of total central-city population, however, the percentage of *total* central-city population below the present poverty level might actually *rise* slightly. It is possible that nonwhite incomes might increase faster than in this forecast. Yet it is almost certain that the substitution of a relatively poor nonwhite group for a middle-income white group in central cities under a status-quo strategy will counterbalance likely increases in the incomes of nonwhites.

As a result, the electorate that will exist in major cities when Negroes become a majority will probably be just as poor as it is now (in real income terms). In contrast, the population in surrounding suburbs will be much wealthier than it is now. Thus, even if nonwhite incomes rise rapidly, there is still likely to be a significant "gap" between central-city and suburban income levels at that time—probably larger than at present.

Yet even under *present* conditions, many large central cities are critically short of revenue. Furthermore, in a generally wealthier society, it is highly probable that most central-city electorates will demand higher-than-existing levels of public service. Finally, the general cost of all government services will have risen sharply because of the productivity trends explained earlier. Hence, future central-city governments will have much higher costs, but not much greater resources than they do now. So rising incomes among nonwhites will not remove the fiscal pressure on central-city governments that is a key ingredient in the "confrontation" described above.

Moreover, the population group most responsible for violence and disturbances in central cities appears to consist of young Negro men between fifteen and twenty-four years of age. A high proportion of these people are unemployed because they lack skills (many are high school dropouts) and elementary training and motivation. This group will undoubtedly grow larger through natural increase and in-migration. Its problems are not likely to be solved under a status-quo strategy. Hence, even if the vast majority of nonwhites in central cities have increasing reason to abhor violence and riots, the *absolute size* of this more alienated group in 1975 will be 40 per cent larger than in 1966, and even larger by 1985.[30] This implies that at least part of this group might start actions forcing the kind of "confrontation" I have described.

Most of the other possible developments under a non-enrichment strategy that would avoid any major "confrontation" involve abandoning concentration of Negroes in central cities. Thus, some observers argue that members of the Negro middle class will increasingly move out to suburban communities as their incomes rise with no further encouragement from public programs. In this way, Negroes would be following the precedent of other ethnic groups. Up to now, there is no evidence that this has started to occur, even though a large Negro middle class already exists. But if such a pattern did evolve, it would amount to dispersal rather than the concentration implicit in the present-policies strategy.

Can Present Policies Be Sustained?

In any event, there appears to be significant probability—which I subjectively judge to be at least 25 per cent and perhaps as high as 75 per cent—that the present-policies strategy will prove unsustainable. If adopted, it would probably generate major repercussions that would force it to be abandoned. Society would be compelled either to suspend traditional individual rights and adopt martial law in cities or to institute major programs to improve ghetto conditions or to move toward wider dispersal of the Negro population, or some combination of these. Admittedly, there is no certainty that the present-policies strategy will lead to these outcomes. Nevertheless, I believe the probability that it will is high enough to make this strategy essentially self-defeating. Modern life is too dynamic for the status quo to be preserved for long.

Yet the present-policies strategy is the one society has so far chosen. Almost all current public policies tend to further concentration, segregation, and non-enrichment, as mentioned earlier. The few supposedly anti-concentration devices adopted, such as open-

ANTHONY DOWNS

occupancy laws, have proved almost totally ineffective. All we
have to do to confirm our choice of this strategy is to continue
existing policies. In fact, avoiding this strategy will be difficult,
because doing so will require major changes in present attitudes
as well as in existing resource allocations.

The "Black Power" Case for the
Enrichment-Only Strategy

The enrichment-only strategy is consistent with a current ideology that has come to be called the "Black Power" viewpoint. This
viewpoint has been criticized by many, and some of its proponents
have misused it to incite violence. Yet it is certainly an intellectually
respectable and defensible position containing some persuasive
elements.

The "Black Power" argument states that the Negro American
population needs to overcome its feelings of powerlessness and
lack of self-respect before it can assume its proper role in society.
It can do so only by exerting power over the decisions that directly
affect its own members. According to this view, a fully integrated
society is not really possible until the Negro minority has developed
its own internal strength. Therefore, the ideal society in which race
itself is not an important factor can only come much later. It could
exist only after Negroes had gained power and self-respect by
remaining in concentrated areas over which they could assume
political and economic control and direction. Hence this view contends that a future in which central cities become primarily Negro
and suburbs almost entirely white would be an advantage rather
than a disadvantage.

The "Black Power" view has several notable strong points. First,
such assumption of local power would be fully consistent with the
behavior of previous nationality groups, such as the Irish in New
York and Boston. They, too, came up from the bottom of the
social and economic ladder, where they had been insulted and
discriminated against. And they did it by gaining political and
economic control over the areas in which they lived.

Second, it is unquestionably true that one of the two most
important factors providing Negroes with all their recent gains in
legal rights and actual welfare has been their own forceful presentation of grievances and demands. (The other factor has been
high-level prosperity in the economy in general.) Negro-originated

marches, demonstrations, protests, and even riots have had immensely more impact in improving their actual power, income,
and opportunities than all the "purely voluntary" actions of whites
combined—including those of white liberals.

Third, time is on the side of the "Black Power" argument if
current population growth and location trends continue. As pointed
out earlier, Negroes are likely to become a majority of the electorate
in many large American cities within the next fifteen years, unless
radically new policies are adopted. By giving Negroes political
control over these cities, this trend would provide them with a
powerful bargaining position in dealing with the rest of society—a
tool they now sorely lack.

Fourth, the "Black Power" viewpoint provides many key ideological supports for Negro self-development. It stresses the need
for Negroes to become proud of their color and their history,
more conscious of their own strengths. It also focuses their attention
on the need for organizing themselves economically and politically.
Hence it could provide a focal point for arousing and channeling
the largely untapped self-development energies of the Negro
American population. One of the greatest difficulties in improving
ghettos is discovering effective ways in which the lowest-income
and most deprived residents can develop their own capabilities by
participating more fully in the decisions and activities that affect
them. Such "learning by doing" is, in my opinion, a vital part of
the process of bringing deprived people into the main stream of
American society. Insofar as "Black Power" proponents could develop such mechanisms, they would immensely benefit American
society.

There are, however, also significant flaws in the "Black Power"
argument. First, Negroes do not in fact have much power in the
U.S. Nor is it clear just how they can obtain power solely through
their own efforts, particularly in the near future. "Black Power"
advocates constantly talk about "taking what is rightfully theirs"
because they are dissatisfied with what "whitey" is willing to turn
over to them voluntarily. They also reject the condescension inherent in whites' "giving" Negroes anything, including more power.
But what bargaining power can Negroes use to compel whites to
yield greater control over the economic and political decisions that
affect them?

There are two possible answers. First, they could organize
themselves so cohesively that they would become a potent political

and economic force through highly disciplined but fully legal action. Examples would be block voting and economic boycotts. So far, nearly all efforts at such internal organization have foundered on the solid rocks of apathy, lack of funds, internal dissension, and disbelief that anything could be accomplished.

Second, Negroes could launch direct action—such as demonstrations and marches—that would morally, economically, or physically threaten the white community. This approach has so far proved to be the most successful. But many Negroes believe it has not improved their situation as fast as is necessary. Hence, there is a tendency to shift the form of threat employed to more and more violent action in order to get faster and more profound results. This tendency need only influence a small minority of Negroes in order to cause a significant escalation of violence. Yet such an escalation might result in massive retaliation by the white community that would worsen the Negroes' position. What is needed is enough of a threat to cause the white community to start changing its own attitudes and allocation of resources in ways far more favorable to Negroes, but not so much of a threat as to cause withdrawal of all white cooperation and sympathy.

This conclusion points up the second flaw in the "Black Power" case: Ultimately, U.S. Negroes cannot solve their own problems in isolation, because they are fully enmeshed in a society dominated by whites. The solution to Negro problems lies as much in the white community as in the Negro community. This is especially true because whites control the economic resources needed to provide Negroes with meaningful equality of opportunity. Hence, any strategy of action by Negro leaders that totally alienates the white community is doomed to failure.

Yet "Black Power" advocates are probably correct in arguing that Negroes must develop an ideology that focuses upon self-determination and therefore has some "anti-white" tinges. They need an "enemy" against which to organize the Negro community. History proves that organization *against* a concrete opponent is far more effective than one *for* some abstract goal. They also need an abrasive ideology that threatens whites enough to open their eyes to the Negroes' plight and their own need to do something significant to improve it. The question is how they can accomplish these goals without going too far and thereby creating violent anti-white hostility among Negroes and equally violent anti-Negro sentiment among whites.

Alternative Futures for the American Ghetto

In the past few years, many Negro Americans—including prominent community leaders—have shifted their sights away from direct racial integration as a goal. Instead they have focused upon other goals more consistent with the "Black Power" viewpoint. They want better housing, better schools, better jobs, and better personal security within all-Negro areas—and a much stronger Negro voice in controlling all these things. These enrichment-only objectives have apparently eclipsed their desire for greater ability to enter directly into white-dominated portions of the society. This rather dramatic change in values appears to rule out much possibility of Negroes' accepting either dispersal strategy.

In my opinion, the main cause of this shift in objectives is the failure of white society to offer any real hope for large-scale integration. After years of seeking equality under the law, Negro leaders have discovered that even removal of legal barriers is not producing much progress toward a true sharing in the life of white-dominated society. Why should they keep knocking on the door if no one will answer? Why not turn instead to existing all-Negro communities and try to improve conditions there? Indeed, I believe continued white refusal to engage in meaningful, large-scale integration will make it impossible for any self-respecting Negroes to avoid espousing some version of the "Black Power" viewpoint. Understandably, they will not be able to accept the conclusion that most of the millions of Negroes whom whites force to live racially segregated lives must therefore be condemned to inferior educations, housing, culture, or anything else.

Rather, they will reason, there must be some way to make the quality of life in all-Negro portions of a racially segregated society just as good as it is in the all-white portions. And if equality in terms of the indices of desirability accepted by whites cannot be achieved, then some of these "Black Power" advocates will be willing to attain at least nominal equality by denouncing those indicators as specious. They will further claim—with some justification—that life in all-white portions of society cannot be better and may be morally worse because whites suffer from racial blindness.

The reason why this argument is and will be advanced so strongly is certainly understandable. Those who advance it would hardly be human if they were not at least tempted to do so. As long as present white attitudes and behavior persist, adopting any other view amounts to despairing of any chance at equality for most Negroes.

Can the Enrichment-Only Strategy Create "Separate But Equal" Societies?[31]

The "Black Power" viewpoint essentially argues that racially separate societies in America can provide equal opportunities for all their members if Negroes are able to control their own affairs. Yet there is a great deal of evidence that this argument is false.

Certainly concerning employment, equality of opportunity for Negroes cannot possibly be attained in a segregated labor market. Negroes must be provided with full freedom and equality regarding entry into and advancement within the white-dominated enterprises that are overwhelmingly preponderant in our economy. Only in this way can they have any hope of achieving an occupational equality with whites.

In education, the evidence is far more ambiguous. The recent reports of the Office of Education and the Civil Rights Commission contend that both racial and economic integration are essential to the attainment of educational equality for Negroes.[32] Yet critics of these reports point out that many types of enrichment programs were not tested in the studies conducted by the authors. Unfortunately, most alternative approaches have not yet been tried on a scale large enough to determine whether any of them will work. Yet one conclusion does seem reasonable: Any real improvement in the quality of education in low-income, all-Negro areas will cost a great deal more money than is now being spent there, and perhaps more than is being spent per pupil anywhere.

Thus, society may face a choice between three fundamental alternatives: providing Negroes with good-quality education through massive integration in schools (which would require considerably more spending per pupil than now exists), providing Negroes with good-quality education through large-scale and extremely expensive enrichment programs, or continuing to relegate many Negroes to inferior educations that severely limit their lifetime opportunities. The third alternative is what we are now choosing. Whether or not the second choice—improving schools in all-Negro areas—will really work is not yet known. The enrichment alternative is based upon the as-yet-unproven premise that it will work.

Regarding housing, the enrichment-only strategy could undoubtedly greatly improve the quantity, variety, and environment of decent housing units available to the disadvantaged population of central cities. Nevertheless, it could not in itself provide Negroes of *any* economic level with the same freedom and range of choice as whites with equal incomes have. Clearly, in this field "separate but equal" does not mean *really* equal. Undoubtedly, all-white suburban areas provide a far greater range and variety of housing and environmental settings than can possibly be found in central cities or all-Negro suburbs alone.

Moreover, there is an acute scarcity of vacant land in many of our largest central cities. Therefore, greatly expanding the supply of decent housing for low-income families in those cities at a rapid rate requires creating many new units for them in the suburbs too.

Thus, if society adopts one of the many possible versions of the enrichment-only strategy, it may face the prospect of perpetuating two separate societies—one white and one Negro—similar to those that would develop under the present-policies strategy. If the enrichment programs carried out proved highly effective, then the gap between these two societies in income, education, housing, and other qualities of life would be nowhere near so great as under the present-polities strategy. Hence, the possibility of a potentially catastrophic "confrontation" between these two societies sometime in the next twenty years would be greatly reduced.

Nevertheless, I do not believe it will really be possible to create two separate societies that are truly equal. Therefore, even if the enrichment-only strategy proved extraordinarily successful at improving the lot of disadvantaged central-city residents of all races and colors (which is by no means a certainty), it would still leave a significant gap in opportunity and achievement between the separate white and Negro societies which would continue to emerge over the next twenty years. This gap would remain a powerful source of tension that might lead to violence, for experience proves that men seeking equality are not placated by even very great absolute progress when they perceive that a significant gap remains between themselves and others in society who are no more deserving of success than they. And that would be precisely the situation twenty years from now under the enrichment-only strategy—whether linked to "Black Power" concepts or not.

Why Dispersal Should Be Seriously Considered

As pointed out earlier, either of the two dispersal strategies would require radical changes in current trends and policies concerning the location of Negro population growth. Moreover, it is likely that massive dispersal would at present be opposed by *both* suburban whites and central-city Negroes. Many of the former would object to an influx of Negroes, and many of the latter would prefer to live together in a highly urbanized environment. Why should we even consider a strategy that is not only socially disruptive, but likely to please almost nobody?

In my opinion, there are five reasons why we should give enrichment plus dispersal serious consideration. First, future job-creation is going to be primarily in suburban areas, but the unskilled population is going to be more and more concentrated in central-city ghettos unless some dispersion occurs. Such an increasing divergence between where the workers are and where the jobs are will make it ever more difficult to create anything like full employment in decent jobs for ghetto residents. In contrast, if those residents were to move into suburban areas, they would be exposed to more knowledge of job opportunities and would have to make much shorter trips to reach them. Hence they would have a far better chance of getting decent employment.

Second, the recent U.S. Office of Education and U.S. Civil Rights Commission reports on equality of achievement in education reach a *tentative* conclusion that it is necessary to end the clustering of lower-income Negro students together in segregated schools in order to improve their education significantly.[33] As I understand these reports, they imply that the most significant factor in the quality of education of any student is the atmosphere provided by his home and by his fellow students both in and out of the classroom. When this atmosphere is dominated by members of deprived families, the quality of education is inescapably reduced—at least within the ranges of class size and pupil-teacher ratios that have been tried on a large scale. Therefore, if we are to provide effective educational opportunities for the most deprived groups in our society to improve themselves significantly, we must somehow expose them to members of other social classes in their educational experience. But there are not enough members of the Negro middle class "to go around," so to speak. Hence this means some intermingling of children from the deprived groups with those from not-so-deprived white groups, at least in schools. Because of the difficulties of bussing large numbers of students from the hearts of central cities to suburban areas, it makes sense to accomplish this objective through some residential dispersal. This consideration tends to support the integrated-dispersal strategy to some extent, even though these reports have received significant criticism, as noted above.

Third, development of an adequate housing supply for low-income and middle-income families and provision of true freedom of choice in housing for Negroes of all income levels will require out-movement of large numbers of both groups from central cities to suburbs. I do not believe that such an out-movement will occur "spontaneously" merely as a result of increasing prosperity among Negroes in central cities. Even the recently passed national open-occupancy law is unlikely to generate it. Rather, a program of positive incentives and of actual construction of new housing in suburban areas will be necessary.

Fourth, continued concentration of large numbers of Negroes under relatively impoverished conditions in ghettos may lend to unacceptably high levels of crime and violence in central cities. The outbreak of riots and disorders in mostly nonwhite areas in our central cities in the past few years is unprecedented in American history. As the report of the National Advisory Commission on Civil Disorders indicates, continuing to concentrate masses of the nonwhite population in ghettos dominated by poverty and permeated with an atmosphere of deprivation and hopelessness is likely to perpetuate or intensify these disorders. This could lead to the disastrous outcome already discussed in connection with the present-policies strategy.

Fifth, a continuation of ghetto growth will, over the next three or four decades, produce a society more racially segregated than any in our history. We will have older, blighted central cities occupied by millions of Negroes, and newer, more modern suburban areas occupied almost solely by whites. Prospects for moving from that situation to a truly integrated society in which race is not a factor in key human decisions are not encouraging. In fact, by that time we will be faced with a fantastically more massive dispersal problem than the present one if we really want to achieve a society integrated in more than just words.

Thus, only the two enrichment-plus-dispersal strategies explicitly seek to create a single society rather than accepting our present perpetuation of two separate societies: one white and one Negro. Dispersal would involve specific policies and programs at least starting us toward reversal of the profoundly divisive trend now so evident in our metropolitan areas. It may seem extraordinarily difficult to begin such a reversal. But however difficult it may be now, it will be vastly more difficult in twenty years if the number of Negroes segregated in central cities is 8 million larger than it is today.

The Difficulty of Gaining Acceptance for Dispersal

I am fully aware that any strategy involving significant dispersal may now seem wholly impractical to responsible politicians and social leaders. The voluntary movement of large numbers of Negroes from ghettos to the suburbs encouraged by federal programs presupposes radical changes in existing attitudes among both suburban whites and central-city Negroes.

In spite of our social mobility, Americans are extremely sensitive to class differentiations. We have deliberately developed class-stratified suburban areas. Residents of each suburb use zoning, tax rates, lot-size requirements, and other devices to exclude persons considered farther down the ladder of social and economic prominence. As each group and each family moves upward in our mobile society, they become more concerned about creating social distance between themselves and those now below them—including those who were once equal to them.

I certainly do not deplore the historic traditions of self-improvement and protection of amenities and privileges that have been won through hard work and perseverance. These traditions should and will continue in some form, because it is proper for successful people to enjoy the fruits of their efforts.

Nevertheless, it is at least possible that the social objective of upgrading the lowest and most deprived groups in our society cannot be accomplished if we simultaneously insist upon excluding those groups from nearly all daily contact with other more fortunate people—as we do now—by maintaining extremely rigid class distinctions by geographic area. Thus, the best dispersal policy might be one that promoted day-to-day inter-class and inter-racial experiences without changing the dominant socio-economic character of the receiving suburban areas. This would allow persons moving out from the inner city to benefit from the existing character of those suburbs. Such a policy implies that the newcomers would comprise a minority in each area into which they went. This means that an integrated-dispersal strategy might ultimately provide the most desirable form of dispersal. It would enable the group that was already there to maintain nearly intact their conception of the proper standards for that community, while sharing the benefits of those standards with others.

Even this change in attitude, however, presupposes a shift in values of profound magnitude among white middle-class Americans. Furthermore, I doubt that most Negroes today want to live in white communities in which they would be relatively isolated from other Negroes. Hence they might prefer a segregated-dispersal strategy, if they were willing to accept dispersal at all. Yet, since most suburban areas are already incorporated into predominantly white communities, where and how could such a strategy be initiated?

Some Tactical Mechanisms for Encouraging Dispersal

Any attempt to achieve dispersal must involve specific answers to two basic questions:

What *mechanisms* can be designed to encourage voluntary out-movement of large numbers of Negroes into the suburbs and their peaceful acceptance and welcome by whites there?

What *incentives* can be developed leading particular interest groups in society to press politically for—or at least support—employment of those mechanisms?

Let us consider the mechanisms first. Americans have always used one basic approach to get people to overcome inertia and make voluntarily some socially desirable change. It consists of providing a significant economic or other reward for persons who behave in the desired manner. That reward might be free land (as for homesteaders and railroads in the nineteenth century), or tax reductions (as for homeowners or investors in equipment in the past few years), or direct payments (as for farmers), or services and income supplements tied to participation in specific programs (as for users of the G.I. Bill in education).

In the case of dispersion, I believe the system of rewards used should probably have the following characteristics[34]:

1. Advantages should accrue both to the Negro households moving out from central cities and to the suburban households into whose communities the newcomers move.

2. Whenever possible, these advantages should consist of rewards administered under metropolitan-area-wide organizations specifically set up for such a purpose. These organizations could be quasi-private bodies able to cooperate directly with existing local governments and other geographically limited organizations. Hence they would *not* be metropolitan governments.

3. Advantages to out-moving households might include the following:

> The possibility of sending their children to top-quality schools that receive special grants because of participation in programs involving out-moving children.

> Home-buying or renting financial aids available only to out-moving families or at least with assigned proportions of their total funding available only to such families.

> Top-priority access to special programs concerning employment and on-the-job training in suburban industrial and other firms. In my opinion, such programs might be effectively built around the self-selection principle embodied in the G.I. Bill—that is, eligible persons would be given certificates enabling those firms who hire them to receive special benefits to compensate for their lower productivity or training costs. Such benefits might include tax credits or direct payments. The persons receiving these certificates would then make their own choice of employers among firms participating in such programs. This would preserve maximum individual choice among program participants.

4. Advantages to households already living in the receiving areas might include:

> Special aid to schools receiving children of out-moving Negro families. Such aid should consist of funds linked to the students in such families (as Title I funding under the Elementary and Secondary Education Act is now linked to low-income families). But the per-student amount of aid given should greatly exceed the added direct cost of teaching each out-moving student. Hence

the school district concerned would have a positive incentive to accept such students because of the financial "bonuses" they would bring with them. Those bonuses could be used to upgrade the entire receiving school or cut locally-borne costs therein.

"Bonus" community financing to participating suburban local governments. Again, the payments involved should significantly exceed the added costs of servicing in-coming families, so that each participating community would be able to improve other services too.

Giving higher priority in other federal programs to communities participating in out-movement programs than to those refusing to participate. These related programs could include sewer and water financing, planning aid, and selection as locations for federal installations.

5. Benefits available for out-moving families and receiving areas could be restricted by geographic area to avoid either paying people discriminately by race or wasting funds paying families who would move out anyway. A precedent for giving residents of certain neighborhoods special benefits already exists in the urban renewal and Model Cities programs. Thus, specific ghetto neighborhoods could be designated "origination" areas and largely white suburban communities designated "receiving" areas. Benefits would accrue only to persons moving from the former to the latter or to residents of the latter participating in reception programs.

6. If these programs were part of an integrated-dispersal strategy, they could be linked to quota systems concerning newcomers to each school or community involved. Thus, the special bonus aids would be available only up to a certain fraction of the total school enrollment or residential population of a given receiving community. This restriction would be aimed at retaining in the schools or communities concerned the dominance of the groups originally residing there. It is to be hoped that the result would be suburban integration, rather than a shift of massive neighborhood transition from central cities to suburbs.

The above suggestions are highly tentative and exploratory. Yet

297

I hope they at least indicate that practical mechanisms can be created that might achieve a substantial amount of peaceful Negro out-movement—*if* they were adopted in a general atmosphere of social encouragement to dispersal.

Some aspects of the basic approach described above may seem terribly unjust. In particular, this approach rewards the advantaged (those already living in suburbs) as well as the disadvantaged (those moving out of deprived areas into suburbs) in order to get the former to accept the latter. Yet that is a key mechanism, one which free-enterprise systems have always employed when they seek to attain high-priority ends through voluntary action. Our society abounds with arrangements that provide special economic advantages to those who are already privileged, presumably in order to evoke socially desired behavior from them. Examples are oil depletion allowances, stock option plans for top executives, profitable contracts for defense firms, lower tax rates on capital gains, and subsidy payments to wealthy farmers. I am defending neither the equity nor the effectiveness of these particular examples. Yet they illustrate that we often adopt public policies that pay the rich to undertake behavior which presumably benefits society as a whole.

A second aspect of the approach to dispersal I have described which might seem harsh is that no benefits apparently accrue to disadvantaged persons who fail to move out to the suburbs. As stated earlier, however, I believe dispersal programs should only be undertaken simultaneously with large-scale ghetto enrichment programs. The latter would provide comparable, or even greater, benefits for those "left behind" in central cities—who will undoubtedly comprise the vast majority of Negroes in our metropolitan areas for many years to come.

Developing Political Support for Dispersal

The concept of dispersal will remain nothing but an empty theory unless a significant number of Americans decide their best interests lie in politically supporting specific dispersal mechanisms. It is conceivable that such support might result from a massive "change of heart" among white suburbanites. They might view dispersal as a way to "purge themselves" of the kind of "white racism" which the National Advisory Commission on Civil Disorders described. I do not think this will occur. In fact, I believe recent urban violence has tended to make white suburbanites more hostile than ever to the idea of having Negroes live next door to them.

Yet, on the other hand, several specific groups in society are beginning to realize that dispersal might benefit them immensely. The motivation of persons in these groups varies widely, from pure moral guilt to sheer self-interest. But almost all significant social change in the United States has occurred because a wide variety of different types of people with diverse motives have formed a coalition to accomplish something. In my opinion, only through that kind of process will any of the basic strategies I have described (except the present-policies strategy) ever be achieved.

I believe the groups favorable to dispersal now include, or soon will include, the following:

> Suburban industrialists. In many metropolitan areas, they are experiencing acute labor shortages, particularly of un-skilled workers. They will soon be willing to provide open and powerful political support for the construction of low-income and moderate-income housing for Negro workers and their families in currently all-white suburbs.

> Downtown-oriented retailers, bankers, restaurant opera-tors, hotel operators, and other businessmen in our larger cities. In cities where disorders have penetrated into cen-tral business districts (such as Milwaukee and Washing-ton), many former patrons have stopped visiting these areas altogether—especially at night. If disorders in these areas get worse, the impact upon both consumer patron-age and future capital investment in big-city downtowns could be catastrophic. Those whose enterprises are "locked in" such areas will soon realize they must vigorously support both stronger law enforcement and positive pro-grams aimed at alleviating Negro discontent. At first, these programs will consist primarily of ghetto enrich-ment, but these groups will soon begin to support dispersal too.

> Home builders. They would benefit from any large-scale programs of housing construction. But the delays and difficulties of carrying out such programs within central

cities are much greater than they are on vacant suburban land. Hence they will eventually exert at least low-level support for dispersal if it means large-scale subsidy of privately built homes.

White central-city politicians in large cities. As the populations of their cities shift toward Negro majorities, they will be more and more willing to support some dispersal policies, as well as the enrichment programs they now espouse.

Businessmen in general with plants, offices, or other facilities "locked in" large central cities. An increasing number of such persons will realize that they will emerge losers from any major "confrontation" between black-dominated central cities and white-dominated suburbs, as described earlier.

Persons of all types whose consciences influence them to accept the National Advisory Commission's conclusion that dispersal of some kind is the only way to avoid perpetuating two separate societies, with the Negro one forever denied equality.

Since these groups now constitute a small minority of Americans a great many other Americans must change their existing values considerably if large-scale dispersal is ever to occur. Yet the alternatives to such a strategy—especially the one we are now pursuing—could conceivably lead us to equally grave changes in values. For example, if there is an extremely significant increase in violence in Negro ghettos which spills over into all-white areas, the white population might react with harshly repressive measures that would significantly restrict individual freedoms, as noted above. This, too, would call for a basic shift in our values. But it is a shift which I regard with much more alarm than the one required by a dispersal strategy. In fact, in this age of rapid technological change, it is naïve to suppose that there will not in the future be significant alterations in attitudes that we presently take for granted.

The Scale of Efforts Required

The foregoing discussion emphasizes that any strategy likely to have a significant impact upon ghettos will require a very much larger effort than we are now devoting to this problem. Even a "pure" ghetto-enrichment strategy, which does not eliminate or even slow down the growth of the racial ghetto, would require a significantly greater allocation of financial and manpower resources to coping with the problems of the urban poor. A dispersal strategy that addresses itself to breaking up or at least slowing down the growth of the racial ghetto would also require even more profound changes in values and attitudes. Only the first strategy—that of continuing our present activities—requires no immediate change in effort or values. But it may eventually result in significant value changes too—and perhaps far less desirable ones than are required by the other two alternatives.

Thus, there is simply no easy way to cope with this problem. In my opinion, past federal programs and many currently suggested approaches have suffered from the desire to find a cheap solution to what is an extremely expensive problem. The problem is expensive in terms not only of money, but also of our national talents and our willingness to change our basic values. In one way or another, we must and will accommodate ourselves to this problem. We cannot evade it.

Creating the Programs and Incentives Necessary to Achieve Any Desired Ghetto Future

Each strategy contains two basic parts: a desired outcome and a set of actions designed to achieve that outcome. I have not placed equal emphasis on these two parts in discussing each of the five strategies concerning ghetto futures. For example, the present-policies strategy as I have described it is essentially a set of actions—the continuation of present policies. Hence it does not emphasize a desired outcome. In fact, I have pointed out several reasons why its outcome might be quite undesirable. Conversely, my discussion of the enrichment-only strategy has focused upon its outcome. Hence I have not made many suggestions about how that outcome might be brought about. Similar emphasis upon the outcome rather than the means of attaining it also marks the discussion of the integrated-core strategy. Even my tentative analysis of how dispersal might be carried out hardly represents a complete blueprint for action.

Any strategy is really just wishful thinking until it links the outcome it envisions with some feasible means of attaining that outcome. This is especially true regarding several of the ghetto futures I have described, since they embody such radical changes in society. They are likely to remain largely fantasies, rather than real alternatives, until specific programs for achieving them can be defined. I have made some program suggestions in connection with dispersal strategies in order to prove that dispersal is not totally unrealistic. Unfortunately, the complexity of developing similar suggestions for the other strategies involving social change prevents my attempting to do so in this article.

Nevertheless, there are five basic principles crucial to formulating such programs.

1. No proposed "solution" to ghetto problems that is not eventually supported by the majority of the white middle class can possibly succeed.[35]

2. The actions designed to bring about any desired outcome must be linked to incentives that will appeal both to the self-interest of all groups concerned and to their consciences. In fact, the most difficult part of implementing any strategy (other than the present-policies strategy) will be providing effective incentives for the relatively well-off white majority. This group must be persuaded to expand many resources, and alter its own traditional behavior, in order to produce outcomes that appear to benefit mainly a small minority of the population. As indicated in the discussion of dispersal, each segment of the white majority (such as business, labor, suburbanites, senior citizens, farmers, and so forth) must be presented with arguments and incentives which appeal specifically to its interests. An example is the argument that business suffers great losses of potential profits and output because of the failure of poor Negroes to engage in high-level consumption and the inability of poorly educated Negro workers to help meet high demands for skilled labor.

3. Any program designed to achieve a given outcome should involve significant action by the private sector. Otherwise, society may relegate ghettos to a position of dependency upon government that is inconsistent with full equality in American life. On the other hand, it is naïve to suppose that the private sector can or will bear the huge expense of

coping with ghetto problems unaided. Society as a whole must pay the extra costs of on-the-job training programs, new factories located in ghettos, union training of unskilled Negro apprentices, and other actions aimed at helping the unskilled or otherwise "left out" enter the main stream of our economy. These actions must be carried out by non-governmental organizations, but financed by the government through direct payments, tax credits, or other means.

4. No program involving ghettos can be effective unless it involves a high degree of meaningful participation by ghetto residents, and significant exercise of power and authority by them. We must realize that ghettos cannot be drawn into the main stream of American life without some redistribution of authority and power, as well as income, for equality in America means exercise of significant self-determination. Admittedly, lack of skill and experience may cause that exercise to be disorderly, inefficient, and even corrupt at first—as it was among the Irish, Italians, Jews, and others in the past. Therefore, turning over more power in ghetto areas to local residents may actually cause a short-run decline in the professional quality of government there—whether in schools, the police, or local government in general. Yet it will greatly alter the attitudes of residents toward those institutions and begin to draw them into the real functioning of our society. So it should and must come.

5. The more benefits that most ghetto residents receive through programs aimed at helping them, the more dissatisfied and vocally discontent certain small parts of the ghetto community are likely to become. This makes the problem of persuading the white majority to support large-scale aid programs doubly difficult. It also means that socio-economic programs will have to be accompanied by greatly enlarged and improved law-enforcement efforts, particularly those in which ghetto leaders themselves play significant roles. Yet emphasis on improving law enforcement alone, without massively trying to meet the other needs of ghetto residents, will probably prove disastrous. Such one-sided emphasis on "law and order" could easily provoke steadily rising violence shifting in form toward guerrilla warfare. The need to avoid

this outcome further emphasizes the importance of relying more and more on ghetto communities to develop their own internal controls of violence, with outside aid, as is consistent with the preceding principle of greater self-determination.

Merely stating these principles emphasizes how far we are from having designed practical programs to achieve most of the outcomes set forth in this article. In my opinion, one of the most important tasks facing us is the formulation and public discussion of the specific ingredients needed for such programs. But even that cannot be done until we have recognized more explicitly the various possible futures of American ghettos and weighed their relative advantages and disadvantages.

At present, most public discussion and thought about racial and ghetto problems in America suffer from a failure to define or even to consider explicit possible long-range outcomes of public policy. This is one reason why such discussion seems so confused, inchoate, and frustrating. I hope that the ideas set forth in this article can serve as a nucleus for more fruitful public discussion of this crucial topic, for the future of American ghettos will determine to a large extent the future of America itself.

REFERENCES

1. The first draft of this essay was written in the early summer of 1967. Subsequently, the author became a consultant to the National Advisory Commission on Civil Disorders. In that capacity, he wrote the rough drafts of several chapters in the Commission's final report. One of these (Chapter 16) contains many of the ideas set forth in this essay. Nevertheless, there are sufficient differences between the contents and presentation of Chapter 16 in the Commission's Report and this essay to warrant separate publication of the latter. The contents of this essay express the thoughts of its author only and do not necessarily represent the views of either the National Advisory Commission on Civil Disorders or Real Estate Research Corporation.

2. Data from the Social Security Administration.

3. *Report of the National Advisory Commission on Civil Disorders* (Washington, D. C.; March 1, 1968), p. 127. This document will hereafter be referred to as the *NACCD Report.*

4. *Ibid.*, pp. 121, 127.

5. Based upon the Census Bureau's Series D projections of future population—the ones assuming the lowest of the four levels of future fertility used by the Census Bureau. See U. S. Bureau of the Census, *Statistical Abstracts of the United States, 1967* (88th Edition; Washington, D. C., 1967), pp. 8-10.

6. *NACCD Report*, p. 121.

7. *Ibid.*

8. *Ibid.*

9. Open-occupancy legislation appears to be aimed at shifting the location of some future nonwhite growth to presently all-white areas. Experience in those states which have had open-occupancy ordinances for some time indicates, however, that they have little, if any, impact in altering the distribution of nonwhite population growth.

10. *NACCD Report*, p. 227.

11. Surveys conducted annually by Real Estate Research Corporation, results unpublished.

12. *NACCD Report*, p. 216.

13. See Raymond J. Murphy and James M. Watson, *The Structure of Discontent*, Mimeographed, Los Angeles: University of California at Los Angeles, June 1, 1967.

14. *NACCD Report*, pp. 123-31.

15. Specific recommendations concerning these subjects are set forth in the *NACCD Report*, Chapter 17.

16. See John F. Kain, "The Distribution and Movement of Jobs and Industry," in *The Metropolitan Enigma*, ed. James Q. Wilson (Washington, D. C., 1967).

17. These include legislative proposals made by Senator Javits, the late Senator Robert Kennedy, and Senator Percy.

18. William Baumol and William Bowen, *The Performing Arts: The Economic Dilemma* (New York: 20th Century Fund).

19. *NACCD Report*, p. 217.

20. Insofar as I know, this principle was first formulated by my father, James C. Downs, Jr.

21. Two well-known urban specialists with such views are Jane Jacobs and Victor Gruen. See Jane Jacobs, *The Life and Death of Great American Cities* (New York, 1961), and Victor Gruen, *The Heart of Our Cities* (New York, 1964).

22. This phenomenon explains why it is so difficult to halt "massive transition" from white to nonwhite occupancy once it begins. It tends to continue

even when whites originally living in the area concerned do not "panic" at all. As long as normal turnover continues to produce vacancies, and only nonwhites fill them, such transition is inescapable. The key persons whose behavior must be affected to stop transition are not the whites living in the area at the outset, but those living scattered elsewhere in the metropolitan area or even other parts of the nation. They are the persons who must move into the areas as vacancies appear in order to maintain racial balance therein. Thus, attempts to organize existing white residents so as to prevent them from fleeing almost always fail to halt transition. Organizers can rarely identify "the whites who aren't there yet," so they cannot influence the decisions of these potential future occupants, and transition continues relentlessly.

23. The U. S. Supreme Court will soon have to face up to the consequences of this "Law." In order to attack *de facto* segregation effectively, it must recognize racial discrimination in the form of school quotas as Constitutional. At present, our society cannot achieve integration or end segregation without deliberate and explicit racial discrimination by public authorities. This is true in relation to other public facilities besides schools, including hospitals and housing.

24. This term and usage were coined by Charles E. Lindblom. See Lindblom and David Braybrooke, *The Strategy of Decision* (New York, 1963)

25. See the *NACCD Report*, Chapter 17.

26. See their statements as quoted in the Chicago *Daily News*, August 25, 1967.

27. *NACCD Report*, p. 227.

28. *Ibid.*, p. 121.

29. These figures are based upon the Census Bureau's Series D population projections. If higher fertility projections are used, the suburbs would contain slightly higher proportions of total population in 1985. See the reference cited in footnote 5.

30. *NACCD Report*, pp. 216-17.

31. This section of the article was written after Chapter 16 of the *NACCD Report* had been completed and closely parallels the contents of certain parts of that chapter.

32. See James Coleman *et al.*, *Equality of Educational Opportunity* (Washington, D. C., 1966), and the U. S. Civil Rights Commission, *Racial Isolation in the Public Schools* (Washington, D. C., 1967).

33. *Ibid.*

34. Many of the programs described in this section have been recommended by the National Advisory Commission on Civil Disorders. See the *NACCD Report*, Chapter 17.

35. This fact is recognized by most Negro leaders not committed to zealously militant separatism. For example, see Kenneth Clark, *Dark Ghetto* (New York, 1965), p. 222.

RICHARD E. RUBENSTEIN

Urban Violence and Urban Strategies

I

ALMOST EVERY day brings forth a new batch of proposals by social scientists, political figures, businessmen, and community groups to alter the conditions of life in the nation's black ghettos. Recently, amidst an accumulating mass of paper schemes and pilot projects, the general outlines of a major debate over urban policy have begun to emerge. It is to elucidate and evaluate arguments which will soon disturb the lives of Congressmen and Senators as well as professors, journalists, and community organizers that I hearken back here to the wave of ghetto uprisings which began in the summer of 1964. Since almost all proposals for the reconstruction of the ghetto, whether "short-term" or "long-term," are in large measure responses to urban violence, analysis of the relationship between such violence and urban strategies seems appropriate.

Three principal responses to the uprisings can be identified, each of which produced, by necessary implication, a strategy for coping with what is now euphemistically called "the urban crisis." For purposes of simplification, we may call these views "conservative" and "liberal."

1. The conservative position, summarily stated, held that ghetto riots were produced by a combination of explosive material—the black mob or "underclass" consisting of the unemployed, those with criminal records or tendencies and lawless youth—and a spark—the rhetoric of local gang leaders or outside agitators. Reactionaries like George Wallace of Alabama stressed the role of the agitators, seeking to explain their activities as part of a sinister, conspiratorial design to disrupt American society. More sophisticated conserva-

tives emphasized those characteristics of the mob which made them vulnerable to demagoguery and "acting out." For example, the McCone Commission report on the Watts uprising underlined the impatience and "nothing to lose" recklessness of those without a stake in society.[1] Other commentators blamed the mass frustration, engendered by failure to deliver, on liberal promises or the absence of social controls within the black community produced by centuries of slavery and social disorganization.[2] The common element which justifies labeling these diverse views "conservative" was the assumption that the causes of the violence lay ultimately in the group itself—that ghetto rioting could be attributed to characteristics indigenous and peculiar to certain segments of the urban black community.

The short-term strategies dictated by conservative views were the immediate suppression of actual riots or revolts by the use of *force majeure*, and the avoidance or limitation of potential uprisings by means of police counter-insurgency techniques: surveillance or jailing of agitators, infiltration of gangs and community organizations, the training of specialized riot squads and their equipment with sophisticated anti-riot weapons, adoption of preventive detention and high-bail policies intended to keep certain persons off the streets during periods of tension, and so forth. The assumption underlying the strategy of *force majeure* was that black violence, however started, was at bottom expressive rather than instrumental, and that rioters or potential rioters would respond to superior force on the basis of a fairly simple pleasure-pain calculus.

Long-term conservative strategy, however, was more complex. Whether the lumpenproletariat constituted a minority of the urban black community (as many conservatives believed) or not, its existence as a cause of civil disorder dictated the adoption of economic and political measures designed to eliminate it. One way in which this could be done was to give the rascals a stake in society by providing them with jobs, decent housing, and education. On the other hand, since unfulfilled promises tended to inflame the mob, and since many of the lumpenproles were probably beyond salvation (confirmed criminals, inveterate shirkers, and so forth) it was necessary to slow down, rather than accelerate, the pace of reform. The dilemma was very much like that faced by counter-insurgency practitioners in Vietnam in their attempt to change South Vietnamese society rapidly enough to provide an alternative to Communism while keeping popular expectations "realistically" low. Precisely as in Vietnam, a clear short-term military strategy tended to dominate a vague long-term political strategy. In Chicago as in Saigon, counter-insurgency outweighed reform in the municipal budget for the "hot" season.[3]

2. Immediately after the Watts uprising, the liberal view of urban violence, soon to become the quasi-official governmental interpretation, was also given voice. Critiques of the McCone Commission Report by Robert M. Fogelson, Bayard Rustin, and others,[4] as well as fresh analyses of later uprisings in other cities, undermined the view that the rioter was a lumpenprole stirred up by lawless despair or outside agitation, emphasizing instead the instrumental nature of civil disorder. The liberal masterwork, the Report of the National Advisory Commission on Civil Disorders, found that the rioters were not "criminal types, overactive social deviants, or riff-raff," but ordinary blacks born in the city in which the riot took place, economically on a par with their non-rioting neighbors and generally better educated and more politically aware than non-rioters.[5] (Subsequent studies found not only that rioters were "representative" of ghetto comunities, but that non-rioting members of the community often responded positively to outbreaks of violence in which they did not participate.)[6]

The Kerner Report viewed the 1967 outbreaks primarily as a form of protest against the rejection of blacks by American society. It laid very heavy emphasis on patterns of discrimination which kept blacks out of better paying jobs, higher quality housing, and competent educational institutions. Noting that, relative to whites, the position of blacks in terms of income, health, education, and job employment was worsening rather than improving, it explicitly linked the termination of urban violence to integration of blacks into the white working and middle classes and elimination of the barriers separating the "two societies." Finally, the Report recognized that violence was engendered, in part, by the unresponsiveness of local, white-dominated institutions to black demands for redress of grievances, and offered several suggestions aimed at improving communications between blacks and local government agencies.

With respect to short-term solutions to the problem of racial violence, the liberal position varied somewhat from that of the conservatives. The Kerner Report emphasized more effective riot-control training, stricter discipline and command of police and troops in the field, and better planning to avoid disorders or to cut them short after an initial outbreak. The principal departure from the conservative view involved recommending alternatives to deadly force and the use of community assistance in crisis situations as a way of avoiding escalation of riots. In addition, the Report recommended the establishment of intermediary institutions which would open channels of communication between city governments and ghetto residents, for example, neighborhood action task-forces, better grievance-response mechanisms, expanded legal services to the poor, and so forth. The combination of short-term recommendations was strongly reminiscent of "pacification" programs employed by the United States in connection with the Vietnamese insurgency. If the conservatives' position in this regard was akin to that, say, of General LeMay, the liberals' position was closely analogous to that of Dean Rusk.

On a longer-term basis, the liberal strategy for the city, aimed as it was at terminating the "two societies" postulated by the Kerner Report, dictated massive federal efforts to improve the status of blacks relative to whites in the field of jobs, housing, and education. This represented a rededication to, rather than an alteration of, political principles espoused by every United States President since Franklin Roosevelt; to wit, that the federal government should should take primary responsibility for improving the standard of living of the poor, and ending racial discrimination. The twin principles of governmental centralism and racial integration, which dominated subsequent liberal proposals for reconstruction of the ghetto, shaped the Commission's recommendations as well. While advocating large-scale federal progams to solve the unemployment, housing, and education problems, the Report was vague in recommending measures to increase the collective power of urban blacks at the expense of existing white economic and political interest groups. It therefore contained within itself the seeds of an explosive controversy, which we will discuss in a moment, between centralists and decentralists, integrationists and advocates of Black Power.

II

The real significance of the election in 1968, as several commentators have noted, lay less in Richard Nixon's narrow victory over

Hubert Humphrey than in their joint victory over George Wallace —a triumph of what Louis Hartz has called "the liberal tradition in America." In an election year plagued by civil disorder and assassinations, the two parties of the center performed the extraordinary feat of holding challenges from both right and left to approximately 14 per cent of the total votes cast. Paradoxically, despite the political divisions created by accelerating social change, Mr. Nixon's victory represented a mandate for continuity rather than for change.

Nixon the Campaigner had moved to silence protest from the right by paying rhetorical obeisance to the theme of "law and order." But with the conservative view of urban violence temporarily eliminated as a politically potent force, Nixon the President acted to consolidate the liberal center, pledging to continue federal efforts aimed at attacking the "big three" urban problem areas —jobs, housing, and education. His appointment of Daniel P. Moynihan as chief White House Advisor on Urban Affairs was the clearest indication that what might be called "establishment liberalism" was to become the policy of the new administration. A certain subtle shift of emphasis away from the blatant centralism of New Deal Democracy was also apparent in official declarations of intention to rely more on private enterprise, in the appointment of Robert Finch to reorganize the Department of Health, Education, and Welfare, and in the launching of such "trial balloons" as the Community Development Bill of 1968. Nevertheless, excepting this twist, the basic urban policies of the new Administration seemed identical to those of the Democrats. In fact, the keynote of the "new" policy might well have been expressed by James Q. Wilson of the Harvard-M.I.T. Joint Center for Urban Studies. In *Varieties of Police Behavior,*[7] Wilson suggested that urban police departments should be functionally rather than politically decentralized. Functional decentralization—the devolution of discretionary power downward within an otherwise unchanged central power structure—seemed a likely tack for the new administration to take.

As the first phase in the debate over urban violence and urban strategies was ending, however, a second phase began. In New York City, experiments in school-system decentralization ended in near bloodshed, a crippling Teachers' Union strike and the estrangement of New York's Negro and Jewish communities. Indeed, it seemed to some that the consequences of attempted school decentralization verified entirely the principles of strategy defended in *Maximum*

311

Feasible Misunderstanding,[8] wherein Daniel P. Moynihan had ex-coriated intellectuals and radicals whose concern for the exercise of political power by the poor—"maximum feasible participation"—pro-voked political reprisals against the Poverty Program. Nevertheless, a new and growing school of thought (herein called "radical") insisted upon the proposition that urban peace could only be achieved, in the long run, by maximizing the power of ghetto dwellers to govern themselves—to control their own schools, police forces, businesses, and unions and their own institutions of local government. Like the conservative and liberal strategies, the radical approach reflected a particular view of urban violence—one which emphasized the powerlessness rather than poverty of rioters, and analogized the ghetto uprisings to struggles for national liberation being waged in the Third World. In this view, the chief villain of the piece was not lawlessness, poverty, ignorance, or poor housing, but a system of interlocking elites, operating at the local level through the machinery of government, to keep blacks in a state of quasi-colonial subjection. We shall consider radical strategies for the city a bit later. First, since this view is so new and little known, relatively speaking, it may be worth exploring at greater length its theoretical basis.

III

Despite their many disagreements, liberals and conservatives interpreting the violence of the 1960's had agreed that the problem was uniquely racial.[9] Although conservatives tended to blame the disorders on the blacks and liberals on white racism, their shared assumption was that the inability of blacks to make rapid, non-violent progress in American society was historically anomalous—or, to put it in another way, the blacks were the great deviation from the norm of peaceful progress. The liberals' concern for inte-gration, and their faith in the potency of central government to achieve it, followed directly from this assumption; to correct an anomaly one adjusts rather than reconstructs an existing system.

The New Deal's legitimate successors and heirs, impressed by the ability of central government to bring farmers, labor unions, and some urban immigrant groups to power, could not imagine that the "failure" of the Negro to achieve the same success might reflect on the adequacy of the centralist approach. It was comforting to assume that the "racial problem" was something special in American history, that it was the intractability of the problem rather than the method of solution which was at fault. The liberal solution to the problem of black violence therefore concentrated almost exclusively on the fulfillment of unfulfilled promises. More civil rights, more integration, more government programs, and more sophisticated anti-riot devices were the answer.

Radical scholars, however, were coming to their own conclusions with respect to the role of group violence in American history—conclusions which tended to support the position of black leaders like Stokely Carmichael and Eldridge Cleaver, who saw racism not as a temporary anomaly but as part of a well-established pattern of internal colonialism. In the general assault on the "consensus school" of historians and social scientists, it was discovered that other large, excluded groups—from the Appalachian farmers of the 1770's and 1780's and the Indians of the early 19th century to the white southerners of Reconstruction and post-Civil War labor unionists—had resorted to mass violence of a high intensity in order to gain the freedom and power which years of non-violent struggle had not achieved. Attention to the history of urban disorder led to a renewed interest in the riots and demonstrations of the Revolutionary era, the tumultuous disorders of the 1790's, the ferocious anti-Catholic rioting of the 1840's and 1850's, the immigrant-group violence of the New York Draft Riots and other affrays, the use of organized crime and gang warfare by Irish, Jews, Italians, and other immigrants to gain economic advancement and political influence, and the resort to violence by urban political machines to maintain their control over local territory and local elections.[10]

These diverse riots, insurrections, and terroristic movements were of interest, among other reasons, because they demonstrated the critical importance to excluded groups of *local* power. In case after case, violent uprisings seemed to be directed against the agents of authority found on the territory of the insurgent groups, or outsiders invading their "turf." Whether one considered the Massachusetts and Pennsylvania farmers who ran tax collectors and court officials out of their territory, the KKK terrorists who helped drive Reconstruction governments from southern soil, the violent labor unions which attempted to clear their territory of scabs, Pinkerton men and company spies, the nativists and immigrants who fought for control of schools and city neighborhoods or the black rebels of the 1960's, the same theme emerged; the importance of local autonomy.

One could theorize, then, that when traditional roads to political and economic advancement were blocked by established elites, the control of local territory was one way in which a group could assure its cultural survival while mobilizing the collective strength needed to engage in political bargaining. And, conversely, it seemed that where groups otherwise alienated and oppressed had *not* resorted to mass violence to obtain their ends, this was, in many cases, because they had already achieved the security of strong local power bases.[11] The New York Irish, who destroyed large parts of the city in the 1863 riots, gained control of Tammany Hall and the police force during the next two decades, vitiating the need for further revolt. The German-Americans of Cincinnati, whose 1884 riot was one of the bloodiest in American history, became model citizens after capturing the Mayor's office a decade later. Farmer rebellions decreased despite a plenitude of "hard times" and national political defeats after Populists took over state and local governments in the West and South. Later immigrant groups—Italians, Jews, Poles, Greeks, and so forth—were fortunate enough to arrive in America when it was relatively simple for large groups of newcomers to assume *de facto* control over housing, schools, churches, small business, unions, and industrial jobs located in their territory, not to mention the local operations of the mob and the machine.[12] But, even for them, the "occupation" of territory was critically important— important enough to make gang war part of the American urban way of life.

All of this made one wonder, of course, whether the advocates of Black Power—the doctrine which asserts that the black community must control the political machinery, economic opportunities, and social and educational institutions found on its own soil—were not closer to a solution to the urban crisis than the liberals. To radicals, black and white, the revolt of the ghetto was not just a protest over poor living conditions and the existence of the "two societies," but an inevitable reaction to the increasing colonial dependence of blacks upon whites. That the uprisings were unplanned and uncoordinated, that they involved so many young people, working men, and even members of the middle class, and that their targets were indeed the properties and persons of those considered to be absentee oppressors suggested that blacks were, in fact, struggling for local power and communal solidarity. The black rioter did not come a-knocking on the door of white society, hat in hand, to beg for a better job or a more decent dwelling; he *demanded* that the white oppressor get off his back. Positively stated, this constituted a demand that definable ghetto communities, considered as political-economic units, be given the right to manage their own affairs on their own territory.

Naturally, the Kerner Report and other liberal analyses of the crisis avoided this interpretation and dodged its implication, for if the demand for group liberation were serious, more than new jobs and houses would be needed to satisfy it. For those who viewed the uprisings as a struggle for self-determination, however, the policy implications were clear. On a short-term basis, white landlords, shopkeepers, ward healers, welfare workers, and policemen—the whole colonial apparatus—should begin to abandon the ghetto. Harrassment, infiltration, and the use of police terror against street organizations and militant leaders should cease. Where further disorders occurred, the black community as well as the white would insist that order be restored, but blacks should be allowed to do the job themselves (as in Cleveland in the summer of 1968) and afterward to continue to police their own communities without the aid of the white police. In short, white meddling in the ghetto should end, with blacks (as well as Puerto Ricans, Mexican-Americans, and other oppressed urban minorities) freed to organize socially and politically, to select new leaders and to improvise new representative institutions.

On a longer-term basis, radicals proposed that the ghettos be treated, in certain respects, as cities in themselves, that business enterprises and real property within be turned over to black ownership (preferably by community organizations), that control over ghetto schools be vested in school boards representing ghetto parents, that police forces operating in black territory be made directly responsible to those inhabiting that territory, that the stranglehold of white-dominated political machines over ghetto political life be broken, and that local housing, health, education, and welfare programs be administered whenever possible by blacks. Each of these proposals, it was recognized, would require serious shifts in the distribution of power in urban areas. Slumlords would be compelled to give up valuable property and businessmen profitable businesses. Urban political machines allied with racketeers would be compelled to abandon a rich vein of political power and graft. An army of welfare workers would be forced to seek other employment and unionized school teachers would become responsible to local boards rather than to more acquiescent central authorities. Little wonder that the Kerner Report (whose members included seven politicians, the presidents of a union and a business, a chief of police, and a civil-rights lawyer) avoided these issues.

At the same time, radicals believed, federal and state governments must increase their efforts to end poverty, to upgrade schools and housing, to improve urban social services, and to end racial discrimination à la the Kerner Report. The apparent inconsistency between this position and the advocacy of Black Power strategies deserves brief comment. Theoretically, the inconsistencies vanish when one recognizes that communities, like nations, may retain their independence while receiving "foreign aid," provided that the aid is consistent with their own development plans. There is no reason why federal aid cannot be given to a community-controlled school (it will soon be given to parochial schools!) or to a community-controlled police force. Similarly, there is no reason—in theory —why the central government should not attempt to create jobs in the ghetto by luring industry in, provided that the relevant unions are entirely open to blacks, and that industrial development plans have community support. (To increase white power in the ghetto under the guise of reform without simultaneously increasing black power is an invitation to disaster.) On the other hand, the *political* inconsistency between demands for local autonomy and governmental aid remains. Can one ask white landlords driven out of black communities to pay increased taxes to improve ghetto housing? Can one expect white industrialists to locate in areas possessing powerful black-dominated labor unions, when the same industrialists are moving South in droves to escape strong *white*-dominated labor unions?

These difficulties cannot be wished away. Urban renewal, which has been a bonanza for white construction industries and unions, may lose their powerful support if black demands for control over urban-renewal planning and for a piece of the action (through black construction companies and building-trades unions) are met. Federal aid to education has had the strong support of local, state, and national teachers' organizations, few of which would be inclined, say, to fight for aid to Rhody McCoy in the Ocean Hill-

Brownsville District of New York. Notwithstanding their reported demise, urban political machines still proved healthy enough to block the implementation of "maximum feasible participation" in Federal Community Action programs; presumably they are healthy enough to control the local administration of federal aid to the ghettos in 1969. And what of Mr. Average White American? Will he be inclined to foot the tax bill to support black independence in a newly divided city?

No—the political powers-that-be cannot be wished away. Unfortunately for them, however, neither can the desire of the powerless for power and of the dependent for self-rule. One is thus confronted with an inescapable strategic choice: to fight for black liberation at the risk of alienating white support for social welfare programs, or to fight for welfare programs at the risk of increasing relative deprivation and further alienating blacks seeking local power. The radical position, of course, is to place primary emphasis on increasing black power at the local level while attempting simultaneously to educate the white public to the need for "foreign aid" to the ghetto. This will be a difficult task, but, *pace* Mr. Moynihan, not an impossible one.

There is evidence, for example, that urban and suburban whites *are* capable of distinguishing their interests from those of the slumlords, exploitative merchants, political bosses, police fraternal associations, teachers unions, and other satraps of the ghetto. Conflicts like that over the New York school-decentralization program tend to polarize opposing forces, but not necessarily to the advantage of racist pressure groups; in New York, polarization helped elect John Lindsay mayor over the right-wing candidates of both parties. Similarly, police political organization in various localities has revealed the narrow ideological base and self-interested machinations of that particular pressure group. Already, liberals are beginning to concede the necessity for turning ghetto businesses over to blacks, getting rid of slumlords and replacing the welfare system with some form of more direct and less humiliating income-maintenance program. And, most important, white and black political interests are seen to overlap at critical points. Most of the poor requiring more income, most of the schools needing grants-in-aid, most of the unemployed, and most of these requiring free medical treatment are *white*. Moreover, most whites, like most blacks, remain interested in achieving urban peace without genocide. The relationship between Black Power and a *paix des braves* in American cities is therefore coming into focus for many whites.

This is not to deny Mr. Moynihan's point that the struggle for local autonomy may alienate some whites and even prevent immediate implementation of worthwhile programs. What no analysis can now overlook, however, is the degree to which blacks have begun to question the price tag attached to social programs planned and administered by federal bureaucrats and city bosses. If the price is increasing dependence, and therefore increasing guilt and rage in their community, more and more black people, even those formerly considered "safe and reliable," will not buy the package. In other words, they are prepared to postpone the enjoyment of some immediate benefits if, in a few years, a proud and independent black community may gain them on its own terms. They do not fear political conflict if its result will be to awaken America to the need for liberation of all the oppressed. And they know that in 1972, and even more in 1976, a new generation schooled not in depression and war, but in struggle against paternal authoritarianism, will swell the voter rolls.

IV

To enter more deeply into the liberal-radical debate, it will be useful to consider the problem of the police in the ghetto, and the growing controversy over community control of urban police forces. The problem, as most analysts recognize, has two faces: first, deteriorating relations between the police and the residents of black communities are a cause (often the most immediate cause) of ghetto uprisings; and second, law enforcement has not secured the persons or property of either blacks or whites in the ghetto and surrounding areas. Liberals have tended to treat these as separate issues. In order to prevent real or alleged acts of police brutality from triggering riots, better communications between police departments and black citizens, improved "community relations," and more efficient grievance-response mechanisms are prescribed. In order to control "private crime," on the other hand, liberals and conservatives alike recommend a war on criminals—more and better-trained policemen, increased use of crime-fighting technology, a crackdown on street gangs, and so forth. To radical analysts, this separation of issues rests upon a fundamental failure of preception and of nerve. Misconception of the problem, moreover, foredooms both proposed solutions.

The radical position[13] is based upon the perception that the police function in urban ghettos like a colonial army of occupation. The analogy operates on at least three levels: (1) The law which is enforced by policemen and other government functionaries in the ghetto is not based on the consent of the colonized. In most cities it represents the interests of powerful white pressure groups and, in some cases, those of a black bourgeoisie. (2) Methods of law enforcement in the ghetto differ radically from methods of law enforcement in white and middle-class areas of the metropolis. These differences are either improvised by the police or imposed by the white majority; again, they are not based upon the consent of the colonized. (3) As is customary in such cases, the mother country often loses control over its *colons*; the ghetto police exercise a wide discretion which often includes violation of the law. Neither police personnel nor police practices are based upon the consent of the governed, who have no more power to select police officials and personnel than they do to make the law.

For these reasons, radicals argue, it is useless to prescribe better community relations as a cure for riots and a war on criminals as a cure for private crime. In both cases, what is lacking is the consent of the colonized, and what requires transformation is the colonial relationship itself. We are familiar with the high rates of crime and corruption in colonized societies and with their causes—the combination of economic deprivaton, physical brutalization, political and psychological powerlessness, which turns a people against itself, and changes cities into jungles.[14] We are also familiar with the process whereby societies starting out on the road towards self-determination choose as initial targets for attack the colonial police—the front-line troops in the unheralded daily war between oppressors and oppressed. The end product of such a process, as examples from American and contemporary international history show, is either some form of self-determination or some form of genocide. The implication, then, is that both private crime and the incidence of violent uprisings will decline when the residents of black communities have taken control of the machinery of law enforcement on their own territory.[15]

With this as introduction, let us see how liberals deal with the demand for community control of the police. Our purpose is not so much to explore this particular issue as to discuss the ideology underlying opposition to community control of the institutions of local government in general. For this purpose, James Q. Wilson's *Varieties of Police Behavior*[16] may serve as a model; although his subject is police-force organization, Wilson recognizes (by mentioning in the same breath "control of the police or the schools") that his arguments may be directed against any proposals to treat the ghetto as a political unity, whether for electoral, law enforcement, educational, or other purposes. In order to avoid misrepresentation, I quote, at length, from his chapter "Conclusions and Policy Implications":

1. For one thing, a central city cannot be fully suburbanized however much we want to—it is, by definition, *central*, which means that many people from all over the metropolitan area use it for work, governing, and recreation and that, as a result, competing life styles and competing sets of community norms come into frequent and important contact. Necessarily, this generates political pressures to maintain order at the highest level expected by groups who use the city . . .[17]

2. Giving central city neighborhoods, many bitterly apprehensive of and hostile towards adjoining neighborhoods, control over their own neighborhood police would be to risk making the police power an instrument for inter-neighborhood conflict. Proposals for communal police often are based on the tacit assumption that, somehow, only Negroes, and poor Negroes at that, would get control of the police. In fact, legislation that would give the police to Negroes would, out of political necessity, give it to others as well . . .[18]

3. Besides deep racial divisions, there are issues of order maintenance and law enforcement in the central city that are of such emotional and political significance that the police are already under intense political pressure from competing forces seeking to exploit these issues. Allowing them to be governed by neighborhoods could only intensify that pressure, putting the police at the mercy of the rawest emotions, the most demagogic spokesmen, and the most provincial concerns . . . if the unit of government becomes the neighborhood . . . the opportunities for a small, self-serving minority to seize control of police or the schools will become very great indeed.[19]

4. When the community is deeply divided and emotionally aroused, the proper governmental policy is not to arm the disputants and let them settle matters among themselves; it is, rather, to raise the level at which decision will be made

to a point sufficiently high so that neither side can prevail by *force majeure* but low enough so that responsible authorities must still listen to both sides . . .[20]

5. Some advocates of communal law enforcement seem inclined to defend the model precisely on the grounds that it avoids the "middle-class bias" of the legal code and the moral order. If by "middle-class bias" is meant a concern for the security of person and property and a desire to avoid intrusions into one's privacy and disturbances of one's peace, it is not clear why it is a "bias" at all. . . . We have had some experience in this country with the notion that different neighborhoods should be allowed to have radically different levels of public order, and the results have not been altogether encouraging . . .[21]

Although expressed gracefully and thoughtfully, these arguments are founded upon certain fallacies which inevitably arise when one attempts to apply the political philosophy of the New Deal to the facts of urban life in the 1960's. The first among these I would call the *fallacy of objective order*: the doctrine which assumes that since all major economic classes and ethnic groups in America share certain values—such as "a concern for the security of person and property, and a desire to avoid intrusion into one's privacy and disturbances of one's peace"—there is a "highest and best level of order," which may be enforced by a neutral central government. However accurately this consensus theory may describe the shared values of various groups which the New Deal attempted to conciliate and order in the 1930's, as applied to the divisions between ghetto dwellers and middle-class whites in the contemporary metropolis it is simply inapplicable. Of course the poor and rich share certain values, like the desire not to be robbed and murdered. But the existence of such a commonality, in which Fiji Islanders and Albanians also participate, hardly proves the existence of an objective "order" enforceable in all these communities. Given the necessity of establishing priorities in order to make use of scarce order-maintenance resources, the fact is that black communities and white communities have different priorities, and therefore different concepts of order.

For example, to talk about "security of persons and property" in the context of the ghetto, where the security of the landlord's or creditor's property is tenderly protected against the rights of the tenant or debtor, and where the police themselves are a principal threat to the security of persons, is absurd. The values *are* shared *in abstracto*, but even without discriminatory laws and law enforcement, their concrete implementation would necessitate radically different kinds of order-maintenance in different communities. Similarly, to claim that "intrusions into one's privacy" and "disturbances of one's peace" have identical or even remotely similar meanings in the ghetto and the suburbs is clearly fallacious. Most ghetto residents would probably list as the primary intrusion into their privacy the practice of police officers, welfare workers, and others of stopping them for questioning, frisking them, and searchtheir apartments without their consent. (And every ghetto dweller knows what "disturbance of the peace" means—it is what you are charged with when booked without evidence!) No "middle-class bias" in order maintenance? Then why are black street organizations openly harrassed while the American Legion is not? Why are poor drunks tanked while middle-class drunks are released with warnings? Why are dragnet arrests, preventive arrests, and arrests on suspicion carried out only in the slums? Why does contract law favor sellers; landlord-and-tenant law owners of property; real property the banks; and election laws the party in power?

The point, of course, is that the exponents of consensus refuse to recognize value-differences between domestic groups serious enough to warrant institutional expression. Those intergroup differences which are acknowledged, are treated as evanescent in light of the inevitability of lower-class groups becoming middle class: "Throughout history the urban poor have disliked and distrusted the police, and the feeling has been reciprocated; the situation will not change until the poor become middle class, or at least working class . . . "[22] This sounds plausible, but, again, it is not. The Irish poor, for instance, rioted in New York in the 1860's, when they had not achieved control over the police or the machinery of city government; a few years later, not much richer, they began to take over both the police department and Tammany Hall, and the "wild Irishman" was no more. The Germans of Cincinnati experienced a similar transformation between 1880 and 1900. Many other domestic groups, as previously noted, resorted to violence in order to gain or protect their control over local government and to build their particular notions of "law and order" into the legal system, after which violence declined or ceased.

It is important to recognize that, throughout our history, groups seeking embodiment of their group values in governmental form have been compelled to improvise *new* institutions to do so—the political party, the political machine, the farmers' cooperative, the labor union, the suburb. There is no reason to believe that blacks labor under a necessity any less pressing, or that the existing political system is any more capable of accommodating their demands now than in the past.

Wilson's warning against "making the police power an instrument for inter-neighborhood conflict" suggests a second and related fallacy, which I would call *the consensus model of the city*. The warning assumes that the urban police are not now such an instrument, and that through central-city government, decisions may be made at "a point sufficiently high so that neither side can prevail by *force majeure* but low enough so that responsible authorities must still listen to both sides." This model describes the operation of no major American city past or present; in fact, it is not even a sensible utopia. When a city contains within its jurisdiction, as ours have always done, groups differing radically in wealth, power, and degree of political development, the chief purpose served by "raising" the level of decision-making is to permit ruling groups to govern through the impersonal machinery of legal bureaucracy—in effect, to disguise the exercise of coercive power. As practiced under such circumstances, "coalition government" (including balanced tickets, patronage-sharing, and so forth) is part of the masquerade, since the representatives appointed for, or elected by, poverty-stricken politically unawakened groups are easily led to serve the interests of the more powerful (or where they do not, they meet the fate of Adam Clayton Powell or Vito Marcantonio). In short, the inter-neighborhood conflict, that moderates so fear is part and parcel of American urban life. By "raising" the level of decision-making to the level, say, of Mayor Yorty's office, or Mayor Daley's, one neighborhood or set of neighborhoods is permitted to dominate another so completely that conflict does not seem to exist at all.

In fact, the fear of conflict runs like a sombre thread throughout the work of consensus scholars. Strangely, they seem to prefer the present type of urban government, in which conflict is ignored or "managed" in totalitarian fashion, to one in which very real differences between large racial and economic groups would be embodied in systemic form. I say "strangely" because institutionalization of political differences seem a likely way to lessen rather than to increase violent conflict. For example, if governmental power devolves systemically downward to the black, Spanish-American, or Appalachian ghettos, meaningful bargaining and coalition government becomes a possibility, since only then do the poor have something to bargain with. Similarly, although "making the police an instrument of inter-neighborhood conflict" may seem a frightening prospect to some, to the residents of various ghettos the police are already *the* instrument of inter-neighborhood conflict (disguised as a conflict between law-enforcement and law-breakers). It is for this reason that they feel constrained to support the activities of anti-police neighborhood organizations, citizens' patrols, and political organizations like the Black Panther Party.

In this respect it is particularly important to emphasize that blacks seeking local power want what whites, whether in urban or suburban areas, already possess. The third fallacy is *the false black-white analogy*—the notion that the present structure of urban government seriously limits white power, and that the extension of community-control principles to the white community will therefore lead to weakening of the position of minorities. ("In fact, legislation that would give the police to Negroes would, out of political necessity, give it to others as well . . .") In the first place, a downward devolution of power *within* the majority community need not occur if whites are satisfied with the extent to which the institutions of local government now respond to the demands and desires. For example, it is perfectly possible to imagine Harlem or Bedford-Stuyvesant with its own police force (or, for that matter, with its own mayor) without the Bronx feeling it necessary to secede from Queens or Staten Island. The idea that solutions to the problems of less-developed political groups must be applied without discrimination to better-developed groups is unsupportable.

More important, however, most white groups which have sought community control of local institutions have obtained it, or can obtain it on demand. When white parents remove their children from urban schools and send them to private or parochial schools this is not called "community control." It produces no strike and no headlines—but the upshot is that white parents control their children's schools. When whites move to the suburbs in order to gain both a sense of community and control over the environment, this does not create great debate or raise questions in state legislatures. Moreover, urban groups like the Jews of New York, the

Poles of Chicago, the Irish of Boston, and the WASPS of Dallas are seen on closer examination to control not just their own schools or police forces, but segments of industry and the professions, labor unions, churches, networks of fraternal and voluntary associations, as well as organized rackets and political organizations. It would be difficult to show how the present structure of urban government constrains dominant groups or limits their power locally.[23]

The final fallacy which deserves comment is contained in the statement that, with community control a reality, "the opportunities for a small, self-serving minority to seize control of the police or the schools will become very great indeed . . . ." This is the familiar argument used by every colonial power against those seeking a redefinition of the colonial relationship: "If you think we are bad, wait until your own people take over!" As applied to local government in the United States, it is based on an outmoded reading of history which assumes that "that government is best which governs most," and that the worst thing one can do is to permit government to get too close to the people. "If the study of urban politics has taught us anything, it is that, except on referenda, and perhaps not even then, 'the people' do not govern—organizations, parties, factions, politicians, and groups govern. . . ."[24]

Is this true? Is it so easy to destroy all distinction between elitism and democracy? In the real world, I would have thought, one could attempt, fairly successfully, to rank various governmental types and arrangements along a continuum leading, let us say, from the relative elitism of Saudi Arabia to the relative democracy of Sweden. On analysis, however, the quoted statement simply begs the question. If, indeed, "groups govern," the question remains whether it is possible and advisable for specific groups to govern themselves, or to be governed by indigenous rather than exogenous subgroups. And the question suggests an answer: It is the state of political consciousness of the group governed, as much as the form of government, which decides the extent to which "the people" govern, either directly or indirectly. One cannot "prefer" central governmental power to local power, or vice versa, as a matter of principle for all time. Under some circumstances, maximizing human freedom may require that the central government assume vast new powers in order to counterbalance increased private power; in others it will require that oppressed and alienated minority communities become more self-determining. The argument between Hamilton and Jefferson is unending precisely because the source of un-freedom shifts over time. At the moment, its focus lies in the coali-tion of white interest groups dominating urban governments.

The fear of the small, pernicious minority which will take power under communal government in order to oppress the com-munity is a phobia generated by certain specific traumae. In the last century the chief advocates of strong local government were either Southerners, to whom "states rights" meant white rights; industrialists, to whom "freedom of persons" meant freedom of corporations to ride roughshod over workers and consumers; or urban bosses, to whom "strong city government" meant vote-buying and endless opportunities for graft. In 1969, however, the fear seems more and more irrelevant. Strong local government under conditions of political somnolence means that power will be grabbed by those piratical enough to grab it, and utilize it. Under conditions in which the governed are awakening to their collective identity, history, suffering, and rights, the situation is reversed, and the traumatic precedents mentioned above do not bind. Others, more relevant to the case at hand, come to mind: local government after the Jeffer-sonian revolution, when state legislatures and town meetings struck down property qualifications for voting and religious tests, estab-lished state universities and began, for the first time, to reflect the demands of the "little man"; state legislatures in the South under Reconstruction, which pioneered in the fields of social legislation and racial reform; state and local legislatures under Populist rule, which sixty years before the New Deal attempted to regulate indus-try and to control the quality of food sold to the public; cities under Socialist or Progressive mayors early in the present century, which initiated modern city planning and "good government"; and those state legislatures in the 1920's and 1930's that attempted to secure the rights of labor and to legislate for the poor.

Community-controlled government is not inevitably vicious, corruptible, or elitist. Often the fears of moderates to this effect reflect a displacement of other, better-founded fears—for example that the community's new leaders will mobilize large numbers of people to seek a radical change in the distribution of power. Of course, there is some truth to the proposition that new governments are often unstable and unpredictable. Where an out-group begins rapidly to develop a self-consciousness and consciousness of the world, initial attempts at self-government frequently involve turbulence and even internal violence, since new constituencies are in the process of formation and new leaders competing for their loyalty. Ordinarily, the turbulence passes as the community becomes organized. For blacks, struggling for power and dignity, to enslave themselves anew to black masters is unlikely, but even if this should happen, it is, after all, their mistake to make. Surely it is time for domestic colonialists to stop worrying about their benighted wards, and to give up the white man's burden.

The arguments against political decentralization and community control, therefore, appear to rest on a series of fallacies—elaborate rationalizations, really, for preserving the *status quo* and the hegemony of existing ruling coalitions. Admittedly, there are difficult questions to be solved before community control of the institutions of local government can become reality—for example, how shall we define the "community"? Who will pay the tax bill for self-government by the poor? (To attempt to answer such questions, there are studies now in progress on the balance of trade to and from ghettos, the real value of minority communities as markets, the real value of ghetto real estate, and so forth. With community control over the economy, the potential ghetto tax base may not be as narrow as had been thought!) The recent experiment in school-system decentralization in New York has demonstrated the critical importance of advance planning for resolution of the interest-group conflicts which decentralization will inevitably generate. But it has also demonstrated something else: the need to establish local control not just over school systems, but over all institutions established to serve local communities, from political organizations to business enterprises, and from police forces to housing projects. A little independence may be more dangerous to the peace of the cities than none at all. Clearly, the crisis through which we are now passing is not merely political, but, in the broadest sense, constitutional. Transcending the myths of consensus, it may not be too late for men of imagination and good will to agree on a new constitution for the American city.

REFERENCES

1. California Governors' Commission on the Los Angeles Riots, *Violence in the City—an End or a Beginning?* (1965).

2. See, for example, William V. Shannon, "Negro Violence vs. the American Dream," *New York Times* (July 27, 1969) and "Two Faces of the Negro Revolution," *New York Times* (July 30, 1967). On the tendency of liberal social science to play into conservative hands by focusing on group characteristics rather than system characteristcs, see Lee Rainwater and William L. Yancey, *The Moynihan Report and the Politics of Controversy* (1967).

3. See the data collected in Gary Wills, *The Second Civil War: Arming for Armageddon* (1968).

4. Robert M. Fogelson, "White on Black: A Critique of the McCone Commission Report on the Los Angeles Riots," *Political Science Quarterly* (September, 1967); Bayard Rustin, "The Watts Manifesto and the McCone Report," *Commentary* (March, 1966); Robert Blauner, "Whitewash Over Watts," *Transaction* (March–April, 1966); Stanley Lieberson and Arnold Silverman, "The Precipitants and Underlying Conditions of Race Riots," *American Sociological Review* (December, 1965).

5. *Report of the National Advisory Commission on Civil Disorders* (1968), Bantam edition, pp. 128–135.

6. See, for example, P. Meyer, "A Survey of Attitudes of Detroit Negroes after the Riots of 1967," The Urban League of Detroit (1967); William McCord and John Howard, "Negro Opinions in Three Riot Cities," *American Behavioral Scientist* (March–April, 1968); T. M. Tomlinson and David Sears, "Negro Attitudes Toward the Riots," *Los Angeles Riot Study* (1967); Nathan Caplan, "The New Ghetto Men: A Review of Recent Empirical Studies," scheduled to appear in the *Journal of Social Issues* (1969).

7. James Q. Wilson, *Varieties of Police Behavior* (1968).

8. Daniel Patrick Moynihan, *Maximum Feasible Misunderstanding; Community Action in the War on Poverty* (1969).

9. See, for example, Richard C. Wade, "Violence in the Cities: An Historical View," in *Urban Violence*, The University of Chicago Center for Policy Study (1969), p. 24; " . . . race riots were always different from other kinds of disorders . . . it is race that is at the heart of the present disorder . . . ."

10. Indicators of awakening interest in the role of political violence in American history are plentiful. See, for example, *Towards a New Past: Dissenting Essays in American History*, edited by Barton J. Bernstein (1968); *The Politics of Protest*, edited by Jerome H. Skolnick (1969); *Violence in America*, edited by Hugh Graham Davies and Theodore H. Gurr (1969). 1969 will also see the appearance of the Report of the National Advisory Commission on the Causes and Prevention of Violence (The Eisenhower Commission) and a series of reprinted documents on violence in American history edited by Robert M. Fogelson and Richard E. Rubenstein to be published by the Arno Press-New York Times.

11. This view is developed at some length in Richard E. Rubenstein, *Rebels in Eden: Mass Political Violence in the United States*, in press (1970).

12. See Chuck Stone, *Black Political Power in America* (1968), pp. 105–148.

13. See, for example, Charles V. Hamilton and Stokely Carmichael, *Black Power: The Politics of Liberation in America* (1967); Jerome H. Skolnick, "The Police and the Urban Ghetto," Research Contributions of the American Bar Foundation, No. 3 (1968); Jerome H. Skolnick, *Law on Trial* (1967); Arthur Waskow, "Community Control of the Police," Adlai Stevenson Institute Collection (1969).

14. The social internalization of violence is explored, *inter alia*, in Frantz Fanon, *The Wretched of the Earth* (1963); Grier and Cobbs, *Black Rage* (1968).

15. Special significance must be attached to law-enforcement strategies adopted in New York, Cleveland, and Chicago in spring and summer 1968. In Cleveland, the police were temporarily withdrawn from the troubled area; in New York, police permitted a limited amount of destruction to occur after the assassination of Dr. Martin Luther King; and in Chicago, following the King assassination, South Side street gangs were permitted, temporarily, to take control of the streets in order to prevent an outbreak there. The relationship between self-policing and civil peace is thus perceived, at least during emergencies. On the relationship between self-policing and the decline in private crime, the reader could do worse than see the *Battle of Algiers* (1968).

16. James Q. Wilson, *op. cit.*

17. *Ibid.*, page 288.

18. *Ibid.*, pages 288–289.

19. *Ibid.*, pages 289–290.

20. *Ibid.*, page 290.

21. *Ibid.*, page 295.

22. *Ibid.*, page 297.

23. Community control or no, the supremacy of the Federal Constitution continues to mean that racial and religous segregation are illegal. It will not do to argue as Wilson does that extending community control to whites will permit local police forces to support segregation.

24. Wilson, *op. cit.*, page 289.

MICHAEL YOUNG

The Liberal Approach: Its Weaknesses and Its Strengths
A Comment on the U. S. Riot Commission Report

THE EVENTS in modern Memphis and Atlanta, followed by their
chorus of funeral fires, have been almost as tragic for distant spectators as they have been for the actors. They have further sharpened
the absorption of the world in the affairs of an America whose title
to world leadership is that it is even more obviously "humanity in
miniature" than when Myrdal used the phrase in 1942. Not only does
it contain a myriad peoples representative of different countries and
of different colours, but these peoples are between them facing in
the concentrated form that underlies all drama the world's most fundamental moral issue: Will the Christian doctrine that we are all
God's children triumph again in race relations as it has done against
always tenacious resistance in so many other spheres? The doctrine
has not just survived the decline of the church and the weakening
of faith in the existence of God; this bit of Christianity has taken
on a new strength in a post-Christian era. The children (at least
if they are of the same colour) espouse their brotherhood more
devoutly after the death of their father. When secularised by the
long line of liberals who followed John Stuart Mill, this mighty
doctrine destroyed the British Empire. The oppressors communicated
the idea to the oppressed, and the oppressed communicated it back to
the oppressors. Could the idea be mightier still and bring together in a
brotherhood a variety of men without "distinction as to complexion"?
We know it has failed to do so in Southern Africa. Will it succeed in
America, now the chief guardian of the old doctrine in the new form
it has taken in the American Creed? The stakes for all of us are gi-
gantic. The chances of moderating colour conflict in the world and,
in the long run, of avoiding the deadliest kind of war, depend upon
the ability of Europe to live in brotherhood with Africa in America.
The chances for humanity in general depend upon humanity in
miniature.

331

This is perhaps as obvious (or more so) writing from today's England as it is from elsewhere. Ten years ago it might have been different; anti-Americanism was so rife and coloured people in the country so few that if the riots had happened then there might have been some perfidious crowing. But now we are a miniature of the miniature. Coloured immigration, the legacy of Empire, has uncovered as much prejudice among limey whiteys as among yankee. The prejudice has helped to create ghettos in Brixton and North Kensington, Sparkbrook and Southall. A Labour Government, deferring to the racism of its own supporters (many of whom are also supporters of Enoch Powell), has done nothing major to prevent these districts from becoming future Notting Hills except to restrict further immigration and this in disregard of promises made to the Kenyan Indians. When we watch the news from American cities on television, we know that we may be seeing our own future. We know, too, that if America can provide a model of reconciliation, it will be one on which we can build.

The report of the Kerner Commission is, therefore, almost a domestic document, even if it has not been produced by Her Majesty's Stationery Office, and I am going to comment on it as freely as if it were. It is immensely welcome. Joe McCarthy is still a haunting presence in Britain, as well as in America, and after the summer of 1967 the fear was that extremism would breed extremism, that the Goneril of a Stokely Carmichael would be matched by the Regan of a Reagan, or worse. The report might have edged that way, as some thought it would when the Commission's membership was first announced; if it had, the dreaded polarisation of black and white would have been pushed a good deal further. The Right would have had an official stance. We can, therefore, take great comfort from what the report is *not* and rejoice that instead of a manifesto for the Right the Commission has issued a mammoth manifesto of liberalism. It is a reaffirmation of the American Creed at a period in the world's history when it could not have been more timely, one that is, if anything, even more so after Memphis. This is such virtue that the report, despite its repetitiveness and other more serious weaknesses, ranks as a great and moving document. This is especially true of Part I, "What Happened?" The whole report sustains faith in America.

But even so one cannot help wishing that it had been something more. The report has avoided the extremism of white and black marvelously well, and yet (as in such critical times it must be difficult to avoid doing) has gone in for a sort of extremism all the same, the extremism of the middle. A certain kind of primitive liberalism is there almost to the last "t". Having decided to attribute the blame to white society, as was surely right and courageous, the Commission has made everything else it says consistent—in fact far too consistent to be convincing. White society created the ghetto: "White institutions created it, white institutions maintain it, and white society condones it." Yes, but white society is not consistent. It also does not condone the ghetto. The report notes that "Burn, baby, burn" was originated by a disc jockey. It does not recognise, or at any rate does not say, that white society and, above all, the ethos of equality I mentioned a moment ago created more than the Kerner Commission. It has sustained Negro protest. It has sustained a civil rights movement that has, after all, enjoyed more success in the last ten years than in the previous hundred. Where else did the ethos come from?—certainly not from Africa. It may seem that again and again nothing fails like success, that expectations are always outpacing achievement, but this should not detract from the achievement, which is primary. If the blame is white society's, so is the credit. If the riots partly stemmed from the Vietnam war (because the war detracted from the legitimation of white society), it is still immensely creditable to have produced a report like this while the war continues.

It is the same with one of the basic diagnoses of the report: That there is a kind of iron law at work that, unless the whole liberal bill is acted upon, will produce a steady worsening of the situation. There is, for instance, "accelerating segregation of low-income, disadvantaged Negroes within the ghettos of the largest American cities," and within them an increase of crime, drug addiction, family instability, and illegitimacy. Schools and housing deteriorate. Needs increase, but the income to meet them goes down as the tax base is eroded by the exodus of white people and industry to the suburbs, and so on.

True enough; but the other side of the picture—the striking economic progress there has been—is not so prominently displayed. For many years now, calves have been calving double in America. Negroes have gained along with whites. The Commission recognises this when it says that "most whites and many Negroes outside the ghetto have prospered to a degree unparalleled in the history of civilization." (Should it not be *most* Negroes though?) But in the next sentence triumph suddenly becomes disaster: "Through television—the universal appliance in the ghetto—and the other media of mass communications, this affluence has been endlessly flaunted before the eyes of the Negro poor and the jobless ghetto youth." The Commission has so fully, and in a way admirably, identified itself with the ghetto people that the members seem to feel their same despair. Neither can gain on the swings *or* on the roundabouts. If America does not get richer, there will not be enough money to spare for the ghetto; if America does get richer, the ghetto people will by contrast feel poorer than ever. Relatively speaking, the poor blacks will whatever happens be as poor as ever.

Yes, yes, one keeps wanting to say, *but* why won't they go on to draw the proper conclusion? Of course poverty can never be abolished. Unless Pareto's Law can be deprived of effect, incomes will continue to conform to a normal distribution, and the people in the bottom tail of that distribution will be in poverty, the same in a hundred years as now. The proper conclusion in this context is surely that a major goal is to bring about the same distribution of incomes among the blacks as among the whites. As far as the poor are concerned, this means that the representation of Negroes in, say, the bottom 20 per cent of income distribution should be reduced to the proportion that they form of the general population; if Negroes are 11 per cent of the total population, there should not be more than 11 per cent of them in poverty. If this be one of the major goals, then a vital social indicator would show how far it is approaching or receding from year to year. Since it does not state the goal, the report naturally does not give any prominence to the indicator. It says that "the proportion of Negroes employed in high-skill, high-status, and well-paying jobs rose faster than comparable proportions among whites from 1960 to 1966." It then relegates to a footnote the statement that "the proportion of non-white families living in poverty dropped from 39 per cent to 35 per cent from 1964 to 1966." There is clearly a long way to go, but at least the movement is in the right direction.

The progress, such as it is, means that there has been some improvement in the Negro standard of life relative not just to their standards in the past, but also to the present standards of whites. The self-blame that liberals are liable to is so evident in the report that this progress is not at any point featured. The missing man, as Nathan Glazer has pointed out, is the Negro who is not in ghetto poverty at all.[1] "Thus, between 2.0 and 2.5 million poor Negroes are living in disadvantaged neighborhoods of central cities in the United States. These persons comprise only slightly more than 1 per cent of the nation's total population, but they make up about 16 to 20 per cent of the total Negro population of all central cities, and a much higher proportion in certain cities." But what of the other 80 per cent? The Commission's focus on the ghetto poor and their belief that things are getting worse there have prevented them from asking this question. It is a crucial one. The Commission seems to recognise this in passing, when it says of the better-off Negro, without giving any weight to it, that "relative affluence seems at least to inhibit him from attacking the existing social order and may motivate him to take considerable risks to protect it," or when it speaks more particularly of the beneficial influence of Negro policemen and counter-rioters, like Hesham Jaaber in Elizabeth, New Jersey, the Positive Neighborhood Action Committee in Detroit, and effective individuals like the twenty-four-year-old E. G. in Detroit, or the two young Plainfield Negroes described as D. H., the newspaper reporter, and L. C., the chemical worker. The outcome of present discontents depends upon the extent to which the 80 per cent become involved in political and other action to relieve the plight of themselves and their fellow Negroes in and out of the ghetto. Without allotting them a central role, there can be no grand strategy for changing the conditions that gave rise to the riots of 1967 and 1968.

These are my first and minor criticisms, and they relate to the general analysis of the place of the Negro in American society. My second set is about the recommendations. They, too, seem to me to embody a primitive kind of liberalism. The members of the Commission are all distinguished men of affairs, with intimate experience of politics and administration. Yet they write as if they were outside instead of inside the establishment; it is not only state and city police who are operating on different wave lengths. Why this should be so I cannot from this distance fathom, unless it be that at the moment there is, apart from this brand of liberalism, no other well-accepted body of thought on race relations for such a body to reflect. It may seem especially strange to me because I am used to reports of Royal Commissions, which lean too far the other way; their members sometimes appear to be so sensitive to the problems of government that they might be its mouthpiece.

The chief marks of the informed outsider's view on almost anything important are these: that a very great deal is attacked as wrong, and very drastic and speedy action is said to be needed to avert disaster. The mark of the insider's view is his awareness of the harsh necessity of choice. No government can ever do a lot quickly. Since resources are always limited, and their possible uses unlimited, policy-makers and administrators have constantly to choose or, in other words, to decide which alternatives have priority. This is obvious stuff of course, and it is only mentioned because the Kerner Report, to take it at its face value, has overlooked the obvious. It has failed to cost its massive list of recommendations either in terms of money or of manpower of different levels of skill, and it has failed to say what priority should attach to each in the use of resources or in the order in time in which they should be acted upon. Its value to governments—federal, state, or local—is therefore bound to be less than it could have been. They all want to know how to make a dollar go furthest; how, that is, to achieve the most for the least. But perhaps it is not too late. Could some of the members of the Commission be recalled—joined this time by some social scientists, with priority for an economist proficient in the cost-benefit analysis for which America is rightly so famous, and for a sociologist well-versed in the debate about social indicators—and asked to say how and why they would spend sums of various orders from the amount at present spent on the Vietnam war downwards? This kind of work is going on in many places, but the results could be usefully pulled together in a second volume of the report. And could the new national commission be matched by a series of local commissions that would have exactly the same task for their cities? It might be objected that this would be to arrogate the functions of government at the national or local level. The objection is not convincing. How much money there will be and how it is spent will be decided in good part by political pressures. But there is still need not just for political pressure on behalf of this or that sectional interest, but for a great deal more thought about the cost-effectiveness of the different steps that might be taken to improve the lot of the Negro American. Continued study is, as the Commission said, essential.

Since I have attacked the Commission on a major point, I feel bound, even as an outsider myself and very much of a one at that, to say something about how I would respond to the same challenge. What would my priorities be? I am going to mention a short list under two main headings: the police and the system of local administration.

The Police

Much of what the Commission says about the police is admirable. The report fully recognises the importance of the part the police play in and out of the ghetto, in times of civil peace as much as in times of civil disorder. Professor Reiss' judgment is endorsed. "The slum police precinct is like the slum school. It gets, with few exceptions, the worst in the system." The worst is too often also the most racist. It is therefore not surprising that the first grievances of the Negro communities in the cities surveyed were police practices. Anyone who reads the horrifying accounts of the behavior of police (whether or not they had Confederate pennants on their cars) in Bridgeton, New Jersey, or in the 10th Precinct Station in Detroit will sympathise. Improvement of police standards would probably do more than any other single change to take heat out of the situation and restore a little of the respect for authority that is evidently so lacking and so needed. More adequate police protection would also encourage the 80 per cent to side more openly with the forces of law and order.

The report thus makes a whole slate of recommendations: for assignment to the ghettos of "officers with superior ability, sensitivity and the common sense necessary for enlightened law enforcement"; for giving them special incentives, getting patrolmen out of the car and into the neighbourhood; and for moderating aggressive "stop-and-frisk" practices. It puts forward an excellent proposal for recruiting as "community service officers" many more young Negroes between seventeen and twenty-one without the ordinary standard police qualifications and then giving them the opportunity to "graduate" into full police officers; and a hundred other proposals besides. The Commission even wants the police to take on more willingly a host of non-police services, including the settlement of marital disputes.

This is all very sensible. Such a new model policeman would certainly make a striking difference to the urban scene. He (or she?) would be the visible representative of authority capable of giving aid and service as well as enforcing the law. But if he is to take on so much more on behalf of society, what more is society going to give him in return? Apparently nothing. The tone of comment on the police is almost uniformly unsympathetic. The Commission has identified with the ghetto Negro, but perhaps just because it has succeeded in that, it has failed to identify also with the police. To appreciate their difficulties as they see them, one has to read between instead of on the lines. No surveys are reported on police attitudes.

The new model police are needed right enough. But where are they to come from in sufficient quantity and, above all, quality? The Commission does not say. It notes, but without any emphasis, that "Blue Flu" raged among the police in Detroit before the riots and that the poor pay of the police is one reason why "better qualified Negroes are often more attracted by other, better paying positions." But why not again draw the obvious conclusion? My first priority would be an improvement in the pay and conditions of the police force at all levels. It would no doubt involve federal subvention. But my guess is that a dollar spent on that would do more than a dollar spent on anything else to reduce the threat of further riots and, more positively, to improve race relations. The relative pay of the police can no longer be considered an index of civil order.

There is an important related matter on which there is no comment at all. Seen from England, the most extraordinary omission in the whole report is the failure to say anything about the need for civil disarmament, and this even though it was written before Memphis. There are unprecedented riots; police and National Guardsmen, with guns everywhere, are terrified of "snipers"; suburban housewives and others start arming themselves; rumours of armed bands marching into or out of the city terrify everyone; and yet even such a report as this does not mention arms control once.

It does say that "a climate that tends towards approval and encouragement of violence as a form of protest has been created by white terrorism directed against non-violent protest." But has not violence also been encouraged by the approval given to its instrument?

To institute arms control would, therefore, be my second priority. I know this is an easy thing to suggest from this disarmed island. The police here can be without guns partly because there are so few guns among the populace, and there are so few of them among the populace partly because hunting was traditionally a prerogative of the aristocracy and landed gentry. The American's right to carry arms is indeed partly a reaction against the aristocratic tradition in England in the eighteenth century. Anyway, you have a National Rifle Association, and we do not. But after the riots and the assassinations (of which we have surely not seen the last) is it not time to take issue with pressure group and tradition? Quite apart from prohibiting Sears Roebuck and the like from selling guns, could not all arms, under pain of penalty, be lodged in police-controlled stores from which they could only be withdrawn "on parole" for specified periods for use on hunting trips or other legitimate purposes? Once the citizenry were disarmed, the police whom they protect could be also. I think that whether and how the police are armed is a better index of the state of civil order than their pay. General Throckmorton ordered the weapons of all military personnel unloaded in Detroit. It would indeed be a day for America and the world if the police could be ordered not just to unload, but to disarm.

Local Administration

"Program" is an American word for which I can find no translation in our brand of English. "Programme" is certainly quite different and "scheme" somewhat so. I am glad there is none. The report is packed with programs for this and that, and full, too, of complaints about the confusions which they engender. The Commissioners are outspoken about the fault.

The spectacle of Detroit and New Haven engulfed in civil turmoil despite a multitude of federally-aided programs raised basic questions as to whether the existing "delivery system" is adequate to the bold new purposes of national policy. . . . There are now over 400 grant programs operated by a broad range of federal agencies and channeled through a much larger array of semi-autonomous state and local government entities. Reflective of this complex scheme, federal programs often seem self-defeating and contradictory: field officials unable to make decisions on their own programs and unaware of related efforts; agencies unable or unwilling to work together; programs conceived and administered to achieve different and sometimes conflicting purposes. . . . The existing welfare programs are a labyrinth of federal, state and local legislation.

To find a way through the labyrinth there has been the usual device of the labyrinthine. "Some two dozen inter-agency committees have been established to coordinate two or more federal aid programs."

But surely what is needed is not 400^{300} new inter-agency programs for coordinating existing programs, not more coordination but more actual unification of administration. To hope for this at the federal or even at the state level is perhaps to hope for too much. Could there not, however, be unification at the local level? The Commission does recognise the need for this at the most local level of all. The Neighborhood Action Task Force it proposes wherever there are many "low-income minority citizens" would be a sort of neighbourhood council. But its proposed functions are vague; it is not even recommended that each Task Force set young Negroes to work during the summer building their own swimming pools and other amenities. Its relationship to the city government is also vague. How could such a "community cabinet," as it is called, focus all those programs if immediately above the neighbourhood the agencies responsible for them remain scattered through a dozen pages of the telephone directory? Should one not aspire to one or at any rate a few for the whole of local bureaucracy? This would imply that most federal aid would be channeled through the city administration and that federal agencies at the local level would be defederalised and made part of the municipality. Such issues are not mentioned by the Commission. Being men of experience in politics, they presumably know what devils they would be letting loose if such issues had been mentioned, and they also realise that any reform of local bureaucracy which was more than tinkering would take so long to accomplish in the face of entrenched opposition that the summer of 1980 could have come and gone before there was very much to show for the expenditure of a great deal of energy. Presumably, therefore, one has to rule out unification of local planning and administration with single local governments covering the areas of whole conurbations, suburbs and all. What I would naturally propose for this tidy England is presumably sheerly impracticable for America. Yet if that is so at least there is a great advantage that can be secured from the plurality of government that exists. It seems to me that the Commission, in preferring the Integration Choice to the Enrichment Choice (as it was surely right to do for the long run), has played down the value that could be derived in the meantime from the deployment of Black Power and its use for constructive work in the neighbourhoods and cities where Negroes are in sufficient density to grasp it.[2] Successful new model governments led by Negroes would be symbols for racial pride to concentrate on, commanding general respect from whites as well as blacks.

My last priority would therefore be for the exercise of the utmost positive discrimination in favour of Negro political leadership, embracing the 80 per cent as well as the 20 per cent in Cleveland or Gary or anywhere else where there is a chance of creating the kind of political machine the Negroes have so far

A Comment on the Riot Commission Report

lacked. It could be aided, too, if private corporations (particularly if the Vietnam war can be ended) were drawn in and given responsibility for organising the employment of Negroes for rebuilding in the ghettos. One of many other priority steps that would help would be the abolition of the lunatic and unjust "Man-in-the-House" rule for the payment of welfare benefits. Many of the ills from which the ghetto suffers derive from fatherless families, and yet here is government actually sowing the dragon's teeth. This same issue was one of the most bitter political issues in Britain in the 1930's. Nothing but good has come from the subsequent abolition of the "Means Test" which used to embody that same residue from the Elizabethan Poor Law. I am sure that a similar reform in America would produce the same benefits for family life.

I said earlier that I was not going to spare criticism, and I have not. But despite that, I want to end by reiterating that this is a great document, even a noble one. It speaks with the voice of an enlightenment that could keep social chaos at bay, for America and for the world.

March 20, 1968   London

REFERENCES

1. Nathan Glazer, "The Real Task in America's Cities," *New Society* (March 21, 1968).

2. For a discussion on all this, see Peter Marris and Martin Rein, *Dilemma of Social Reform: Poverty and Community Action in the United States* (New York, 1967).

MAX LERNER

The Negro American and His City: Person in Place in Culture

I

THE AMERICAN city, in the late 1960's, is caught in three great testings: First: Can racial groups live together not in an uneasy coexistence punctuated by erratic flare-ups of burnings and killings, but in a going community of give-and-take, live-and-let-live? Second: Can a tolerable open society, clinging to the frame and political style of a traditional democracy, absorb and resolve the tensions of social division that are at once racial, class, and generational in character? Third: Is the modern American city viable as a social organism—that is to say, can it meet the minimum needs of the growing-up years so as to achieve a reasonably healthy personality structure with some roots in the city environment?

All three questions are obviously entangled, but I shall concentrate on the third. I should guess that whatever clues we shall find to the first two will largely depend on what clues we find to the third. My assumption in this essay is the rather obvious one—that nothing short of a total coalition of all relevant resources and talents will enable the city and the society to survive these testings. I propose not so much to argue this as to examine some of its implications.

What targets should the coalition energies focus on, by what strategies, with what guiding theories, in what spirit? The usual plea has been to make all programs "action-oriented," a plea voiced by whites and Negroes alike, by people of every political persuasion. The purpose is to avoid bureaucratic obstructions and paper constructs and to be pragmatic rather than theoretical. But action in itself can be a mindless value and in fact retrogressive. To do something about cleaning up the streets and the littered

342

yards, getting new housing and new jobs, keeping kids in school, training and re-training young men and older men—that is obviously necessary. But it will not be adequate unless some questions are asked and answered about the action itself. Who will work at it with whom, and who will make the decisions? By what incentives will the work be sustained?

And for what good—*cui bono?* Take the job-creating task. In a technology in which speed-tape mechanisms are replacing earlier skilled and semiskilled work, the question of what kinds of jobs and for whom is of some consequence. If Peter Drucker is right in his essay in this volume, it would follow that schooling, training, and apprenticeship programs will have different impacts depending on whether the trainees are to be located in the old or the new industries. The building of new schoolhouses becomes less important than the question of what is taught, by whom, and under whose controls. As for housing, it is a truism that urban renewal programs have tended to tear down the dwellings where the poor have lived and to set up middle-income units in their place, thus leaving homeless the very people whose living conditions set the projects in motion in the first place. And if the aim is to break open the ghetto trap, I agree with Melvin Webber that coalition operations might better be focused on making low-income dwelling units available in the larger metropolitan area, especially since the location of industries is bypassing the central city.

In the broadest terms the coalition concept means the deployment of every resource upon whatever target. In a more precise sense it means a working coordination of a number of agencies in attacking the problem of the inner city—more concretely, government units at every level, independent government corporations, private corporate enterprise, banks, insurance companies, trade unions, voluntary organizations, churches, universities, school boards, foundations, media representatives, and *ad hoc* "people's groups" in the neighborhood. America is pluralistic, and every new problem must therefore be attacked by a cluster of organizations working toward a common end. But beyond the cluster itself, a coalition implies a strategy of operation for its members, articulating their roles and their relations to one another and to the program.

In every coalition, however widespread and intricate the net of membership, there are three prime partners who must carry the main burden of the support and strategy. They are government, business, and the neighborhood group. They are *primi inter pares* because among them they have the sinews of action, the first two with the money and the power, the third with the necessary good will and knowledge of life conditions and a hunger for choices. The coalition may prove to be a way of breaking the old impasse about whether government or business should take responsibility and wield power over whatever needs doing. By widening the field of discourse, increasing the partners, linking government and business with the people whose lives in the city are being affected, and by placing the stress on the how rather than the whether, on the strategy of coordination rather than on the conventional legitimacy of the cooperative action itself, the coalition method breaks away from the barren disputes of the past and opens new ground. It also tries to achieve something of that "civic religion" that Tocqueville noted in the participatory democracy of the America he visited.

In a rough typology of strategies, one can isolate five. There is the action by a single corporation (for example, Fairchild-Hiller, Aerojet General, U.S. Gypsum) or by a group of them (a consortium of life insurance companies) for a specific project in the slum area, whether for creating new jobs or building houses or whatever. Often such a project is not calculated to make a profit; although it may not be economic, it is responsive to a larger self-interest that sees corporate health as part of community health. There is the effort to attack the business-incentive problem by grants, subsidies, and especially government guarantees to cover possible losses. (The Javits, Percy, and Kennedy plans belong here, as do many others.) There is the "triggering" government corporation (Governor Rockefeller's innovative plan for New York State is the best example) whereby a government body, funded by a vast bond issue, rides herd on local obstructions and makes initial expenditures and commitments in the hope of triggering further commitments by business itself which may exceed the total governmental fund by a multiple of five or more. There is the *ad hoc* loose business alignment (for example, the National Alliance of Businessmen, under Henry Ford's chairmanship) that serves as liaison between business and governmental groups, mainly for work-training programs. There is the city or neighborhood program (Newark is an example) where a local corporation or coalition, composed of representatives of the dwellers themselves, undertakes a housing construction program on its own, with government and allied funds, instead of having the programs planned and carried out *for* it. In Philadelphia a coalition of white businessmen has pledged an industrial fund, to be administered by a "Black Coalition," aimed at helping the black community to self-help measures.

Cutting across these, on a deeper level, there are several different viewpoints about the target area to which these strategies are directed. The first may see it in economic terms, as a consumption and purchasing power area whose potentials have not yet been tapped, and whose health or unhealth can affect the rest of the nation. Another sees it politically, as an explosive area where further explosions could endanger the fabric of the nation itself, and which must therefore be contained and enriched. A third sees it as an undeveloped region (like the Italian South) or even as an undeveloped country, to which a total development strategy needs to be applied (this comes close to the thinking of Hubert Humphrey), encompassing a set of feasibility studies, the use of loans and investment guarantees for job-creating programs, the dispatch of technical expertise to the city to work under local direction and with a local plan. There are doubtless other viewpoints as well. The only one about which little is said is to view the city quite simply as *a city*, a fusion of earth and ethnos and ethos, of place and personality and life style.

II

What kind of crisis does the American city face? In sheer physical terms the crisis is easy enough to describe: There is the pollution of air and water, the eyesore ugliness of billboards, the littered ugliness of vacant lots and auto graveyards, the chaos of badly planned transport, the strangling of the city by traffic, the violent explosions of the city in riots. No one can question that this chaotic ugliness and this ugly chaos are true of the American city. The city is being choked, clogged, strangled, and burned to death. Nor can anyone doubt that nothing short of a radical redesigning of the physical, social, cultural, and human environment will save the city from the body and spirit of this death.

But that begs the question: *What kind* of a radical redesigning? Conceivably one could finish the choking-strangling-burning job, level the cities of the plain, and start all over again, in different places or the same ones. But one would have to start with the same society, the same historic memories. Leveling the cities is no shortcut to a solution. To reinvent them in a better way one would have to grapple with the question of how they have come to their present situation.

This question must, in turn, be broken down into two related, and yet separable, parts. One is how the existing inequalities developed between the racial groups in the cities—inequalities in income, employment, living standards, and treatment at the hands of the society. The other is why the large-scale violence came when it did and where it did.

The answer to the first has been spelled out in a series of inquiries and reports, both governmental and academic, from President Truman's pathbreaking commission on discriminatory practices in the nation's capital to the post-Watts report in California to the Kerner Commission report. It will be found also as the background social reasoning that bolsters the judicial reasoning in a number of key Supreme Court decisions, notably under the Warren Court. It runs primarily in terms of the social and psychological heritage of slavery and Reconstruction, as well as in terms of the impact both of history and of the badge of color upon racist discriminatory practices by the whites and upon the self-image of the blacks. There can be no question that the only way to make good these injustices flowing from inequalities is through a massive institutionalizing of justice and equality. It must inform every phase of the relations between the "two societies" so as to make them one larger pluralistic society—the work and income phase, food and diet, schooling, housing, the physical setting of neighborhood and city, and above all else the phase of political power without which other gains will seem phantasmagoric.

The whole thing has the simplicity of a geometrical proposition. The only trouble with it is whatever is, at the core, the trouble with the over-rationalist, over-determinist, simplistic thinking of traditional liberalism. The determinist fallacy: Since the present situation has been determined by economic-social conditions, then change the conditions, and all will be well. The rationalist fallacy: Only do away with prejudice, repair people's ignorance, get them to understand one another, and all will be well. The liberal-ethical fallacy: Only deal with objective injustices and replace them with objective justice, and all will be well. Add two others to these: the law-and-order fallacy and the ethnic ghetto fallacy. If the others are determinist and rationalist-liberal, these two are normative. The law-and-order (crackdown) fallacy: Only apply the norms of law and order to those who are breaking both and crack down on the malefactors, and all will be well. The ethnic ghetto fallacy: There have been other ethnic minorities who have lived in ghettos, but they worked hard and educated themselves, and were able to get out; why not the blacks?

Thus the thicket of fallacies surrounding the question of the white-black relationship in the inner city. In every instance what is at fault is reductionism and abstraction—the reduction of a complex problem to one aspect of it, the abstraction of that phase from the whole.

One hears it said often that the American city is being broken apart by the forces of race, or by the forces of class conflict, or by the forces of the power struggle. It is nearer the truth to say that no single force is tearing the city apart, but that these three and several other divisive strains as well are in operation. Since the city is the loose envelope that contains, within its bounds of place, all the going strains and thrusts of American civilization, it follows that the crisis of the city is a crisis of class, race, and power divisions, and that it is also a crisis of the generational conflict and the value rebellion.

If this is true, then there is no easy gimmick that can resolve the crisis of the city. The reason why the coalition attack on it makes sense is that only a total effort could possibly hope to bring to bear a range of measures that would affect the income and daily life of the inner-city dweller as a member of a class, deal with his self-image as the member of a racial group, give him a chance to replace his powerlessness with some power, narrow the gap of generational bitterness and separation, and place within his reach the real life-options out of which a choice of values becomes possible. The existing inequalities have developed not because one particular facet has gone awry in the situation and treatment of the blacks, but in a sense because the whole alignment of the civilization-pattern has gone awry for them. Crucially, an economic, legal, political, and moral task is involved in setting it right.

The second question that I mentioned above—why the violence in the cities should have come when and where it did—is much harder to answer. Correspondingly it is more difficult to resolve in the arena of social action. Although the inequalities have been institutionalized, the discontents have been internalized. An institutional change will affect the inequalities, but not necessarily resolve the discontents.

With startling prescience, Tocqueville saw that the real problem of black-and-white relations would come after the abolition of slavery, and that it would come because the blacks, dissatisfied with formal freedom, would not stop short of anything except complete equality. "The Negroes," he wrote, "might remain slaves for a long time without complaining; but as soon as they join the ranks of free men, they will be indignant at being deprived of almost all the rights of citizens; and being unable to become the equals of the Whites, they will not be slow to show themselves their enemies." Tocqueville understood the dynamics of passionate movements, which we generally call "revolutions." Studying the French Revolution, he saw that it had not come at the point when the condition of the people was at its worst, but when important concessions had been made and conditions were on an upward arc. Every intense social movement, he saw, "grows by what it feeds on." Bukharin saw the same phenomenon much later: "In revolutions, appetite grows with the eating."

Seen thusly, it becomes clear why the great civil rights victories of the 1950's and 1960's, starting with Brown v. Board of Education, were accompanied not by social peace, but by mounting violence. Revolutions come in periods not of stagnation, but of accelerated social change. They come in periods not of apathy and hopelessness, but of rising hope—hope that is not fulfilled rapidly enough and therefore turns to frustration and bitterness. When Myrdal wrote his *American Dilemma*, it was largely an appeal to the conscience of the whites, and he wondered whether the dynamic of American idealism—both from religious and political sources—could operate effectively enough against the resistances of racism. His focus was upon the mind and personality of the whites. The Kerner report, with the same emphasis and the same focus, may be seen as the closing phase of the Myrdal approach, not as the beginning of a chapter in the story of black-white relations, but as the ending of one.

III

The next phase must focus on the psychodynamics of the Negro personality and the voyage of the mind of the blacks. The question is not only of the objective reality of whatever access the blacks get to economic and social life-chances, but also of their subjective perception of it. A good deal of the destiny of the cities will depend on the internal struggle between alienation and trust, especially in the mind of the young Negro as he grows into adolescence and beyond, whether in the ghetto streets and schoolrooms or—in the rarer cases—in middle-class homes and on university campuses.

Even a too summary glance at the development of the Negro personality will show how counterproductive it is to abstract any phase of the problem of the cities from its rich living context—a context that must always be sought at the convergence of person, place, and culture which we call the Negro ghetto. The young Negro, in his growing-up years, is subjected to a barrage of forces that zero in on his career-line. Roughly they can be put under four heads: the family, largely unstructured, mainly matrifocal; the media, at once stimulating and disillusioning, especially TV; the school, in the form of the angry classroom, lunchroom, play-yard; the street, with its cacophony of sounds and sights, its "welter of pathologies" (in Kenneth Clark's phrase), its sexual vividness, and its criminal marginalism in the form of prostitute, dope-pusher, numbers-runner. In later years, one might add to these socializing agencies the church (especially in the tightly cohesive southern communities), more than occasionally the police precinct-house or jail, and of course the Army, and for some the university.

While I have called these socializing agencies, in the sense that they bring the young Negro into the adult community in one way or another, they are not acculturating in the sense of fitting him into the larger culture, although they may in fact fit him into the ghetto subculture. One danger we run in observing the Negro family is to measure it against that of two other ethnic minorities, the Jews and the Irish or Italian Catholics, in another ghetto in the earlier history of the American city.

It is a danger because these two classic instances of access and acculturation present a false norm for the very different Negro family, with its very different historic experience, social and economic location, and life style. The Jews and the Irish, to take the best-studied ethnic minorities, started with what may be called the *dream of access,* which they never gave up. There was a good deal of family stability among the Jews, less of it with the Irish, but in both cases it was directed at "making good." They developed the rooted ties of owning (retail store, skill-shop) and running (precinct, ward); they had a tradition of the life of the mind, whether in intellectual skills or the church; they valued the winning of prestige in their subculture and larger culture. Crucially

349

they could leave the ghetto once they got the means to leave. Although they were kept out of the social Establishment of the owning and governing caste, they did not have color as a residual badge of past subjection to keep them trapped where they were.

The dream of access has proved an eroded dream for the Negro. This is not true of the upwardly mobile middle-class Negro family, but in the other instances equal access to equal life-chances has been a cup offered, but dashed from the lips. The capacity to make use of it is less, precisely because the condition of the poor Negro family in the city—the illegitimacy, the absent father, the working mother, the cruel pressures of the relief rolls—has not been conducive to the exploration of access. There is a temptation for the Negro youth to use the obstacles in the path of access as a rationalization for inaction, a way of opting out of the competitive struggle. The result is often the drifter or operator who lives on his wits—sometimes on the margin of the criminal world, preferring the unpredictable windfalls of such a life to the burdens of an arduous job.

The media role has been disputed among a number of observers of life in the inner city. My own strong feeling is that TV played an important historic role in breaking the Negro household out of its isolation and giving it a new window on the larger world. TV and the auto have been the two ways out of the ghetto, making ghetto life tolerable for those who must stay in it, yet want to escape from it. But as often happens when the walls of isolation are broken down and when traditional culture-elements are rapidly modernized, the result may be an uprooting and confusion of the personality. That has happened a number of times in the new African states, when emigrants have left their village and tribal ties to come to the city, and when the change has left them detribalized, without any new roots and ties to take the place of the old ones. In a sense, the Negro American, torn from the roots of his church-oriented southern community with its larger joint family, a migrant to the big northern city, has used television as a way of enlarging his vistas and has ended in the same confusion of self-image as his African contemporary.

TV lighted up the little Negro flat or tenement with a view from the great world outside. It showed off the seductiveness of that world, its Babylonian surfaces and splendors, its sleek cars, its high living, its expensive fabrics, its consumers' goods, and above all its cash nexus and vendibilities as expressed in TV commercials. The urban Negro, for whom the TV screen had become a necessity no matter how low his income, was at once seduced and repelled by this view. The prizes it held out were attractive, but eluded the grasp of those who reached for them. If anything, TV may have deepened their mistrust of a society so capable of withholding what it seemed to offer, and may have widened their estrangement from it. The homes you saw were not open to you, the consumers' goods were priced beyond your range, the delicious fripperies of kitchen and boudoir could be galling if you were jobless and on the poverty level that the relief check afforded. Perhaps deeper than anything else, the white sexuality displayed was meant for whites, not blacks, and in some states it could mean death if you reached to respond to it. Thus the light that showered into the Negro flat from the TV screen, for all its brilliance, turned out for many to be a light that failed.

The trouble with the school was its inability to make what it taught, and the teachers as well, at all relevant. It was geared to a different way of life, different ordeals and ideals, a different career-line and personality-structure. But it offered a good arena for combat, a good stage on which to disport yourself. As for the vocational skills they were ready to teach you, what was the use of learning them if they fitted you for jobs that were not there or that paid worse for blacks than whites, with unions that often made the admission of blacks intolerably difficult? The Army was another matter: The black soldier or Marine got a chance to show the stuff he was made of, alongside the white, in a democracy of danger and death. Besides, the skills the services taught were skills that equipped you for work in the new electronic age, and the prestige of Army service carried over into civilian life and gave you a good chance at a job. The returned veteran was likely to find himself less estranged from the white society, more in command of himself in the black society, than any other Negro, including the upwardly mobile civilian blacks. But what an irony that the back door by which a black could enter into some kind of social normality should be a door that carried the danger of death.

Thus the career-line: family, street, media, school, Army. The inner fantasy-life that it has carried with it is one that lay ready for the spark of violence to ignite and explode. If one were to say that this fantasy-life counts for the black personality, that the disheartening gap between fantasies and the reality-principle is the clue to the discontents and therefore also to the confrontations with white authority, many "action-oriented" students of the problem might scoff. Yet I venture that there is an arena of action inside the mind and imagination that may be less dramatic than the actions outside, but without it the tearing down and building of structures, clearing and remodeling of decayed areas, the new investment, the revamping of welfare will have little focus and relevance. It forms the *cui bono* for the whole coalition approach.

Obviously I have myself been guilty of a kind of abstraction and reduction in talking as if there were a single universal personality type among the young Negroes growing up in the ghetto. One could suggest a more complex typology: the ambitious, upwardly mobile skill-oriented Negro, including not only the teachers and other professionals, but also the young men returning now from the armed services; the rooted, code-bound, church-oriented Negro, either lower-middle class or proletarian; the alienated Negro, disillusioned about white society, but still willing to move toward integration and ready to believe in the ultimate promise of an open society; the militant Negro personality, not only alienated but separatist, who has given up hope for anything but coexistence with the whites and believes that the best way to get that coexistence is to claim it, not flinching from the gun as a weapon and from fire as a symbolic leveler; the alienated Negro (again) who is not an activist, but a drifter and *Luftmensch,* making his living in the interstices of a loosely organized society, ready to make consumers' goods his own on the right occasion of violence, but uninterested in activism or revolution; and finally the Negro who has not been able to tolerate the gap between his fantasy-life and reality without becoming a drug addict and getting involved in petty crime.

I should add that in the last two types the undue postponement of the work life of the adolescent, which operates in the case of the whites to provide him with skills for a post-industrial (or knowledge-applied-to-industry) era, operates in the case of the Negro adolescent only to cast him adrift exactly when he should be putting down the roots of job, place, home, and defining his sense of selfhood.

I fear that the whites have not begun to understand the inner world of the Negro, or his fantasy-life, or the meaning that modes of personality and behavior have in the life of the Negro which would seem abnormal in the life of the whites. The norms and modalities are different, and the failure to see this has led to a failure of white psychologists and psychoanalysts to make much sense of the Negro personality in their studies of it "in depth." Where the liberal white reformer has seen the Negro on an overly rationalistic plane, the psychiatric studies have tended to see him as a set of case histories in irrationalism and psychosis, partly at least because they have not taken into account the different emotional constitution of the Negro family, the different meanings attached to male sexuality, and the different contexts in which identity is or is not achieved. If one were to take as accurate the picture of the Negro personality emerging from the psychiatric profiles-in-depth, the task of ever getting communication—not to speak of social peace—between the races would be hopeless.

I do not mean to gloss over the difficulties both of communication and social peace. They loom particularly large when you look at the whole sweeping cycle of the Negro role, from his African homeland until today, and see the progression from warrior to slave to proletarian to sullen and smoldering resister of white society and white authority. The Negro American has not passed through the stages of merchant and intellectual that the Jew has passed through, nor of lawyer and politician as in the case of the Irish. We cannot expect to cramp him into the mold of the other ethnic minorities. But it should be clear that one of the problems of the inner city is the exclusion of the Negro from the fruitful roles that have eased the acculturation of the other groups—or at least his failure to assume and fulfill those roles.

No minority can emerge from the caste status until it has been able to move into the significant elites of the society. The upwardly mobile Negro has moved into the elite of the entertainment world and of sports, but not yet into the three elites that characterize the whites: the corporate managerial elite (largely Protestant), the political elite (largely Catholic), and the intellectual and artistic elite (largely Jewish). That is why the recruiting of young Negroes for the small colleges and the great universities makes sense from an overview of the total problem. The Jews did not achieve a fully normalized life until they had shown, in the recent Israeli wars, their capacity as warriors. The Negroes, already rather formidable warriors, may not achieve a fully normalized life until they show their capacity to own, manage, and run, if not the whole city, at least those parts to which they are organic.

It is to this aspect of the Negro and the city that I turn in the final section of this essay. But not until I have asked what is meant by the violence of the Negro encounter in the inner city with the symbols of white ownership, affluence, and authority. Is it fun and games? Is it (as many of the terrified whites fear) racist hatred and death? Obviously it is a little of each. But it is also the expression of a claim on America and its Babylonian splendor. And it is a cry of anguish on the part of those who have not found their true selfhood and have not resolved the tensions between feeling and living as Negroes and feeling and living as members of the larger city and national community. It is all these and perhaps one thing more: a cry of despair at not having found suitable roles—in skills, knowledge, power—that will enable the Negro to lead an expressive life, cherishing the city he is part of, rather than threatening to level it with a flaming sword.

IV

There have been many definitions of the ghetto, some stressing its self-imposed aspect, some its other-imposed aspect. But basically a ghetto is a trap. It is a trap that may have started, as in the case of the Negroes in northern cities, when migrants moved into it to huddle together for warmth, and then continued because no other place was open to them. In some cases, they may want to continue to live there, out of a sense of the familiar and a distaste for the strange new scene. But if exit is not open to them, whether they want to avail themselves of it or not, then the trap aspect makes it a ghetto. It may also be a slum, in terms of congestion, dilapidation, or decay, but that is another matter. Psychologically, it is the ghetto aspect that counts.

Having said this, I should add that mass emigration from the city's ghettos is not necessarily the solution to the inner city's turbulence or its poverty. The whole problem has been brilliantly discussed in Anthony Downs' essay in terms of choices between possible alternative social strategies. I note only the danger we all run of falling into the fallacy that the Negro will be "happier" living elsewhere than where he is. He may or may not be. It depends on whether he can find elsewhere—in the suburbs or in parts of the central city where he is in a minority rather than a majority—the kind of social warmth and the sense of place and belonging that he finds where he is now. But what is crucial is that the Negro should be able to leave the ghettos if he chooses, able in the legal sense of open-housing laws and in the *de facto* sense of having work to do and an income that sustains him there. As for guesses about how many would leave if they had the chance, I find Kenneth Clark's estimate a credible one: that in the first generation perhaps only 10 per cent would leave, in the next 30 to 35 per cent, with enough leaving in the third generation to make it a racially balanced area, rather than a racially segregated one.

It is ironic that many who have written about the city, with the concept of place being necessarily part of it, have never themselves had an empathy for the sense of place. This is especially true of the liberal thinkers who have lived in the city, but have never been attached to a particular city. Like Jefferson, they dislike and fear the mass-city for its mass-culture aspects. Jefferson had a wonderful feeling for the farm and village and small town, and for the interaction of person, place, and culture. But a number of his followers today, although adhering to his radical views of democracy, lack his sense of the organic role of place.

A man defines himself in part by the web of his relations with others, in part by his relation to the place where he lives and works, in part by his relation to his subculture and culture. But, more precisely, what constitutes a sense of place in the city? One might say that a man has a good functional sense of place if his children are growing up there, if he has work, friends, a feeling of familiarity, and a sense of participation and some control over his destiny there. Take the classic case of the New England township in its heyday, and you will find it fulfilling each of these criteria. Take the much maligned suburb of today, with all its conformist pressures, and you will still find it measuring up tolerably. Can the same be said of the situation of the Negro in the inner city?

Only in part. His children are growing up there, but not well—largely without parental or other controls, with a series of too precocious exposures to adult experiences and too few culture-binding exposures to aspects of the larger culture. If he has work, which is a chancy if, it is likely to be elsewhere. He does have friends there and a sense of being at home in a familiar environment. He has little power or control over his destiny there, which is one of the reasons for the desolating sense that nobody cares, which we call "alienation" and which is growing rather than lessening among Negroes.

It has become a truism to say that everything will fall into place if only the Negro poor have a decent income, and there is enough truth in this to make the battle for something like a guaranteed family income a valid one. Yet income alone, or even a job alone, is not enough. It must be *work* rather than a *job*, putting back into the work concept some of the pride and sense of vocation that the Protestant ethic gave it and that, perhaps, the Negro has moved furthest from. When Ralph Abernathy organized a "poor people's march" on Washington, he defined the objective thus: "To plague the Pharaohs of this nation with plague after plague until they agree to give us meaningful jobs and a guaranteed annual income." When Lewis Mumford says that we must stop building vast high-rise urban renewal projects and pushing highway programs, stop looking for technological breakthroughs into the problem of the cities, he tells us to "listen to the poor people in every city—the unemployed, the exploited, the neglected racial minorities who are tired of being treated as subjects for computerized urban research or bureaucratic runaround." In both instances there is the hint of some special mystique of the condition of being poor that I reject.

When Abernathy talks of "meaningful jobs," however, he is talking of work in the sense I have used above. And when Mumford says that we must start not with money or technology but with men, and that we can do nothing "without restoring their self-respect, their self-confidence, and their capacity for self-government," he reaches very close to the heart of the issue, and includes work and place, power and culture.

Work—meaningful, prideful work—can do more than anything else to achieve this restoration. The Negro, migrating from the southern plantations to the cities of the North, hoped to find work and freedom in them. He found jobs in the mass-production plants for a brief spell, and in Detroit and Chicago and Watts he found freedom, but not the sense of community he had left in the more tightly knit Negro communities of the South. But the mass-production jobs needed skills and the kind of steadfast patience that many of the newcomers lacked. After the Detroit riot in the summer of 1967, the auto plants agreed to take on a number of unemployed unskilled Negroes, to open jobs for them and train them, but a dismaying percentage of them dropped out of the training course. Clearly the chances for future jobs lie less with the mass-production industries than with the new ones geared to the new technology. A massive coalition-directed program of training a large number of promising young Negroes intensively for work as technicians in these service and knowledge industries might just possibly succeed in coping with the imperative of prideful work that man needs if he is to be a person in a place. Sometimes in history the same innovating technology that dislocates a going situation and sets up a problem may help resolve it. Without going through an elaborate college education, many young Negroes can be trained by the newest technology to take their places in that same technology.

Along with work nothing can be more effective in restoring self-respect and self-confidence than the sense of having a hand in the destiny of one's neighborhood and city. This might be called participatory power. It goes beyond the voting principle, in choosing those who govern. It operates through a direct self-government on the immediate level: by decentralized school systems in which the neighborhood parents and administrators have a large share in teaching the children; by decentralized state and federal community programs in which the beneficiaries must learn to cope administratively with their own needs; by a direct share in coalition programs for developing small business ventures and for home ownership; increasingly by training more teachers, police, doctors, and politicians from the neighborhood itself so that those who live there feel that they are treated, served, represented, and governed by people with whom they feel at peace because they are their own. The way to stop the burning is to have the propertyless own their own homes, whether privately or cooperatively. The way to stop the looting is to have them own shops and small enterprises. The way to give schooling some standing is to have the schools run by those whom the people of the neighborhood know and trust. The way to anneal the sense of alienation from government and society is to see your own people become councilmen, police inspectors, mayors, governors, senators.

I am not arguing here for "Black Power" in the hostile and exclusive sense of that term, when it becomes an inverse *apartheid* and spreads the kind of *grande peur* that feeds the most extreme forces of reaction. Black Supremacy is no better than White Supremacy, and it is bound to drive whites out of any area in which the blacks seem likely to become strong. But the day is over when the ghetto was a fair preserve for proconsuls and satraps, when the whites had a prescriptive monopoly of the crucial governing posts. Today there are Negro mayors in Washington, Cleveland, and Gary; tomorrow there will be others like them in a half-dozen other great cities whose Negro component is close to a majority, if not actually one. The day after tomorrow there will be black governors, and the day after that the composition of a Presidential ticket will not easily exclude the idea of a Negro for one of the two top posts.

This is the genius of American politics, this capacity for channeling new freshets and even tumultuous currents into the main stream, whether it be in business, politics, education, or innovations in the mores and the arts. Those who speak for the necessity of a separatist Black Power movement in order to achieve a sense of pride and identity tend to forget that true self-confidence does not come when you have locked your opponent out and have your little arena to yourself; it comes when you have shown your capacity to meet your opponent on his own ground in the larger arena or to join in a coalition with him against other opponents. The relation of participant power to the sense of identity is a crucial one, and out of it can come a pride in place and a greater ease and coolness in living in it.

The other aspect of power that bears on the situation of the city is its relation to trust. The powerless cannot trust anyone: They fear the shadows as well as the realities of enmity. But some equality of bargaining power begets trust, which is needed for any coalition activity. One of the difficulties with making coalition action persuasive hitherto has been the scepticism of the Negroes not only about the good will of the whites who form the coalition but—even assuming good will—their capacity to do something about it. Before white good will can be translated into social action, there must be, so to speak, another gear—the conviction of the whites that they have personal and group interests that will be served by the action. One form of such self-interest is the idea, gaining ground steadily, that the rest of the city (or society) cannot prosper if one crucial part of it languishes. Another form, as many black militants assert, is the fear of the burning and looting that will occur unless the action is taken. Still another form is the feeling that a Negro power base—economic and political—must be wooed by actions rather than words and good will. Some whites may have as their "other gear" simply the stirring of their imagination or a more personal sense of self-interest—their image with their own children and their desire to have the approval of the young, who in many cases have identified with the cause of Negro access and power.

The growing number of young Negroes who are being admitted

into the colleges and universities raises questions of the impact the newly emerging Negro intellectual elite will have on the city. The trend among them is not only toward militancy, but a black separatism in residence and classroom and in activism outside the classroom. This is bound to affect the emotional climate of the inner city, to which most of them—as separatists—are likely to return. At the universities they have been learning invaluable lessons in political tactics and in the nature of power and the emotional frame of opinion. They need a chance to apply what they have learned to the participatory politics of city and neighborhood. There is the chance, of course, that their newly found militant separatism may lead to a break in legality and to revolutionary politics in the fragmentizing and sectarian sense. But it is a risk that has to be taken, since only the infusion of new energy and imagination into the inner city can give it the sense of ferment without which place is only location, not living.

It must be living if it is to have any meaning. One of the worst things that the white society has done to the Negro in many of the cities has been to shut him out of community, in its deepest sense of common interests and actions and the sharing of common experience and values. The Negroes had to find some common experience and values of their own. They had done so in the South, in cities like Atlanta and New Orleans. They managed to do it to some extent outside the South, in Harlem, St. Louis, San Francisco. They achieved it almost not at all in Watts, Detroit, and Newark where the Negroes came as uprooted migrants and where they found no subculture of their own to give them definition and warmth. Harlem, for example, developed its own literature, its own arts, its own dance and jazz, its own life style. The Negro in Harlem found himself to be a person not only in a place, but in a culture of his own.

Is it too wild a surmise to say that there may be some relation between this and the incidence of the riots? I have put the question earlier as to why the riots came *when* they did. But there is the added question: Why did they come *where* they did—in Newark rather than Harlem, in Detroit and Watts rather than in San Francisco? The question of the living conditions of the people is not decisive. If it were, how could one account for the trouble in Detroit, where the city administration was relatively liberal, and where the white and Negro community leaders had worked in action programs for years?

The answer about the where is complex, yet one strand of it may run through the existence rather than the absence of a conscious subculture, through some measure of the organic relations of person, place, and culture rather than the uprootedness and alienation that were true of Watts and Detroit, and supremely true of Newark.[1]

REFERENCE

1. I owe a great debt in this essay to the help of Michael Lerner at the Yale Graduate School and to his manuscript "Personality Development in the Black Urban Ghetto."

Part V:

Urban Policy

MARTIN MEYERSON

Urban Policy: Reforming Reform

AFTER TWO thirds of a century, the main stream of urban reform in America is faced with disenchantment. Part of the disenchantment comes from those who feel (wrongly) that no improvement has been made—that cities and metropolitan areas are as dirty, ugly, congested, crime- and corruption-ridden, and as generally degraded as ever. Part comes from intellectuals, professionals, and liberals who no longer see a clear path to reform, for they are only aware of the pitfalls in past and present programs. Part comes from the black and the poor who feel that they have not benefited much from the vast public programs and expenditures. And part comes from the new opinion leaders of the young who reject the administered life, which they claim is a hallmark of twentieth-century urban reform as well as of American society in general. Quite apart from dissident student organizations of the New Left, there is a strong undercurrent among the student young which holds that there is a platitudinous rhetoric of vague, democratic American goals in contrast with unpleasant reality. In this view, the large bureaucracies of city, state, and nation become indistinguishable from the large bureaucracies of corporations, unions, and universities, and all these large bureaucracies are given to depersonalizing human relations and to deciding upon an administered life for others without their consent. Such a view shares many elements with traditional American conservatism.

All this disenchantment comes at a time when, in the news media and in political discourse, virtually all domestic issues are grouped under the rubric of the "urban problem," and many expect the "urban problem" to be solved straightaway as soon as international entanglements in Vietnam are resolved.

Of course, throughout the history of the literate world, men have been self-conscious about creating cities and living in cities, perhaps because an element of willful choice has always been present, or seemed present. Self-consciousness has gone hand in hand with self-criticism. There have always been critics to complain about city immorality or poor sanitation, crime or high costs, overcrowding or governmental incompetence.

The scale and character of the conscience of the city, however, have altered. Near the turn of the century, groups of citizens developed political pressure groups to reform American cities. The reformers, drawn from the upper and middle classes, were appalled by what they saw in the large American city. Thomas Jefferson's slogan at the beginning of the nineteenth century that the city is a cancer on the body politic seemed to have come true by the end of that century. The Anglo-Saxon Protestants who had controlled urban government had been displaced by Irish Catholics and Central, Eastern, and Southern Europeans; graft was common; squalor and congestion were apparent; one wave after another of immigrants clashed with each other and with earlier ethnic groups; low wages accompanied and enabled the rise in manufacturing; and much degradation attended low wages.

The first important efforts to counter the immigrant-based municipal political machines were made at the turn of the century. The commission form of government (started in Galveston in 1901) and later the city manager form of government were espoused as honest governments. Historian Charles A. Beard became the head of the Training School for Public Service, among the first of those agencies which urged municipal decisions based on facts rather than on political favors (although in reality the outcome was usually to select one set of favors rather than another set of favors). Incidentally, the young Robert Moses who became Beard's assistant, went on to develop later a series of public works programs designed for middle- and upper-income rather than lower-income groups.

Frederick Winslow Taylor's experiments at rationalizing production in the Midvale Steel Company and subsequent assignments captured the imagination of many good government reformers. Other reformers became entranced by civic centers, broad avenues, and other examples of civic grandeur and affluence, an interest largely stimulated in the period between the 1893 Columbian Exposition, designed by Daniel Burnham and his associates, and the 1909 plan for Chicago, done by some of the same group. Meanwhile the municipal engineers of Germany were improving utility systems, and the American city planners who sprang from the city grandeur movement were pleased to adopt the utilitarianism of the German-type engineer to prove their practicality.

The civic reform movements mainly had as a goal efficiency (which sometimes was a euphemism for the elimination of graft and nepotism) and to some extent the very reverse of efficiency, namely ostentatious city beautification. Social concerns for the poor and the handicapped were not entirely absent, however. The first important public health and tenement laws were passed near the turn of the century, and settlement houses were established in city after city. But the rhetoric of the reformers in relation to the poor was reminiscent of Puritan John Locke: Helping the poor demolished their character and should only be resorted to in desperation. Self-help and self-reliance were, after all, the virtues which brought success in the Protestant Ethic.

For the first third of the twentieth century, urban reformers had minor successes (and they were minor, as Lincoln Steffens and others attested) through pursuing efficient government and, occasionally, civic aggrandizement schemes. Assumptions about the limits of appropriate public actions were severely shaken, however, by the Depression of the 1930's.

Even though William Green, the head of the American Federation of Labor, proclaimed to the 1930 AF of L convention (after the Depression had begun) that the pride of the American workman would make him unwilling "to make himself a ward of the State," American political sentiment and political action soon altered and altered greatly. The policies preached by John Maynard Keynes gradually came to be accepted. By compensatory expenditures, the tendency of a capitalist economy to become sluggish and run down could be overcome and another great depression avoided. At the required scale of governmental intervention, only the national government could have great impact. The importance of local affairs dimmed while at the same time the national government became more involved than ever before in urban questions through housing programs, the National Resources Planning Board, and other agencies and programs.

By the middle of the century, urban reformers who had abandoned neither the vocabulary nor the programs they evolved in the beginning of the century began to concentrate more and more attention on federal activities. Although urban reformers had learned the lessons of Keynes, they had not recognized that in important respects a policy of compensatory government expenditure is value free: Such expenditures can keep Gross National Product high or for that matter raise it very significantly by helping either the well-off or the poor. With the general middle-class bias of the United States, the programs of the New Deal, the Fair Deal, the Eisenhower Administration, and subsequent administrations predominantly aided, despite their claims, the middle-income groups. Indeed, one of the glaring discrepancies in American political life is between manifest purposes and actual benefits. Presidential and political speeches and almost every important piece of national legislation in our generation abound in promises to the poor and deprived. For example, the preamble of the Housing Act of 1949 proclaims "the realization as soon as feasible of the goal of a decent home and suitable living environment for every American family. . . ." A score of years later, the promises appear shallow.

Programs run by middle-class professionals have evolved so that middle-class people have benefited the most. An original purpose of Federal Housing Administration mortgage insurance, for example, was to improve the position of the low-income consumer of housing. Instead, if it strengthened the position of the consumer of housing at all, it was the middle-income household that benefited. But mostly the program has become one for removing risk for home builders and mortgage lenders. As for urban renewal, it has cleared slums; but after the poor were displaced, the new facilities erected were often for high-income families or for commercial and governmental purposes. Much of the high-income housing and commercial and governmental development probably would have taken place anyway, without the incentive of subsidized urban renewal land. While this claim may be debatable, it is not debatable that much of urban renewal has caused inconvenience and suffering to the low-income families who lived in the slums, particularly low-income black families who have had the least opportunity for alternative housing of any kind, let alone superior housing.

Vast publicly supported federal highway programs have made it easy for middle-income families, particularly white families, to leave behind an obsolescing urban plant and difficult social and economic conditions and live in newly built suburbs. The recent afterthought of federal aid for mass transportation is at a puny level. In the few cities where actual rapid transit investment is taking place, it turns out once again to provide subsidies for middle-income families. The urban mass transportation systems generally are designed to serve downtown and other white-collar areas more than industrial ones. Furthermore, in most urban areas the poor are already current users of the transit systems; the new subsidies will extend service to higher-income groups (who like to have mass transportation on a standby, supplemental basis when the car is in the repair shop, or in use by another family member, or the weather is poor, or for some other occasional reason).

A similar class bias exists for the National Park Service recreation facilities. They serve mostly people from urban communities, but their locations and the kinds of facilities they provide and the money and time costs associated with their use make the national parks attractive to families of relatively high income.

In 1954 the Supreme Court proclaimed the necessity for racial integration in the schools. Since then the agencies of the federal government have proceeded to implement the judicial decree. So far, the results have mainly meant that what racial integration has taken place has been for low-income whites and low-income blacks, both of whom come from poor educational backgrounds. Children of well-educated white families have rarely experienced integration by fiat; the parents could either move to the suburbs or send their children to private or parochial schools if they did not wish the integration experience.

Even policies which have had as manifest ends the redistribution of rewards in our society have generally reinforced the given system of allocation. The War on Poverty scarcely deserves such a grandiloquent title. The funds so far have gone less to redistribute income than to elaborate overhead activities.

Ironically, in reducing unemployment in recent years, we have done so primarily for college graduates, professionals, and business men and women. One of the striking differences between poverty in the 1960's and poverty in the 1930's is that in the 1930's the unemployed came from a variety of social strata, and now they do not. Then there were unemployed bankers and engineers as well as unemployed laborers. When unemployment gripped people of a wide range of skills and backgrounds, the unemployed probably did not feel the same sense of personal failure as they do when only a selective group is affected.

I raise these points not because I believe that all urban reform should lead to policies and programs which will redistribute rewards, but because reformers who advocate and reformers or bureaucrats who administer urban programs have engaged in unwitting hypocrisy. The tendency to favor the center majorities is inherent in the political power structure of the United States and in our definitions of the public interest. Though public policy is largely responsive to the expressed preferences of specific interest groups, the most vocal, articulate, concerned, self-selected urban spokesmen have come from the middle- or upper-income groups: The goals they have urged and the programs as they have been effectuated have reflected their class bias. They have not advanced policies and programs in their own self-interest; they have merely assumed that all people view the world, or ought to view the world, as they do. Indeed, in large part they have been right—one of America's greatest achievements has been the rapid movement of millions of persons into the middle class.

However, the new conscience about the city has recognized the poor and the unemployed (they are not synonymous) and the non-whites who make up such a high proportion of the unemployed and the poor. These formerly disenfranchised groups and their supporters demand a new set of priorities partly on the basis of justice (and much of conscience depends on a sense of justice) and partly on the basis of expediency. The poor, the unemployed, and particularly the blacks are demanding public programs to assist them—and now. They are speaking up, sometimes eloquently, sometimes through traditional political power, sometimes through violence—for their share of the historical American dream.

The appropriate response might seem to be simple: Let the middle-class reformer refrain from urban proposals, if what he proposes is no longer applicable in helping the poor and the black, and let the poor and the black frame their own reform proposals. But the answer is not that simple. For one reason, the poor and the black have been surrounded so long by the rhetoric of urban reform that they may adopt for themselves hand-me-down programs that are no more applicable to their own self-interest than the proposals of the middle class. For another reason, resources are not unlimited, even should the funds now consumed by the Vietnam conflict be released for urban and social welfare goals. A broad spectrum of goals—better health, improved education, better housing, elimination of unemployment and poverty, in-

367

creased recreation provisions, reduction of crime, coordination of transportation, better municipal services, superior government employees, amenities of clean air, water, variegated facilities and services, and pleasing vistas and beautiful buildings—these goals and more could all be sought in every community by the poor and the black as well as those who are currently well off. But certainly not all are attainable at once. They are not attainable because there simply are not enough resources to provide immediately for everything that is desired. Also, it is doubtful whether the poor or the rich will want to change their habits of life sufficiently to achieve all they say they want. Slum housing, for example, provides considerable satisfactions. (It is possible to spend less of one's money and one's energy on slum housing than standard housing.) If air pollution is to be reduced significantly, not only must industry change its production practices and raise costs, but so must individual home owners (who must burn fuel more efficiently and refrain from burning trash and leaves) and all automobile drivers alter their habits. In some areas, the density of the settlements themselves would have to be changed—either greater concentrations of persons, served largely by mass transportation facilities, or more dispersed settlements (where the pollutants would be dissipated in the air) would be preferable to our present medium-density existence, if air pollution is to be reduced. But people are reluctant to change their life patterns.

A third reason why the black and the poor cannot be left to do the urban tasks alone is that they are a minority. The blacks will increasingly become a very substantial minority and in many cases a majority in numerous central cities. They will never, however, succeed in achieving their demands without the cooperation of the majority. Black mayors, as in Cleveland and Gary, have to draw upon the skills and the purses of the whites as well as the blacks in the entire metropolitan area. Furthermore, a substantial part of black America is itself middle class in terms of income and behavior. Many of the most vocal leaders (Martin Luther King was an example) come from that middle class.

What is happening is that a coalition is forming between the middle-class or upper-class white reformer and the black militant. In Detroit—and nationally—automotive and other corporate magnates are beginning to work with black militants. Working alliances are being established, despite mutual mistrust and hostility. Fortunately, in our society where there is much prejudice against skin color, there is undoubtedly a decreasing amount of prejudice among those with high education and influence. These people do not confuse racial behavior with class behavior; they know that if a poor black man commits a crime, it is not because he is black. They are able to recognize that protest rather than gratitude goes with improvement in the lot of those at the bottom of the economic scale. They realize that Black Power groups are asking for more concessions because life is improving for Negroes, not because it is worsening; that the gap between the whites and the blacks is more galling when the appetite for amenities and opportunities is whetted.

The new alliances will have to evolve new sets of urban priorities, and they will need to adopt changes in style. Psychic and attitudinal changes are altering the perceptions of urban life and the scope, the manageability, the emphasis of action. The new urban reform ought to focus on process rather than on huge public programs; on the humanity of the person to be served, rather than on the service to be rendered. It should aim to create an environment in which change can take place and should try public remedies on a well-funded experimental basis rather than through massive, across-the-nation, all-or-none types of programs.

For example, there seems to be widespread agreement among economists, political leaders, and social reformers that the present welfare system is degrading and ineffectual. It depends on a large supervisory staff, who act like policemen to see that no one has any funds outside the welfare handout; it discourages the presence of a male adult in the household, since his wages, if any, would reduce the welfare benefits. An income bolstering scheme, given simply, as a matter of right, with no necessity for elaborate review, supervision, or the invasion of privacy, could provide an individual or a household with a minimal standard of food, shelter, clothing, and medical care with a maximum standard of human dignity.

The changing political climate is such that in 1969 the new reformers began working toward some kind of income bolstering system as a substitute for our elaborate public welfare system. One might favor a negative income tax; another, a family allowance; a third, a wage supplement; a fourth, a combination of these. The wage supplement plan has much to commend it; in this arrangement, every adult who is physically able to do so works, and work, after all, is a key part of the American cultural tradition even for the rich. If he is unskilled and uneducated, the employment market may not pay him much; in many cases, it may have to be less than the minimum wage, but millions of jobs are not covered by minimum wage legislation anyway. The government would pay the difference between the going market rate for unskilled labor and what is needed to raise a family above a poverty level. The arrangement has political appeal to taxpayers at large since work is rewarded, and the poor person is partially paying his own way. It has appeal to poor people for the same reasons, and because the status position of the male head of a household is reinforced. Unions may be wary of the proposal, however; they may hold that employers would depress the wage scale and would have an incentive to downgrade jobs. Yet in an economy where skilled people are in short supply, such an argument is not valid; the employer has an economic inducement to pay a good wage, far above the one that needs to be supplemented, if he can only attract or train the capable worker.

The new alliances for urban action find support from a variety of unexpected sources. Much of what disturbs intellectuals, protesting students, and spokesmen for the black and the poor also disturbs a large bloc of American conservatives. They all are suspicious about the corruption and bureaucracy of big government, big unions, and big corporations. They all see a moral deficit and hypocrisy in the regulations, red tape, ineptitude, and lack of responsibility which they believe accompany large-scale bureaucracies of any kind. They all object to the administered life. Where the old conservative, borrowing from American populism, differs from the new reformer is on the matter of responsibility to the poor: The conservative accepts the class system as just; the new reformer rejects it as cruel and immoral. The liberal reformer believes there must be compensatory help for the disadvantaged; the conservative believes that the disadvantaged should work harder and help themselves.

If new alliances are emerging, to what ends are they to work? I mentioned that income bolstering appeals to the new reformer. But is income bolstering an urban problem? Surely the present distribution of income has the most profound effects upon life in urban areas. If there were not so many poor people living in central cities, there would not be the same intensity of problems that now perplex us: under-utilization of employment capabilities, crime, poor health, decayed housing and other facilities. (Of

370

course, if poverty is to be defined statistically as the bottom third or fifth or any other portion of the population, it could never be eliminated; but the poverty that is so distressing now in our cities is measured more concretely as an economic level that cannot provide people with basic housing, medical care, and even diet.) Although poverty is found in cities and has profound and multiple effects on cities, it is a national problem that is localized in cities rather than one that is peculiar to cities or susceptible to correction by cities acting on their own. Similarly, the life-style disparities, the educational irrelevancies, the family disruptions, the maldistribution of services are not peculiarly urban problems, although they are observed in urban places.

Too many problems are called urban today. People are simply not talking about the same things when they lump a traffic bottleneck into the category that contains technological unemployment, the existence of dozens of conflicting building code regulations in a metropolitan community, and the fact that the amount of new housing is dependent upon credit rates influenced nationally by the Federal Reserve Board to encourage or to decelerate economic expansion, employment, and other economic phenomena.

With so much called urban (the only subjects that escape are foreign relations, agriculture, and natural resources), it can be argued that it is impossible to set national policy for urban development because such a task is tantamount to setting national policy on domestic development. Would new urban reformers be courageous enough to relinquish the catch-all approach of calling every social, political, physical, or economic problem that occurs in cities urban? Is it possible to distinguish at least tentatively those problems that are national in causation, distribution, and solution from those that are state or metropolitan or those that are the problems of individuals? Which issues are associated uniquely with the urban community?

Is it possible in the redefining of urban problems to cast them into manageable units? When physical actions or solutions were prominent in the earlier era of urban reform, cities had at least the fiction of coping with specific problems. When transportation was thought of in physical terms of highways and mass transportation facilities instead of in terms of accessibility, when employment was thought of in terms of industrial plants and retail stores instead of human skills, when housing was thought of in terms of bricks and mortar instead of a community environment, the tasks were

371

measurable. Now that we seek social and economic solutions, we are properly unsure of the measures of success.

I do not suggest returning to a simplistic concern with physical facilities rather than the conditions and processes of urban life. What I do suggest is that the new concern be made operational. If human relations in cities are to be improved, it must be determined which kinds of clashes are in fact racial and which are something else—like youth against age or the poor against those they think are exploiting them—and which kinds of actions seem to change behavior and attitudes and how. Manageable and assessable tasks could give a sense of purpose for the vast, vague, limitless social, economic, and political problems we seem presently to be setting for our agenda.

Unfortunately, the new urban reformer is not ready to articulate a set of priorities. He knows what he does not like; he has become disillusioned with past programs, but imbued with rising expectations; he craves an environment in which national resources will proliferate for the domestic good, but decentralized decisions will predominate. I cannot guess what will be attractive ultimately to the new urban reformer, but I do suggest the following policies as being consistent with minimal administrative interference and maximum participation by diverse community and national interest groups. These initial policies are modest, yet their effects might be profound. More than anything, they would free both local communities and the national government to select from among many possible alternative paths for urban development and set in motion a new style of dealing with urban problems.

A. *National leadership in urban development.* It is not paradoxical that, after speaking of the suspicion toward bureaucracy and the administered life, I place first national leadership. It is precisely because the new urban reformer is suspicious and seeks a sense of national commitment that national leadership must come from the very highest office of the land. The President ought to be persuaded that his role is to lead the nation in dealing with urban problems and achieving urban potentialities. His role should not be to set up and administer monuments—so frequently they tarnish anyway—through legislation and huge federally funded and staffed programs, but rather to convene appropriate groups and to develop suitable courses of action, in which the federal establishment might possibly have no other major part. For example, the construction industry is notoriously deficient in hiring, training, and retaining skilled and semiskilled Negro labor, yet it is an industry eminently suited to such employment. Even though the federal government maintains fair employment policies and despite the recent heroic efforts by the Secretary of Labor, little progress has been made in getting and holding black people. The unions, the archaic practices of the construction industry, the traditional hazing of apprentices, the lack of enthusiasm among contractors—all contribute to maintaining the present situation. If the President were to use the influence of his office to explore with the unions, the construction industry, and black groups ways of revamping construction techniques in general and training of Negro labor in particular, he ought to elicit more practical steps and get more people actually on the job than has happened through all the contract requirements.

Obviously the President cannot become personally involved with all specifics, but he can become involved with certain symbolic specifics. The construction industry is a case in point. American industrial capitalism has largely forgotten the construction and home-building industry, which is among the least mechanized, rationalized, and technologically advanced industries. Every year construction costs go up by as much as 5 per cent; if a city defers a capital expenditure and still wants it eight or nine or ten years later, its costs may have doubled. If the President were to participate actively in working through the steps to increase the spread of information, spur innovations, modify and unify building codes, and in other ways remove the impediments to rationalizing the construction industry, people in cities would be the greatest benefiters. Incidentally, one of the major ways to help rationalize home-building and other parts of the construction industry would be through federal credit policy (which, instead of encouraging an ever normal level of building, now stimulates a cyclical ebb and flow that has disastrous effects and hardly achieves the economic stability toward which the Federal Reserve Board and other agencies aspire).

B. *Shifting welfare and education costs from the locality to the federal government and the state government.* It is nonsense to consider welfare (including health care) as a charge against the local community. Poverty, health, unemployment are not issues with which localities are competent to deal; the main local options are ones that might make a community somewhat more humane than its neighbors and thus act to penalize the community by attracting others in need. Welfare should be recognized as a national problem, despite its long history of local responsibility, and funded accordingly. A national income bolstering scheme, particularly a wage supplement, would have the advantage of simple administration and a great deal of reliance on the individual decision-maker, the family head.

Nor should education any longer be considered a fiscal matter for the locality; with population mobility what it is, no community can reasonably expect to reap the benefit of the education received by its children. Since people fear federal control if there is federal funding for elementary and secondary education, such monies would probably have to funnel largely through the states, and the states should bear most educational costs with the federal government providing block grants to help equalize opportunities among the states. I am not arguing for the abandonment of local control in education, however. Indeed, it would be a great advance if many more options were opened to parents, pupils, and teachers. I suggest that funds be made available to students at private and parochial schools as well as public ones; that all kinds of experimentation be encouraged, with some public schools going metropolitan, drawing center-city residents to the suburbs; that some schools be started by black parents; that some emphasize learning machines and some large numbers of volunteer teachers. What is needed is a great deal of unequal education (after basic minima are met) with many choices to be made available for the best learning process for groups of children and particular children.

Education and welfare make up more than half of the general expeditures of local communities; if these two burdens were lifted from communities, they would have the resources to contend with some of their other social, economic, physical, and governmental issues.

C. *The elimination of slums within a decade.* Throughout the century the slum has been the symbol of urban woe. By now we recognize that the slum is not only a rotting structure, but also the effect of a particular social structure. Therefore it is not enough just to protect people from rats, lack of sanitary facilities, and leaking roofs; they must also have protection against crime and drugs and people who prey upon them. There would be little political opposition to the national goal of eliminating physical slums in a decade, but altering the social structure is more difficult.

In terms of the physical structure, the operational definition of a slum could not include those houses which a critic merely finds less satisfactory than others. Also, since better housing will generally cost more, an income bolstering device to raise consumer purchasing power would be necessary. Of course, the volume of new housing construction would have to be commensurate with population increases and the demolition of old dwellings, and aging dwellings would have to be conserved so that they would not rapidly spiral into slums. But the simplicity of the goal, the modest successes over the years, the known methods to achieve such an aim, and the widespread habituation to the goal as part of the American dream would all contribute to its achievement. The legal doctrine that has so far prevented the federal government from adopting a national housing code has become so dented that it may now be feasible to make national provisions for housing and building regulations. The ideal housing inspector would be one who could teach as he inspected, giving advice on how to make simple necessary repairs and referring to other sources if the problem was complicated. A training program utilizing manpower from the slum areas might be desirable.

Increases in traditional policing of slum areas would probably be less satisfactory than trying to develop neighborhood and other indigenous cooperative protection associations. In some of the largest cities, former gangs of delinquents turn into gangs of guards.

D. *Research and experimentation.* It would be highly desirable if present massive governmental spending could be leavened by experimentation. In the United States, and probably in most countries, we adopt all-or-none approaches to public works programs and to such service programs as medical care. We do not develop manageable models nor analyze experiments. We have uniform and unified policies and programs. Later we may modify them or repeal them or set up countervailing policies. But we ought to be able to try out innovations and test them. Some activities do not lend themselves to small tests; it would not help much, for example, if every twentieth automobile had an air pollution device, and the other cars were uncontrolled. But experimentation could be tried in a single community in an intensive way without having

375

a policy or a program uniformly applied to all communities. It is time that we truly had a model city program; that we selected one or several communities for experiments on issues that perplex us. For instance, we do not have examples of good mass transit compared to good highway development. In the United States we invest over twenty times as much in highways as in mass transit. I do not suggest that we rush in to make the expenditures equal, but we ought to have the courage to do so in a selected community or two.

Similarly, if communities could use tax policy imaginatively, they might be able to achieve far more through incentives to private enterprise than they could through direct public investment programs. If, for example, property improvements were not penalized by additional taxation (taxes on land and on improvements should be handled differentially), then more rehabilitation, remodeling, and renewal could be accomplished than through public governmental renewal. Rather than put this belief into massive programmatic action, however, it would be far preferable to free some community from its restraints to test out over a period of years what a differential tax on land and buildings could accomplish.

Social and technological research on urban matters has lagged behind biological, industrial, communications, and agricultural research. No one locality or industrial firm—or even a group of localities or industrial firms—could afford the kinds of technological and managerial research in transit, waste disposal, and the housing industry that are required. No individual groups have the initial capital, the know-how, or the staying power to make the significant advances. The federal government is beginning to recognize the importance of research in air pollution control, in the desalinization of water, in self-contained and self-cleansing waste disposal systems, in transit.

If the federal government can extend its research funds—perhaps in partnership with private industry—to a variety of urban functions, and if it can sustain these funds over a number of years, improvements in urban life should occur. Not all improvements are technological, of course, and I see the greatest benefits deriving from social, economic, and governmental research. Many entrepreneurs do not lack capital so much as adequate research and information; many do not require the props of guarantees so much as the buttress of market and trend analysis.

Much of the information about metropolitan areas is collected by the federal government. Other than census material (and that only on special request if it is wanted in more detailed form than generally published), the information seldom returns to the community for its own self-appraisal. Furthermore, the federal government is in the best position to collect information from the many diverse groups within metropolitan areas, should communities and private groups desire it, and to help provide data on the questions they wish answered on investment, population, density, employment, education, consumption, and other trends. This kind of service may be regarded as a low level of research, if it is that at all, by those mostly interested in intensive university-type research, but it can be tremendously valuable.

Thus far I have indicated that there is considerable disillusionment with twentieth-century urban reform and on this matter have stressed, in particular, the disillusion coming from public programs ostensibly for the not-so-well-off which have, in fact, subsidized the middle class. I have suggested that there are beginnings of a new urban coalition or coalitions to which both various liberals and various conservatives may be drawn. (The Urban Coalition in capitals and its local affiliates may or may not become identical with the less formal coalition or coalitions to which I refer.) I have indicated a few policy areas on which I think there can be immediate agreement and raised some issues the next generation of urban reformers may have to face.

I am not an innocent bystander in the process of the reformation of urban reform that I believe is taking place and the new political constellations that may result. As a summary, I shall indicate several themes that I advocate as the basis for a new style of urban reform and for a fairly wide and politically feasible alliance or coalition of forces to achieve it.

1. For twenty years some of my former students and I have been urging that urban services and facilities be responsive to their users or customers or clients. Schools unfortunately are often run for the satisfaction of superintendents, principals, and teachers rather than for students. Hospitals are frequently managed to satisfy the physician and the administrator rather than the requirements of the patient. Parks and playgrounds, similarly, have been designed for recreation workers. The list could be extended to virtually every

377

aspect of urbanism. Fortunately, the few voices of a score of years ago are now many voices, and urban services, if we continue our advocacy, can at last become essentially user-based in the years ahead.

2. Linked to the first point is a growing sense that decisions should be decentralized to bring them closer to those affected by them and to achieve greater participation by those affected. Corporate enterprise has begun to decentralize authority extensively. Public enterprise, recently, has been much less ready to make such a shift. Bold proposals, such as McGeorge Bundy's on the decentralization of schools with its accompanying user orientation, however, are shaking past practices of public administration. The new strategies of urban reform will need to take into account which roles and activities can best be decentralized and which ought properly not to be. For example, as I suggested above, the role of the President of the United States as a leader in urban affairs rather than as an administrator of urban programs should properly increase. Similarly, much of the funding of urban activities should be provided nationally and, to some extent, through state sources and fiscal actions, with resources going largely as block grants to localities. At the same time, greater responsiveness to many purely local questions should grow and flourish.

3. As a user orientation comes more into being and decentralization is regarded with more affection, class biases and race biases will dim. A user orientation and decentralization will mean that low-income groups, black groups, and other groups will devise programs for themselves which may differ significantly (although they need not do so) from what the white middle class chooses. Some young white students seem to be opting out of a society of material consumption while many black youths may be seeking it. This option for differentiation has heretofore existed largely for the rich, and even they have not always availed themselves of it.

4. There will be a growing sense that the best administration is the least administration. I expect that in such fields as welfare there will be a tendency to supplement wages or

in other ways provide income which the recipient can largely spend as he sees fit. In public aid programs there would thus be less administration and a kind of consumer sovereignty that would not force an administered life on any citizens but the chronically deranged or diseased. A social system operating as though run by an invisible hand of a kind Adam Smith envisaged would come into being— an achievement Smith's market place was not able to produce by itself. As a concomitant, the disdain for negative governmental acts should decrease; more and more people may realize that negative acts, such as strong enforcement of housing codes to eliminate slum properties, may have more democratic safeguards than so-called positive programs which have failed to eliminate slum housing.

5. Similarly, the next stage in urban reform could lead to more competition among urban choices than has ever existed before. Diversity of choice will become increasingly sought. Housing of the most varied kinds, locations, and types of tenure (including the ownership-rental-cooperative forms we know today) would become available. The United States has not yet offered the kind of housing Scandinavia could offer a generation ago with provisions made for the children of working mothers and for the care of dwellings which working mothers could not otherwise tend. Competition could result in mass transportation once again becoming a major factor in the urban pattern—less to reduce the use of the automobile and more to provide alternative means of movement and accessibility for the young, the old, the ill, and those who may prefer to use their automobiles to go out into the countryside rather than for daily trips to work or schools or shops. Competitive means for providing municipal services may even come into being. Municipalities in their staffs, for example, are leaning on the engineers they recruited in the Depression of the 1930's. (They have not been able to hire many since.) Much of the future municipal engineering may thus have to be done by outside firms. Similarly, many firms might be far more effective than single communities in handling complex systems of waste disposal since they could provide shared parts, staffs, and other savings for a number of localities. Or in

some areas urban functions may be best performed by the states or by federations of counties and other governments.

6. Along with competition may come the growth of the voluntary sector of services and the rise of groups which are neither governmental nor private organizations, but which can increasingly develop the advantages of both or avoid their disabilities. The voluntary service organization in health and education, in job development, and in religion and recreation is becoming more valued, particularly among the young.

7. I stated above that experimentalism ought to be substituted for the all-or-none approach that has characterized American national policy toward urban questions. Thus, instead of deciding on a particular program or approach and applying it to all the cities in the land, we would devise experiments in which the program or activity would be tried out in one city or a small group of cities. We would try out alternative approaches and assess the lessons we learn from each demonstration. Successful experimentation requires the fullest collaboration of all levels of government, of industry, of unions, of voluntary associations, of foundations, and of research groups. Prototype new cities and towns would be among the most fruitful of experiments to develop and test social, economic, and technological innovations.

8. There ought to be a greater emphasis on urban research, which is not the same as the experimentalism I have just mentioned. The days may be over when we would say that more money is being spent on research for Lespedeza grass than for cities. Through the new national Urban Institute, as well as through a tremendous number of efforts by universities, governments, and other agencies, we shall achieve a better knowledge base for urban decisions than ever before. This knowledge should include knowledge of the consequences, including the unintended consequences, of previous policies and actions. Crude efficiency as a basis for urban action will give way, partly through research, to a concept of adequacy.

9. The concept of adequacy will come to cover two great neglects of the American scene: beauty and amenity. Not only have American men of influence not been men of visual taste, but Americans generally have not been visual partly because of our Puritan heritage. Here, too, a great change is taking place. In the new concern for affect, the visual, the auditory, the olfactory, and other sensory responses are being rediscovered. Similarly, that sense of amenity that enables a city, such as Copenhagen, to have its Tivoli Gardens with their marvelous mixture of popular and high culture is being discovered by Americans. As they become internationalized, Americans will admire in other countries throughout the world a level of amenity that will become part of their set of domestic expectations and aspirations.

10. Finally, in a nation that has always held that opportunity can best be achieved through education, I believe that education will be seen as the means for creating that set of sentiments and that climate in which a new urban reformation can best be furthered. Ours is the only country in the world in which young men and women are virtually at the point where most of them will have some kind of higher education. We even have more Negro college students in the United States, small as the proportion is, than there are total students in higher education in England. As more and more Negro mayors get elected—and they will be—they will soon find an increasing number of educated Negroes to serve the black political machines that will displace the succession of Yankee, Irish, Jewish, Italian, or Polish political machines. The challenge, however, will be less through quantity of education than through a quality of education enabling the students to understand the urban environment in which over 90 per cent of them will live, to understand the options available to urban America, and to see that their individual and group efforts are relevant and indispensable for the changes which can take place.

The urban reformation outlined above will not take place automatically. If a broad alliance were to be formed, however, this new style of urban reform and of local, state, and national urban policy could be effectuated by many people. If this were done by 1976, we could truly celebrate the two-hundredth anniversary of the Declaration of Independence.

Notes on Contributors

EDMUND N. BACON, born in 1910, is executive director of the City Planning Commission of Philadelphia and visiting lecturer at the University of Pennsylvania. Mr. Bacon is the author of *Design of Cities* (1967) and a member of the President's Citizens' Advisory Committee on Recreation and Natural Beauty.

EDWARD C. BANFIELD, born in 1916, is Henry Lee Shattuck Professor of Urban Government at Harvard University. Mr. Banfield is the author of *Political Influence* (1961) and *Big City Politics* (1965); the co-author of *City Politics* (1963) and *Boston: The Job Ahead* (1966); and the editor of *Urban Government* (1961). Mr. Banfield is also a member of the Joint Center for Urban Studies of Harvard University and the Massachusetts Institute of Technology.

KENNETH E. BOULDING, born in 1910, is professor of economics and director of the Program on General Social and Economic Dynamics at the Institute of Behavioral Science at the University of Colorado. Mr. Boulding is the author of *The Image* (1956), *The Meaning of the Twentieth Century* (1964), *Impact of the Social Sciences* (1966), and *Economic Analysis* (4th ed., 1966).

STEPHEN CARR, born in 1935, is assistant professor of urban design at the Massachusetts Institute of Technology. Mr. Carr is also director of a study on visual communication in the city being conducted under the auspices of the Department of Housing and Urban Development and the Boston Redevelopment Authority.

JAMES S. COLEMAN, born in 1926, is professor of social relations at the Johns Hopkins University. He is the author of *The Adolescent Society* (1961), *Introduction to Mathematical Sociology* (1964), *Community Conflict* (1957), and co-author of *Equality of Educational Opportunity* (1966).

ROBERT COLES, born in 1929, is research psychiatrist at the Harvard University Health Services. Dr. Coles is the author of *Children of Crisis: A Study of Courage and Fear* (1967), *Dead-End School* (1968), and *Still Hungry in America* (1968). For ten years, Dr. Coles has worked with rural and urban poor, both white and black, northern and southern.

ANTHONY DOWNS, born in 1930, is senior vice president and treasurer of the Real Estate Research Corporation in Chicago, Illinois. Mr. Downs' publications include *An Economic Theory of Democracy* (1957) and *Inside Bureaucracy* (1967). Mr. Downs is a member of the President's National Commission on Urban Problems and a consultant to the National Advisory Commission on Civil Disorders.

PETER F. DRUCKER, born in 1909, is professor of management at the Graduate Business School of New York University. Mr. Drucker is the author of *America's Next Twenty Years* (1958), *Landmarks of Tomorrow* (1960), *Managing for Results* (1964), *The Effective Executive* (1967), and *The Recent Future* (1968).

LYLE C. FITCH, born in 1913, is president of the Institute of Public Administration in New York City. He is the author of *Urban Transportation and Public Policy* (1964) and "Social Planning in the Urban Cosmos," in *Urban Research and Policy Planning* (1967). Mr. Fitch is a member of the Committee for Economic Development's subcommittees on Goals for Metropolitan Areas and Problems of Urban Poverty.

ALEXANDER L. GEORGE, born in 1920, has for many years been a political scientist at the Rand Corporation. He is now professor of political science at Stanford University. Mr. George is the author of *Propaganda Analysis* (1959) and *The Chinese Communist Army in Action* (1967). With his wife, he wrote *Woodrow Wilson and Colonel House* (1956).

MAX LERNER, born in 1902, is professor of American civilization and world politics at Brandeis University and a syndicated newspaper columnist. Mr. Lerner is the author of *America as a Civilization, The Age of Overkill, Ideas Are Weapons, The Unfinished Country, The Mind and Faith of Justice Holmes,* and *Education and a Radical Humanism.* Mr. Lerner is also co-editor of a new edition of de Tocqueville's *Democracy in America.*

FRANKLIN A. LINDSAY, born in 1916, is president and director of Itek Corporation in Lexington, Massachusetts. Mr. Lindsay is a trustee of the Committee for Economic Development and a research associate of the Institute of Politics at Harvard University.

KEVIN LYNCH, born in 1916, is professor of city planning at the Massachusetts Institute of Technology. He is the author of *The Image of the City* (1960) and *Site Planning* (1962), and the co-author of *The View from the Road* (1964).

RICHARD L. MEIER, born in 1920, is professor of environmental design at the University of California, Berkeley. Mr. Meier is the author of *Modern Science and the Human Fertility Problem* (1959), *A Communications Theory of Urban Growth* (1962), *Developmental Planning* (1965), and *Science and Economic Development* (rev. ed., 1966).

MARTIN MEYERSON, born in 1922, is president of the State University of New York at Buffalo. He is a former dean and acting chancellor of the University of California at Berkeley and was Williams Professor of City Planning and Urban Research at Harvard University. Mr. Meyerson was formerly director of the MIT-Harvard Joint Center for Urban Studies. His most recent book, of which he is the co-author, is *Boston: The Job Ahead* (1966).

DONALD A. MICHAEL, born in 1923, is professor of psychology at the University of Michigan and professor of natural resources at the same university. Mr. Michael is also program director of the Center for Research on Utilization of Scientific Knowledge at the Institute for Social Research. Mr. Michael is the author of *Cybernation: The Silent Conquest* (1962), *The Next Generation: Prospects Ahead for the Youth of Today and Tomorrow* (1968), and *The Unprepared Society: Planning for a Precarious Future* (1968).

RICHARD E. RUBENSTEIN, born in 1938, is associate professor of political science at Roosevelt University and assistant director of the Adlai Stevenson Institute. Mr. Rubenstein is the author of *Rebels in Eden: Mass Political Violence in the United States* (1970) and co-editor of *Legacy of Conflict* (1969).

JOHN R. SEELEY, born in 1913, is dean of the Center for the Study of Democratic Institutions in Santa Barbara, California. He is the author of *Crestwood Heights* (1956), *Community Chest* (1957), *The Alcohol Language* (1958), and *The Americanization of the Unconscious* (1967).

MELVIN M. WEBBER, born in 1920, is professor of city planning and chairman of the Center for Planning and Development Research at the University of California, Berkeley. Mr. Webber is also program director for the new Social Policies Planning doctoral program at Berkeley. He is the co-author of *Explorations into Urban Structure* (1964) and the author of "Order in Diversity: Community Without Propinquity," in *Cities and Space*.

ADAM YARMOLINSKY, born in 1922, is professor of law at the Harvard University Law School and a member of the Institute of Politics at the John Fitzgerald Kennedy School of Government at Harvard. Mr. Yarmolinsky is the editor of *Case Studies of Personnel Security* (1955) and the author of *Recognition of Excellence* (1960). Mr. Yarmolinsky was special assistant to the Secretary of Defense, 1961-64; Deputy Director of the President's Task Force on the War Against Poverty, 1964; and Principal Deputy Assistant Secretary of Defense for International Security Affairs, 1965-66.

MICHAEL YOUNG, born in 1915, is director of the Institute of Community Studies and chairman of the Social Science Research Council in Britain. He is the author of *Family and Kinship in East London* (1957), *The Rise of the Meritocracy* (1958), and *Forecasting and the Social Sciences* (1968).

INDEX